Secular States and Religious Diversity

Ethnicity and Democratic Governance Series

How can societies respond to the opportunities and challenges raised by ethnic, linguistic, religious, and cultural differences and do so in ways that promote democracy, social justice, peace, and stability? The volumes in this series seek answers to this fundamental question through innovative academic analysis that illuminates the policy choices facing citizens and governments as they address ethnocultural diversity. The volumes are the result of a collaborative research project on ethnicity and democratic governance under the general editorship of Bruce J. Berman.

Volumes in the series

Avigail Eisenberg and Will Kymlicka, eds., *Identity Politics in the Public Realm: Bringing Institutions Back In*

Bruce J. Berman, Rajeev Bhargava, and André Laliberté, eds., *Secular States and Religious Diversity*

Kristin R. Good, Triadafilos Triadafilopoulos, and Luc Turgeon, eds., *Segmented Cities?: How Urban Contexts Shape Ethnic and Nationalist Politics*

Avigail Eisenberg, Andrée Boisselle, Glen Coulthard, and Jeremy Webber, eds., *Recognition versus Self-Determination*

Volumes planned in the series

Bruce J. Berman, André Laliberté, and Stephen J. Larin, eds., *Ethnic Claims and Moral Economies*

John McGarry and Richard Simeon, eds., *Assessing Territorial Pluralism*

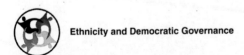 **Ethnicity and Democratic Governance**

Edited by Bruce J. Berman,
Rajeev Bhargava,
and André Laliberté

Secular States and Religious Diversity

UBCPress · Vancouver · Toronto

21 20 19 18 17 16 15 14 13   5 4 3 2 1

Printed in Canada on FSC-certified ancient-forest-free paper
(100% post-consumer recycled) that is processed chlorine- and acid-free.

Library and Archives Canada Cataloguing in Publication

Secular states and religious diversity / edited by Bruce J. Berman, Rajeev Bhargava, and André Laliberté.

(Ethnicity and democratic governance series, 1927-0720)
Includes bibliographical references and index.
Issued in print and electronic formats.
ISBN 978-0-7748-2512-2 (bound). – ISBN 978-0-7748-2513-9 (pbk). –
ISBN 978-0-7748-2514-6 (pdf). – ISBN 978-0-7748-2515-3 (epub)

1. Religion and state. 2. Religion and politics. 3. Secularism – Political aspects.
4. Religious pluralism – Political aspects. I. Berman, Bruce J., editor of compilation.
II. Bhargava, Rajeev, editor of compilation. III. Laliberté, André, editor of compilation.
IV. Series: Ethnicity and democratic governance series

BL65.S8S43 2013   322'.1   C2013-905269-0
                                                             C2013-905270-4

Canadä

UBC Press gratefully acknowledges the financial support for our publishing program of the Government of Canada (through the Canada Book Fund), the Canada Council for the Arts, and the British Columbia Arts Council.

This book has been published with the help of a grant from the Canadian Federation for the Humanities and Social Sciences, through the Awards to Scholarly Publications Program, using funds provided by the Social Sciences and Humanities Research Council of Canada.

UBC Press
The University of British Columbia
2029 West Mall
Vancouver, BC V6T 1Z2
www.ubcpress.ca

Contents

Preface / vii

Acknowledgments / ix

Introduction: Globalization, Secular States, and Religious Diversity / 1
Bruce J. Berman, Rajeev Bhargava, and André Laliberté

Part 1: Historical and Theoretical Approaches

1 Religious Pluralism as a Self-Evident Problem in the Context of
Globalization / 29
Peter Beyer

2 Secular Modernity, Religion, and the Politics of Knowledge / 45
Bruce J. Berman

3 Can Secularism Be Rehabilitated? / 69
Rajeev Bhargava

Part 2: Secularisms in the West

4 Between Secularism and Postsecularism: A Canadian Interregnum / 97
Paul Bramadat and David Seljak

5 Tolerance and Accommodation as Vestiges of the Empire / 120
Lori G. Beaman

6 In God We Trust? Secular States, Diversity, and the "Clash" within
North America / 136
Yasmeen Abu-Laban and Claude Couture

7 Ideologies, Institutions, and Laws: Religious Freedom in Secular States / 165
Ahmet T. Kuru

Part 3: Secularisms beyond the West

8 State Intervention in the Reform of a "Religion of Rules": An Analysis
of the Views of B.R. Ambedkar / 187
Rinku Lamba

9 Something Got Lost in Translation: From "Secularism" to "Separation
between Politics and Religion" in Taiwan / 207
André Laliberté

10 The Changing State Monopoly on Religion and Secular Views in
Thailand / 232
Manuel Litalien

11 State-Society Structures and the Frustration of Movements for Secular
Reforms in Lebanon: Civil Marriage and Youth Activism / 265
Elinor Bray-Collins

Conclusion: Secularism, Religious Diversity, and Democratic Politics / 293
Anna Drake

List of Contributors / 310

Index / 314

Preface

The EDG Series: Governing Diversity

The volumes in the Ethnicity and Democratic Governance series are the product of an international Canadian-based Major Collaborative Research Initiative (MCRI) begun in 2006 under Bruce J. Berman of Queen's University as principal investigator. Over the course of six years thirty-nine international researchers and other associated organizations pooled their research and knowledge of one of the most complex and challenging issues in the world today – governing ethnic diversity. The EDG project began with one foundational question: How can societies respond to the opportunities and challenges raised by ethnic, linguistic, religious, and cultural differences and do so in ways that promote democracy, social justice, peace, and stability?

To approach the complex issue of governing ethnic diversity our academic investigations were broken into four interrelated research streams represented by four main research questions:

- What are the causes of ethnic community formation, political mobilization, and conflict?
- What are the institutional strategies and policies available to states for developing democracy in multiethnic societies?
- To what extent can the international community facilitate the peaceful resolution of ethnic conflicts?

- What normative principles of justice and democracy should be used in formulating or evaluating the governance of diversity?

The themes around which our work has coalesced include nationalism, multiculturalism, federalism, ethnicity and moral economy, recognition and identity, accommodation and integration, conflict resolution, democratic governance, secularism and religious pluralism, citizenship, international intervention, immigration, social integration, self-determination, and territory.

Core funding for the Ethnicity and Democratic Governance MCRI comes from the Social Sciences and Humanities Research Council of Canada. The project is headquartered at Queen's University and conducted in partnership with the Université du Québec à Montréal, the University of Toronto, and the University of Victoria. It is our hope that readers will discover within all of our volumes – and in other project outputs – new understandings of previously neglected or understudied aspects of the nature of ethnic identity formation, the causes of ethnic conflict, and the relationship between ethnic conflict and democratic governance in the contemporary globalized world. For more information on the EDG project and for a list of other EDG publications, see http://www.queensu.ca/edg/.

Acknowledgments

Earlier versions of the chapters in this volume were presented at a workshop of the Ethnicity and Democratic Governance (EDG) project held at the University of Ottawa in October 2008. The editors are grateful to the authors for their enthusiastic participation in the project and their cooperation in revising the papers for publication. We would also like to thank the commentators and participants at the workshop – José Casanova, Avigail Eisenberg, Ruth Marshall, Tariq Modood, Shaheen Mozaffar, and Razmik Panossian – for their valuable insights and contributions. Thanks also to Anna Drake for her assistance in preparing the manuscript and to Emily Andrew of UBC Press for her guidance through the publication process. We would like to extend our warm gratitude to Jennifer Clark, the EDG project manager, and Anne Linscott, the managing editor of this book series, for their advice and assistance in relation to every aspect of this project, including the planning of the workshop and the editing of this volume. Your support has been indispensable!

Secular States and Religious Diversity

Introduction
Globalization, Secular States, and Religious Diversity

Bruce J. Berman, Rajeev Bhargava, and André Laliberté

This book developed from the realization that religion was too often left out of discussions of the issue of democratic governance of ethnic diversity and that this exclusion was untenable in the context of recent controversies in Canada and other Western democracies over the secular state and the challenges allegedly attending the unprecedented ethnic and religious diversity caused by recent immigration. It comes from a conference on "the secular state and religious diversity" organized by the Ethnicity and Democratic Governance program, which was convened at the University of Ottawa to think about this issue. It quickly emerged from the papers presented that for many contributors the changes produced by globalization constituted too important a contextual framework to ignore. This followed logically from the original impetus for the conference, which was the realization that debates on the secular state were Eurocentric and failed to capture the political realities faced by a majority of the world population. China, the largest country in the world, has been ignored for too long in this debate, and India, the largest democracy in the world and perhaps the most important experiment as a secular state in a diverse society, has too often been marginalized as peripheral to it. The book seeks to address these lacunae and to enlarge the framework of critical and comparative analysis by paying attention to these two countries and other non-Western societies, as well as to the different modalities of Western secularism, in order to enlarge discussion of religious diversity and the secular state.

Although the three editors of this volume are political scientists, they come from different horizons: Bruce J. Berman is an Africanist who has worked on the state and development and has recently focused on nationalism, ethnicity, and multiculturalism; Rajeev Bhargava is a prominent public intellectual in India who has written extensively on secularism and secular democracy; and André Laliberté is a sinologist who has written on the state and religious affairs in China and Taiwan. The contributions to this book reflect scholarship in political science by a new generation of scholars working on religion and the secular state: Yasmeen Abu-Laban, Elinor Bray-Collins, Claude Couture, Ahmet T. Kuru, Rinku Lamba, and Manuel Litalien. Abu-Laban and Couture compare the United States and Canada, and Bray-Collins writes on Lebanon, Kuru on France and Turkey, and Litalien on Thailand. This book also includes prominent scholars of religious studies who focus on the effects of globalization and the legacy of postcolonialism for religion and secularism in Canada: Lori G. Beaman, Peter Beyer, Paul Bramadat, and David Seljak.

In this introduction we present the challenges faced by the secular state in the context of globalization, with particular attention to the issue of religious diversity. Then we address the normative issues raised by these challenges by presenting an approach inspired by the experience of India that represents a break from traditional academic analyses using the United States or France as models of secular states. We believe that India also deserves consideration as a source of inspiration as a model of a secular state, as it is the largest democracy in the world and one of the most religiously diverse societies. Then we sketch the diversity of the social, cultural, political, and historical contexts of different regions in the non-Western world to remind us that the contextual secularism inspired by India may not be easily replicated elsewhere. India can serve as a model of interreligious coexistence as long as one accepts the premise of religion's relevance in the public sphere, but for those who reject this view and for those who think that religion's involvement in politics is problematic, the Chinese model of state control over religion, which *is not* what we mean by a secular state, is an alternate model for many authoritarian regimes that we cannot afford to ignore.

The Secular State and the Political Resurgence of Religions

It is no secret that social scientists, Western and non-Western governments alike, and international institutions were surprised by the powerful political resurgence of religion and radical religious movements during the past thirty years. In the mid decades of the twentieth century religion was widely thought to be a declining force in human societies in the face of the relentless advance of secular modernity expressed in the global development of nation-states and economies, both capitalist and socialist, based on scientific knowledge and instrumental reason. Anticolonial and national liberation movements were overwhelmingly grounded in the ideologies and goals of this secular modernity (Fox 2004). The resurrection of aggressive political religion came to the fore with worldwide events: the 1979 Iranian Islamic Revolution, which displaced the modernizing regime of the shah; the rise of Islamist parties from the Maghreb to South Asia; the rise of Hindu nationalist parties and their affiliates within mainstream Indian politics; and the deepening of the political influence of the "religious right" in the United States during the administration of President Ronald Reagan. These events indicated that secularization had not in fact unseated religion as a dominating political and cultural influence, although they were perceived by many at the time to be the last gasps of an old order whose anomalous, backward-looking reactions to modernity went against the grain of the global trend towards secularization. By 1999, however, it had become increasingly difficult to hold this perception when China, a country viewed as thoroughly secularized, saw the emergence of the spiritual movement Falun Gong. The resurgence of such multifaceted, subterranean, and at times militant religiosity did not make sense to outsiders, occurring as it did in a country subjected to a very aggressive form of state atheism propagated for decades at all levels of society. In Canada, another state viewed from afar as secularized and a leading example of modern multiculturalism, controversy erupted in 2007 over demands for "reasonable accommodation" of religious minorities (particularly Muslim minorities) that revealed both ugly expressions of intolerance and deep-seated insecurities about the place of religion in the public sphere. Although the Chinese and Western situations differ widely from each other, and from those in other parts of the world, they underscore the fact that secularism – which in principle defines the proper place of religion in modern societies – has not achieved the universal acceptance and hegemony once expected.

Although the challenges to the secular state can be seen as global in scope, three different types of configuration emerge from the preceding observations: Western states that have established certain forms of secular state; postcolonial states that have inherited these institutions from previous colonial rulers and have come to terms with them in ways ranging from adaptation to rejection; and states that did not experience direct colonialism from the West and therefore find themselves least affected by the direct impact of Western secular states. The book's chapters reflect these three different situations by addressing different forms of secular state in Western countries such as Canada, the United States, and France, in countries such as India and Lebanon that have been relatively westernized due to colonialism and have adapted or rejected the forms of secular state imposed on them by Western states, and in countries such as China, Turkey, Thailand, and Taiwan that are adopting some aspects, in whole or in part, of the Western secular states into dramatically different religiocultural backgrounds.

This volume is also based on three premises. The first is that religion in all societies – North, South, East, and West – continues to provide inspiration for many people with a wide variety of political agendas. This religious inspiration has led to a variety of political programs, some of which aim to influence an entire society with a particular religious agenda, whereas others reject institutionalized religious domination, defending only the right of their own communities to greater inclusion in mainstream society or the right to live apart. Others tackle issues such as the defence of the civic rights of those outside of their own faith. The fight for religious domination and/or inclusion takes many political forms, ranging from democratic participation in mainstream political parties[1] to the development of militant antisecular organizations.[2] Chapters in *Secular States and Religious Diversity* strive to illustrate a variety of civilizational and political contexts beyond Canada and the two countries to which it is most frequently compared: the United States and France. Case studies in this volume also extend beyond the type of European country where established religions coexist with freedom of conscience and where religion's influence has been significantly reduced, as well as beyond states deeply influenced by Christianity and Judaism. Chapters examine secularism and the secular state as they are experienced in the Middle East and in South, Southeast, and East Asia and as they are influenced respectively by Islam, Hinduism, Buddhism, and Confucianism, among others. Chapters explore how non-Western states interpret "separation" of religious and political institutions, to the extent they do so at all.

The second premise underlying the work of this volume is that religious diversity is a major characteristic of modernity at the global level. Religious diversity can be analyzed along two dimensions: diversity *of* religions and diversity *within* religions, both of which are examined in more depth in Bhargava's chapter and, to a lesser degree, in Laliberté's and Bray-Collins's chapters. The former dimension considers the differences between religions with backgrounds in different civilizations, whereas the latter looks at differences within religious communities, whether between leaders and followers (i.e., clerics and lay persons), men and women, caste and racial hierarchies in India, or different interpretations and practices of a given religious tradition. These differences have led to the diverse worldviews of people with varying levels of religiosity, ultimately also including those at the far end of the spectrum, such as secular Hindus or Jews, who may feel only loosely attached to communities of people associated with the strict practice of a religious tradition, as well as practitioners of body-cultivation techniques like Qigong who may consider themselves nonbelievers or even atheists.

A third crucial underlying premise developed in the chapters by Berman, Beyer, and Beaman is that secularism originated in a distinctive Western historical experience. Along with the liberal revolution in the United States, which generated a regime of separation between church and state, and the more radical French variant, there has also been a gradual evolution away from religious establishment in states such as the United Kingdom and the states of continental Europe. These forms of relationship between religion and state were also imposed through colonialism on societies with other historical, religious, and political traditions in which there were no churches to separate from state institutions. Colonialism also brought the secular knowledge of the state and market and, through the activities of Christian missionaries, a degree of religious pluralism, both of which have seriously undermined indigenous forms of political and religious authority.

The rising religious-secular tensions have taken place within a rapidly changing and increasingly unstable global context, which experienced a tectonic shift with the emergence of China and India as economic powers. Berman notes that globalization has generated widespread socioeconomic and political crises in non-Western societies that have threatened established religious communities and have led to the widespread belief among many Muslims that they are under deliberate attack by Western secular modernity in a "war on Islam." Bray-Collins discusses youth movements in Lebanon and the country's inability to break the shackles of communal leaders' domination, aptly illustrating the consequences of the threat felt by traditionalist religious leaders. Berman also points to the rise of ethno-religious political movements and fundamentalism (as two distinct phenomena) within world religions that may lack a history of functioning within secular states or may have found increasing secularity a challenge to their beliefs. Such movements have threatened nation-states and have led some to believe in the essential incompatibility between the secular liberal-democratic modernity of the West and the rest in what has been termed the "clash of civilizations" (Huntington 1996; see also Berman's and Beyer's chapters). There is no doubt, as Beaman notes, that unprecedented international migration and rapidly increasing ethnic and religious diversity in Europe and North America have made migration, integration, and accommodation of new ethnoreligious minorities central issues of national politics. As Beyer documents, these tendencies were reinforced by the collapse of the Soviet Union and its satellites from 1989 to 1991, bringing an end to the most militant secularist atheist states and the death of the socialist option in the global economy. These trends are also relevant to China, even if the People's Republic remains nominally socialist and committed to its own authoritarian version of secularism (Goossaert and Palmer 2011). Conflicts between secular and religious authorities there need to be seen in terms of a competition for international legitimacy between, on the one hand, the Chinese state and, on the other hand, the global Chinese diaspora and the democracies influenced by Chinese culture such as Taiwan, as well as Japan and South Korea.

In the context of the now interlocked global and local confrontations, Berman notes that neoliberalism may itself have taken on the ideological form of a millennial cult, tending towards homogenization in the name of a global-market universalism, and that religious fundamentalists exhibit increasingly militant lines of differentiation between the infidels and the true believers – even among their own followers. The most visible, overtly menacing, and violent aspect of religious extremist movements – global terrorism – can undermine the stability of weaker nation-states but ultimately involves only a very small proportion of the adherents of the major world religions and tends to obscure the broader and deeper issue of the development of relations between secular states and religious communities and institutions, as well as how this development will shape not only the direction of public policy but also the very course of liberal democracies in the future. In these confrontations we find the contemporary challenges to secularism, empirical and normative, and its ability to encompass the increasingly complex and divisive intersection of religious institutions and public life.

Existing secular states now face several challenges. First, some religious institutions do not accept the authority of the secular state, whereas many others, having accepted it reluctantly, now question its legitimacy through militant religious contestation. Second, some supporters of the secular state argue that states are not in fact "secular" enough and should not concede to even the milder demands of religious actors. The tension between these two perspectives has been exacerbated by the consequences of decolonization, the end of the Cold War, and increased global mobility. Finally, and most relevant to this volume, increasing religious diversity compels the secular state to rethink its purpose and its position relative to religion. The presence of growing religious diversity was briefly obscured by the rise of the nation-state and the accompanying conceptual ideal of culturally homogeneous political communities. Today, however, diverse religious communities with differing conceptions about the place of religion in public affairs have helped to reignite debates about the secular state. Moreover, modern ethnonation-alist movements and ethnic conflicts have increasingly become religiously grounded and have reinforced religious militancy (Juergensmeyer 2008; Fox 2004). Beyond the diversity of views on the secular states, there is one issue on which opponents and proponents alike agree: the historical development of the different models originated in the West and relied on the subsequent "Europeanization" of the world.

The Secular State as Western Hegemony

Beyer notes that, over a period of more than a thousand years, Western societies have moved from an experience of fragmented political pluralism and the religious universalism of the Catholic Church to the modernity of a small number of unified and sovereign nation-states containing a diversity of religious communities that are nonetheless primarily Catholic, a wide variety of Protestant churches, and small communities of Jews. Societies of western Europe and societies in the settler colonies of the New World, which had in common the dominant influence of Christianity, either adopt-ed variations of the American and French models or gradually modified regimes of established state churches to give religious freedom and full civic rights to other religious communities. Although secularism situates the state as the dominant agent in the regulation of religious institutions, in practice this has resulted in state responses ranging from the minimal regulatory approach of the United States to the stronger state interference imple-mented in France. American secularism is characterized by what Alfred Stepan (2000) has termed "twin toleration" – noninterference of the state in religious affairs but also nonintervention of religious institutions in gov-ernment (although enforcement of the latter implies that the principle of noninterference by the state may be impossible to implement in its entire-ty). Implementation of these two principles of noninterference has not ne-cessarily meant the rejection or deliberate negation of religion but rather constitutional measures that prevent religious institutions from directly exercising political power and also limit state control over any religious community.

Beyond these differences, there is little question that secularism – as a discourse and an institutional practice positing that religion should not be the final determinant of political outcomes and that religious institutions should not directly exercise secular power – still stands out globally as a hegemonic approach supported at least overtly by the overwhelming majority of states, whether authoritarian or liberal. For supporters and critics alike, secularism embodies the essential nature of the modern state and is institutionalized at varying levels almost universally. Western states have adopted a variety of approaches to established churches, denominations, and non-Christian religious institutions, all premised on the idea that states should be the final arbiter in matters of interreligious relations and the ultimate authority in managing secular worldly affairs. Most postcolonial states have adopted some permutation of religiously neutral and distanced state institutions that constrain the role of religious institutions, and most view these institutions as being foundational attributes of their own independence. States such as the People's Republic of China – and until 1989 the Soviet Union – are only quasi-secular because if they have adopted the principle of keeping religion strictly out of the state and have relegated it to the private sphere, they have not implemented freedom from state interference in religious affairs, the other part of the ideal relationship between state and religion implied in the notion of secularism.

Of course, not all contemporary states are secular. The obvious exceptions are the Islamic Republic of Iran and the Kingdom of Saudi Arabia; both states also greatly impact the global economy and the international balance of power. In addition, the precarious situation of Pakistan, which appears to be veering ever closer to the status of an Islamic republic due to its internal Taliban insurgency, presents the world with a nuclear-armed country of over 170 million people now decisively rejecting a half-century-old secular – although undoubtedly precariously "secular" – state. Recent elections of political parties advocating a greater presence of Islam in public life following the Arab Spring in Egypt, Morocco, and Tunisia represent important tests of the secular state's resilience – or lack thereof – in these countries. As suggested above, the more intriguing but equally, if not more, consequential case relevant to the future of the secular state is the baffling model of China with its own mode of state control over religious affairs. Over the past six decades China has proceeded in a haphazard way to establish five religions under the tight control of the atheist Communist Party;

that is, the state explicitly recognizes five (and only five) religions at the expense of the many others that existed prior to 1949 – and still do outside of the People's Republic of China. In other words, even if China's public intellectuals claim to be secular, due to the absence of freedom of conscience, the Chinese state is not. Whereas the model of an Islamic republic may appeal to some Muslims who are critical of the secular state, it has no attraction at all in societies where the religious background of the majority is Christian, Hindu, or Buddhist. The Chinese quasi-secular model, however, may represent a more formidable challenge to the variants of the liberal secular state because it could inspire authoritarian leaders in societies with a different religious configuration, which are also facing a religious resurgence with the potential to oppose their political regime.

The religious revival and the militant challenge to secular states and culture – as well as the obvious error in "secularization" theory's expectations of an inevitable global process of secularization – have attracted the attention of social scientists, including the contributors to an important collection of papers edited by Ira Katznelson and Gareth Stedman Jones (2010). They and their collaborators recognize secularism as a complex and open-ended process encompassing a wide range of beliefs and increasingly heterogeneous forms of religion. Rather than following a universal trajectory, it is part of larger and more contradictory historical processes. Secularism in state and society is not one thing but takes multiple forms in different societies as the contingent outcome of powerful social forces. In this volume we attempt to explore these processes in broader comparative and historical context, looking in particular at the development of secular states and at their relations with religious institutions not only in Western societies but also in the wider range of major non-Western societies that have been affected by the global impact of Western political and cultural secularism.

Katznelson and Stedman Jones (2010, 12-13) distinguish as well between "political" and "existential" secularism. Here we further develop a distinction between "institutional" secularism – particularly in the dominant institutions of modernity, namely the nation-state and the capitalist market – and "cultural-ideological" secularism. They are closely related but remain distinct in their relationship to religious doctrines and communities. Secular states separate religious institutions from the direct exercise of secular authority and the mutual official sanction of church and state. This is anticlerical rather than antireligious and has actually opened the way for religious freedom as a personal choice and for the legitimation of religious pluralism. Secular culture, however, developed out of the separation of the sacred and the profane – the "disenchantment of the world" described by Max Weber (Habermas 1990, 2) – which rejected religion as "superstition" and grounded human agency in the secular world based on instrumental rationality and science. States and markets have been increasingly dominated by diverse forms of expert knowledge that dismiss the authority of religious knowledge of the sacred. For more than two centuries the growth of the secular culture of modernity (Giddens 1991) has posed a deep threat to religious institutions and doctrines. This confrontation between faith and reason has led to what Berman describes as "the politics of knowledge," and it continues to divide the secular and the religious in conflicts over control of the institutions and practices of the state.[3]

Although secularism remains a dominant global influence despite long historical resistance in the West from religious institutions in battles that have lasted decades, if not centuries, the variety of arrangements found around the world to govern relations between states and religions testifies to the wide array of circumstances under which these struggles have unfolded and continue to do so. This conflict has yet to abate, and although in some parts of the world, notably Europe, it may be on the wane, elsewhere it has experienced a powerful resurgence. Contributors to this volume are interested particularly in one dimension of this resistance that is especially relevant to most societies experiencing the effects of late-capitalist globalization: the phenomenon of greater religious diversity and its effects on social cohesion. This phenomenon affects Canada in many ways, as Lori Beaman demonstrates in her discussion of the power differential embedded in the language of accommodation and toleration. Paul Bramadat and David Seljak clearly underline how deeply secular societies such as Canada are entering uncharted territory as far as the current institutions of secularism are concerned: If not a return to a *status quo ante*, what would be the contour of a postsecular society? In other societies like India, the critique against secularism should not blind us to its considerable benefits; Rinku Lamba underscores this in her examination of the vital impact of secular institutions in battling caste-based discrimination. Likewise, as André Laliberté notes in his observations about Taiwan and East Asia, secularism still benefits from quasi-universal support in this region, although it sometimes takes forms that would not be recognized as such in the West.

This volume addresses the emerging field of multiple secularisms, and because this field remains in its infancy, the volume tentatively introduces different typologies to make sense of a very heterogeneous conceptual field.

In addressing this multiplicity of secularisms, this introduction presents various typologies that apply mostly to Western states – including assertive, passive, and moderate types of secular state – as well as Bhargava's central concept of "principled distance," originally developed in India, a multi-religious state from its beginning in 1947. Although India has adapted much of Western secularism through the influence of colonization and thus may be more easily identified with other Western forms, India's approach cannot be adequately captured by the assertive, passive, and moderate types and propels us into thinking about the relevance of dramatic differences due to non-Western religiohistorical (i.e., Islamic, Indic, and Sinitic) backgrounds. To this end, we introduce a framework that addresses non-Western states that have willingly or unwillingly adapted some forms of the originally Western philosophy and structure of secularism, and we present a typology of Western, Islamic, Indic, and Sinitic "secularisms," with the recognition that much more research needs to be done on the latter three. This is a task whose urgency can hardly be overestimated: a majority of the world popu-lation lives in non-Western societies, and among the latter, China, the most populous country in the world, is travelling a path to modernity that differs from that taken by both Western and postcolonial societies. The particular approach to the management of religious diversity by societies influenced by Chinese culture will increasingly matter since China's growing economic clout is likely to have a "spillover effect" on other institutions of global gov-ernance, such as international covenants on human rights and religious freedom.

Modalities of Western Secularism and Its Challenges

Ahmet Kuru's chapter develops an analytical distinction between the differ-ent forms of secular state experienced in France (assertive secularism) and the United States (passive secularism). Kuru argues that twin toleration rep-resents the basis of passive secularism, and he notes that the United States is the closest approximation to this particular ideal type. France implements an assertive form of secularism that arose out of a distinctive form of anti-clericalism that focused on the management by the *ancien régime* of an es-tablished church that had once actively provided legitimacy to the established order. In both passive and assertive secular states, however, the privatiza-tion of religious belief was as much about protecting religious minorities from religious intolerance and persecution as it was about excluding reli-gious institutions from secular power. In Europe this meant protection for

Protestants where the Catholic Church remained dominant, for Catholics and dissenting Protestant sects where Protestants were dominant, and for Jews everywhere. Relations between states and religious institutions in the West could also follow a third institutional path, which Tariq Modood (2011) calls "moderate secularism" and which we prefer to call "incremental secularism." In countries with established state religions, the fragmented, piecemeal development of liberal democracy was linked to the gradual removal of restrictions on religious minorities' participation in the public arena and on their holding public office but only insofar as these minorities did not act as Jews or Protestants or Catholics in the public sphere. The distinction between passive, assertive, and incremental secularism, as we discuss below, may have an effect on postcolonial societies' receptivity to secularism.

The varying forms of Western secular state are discussed in the chapters that follow. The strongly republican ideological secularism of France and Turkey is discussed by Kuru, and the very different institutional and ideological contours of American secularism are discussed by Berman and by Claude Couture and Yasmeen Abu-Laban. The Canadian experience of a gradual movement – first in the British imperial tradition and later in a more independent fashion – towards tolerance and accommodation of ethnic and religious pluralism is analyzed by Beaman and also by Bramadat and Seljak. These two chapters focus critically on the contemporary development and limits of liberal multiculturalism underpinning the Canadian approach to religious diversity. Beaman notes in particular the hegemonic power differences that remain embedded in notions of tolerance and accommodation and the recent public fixation in Canada on the "limits of accommodation" of ethnoreligious minorities, especially Muslims and Sikhs. Both Beaman and Bhargava note the need to recognize the diversity within and between religious communities embedded in the power relations of these communities and in the wider society. Bramadat and Seljak argue that despite the melding of liberal multiculturalism with the discourse of human rights, liberal multiculturalism alone cannot deal effectively with the new religious diversity, particularly since it fails to understand the internal diversity of ethnic and religious groups and the ambiguity and historicity of their claims.

There are multiple challenges to the management of religious diversity in secular states. Many religious actors think the secular state lacks moral authority and therefore holds no legitimacy to regulate religious affairs; in other cases, religious minorities view the secular state as the protector of minority rights against dominant religious majorities and may therefore pressure the state to act in ways that compromise its neutrality. Finally, secularism faces challenges in its implementation because (as we discuss below) varied philosophical approaches to secularism have led to differing institutional models. This diversity, resulting from different experiences with modernity, exposes societies to widely divergent expectations about the nature of secularism. There is also a historical and cultural specificity to dominant models of secularism – both as institutions and as concepts in the Western world – and therefore questions about the extent to which they can be employed as templates for non-Western societies. The chapters in this volume reveal the complexity of secularism not only in the nations of the West where it "originated" but also in the non-Western societies to which it was often aggressively spread by Western imperialism and colonialism, as demonstrated in Lamba's chapter on India and in Bray-Collins's chapter on Lebanon, as well as in other non-Western societies where elites with very different understandings of modernity adopted it, as illustrated in Kuru's chapter on Turkey, Litalien's chapter on Thailand, and Laliberté's chapter on East Asia. In each national instance the character of secularism and the state was shaped by the earlier historical experience of the relationship between political institutions and religious beliefs and institutions.

This reopening of the confrontation between secular modernity and religion owes much to developments within the Islamic world and – due to increased international migration – to the growth of Muslim communities that are now an intrinsic part of the fabric of societies in post-Christian and postsocialist Europe and, even more so, of societies established by European settlers in the New World. The attachment of a growing segment of the populations of secular states that were once overwhelmingly Judeo-Christian to a variety of religious traditions from non-Western ancestral lands tests the ability of many of these states to respect ostensibly deeply held values such as freedom of conscience, an intrinsic part of which is religious diversity and the capacity of religious adherents to practise their own deeply held religious ideals. Western societies must come to terms with the fact that a majority of the global population – and an increasing proportion of their own citizenries – refer to traditions other than Judeo-Christianity, and this creates the need to look beyond dominant models of the secular state and to consider lessons from non-Western states regarding the management of religious diversity. Meanwhile the confrontation between secular modernity and religion plays out differently in societies like China where the state's project of modernity was not about establishing a secular state through a regime of separation between religious and political authority but rather about asserting state authority to control religious activities. In this case, the state is best defined as quasi-secular, and religious resurgence is often seen, rightly or wrongly, as an assertion of civil society against an authoritarian state rather than as a questioning of the secular state. Understanding the Chinese situation matters to the broader context of world politics and the transmission of norms across cultures because its model of state control of religious affairs appeals to other societies' rulers who consider religious resurgence to be a threat.

And there is no question that this religious resurgence can be especially worrisome when it is accompanied by intolerance against other religions, especially minorities. One of the supposedly great merits of the ideal liberal secular state in Western political philosophy is that it legitimates tolerance of minority religions through its dissociation from the majority religion. However, with the increasing ethnic and cultural diversity of Western societies, this dimension of existing secular states, regardless of their varying forms, is coming under stress. Whether it is the hostile reaction to building a mosque at "ground zero" in New York or to minarets in Switzerland or the ban on the *niqab* in France and Quebec, the ability of secular states to respect religious diversity is coming under increasing challenge. Here the difference of quasi-secular authoritarian states like China matters again. Religious resurgence in China often accompanies more general calls for political liberalization (Yang 2005), and the persecution of religious minorities does not result from the rearguard reaction of populist groups and demagogue politicians but from the state itself and its particular variant of modernity (Tong 2009). In short, the political contexts where religious believers and organizations make demands bring forth the necessity to contextualize the secular state's modalities when discussing the future.

The Future of Secular States, Secularism, and Religious Pluralism

Secular nation-states are confronted with unprecedented ethnic and religious pluralism in the context of a global crisis marked by what Bramadat and Seljak term an "ideological interregnum" when previous hegemonic ideologies, secular or religious, have been dramatically undermined. Neoliberalism – whose hegemony largely embraces the elites of international institutions, major Western nations, and international corporate capital and whose utopian claims to creating global prosperity have produced in many situations quite the reverse – may have tarnished, if not annulled, the credibility of its moral claim to advance justice or equality, whether secular or sacred. On what basis, then, can a global paradigm be constructed that will link both religious communities and secular political forces in commitment to a shared agenda of social justice and equality in mundane secular reality at the local and global levels? Do we need, as Bramadat and Seljak suggest, a "postsecular" paradigm, or do we need, as Bhargava suggests, a "contextual secularism" based on a principled distance between the state and religious institutions and a shared search for a contextually grounded common ethic? This search would take place both within and between religious communities and secular states. How do we deal with communities or movements within the world religions that reject the legitimacy of the secular nation-state, which remains the dominant global political form – particularly the dominant liberal-democratic form – and that may seek either to live in isolation from secular nation-states or to replace them with theocratic states that are agencies of extreme oppression, exclusion, and violence? And finally, how do we avoid tarring with the same brush other communities or movements from within the same world religions that are politically active rejecting only the authoritarian variants of the secular state?

One suggestion, put forth by Bhargava, is that rather than imposing a highly context-specific liberal-democratic secularism or seeking a radical religion-centred alternative, we might construct a new conception of political secularism from the best practices of Western and non-Western states. Bhargava details five features of this contextual secularism based on his understanding of the characteristics of the Indian secular state. First, such a secularism's more explicitly multivalent character would look beyond individualistically construed values of religious and nonreligious liberty and equality to encompass community-specific rights such as peace, toleration, and nonindividualistically construed values of liberty and equality. Second, it would have the capacity to address both inter- and intrareligious domination and would benefit minorities through community-specific political or sociocultural rights, where required.

The concept of principled distance is a third, and perhaps the key, feature of Bhargava's contextual secularism. In contrast to mainstream Western secularism, in which separation appears to have taken the routes of either one-sided or mutual exclusion of religion from state functions, principled distance accepts that although states must not be tied to religious goals and must be kept apart from religious institutions, they do not need to keep religion entirely out of policy and law. Secularism based on principled distance would apply a flexible approach to the question of state inclusion versus exclusion of religion and to the question of state engagement versus disengagement with religion. Religion, then, would be allowed to intervene in the affairs of the state if such an intervention promoted freedom, equality, or other values integral to secularism. For instance, practices banned or regulated by the state for one culture might indeed be permitted in a minority culture because of the distinctive status and meaning these practices have for its members. The important consideration here is whether this intervention occurs as a means to treat all people as equals. However, principled distance is more than differential treatment; it may require state intervention in some religions more than in others, and it takes into account the historical and social conditions of all relevant religions. Thus the state may not relate to every religion in society in exactly the same way or intervene in each religion to the same degree or in the same manner; the state must ensure only that its relationship with each religion is guided by nonsectarian motives consistent with democratic values and principles.

This emphasis on the role of values and principles brings up a fourth aspect of secularism: the commitment to pursue actions that may be perceived as hostile to particular aspects of religion (e.g., caste and gender restrictions) but necessary to other deeply held values such as equality. The final aspect of contextual secularism, referred to in its name, is its highly *contextual* mode of moral reasoning, where the precise form and content of secularism vary from one context to another and where this idea of multiple secularisms opens up the possibility of different societies working out their own form.

One implication of contextual secularism is that, as a multivalue doctrine, its constitutive values do not always sit easily with one another but are frequently in conflict. As a result, internal discord and instability are integral parts of contextual secularism. New interpretations, contextual judgments, and attempts at reconciliation and compromise are therefore central to this form of secular state. From an institutional standpoint, according to Bhargava, this practice of secularism requires a different model of moral reasoning than ones that rely upon what Charles Taylor (1994, 16-43) terms "straightjackets": well-delineated, explicitly stated rules. Bhargava holds that one of the key characteristics of contextual secularism is its capacity to recognize that the conflicts between individual rights and group rights, between claims of equality and liberty, and between claims of liberty and the satisfaction of basic needs cannot always be adjudicated by recourse to general and abstract principles. Rather, they can be settled only case by case and may require a fine balancing of competing claims. Multivalent doctrines such as secularism encourage accommodation and the reconciliation and possible harmonization of different values – in an effort to make each value work without changing its basic content.

Bhargava's chapter defends his concept against possible accusations that it could lead to moral relativity and could elicit watered-down compromises, among other possible criticisms. Whatever contextual secularism's weaknesses might prove to be, it draws on a secularism based on some of India's lived practices in accommodating deep diversity. It is one attempt to further the practical applications of political secularism that asks what the relationship between the state and religion ought to be if the concern is to prevent religious domination and to promote freedom and equality. Although political secularism must be conceived in opposition to institutionalized religious domination, questions remain as to what this entails; for example, Modood (2011, 2) argues that despite their formal recognition of one religion, states with established religions (e.g., Britain) can still "treat the claims of all religions in accordance with multicultural equality." This stands in contrast to states whose political secularism opposes all forms of religion-centred governance – that is, theocracies and states that establish religions – and is equally opposed to amoral and antireligious secular states. Clearly, there is room for future debate as to whether political secularism does in fact require a complete separation of state and religion to fulfill its purpose. Whatever the result of such a dialogue, this volume highlights and critiques the tendency in the literature to equate political secularism with a unique version of governance developed largely in the West. This mainstream conception exhibits the very problems and weaknesses touched upon in this chapter and further explored throughout this volume. The crisis of secularism the world over is also due to certain problems internal to this mainstream version of governance. Although Bhargava's contextual secularism remains to be tested both in this volume and beyond, it exemplifies the idea of multiple secularisms. And because it lies in contrast to forms of secularism that have been studied in much more depth, it strikes deeply at the heart of the question of whether equality requires the accommodation of religious minorities as groups – rather than only as individuals – and it arises from the very lessons learned in India's confrontation with deep religious diversity. As a result, there may be much to learn from contextual secularism.

Non-Western Religious Diversity and Encounters with Secularism

Modern secularism as a culture and ideology and as an institution has come to the non-Western world largely through the experience over the past three centuries of Western imperialism and successive epochs of globalization. The adoption of the secular state in societies with a non-Christian heritage, not surprisingly, proceeded in differing ways. Sometimes, secularism was imposed by colonial rulers in an authoritarian manner often hostile to religion and by states such as France that had implemented in their own countries a radical form of secularism. In countries such as India that were ruled by Great Britain, a colonial power with its own established religion, secularism took a form more accepting of religion and religious pluralism. Finally, as in the cases of China, Turkey, and Iran, secularism was implemented under modernizing revolutions against old elites. This variety of historical trajectories reminds us again why there is no single dominant form of secularism or relationship with religion but rather a variety of distinctive national forms that differ politically, socially, and culturally. This book attempts to widen the comparative scope of analysis beyond what has been attempted before (Katznelson and Stedman Jones 2010, 11-20).

Secularism was sometimes imposed on societies where the very concept of "separation between church and state" was largely irrelevant because the leaders of these societies were also supreme religious leaders, as Laliberté shows in the case of ancient China and as Manuel Litalien shows in the case of present-day Thailand. In these and other cases theocracy was a foreign concept superimposed on societies where the dominant worldviews were not founded on a belief in one God. In non-Western states issues of domination and subordination between religious communities and the tolerance of difference both within and between communities took very different forms. The authoritarian institutions of the colonial state generally did not sanction indigenous religions, which in Africa and the Americas were largely dismissed as primitive and savage and in Asia condemned as backward and decadent. The tools and expertise of industrial modernity, both civil and military, also dismissed indigenous knowledge and practice (Adas 1990).

Contemporary responses to secularism and religious pluralism in the non-Western world are often based on earlier interactions between native traditions and colonial officials, missionaries, and settlers, and these responses have been sharpened by the social and economic crises of globalization and by its hegemonic neoliberal ideology, which challenges the world religions of the Middle East and Asia. We can identify a variety of forms of non-Western secular state. In addition to the distinction between passive, assertive, and incremental secularism in Western states, we can also distinguish between three groups of non-Western secular states according to their civilizational origins. This is not a reiteration of the categories used by Samuel Huntington (1996) but rather an approach closer to that of Schmuel Eisenstadt (2000), who looks at civilizations as metanarratives defined by core sacred texts and traditions with which large groups of people and nations identify and to which they relate their collective histories – even when they are critical of these texts and traditions and even in situations where these texts and traditions incorporate elements of other ones. These three groups of non-Western secular states adhere to metanarratives that can be categorized as *Islamic,* where the central reference is the Quran; as *Indic,* where the foundations can be traced back to the Vedic and Upanishadic tradition; and as *Sinitic,* where the foundations can be traced back to the formative Spring and Autumn periods in China more than twenty-five centuries ago. These forms correlate to the dominant religious and spiritual traditions that prevail in particular areas. It is important to keep in mind that each form contains variants depending on particular historical circumstances, including but not limited to the impacts of inter- or intrareligious warfare; conflict with the state over the establishment or disestablishment of a major religious institution such as a mosque, *mandir, fotang, gurdwara,* or the like; disputes between the state and religious authorities over the legal interpretation of holy scriptures or traditions; conflict with the state over the extent to which secular institutions ought to be established; the legacy of colonial rule in states where Christian missions played a role in conversions; and the complexity of religious diversity. Non-Western societies and governments have employed a variety of approaches in their attempts to implement secular states.

We can identify three different forms of secular state in societies where Islam represents the religious tradition of the majority. This is in addition to those Islamic states where Islam forms the ideological foundation for state institutions.[4] All of these are part of the torturous and deeply conflicted efforts in Islamic societies to come to terms with a secularism that came as an intrinsic component of Western capitalist modernity and imperialism (Tripp 2007). There are *assertive secular states* where Islam represents the religion of the majority but where the state is opposed to a conspicuous presence of religion in the public sphere.[5] There are *passive secular states* where Islam is the state religion but where – similar to western European states with established churches – religious customary law is not the source of legislation.[6] In some significant passive secular states, the Constitution does not make a specific commitment to religion, often due to the intrinsically religiously pluralist makeup of the population.[7] Finally, there are also *majoritarian secular states* where Islam is a crucial aspect of the national identity but only for larger or smaller majorities, a situation that threatens the integrity of the state if extremists aspire to impose their version of Islam on the entire country.[8] In these three types of secular state, political Islam represents an important source of inspiration for political parties, many of which aspire to take power and transform their societies according to their particular interpretation of the tenets of Islam. In those states where Islam coexists with other important religious minorities, the concept of the secular state may feel threatening to the majority religion, especially when it is fragmented along sectarian lines. Such is the situation in Lebanon, whose complex equation Bray-Collins examines in her chapter on the Lebanese youth movements' inability to establish a nonconfessional political system. She points to the difficulty of establishing a passive secular state in the context of deep religious diversity entrenched by a religiously based consociational system and in the context of the resistance of religious leaders to secularism in the absence of a strong state.

Religious diversity has long been a central characteristic of Indic Asia,[9] even though the influence of Christian missions was far more limited there than in other parts of Asia. Countries of this region established their own political institutions influenced by world religions such as Hinduism, Buddhism, and Islam. In South Asia, Hinduism primarily influenced India and Nepal, whereas in continental Southeast Asia, Buddhism constituted the major foundation for state builders in their conceptions of the appropriate relations to encourage between state and religion.[10] Whereas the religious diversity of India and the complexity of its colonial history facilitated the development of a unique and hybrid form of secular state, the religious diversity of Sri Lanka and Nepal led to the creation of established state religions: Buddhism and Hinduism, respectively. In her chapter Lamba argues that the Indian secular state's efforts to maintain neutrality towards different religious beliefs do not (and should not) prevent state intervention in religious affairs to serve goals such as social justice or equality. That is, India is neither assertive nor passive: it does not prevent the intervention of religion in public affairs, and it intervenes in religious affairs. Yet India cannot be defined as an incremental secular state because the republic's founders staunchly resisted proclaiming an established religion.

In continental Southeast Asia, a region influenced primarily by the Indian tradition for more than a millennia, the hegemonic presence of Buddhism has not prevented different reactions to the secular state. Thailand has established Buddhism as the state religion, but Burma, Laos, and Cambodia have not. Burma and Laos appear to have developed assertive secular states, whereas Cambodia developed a passive secular state following the brief dictatorship of the Khmer Rouge, which had implemented an extreme form of assertive secular state. Viewed from afar, Thailand may appear as the Buddhist equivalent of the western European state with an established religion that in effect sustains a passive secular state. However, Litalien's exposé on the close connection between the monarchy and the Buddhist religious establishment demonstrates that Thailand is not a genuinely passive secular state. Although Buddhism may seem more amenable to secularism and more tolerant of diverse beliefs, Litalien points out Thailand's continuing reluctance to recognize religious minorities.

Evidently, not one religious tradition facilitates the management of religious diversity in South Asia and Southeast Asia. In contrast to those societies influenced by Islam, however, societies with an Indic heritage appear to have reacted differently to colonial rule; in India the secular state is not seen as an imposition from the West, and in Thailand resistance to the secular state cannot be attributed to colonialism since this country was never subjected to Western domination.

East Asia demonstrates a form of secular state distinct from those of the West and of Islamic and Indic Asia. We can call it *Sinitic*, as it is deeply influenced by Chinese culture. States in this region have historically supported and sometimes established specific religions, often simultaneously. Governments have lent legitimacy to religious practices that incorporate the liturgy and belief systems of Buddhism, Confucianism, and local national traditions such as Taoism in China and Shinto in Japan, often at the same time and without appearing to favour one over the other. However, following the major divisions created by the Cold War, two different types of secular state developed, mirroring divisions between political regimes in the region: authoritarian, nominally Leninist states became extreme forms of the assertive or quasi-secular state, and liberal, pluralist states moved closer to the model of the passive secular state. The three quasi-secular states – the People's Republic of China,[11] Vietnam,[12] and the Democratic People's

Republic of Korea (or North Korea)[13] – have created societies in which the state gives recognition and protection to a limited number of established religions to the exclusion of others. In these cases, tight state control accompanies recognition. In contrast, Japan, the Republic of Korea (or South Korea), and Taiwan have developed passive secular states that recognize a variety of religions over which little state control is asserted. In all of these cases, the importation of foreign modes of religious regulation – mostly from the United States – has combined with the institutional memory of state control over religious affairs to give each region its distinctive characteristics. States with a Sinitic cultural heritage have an altogether different experience of the secular state than do Western and postcolonial states. As Laliberté argues in his chapter on Taiwan's regulation of religious affairs, the secular state in East Asia, far from being imposed by Western powers, is considered a transposition of a long tradition of state control or state regulation of religious affairs. Decisions in the region to adopt or reject the secular state do not rely on a metanarrative of foreign invasions. The adoption of secularism is partly inspired by an indigenous history in which for centuries states promoted religions whose institutionalized boundaries were often indistinguishable from those of state authority. Because the relation between the state and religions in East Asia was originally one where religion was subordinate to the state, as remains the case in China, Vietnam, and North Korea, these three polities can best be described as quasi-secular states.

To better understand the varieties of secular state in each of the four clusters discussed, it is appropriate to look into the religiously pluralistic situation in which these states were established. It is important to underline that there are few, if any, regions in the contemporary world without some form of religious diversity. We identify four broad forms of religious diversity. The first is the Western form, which has gone through different stages and is familiar due to the vast amount of scholarship on the subject. The second is the Indic form, whose deep diversity is not only unlike that of the contemporary Western world but also arguably more complex because in Indic states the traditions of Hinduism, Buddhism, Islam, and Christianity have comingled for centuries. The third form is the not often acknowledged Islamic pattern of religious diversity, which is evident primarily *within* the dominant religion but is nevertheless important enough to explain the variety of constraints that have influenced the development of different secular yet predominantly Muslim states. The fourth is the Sinitic form of religious diversity, which shares with contemporary Western and

Indic areas a condition of deep diversity that, like in South Asia but unlike in the West, has prevailed for millennia.

Conclusion

The discussion above about different clusters of religious diversity serves to remind us that although the Indian approach of principled distance may appear compelling as a way to assuage conflicts or to reconcile groups with contrasting worldviews in many non-Western or postcolonial societies, it cannot serve as a universal template. Given the stark differences between the religious policies of India and China, it is difficult to see how the latter could seek to emulate the former. In other words, there is likely to be more than one model of secular state capable of reconciling the sometimes conflicting exigencies of freedom of conscience, social justice, and political control. Nonetheless, since the global context produces powerful homogenizing effects that reinforce trends towards a "one size fits all" model of governance for the management of diversity, the idea of contextual secularism appears more relevant than ever. This book contributes to the early exploration of contextual secularism, even when the authors do not use this terminology explicitly. Chapters discuss the fundamental terms of reference, such as the original and historical meaning of secularism, the secular state under contemporary globalization, the changing nature of religious pluralism, and the effects of modernity on the above in the context of sociology, history, and political science. Chapters also question in the Canadian context the limitations of loaded concepts such as tolerance and accommodation, as well as testing the idea of the chasm between secularism and postsecularism. Finally, the comparative case studies provide empirical evidence of the relevance of contextual secularism. Even societies with relatively few cultural differences between them, such as Canada and the United States, can harbour significantly divergent approaches to the secular state. The comparison between the United States, France, and Turkey underlines how much ideological views can mould supposedly universal and value-neutral institutions differently, and the case studies on India, Taiwan, Thailand, and Lebanon confirm that cultural differences are likely to yield even more institutional forms. It is hoped that this book will encourage further explorations of a now global issue.

Notes

1 For every major religion there are affiliated parties. Christian Democrats have their counterparts among Muslims with the Adalet ve Kalkınma Partisi (Justice and Development Party) in Turkey and the Nahdlatul Ulama in Indonesia and among Buddhists with parties such as the Komeito in Japan, among others.

2 The Islamic Hamas and Hezbollah have their counterparts in the Hindu Shiv Sena in India, the militant Buddhists in Sri Lanka, and the far-right Christian militias in the United States.

3 The sharpest contemporary confrontations between secular ideology and religion, particularly in the United States, are over evolution, global warming, and human sexuality.

4 Pakistan, Iran, Afghanistan, Saudi Arabia, and Yemen, all did not experience direct colonial rule.

5 Such states are Turkey and the nations of Central Asia. Although predominantly Muslim the population of Turkey has been profoundly shaped by its contact with the West on a relatively equal basis, in contrast to the former central colonies of the Soviet Union in Central Asia.

6 Such states are Bangladesh, Iraq, Egypt, and those of the Maghreb.

7 Examples are Indonesia and Syria. However, Indonesia sits uneasily in the Islamic context, being shaped deeply by other cultural influences and non-Islamic histories.

8 Examples are Nigeria and, before 2010, Sudan.

9 Indic Asia emphasizes here the influence of religions emerging in India: Hinduism, Buddhism, Sikhism, and Jainism, among others. Indonesia, Pakistan, Bangladesh, and Malaysia could arguably all be included in the Islamic context because the influence of Islam has been pervasive in these countries for centuries.

10 This group includes Thailand, Burma, Cambodia, and Laos. Sri Lanka and Bhutan, although not in Southeast Asia, could be added to the list. Vietnam should be excluded because its traditions and political experiences are more relevant to the Sinitic world.

11 China recognizes Buddhism, Taoism, Islam, Protestant Christianity, and Catholicism.

12 Vietnam recognizes the same religions as China minus Taoism (see note 11). It also recognizes Caodaism and Hoa Hao Buddhism, both of which are indigenous developments.

13 North Korea recognizes Buddhism, Protestant Christianity, and Catholicism, as well as Chondogyo, a religion that emerged on the peninsula.

Works Cited

Adas, Michael. 1990. *Machines as the Measure of Men: Science, Technology and Ideologies of Western Dominance.* Ithaca, NY, and London: Cornell University Press.

Eisenstadt, Shmuel. 2000. "Multiple Modernities." *Daedalus* 129 (1): 1-29.

Fox, Jonathan. 2004. "The Rise of Religious Nationalism and Conflict: Ethnic Conflict and Revolutionary Wars." *Journal of Peace Research* 41 (6): 715-31.

Giddens, Anthony. 1991. *Modernity and Self-Identity: Self and Society in the Late Modern Age.* Cambridge: Polity.

Goossaert, Vincent, and David A. Palmer. 2011. *The Religious Question in Modern China*. Chicago: University of Chicago Press.

Habermas, Jürgen. 1990. *The Philosophical Discourse of Modernity*. Originally published in German in 1985. Boston: Polity.

Huntington, Samuel P. 1996. *The Clash of Civilizations and the Remaking of World Order*. New York: Simon and Schuster.

Juergensmeyer, Mark. 2008. *Global Rebellion: Religious Challenges to the Secular State*. Berkeley: University of California Press.

Katznelson, Ira, and Gareth Stedman Jones. 2010. *Religion and the Political Imagination*. Cambridge, UK: Cambridge University Press.

Modood, Tariq. 2011. "Moderate Secularism: A European Conception." *Open Democracy* 7:1-8.

Stepan, Alfred. 2000. "Religion, Democracy, and the 'Twin Toleration.'" *Journal of Democracy* 11 (4): 37-57.

Taylor, Charles. 1994. *Multiculturalism: Examining the Politics of Recognition*. Princeton, NJ: Princeton University Press.

Tong, James W. 2009. *Revenge of the Forbidden City: The Suppression of the Falungong in China, 1999-2005*. Oxford: Oxford University Press.

Tripp, Charles. 2007. *Islam and the Moral Economy: The Challenge of Capitalism*. Cambridge, UK: Cambridge University Press.

Yang, Fenggang. 2005. "Civil Society and the Role of Christianity in China." In *Civil Society as Democratic Practice*, edited by A.F. Perez, S.P. Guèye, and F. Yang, 197-212. Washington, DC: Council for Research in Values and Philosophy.

Part 1
Historical and Theoretical Approaches

Religious Pluralism as a Self-Evident Problem in the Context of Globalization

Peter Beyer

Chapter 1

Some Self-Evident Assumptions

The common theme of the chapters in this book is "secularism, the secular state, and religious diversity." Although this phrasing may seem both clear and straightforward, it nonetheless contains certain assumptions that, if perhaps obvious to most readers, are worth recalling to underscore their contingency. The first of these interrelated suppositions is that *religion* (or the religious) and *state* are distinct as concepts, as institutions, and as social regimes of communication and action. The second supposition is that the state is or can be *secular* – that is, not religious – and therefore that the term *secular* goes beyond the mere distinction between religion and state to include the idea of some form of nondependence between state and religion. As an idea, secular conceptualizes the structure of this differentiation. Calling a state secular distances it from religion, just as calling a religion apolitical distances it from the political. However, the third supposition is that *secularism* implies, among other meanings, that the state can express its secular character in a variety of ways, only one of which amounts to secularism – which I take to be an orientation of antireligiousness and principled superiority to religion or the religious, expressed perhaps through the idea that religion belongs in a private sphere, whereas the state represents a contrasting public one. Such an attitude is different from, for instance, benign or supportive neutrality, laissez-faire noninterference, or even indifference. The fourth supposition, probably the most significant in the current context, touches on a key basis for the distinction between the state and the religious: the term *state* is in principle determined, clearly formed (hence the nominative grammatical form), and meaningfully employed in the singular, whereas the term *religious* is by comparison fluidly determined, less clearly formed (hence the adjectival grammatical form), and in principle expressive of diversity. Finally, although it is perhaps not an assumption inherent in the common theme of this book, I think that this theme's phrasing also contains the idea that the relation between the secular state and religious diversity is or can be fundamentally problematic and, more specifically, that the nature of this problematic relation is in key ways related to the singularity of the one versus the diversity of the other.

Having enunciated these assumptions, I want to examine more closely exactly why they make sense and specifically why and how they make sense in the current world-historical context that we inhabit. In particular, the hypothesis that I defend is that the "obviousness" of the assumptions I have just outlined has everything to do with this global-historical context. From this starting point, I therefore proceed historically, looking at the development of the concepts, the assumptions associated with them, and the context in which they make sense historically – rather than, for instance, deductively as derived from axioms, principles, definitions, and propositions. The questions then become how, where, and when did the concepts of the secular, secularism, the religious, the secular state, and the state, with their attendant meanings, arise? And how and where do these terms operate today?

The Historical Construction of the Modern and Globalized Categories of State and Religion

The historical narrative could, of course, begin anywhere at anytime, but the most common way of approaching this sort of question is to begin somewhere in western Europe at sometime in the late-medieval or early-modern centuries, even though the terms *late-medieval* and *early-modern* already assume much about the narrative to come. Institutionally, the period after the ninth century saw the development of a *plurality* – I stress the plural – of monarchically defined political units that in form, and often in location, became the precursors of today's nationally defined European political units that we call states. At the same time, and in tandem with these political units, an ever more powerful and *singular* religious institution, in the form of the Roman Christian Church, consolidated and strengthened itself on the basis of structures that were in key ways parallel to those of the states (see Berman 1983) but also manifestly and openly distinct from them. Although the church was in many very important respects a multifunctional body whose mandate did not exclude an increasing claim to political authority, it structured itself primarily as an explicitly religious institution (see Délumeau 1983). That is, the church did not embody apolitical religion, but as self-described, it did embody religion in the singular, in contradistinction to the state and, indeed, society.

The period of the Protestant Reformation initiated a centuries-long process that brought about the mirror-imaging of this situation. For their part, the sixteenth-century reformers, whether Protestant or Catholic, sought to purify the church in the sense of rendering it more purely religious and less multifunctional, even espousing in certain cases an explicitly apolitical religion to bring this about. Several of the principal state actors of the time took advantage of the incipient religious divisions that the reformers represented to consolidate their own *sovereignty,* a word that expresses political differentiation about as well as any word could. The resulting protracted and violent conflict lasted for about a century and eventuated in an institutional structuring of the religious and political domains to the decided advantage of the latter; the Westphalian formula of *cuius regio eius religio* brought an end to the religious wars but only by subordinating the differentiated religious to the differentiated political and thus, in the same stroke, institutionalizing the pluralization of religion. The Westphalian formula, however, was also a compromise position: religion within a given singular state was still conceived of as singular, and the various "Crowns" of the political *saeculum* (temporal) were to determine the assumedly single religion, the domain of the *aeternum* (eternal), but only within *cuius* (their) *regio* (realm). In this regard, as a reflection and aspect of these institutional developments, the dominant conceptualization of both the political and the religious underwent an equally peculiar transformation. The religious during these same centuries gradually came to be conceived of not only as a singular and distinct domain called religion but also as a domain that expressed itself in a plurality of distinct religions (Despland 1979; Feil 1997). The political came to be conceived of in terms of a plurality of states (Poggi 1987) that were parallel to but not consistently isomorphic with the religions. The conceptual and institutional pluralization of both realms is noteworthy, as is the association of this transformation with division and conflict. Somewhat paradoxically – although understood as the realm of the eternal, the foundational, and the encompassing – religion, not just the political realm of the states, is also a source of this division and conflict. Accordingly, the religious and political idea of religious "tolerance" was also introduced, which still carries its meaning of forbearance, endurance in the face of provocation, and a corresponding search for unity or foundational singularity – for instance, in the idea of "natural religion" (Byrne 1989). The syntax of the Westphalian formula, however, indicated that the only location for a practical answer was the regio, which was embedded in the saeculum. It is in this indirect sense that the Europeans found the solution to the wars of religion in "secularization," a logic that worked itself out gradually over the succeeding centuries.

Over the same period two further developments were of critical importance: the expansion of European influence to cover the entire globe by the twentieth century and the shift of *cuius* in *cuius regio* from a term denoting states as expressions of individuals and royal families – that is, absolutist and monarchical rulers – to a term denoting states as necessary expressions of culturally defined peoples or nations. Both of these processes were launched during the nineteenth and early twentieth centuries. The first eventuated in the consolidation of the idea that religion was plural through the "discovery" of more religions, notably but not exclusively Hinduism and Buddhism. In combination with the inherited set of Christian, Judaic, and Islamic religions, this expansion paved the way for the development of the idea of a privileged set of "world religions" that were in principle both universal in offering a vision that included all of humankind and global in their translocality and ability to be found or established (and recognized) anywhere. In the process, religions came to be understood more as "isms" that formed a set of systematic and "reified" life-orienting regimes (Smith 1991) and less as simply the beliefs and customs of peoples and nations, even though this latter association remained very strong until well into the twentieth century (Masuzawa 2005), modelled as it was on an increasingly solidified modern European understanding. This ambiguous relation between *religio* and *natio* has to be seen in light of the second development, which had the effect of transforming states into societies by conceiving of states as geographical units with precise territorial boundaries that nonetheless contained within themselves complete and self-sustained societies centred upon the cultural idea of a unified and singular people: the nation. Within an individual state, society was therefore singular, and differences within this society, however conceived, had to be understood and incorporated with reference to this identity. The role of the state – or governmental regulatory structures – in these societies was variable, as was the place and importance of religion. However, in all but a few of the European cases of developing nation-states and national societies, an inheritance of the Westphalian regime was the continued dominance of a single religion in the form of Protestant, Catholic, and then also Orthodox Christianity – whether recognized as the de facto cultural characteristic of the nation or the de facto identity of the large majority of the people of the nation, as a de jure religious establishment, or as both. States that had "religious minorities" – Protestant dissenters from the national Protestant Church, Protestants in Catholic countries, Catholics in Protestant countries, either Protestants or Catholics in Orthodox countries, the Orthodox in either Catholic or Protestant countries, and Jews in nearly all countries – almost invariably had histories of contestation, sometimes severe, over how to deal with such "anomalies," indicating just how close religious identity and national identity were still conceived to be. The solutions from one state to the next were variable since they depended on the peculiarities of local circumstances; the core problem, however, was not variable since it resulted from a shared conceptualization of the situation and its corresponding institutionalization.

Beginning no later than the end of the eighteenth century, and in various respects even before then, these European developments with respect to the state and religion gradually ceased to be merely *European*. As the influence of the Europeans expanded, the responses of non-European parts of the world emerged, consolidated, and in their turn transformed these ideas into a range of particularizations. Although the possibility of rejecting or ignoring the Europeans and what they carried seemed possible during the earlier portions of this period, the increasingly evident power differential eventuated in the selective appropriation of European ideas and institutions but not, over time, in a simple imitation of them. The political, cultural, and societal concepts and institutions at issue here – those of the nation, the nation-state, and the national society – have been more universally and thoroughly appropriated than have the concepts and institutions of religion (and the religions), but the difference is not so great. What is important in the current context is that these appropriations happened not as part of a straightforward imperialist and colonialist process of global diffusion and homogenization but – just as was increasingly happening at the same time among the Europeans themselves – as ways of integrating into an ever more global social system on the basis of differences, specifically national differences that bore a corresponding relation to religion and religions. Globalization did not erase differences but brought about their reconstruction through ever-transforming global models, including models of state, nation, society, and religion. Key in all of this is that – at least after about the middle of the eighteenth century, if not before – these transformations and reconstructions did not affect Europe first and then everybody around the world subsequently; rather, the European transformations paralleled the globalizing processes elsewhere and were an aspect of them. This is above all the case with respect to "world religions" and "nation-states/ national societies." Moreover, and just as significantly, the reconstruction of these differences occurred in large measure as a process of mutual identification since states, nation-states, nations, national societies, and religions conceived of and institutionalized their differences in relation to and in comparison with one another. Such comparative imagination did not necessarily occur on a very broad scale in each case; the identifying differences of one nation, state, or religion could be based on comparison with only a few of the others. For instance, concerning religion, many differences were styled primarily in contrast to Christianity. In any case, the process could not and did not happen independently and, above all, was not an *inevitable outcome* of what the nation or religion essentially was, despite what most discourses of identification claimed.

Institutional Differentiation of Societal Systems and the Idea of Secularization

A further dimension must be added that corresponds to and parallels these semantic developments, namely that the same late eighteenth- to twentieth-century period witnessed an increasing differentiation between the state and religion as systematic social structures – a differentiation that expressed itself in various ways. One of these ways was propagation of the idea that states, and thereby national societies, should be and were becoming increasingly secularized, which meant quite specifically the progressive weakening of religion as a force within them. This development was not the straightforward and logical working-out of the difference between the saeculum and the aeternum, as though these two qualities had not always been conceived of as an intimately related polarity in Western sensibilities. Rather, it reflected the emergence of different institutional rationales for framing the political and the religious, among other dimensions, as societal systems. It also reflected an increasing power differential between societal systems in favour of those that were secular rather than religious. In other words, the perceived "secularization," or nonreligiousness, of states and societies from the late eighteenth to the twentieth century was a multidimensional outcome characterized less by a real decline in the presence and power of differentiated institutional religion – although this occurred to some extent here and there – and more by an increase in the presence and power of ever more clearly structured nonreligious institutional domains, which included not just the state but also, and at least as importantly, (capitalist) economy and (empirical) science (Beyer 2006).

For two reasons, I now turn to the idea of societal systems, and here my conceptualization draws a great deal from that of Niklas Luhmann (1995, 1997). The first reason is that the idea of societal systems provides an observational and theoretical point from which to understand how religion and state, in the reconstructed sense and form that they acquired over these centuries, were both sociostructurally analogous, although increasingly different, and historically highly contingent. The second reason is that the idea of societal systems enables an articulation of how modern states and modern religions differ from nations and national societies as social realities. Unlike the former, the latter have not been institutionally constructed as societal systems; rather, nations and national societies are more like cultural ecologies since they comprise loosely interconnected sets of communicative styles and themes that coalesce in coherent self-descriptions and attain much of their definition through expression in various institutional societal systems – above all, through state, law, information media, education, art, and religion.

It was in this context of the rising power and independence of nonreligious systems that the idea of secularization gradually took hold. Among other ways, it manifested itself, as it continues to do, in the notion that the state is or should be secular, meaning independent of differentiated religion, and in the notion that this independence expresses itself in a self-conceived superiority of the rationality of the state vis-à-vis the (ir)rationality of religion. Yet *secular* in this case does not necessarily mean *secularist* in the sense of the deliberate negation of religion, although this has clearly been an option. In fact, the secular state can incorporate within its structures a great deal that is religious, both in the sense of systematic religion and in the sense of seeking to embody foundational or "ultimate" concerns; the saeculum can and does seek to incorporate the aeternum but on its own terms, which often carry strong and obvious "religious" connotations. It is for this reason that different states have historically arrived at quite different arrangements with respect to religion as a differentiated institution. These arrangements include express atheism and secularism such as in the Soviet Union and the People's Republic of China, state neutrality such as in India and the United States, and varying degrees of establishment such as in Muslim and many European states. In almost all of these solutions, however, a particular feature of the Westphalian formula remains a key part of the now increasingly global model: dominant discourses consider the state, as an institution, to represent the "national society" more closely (or at least more immediately and practically) than does religion, meaning that the state is the arbiter of how religion is accommodated and, above all, how religious difference or diversity – along with other more clearly cultural diversities like ethnicity – are accommodated. Such societies are, or conceive themselves to be, "state-centred," and indeed their staus as societies depends largely on the fiction that the boundaries of the state are somehow the boundaries of society, even though a great deal of social process (e.g., transnational networks, information media, science, and especially economy – not to mention religion) does not obey the same boundaries; moreover, internal divisions are often at least as salient as the ones represented by state boundaries. In fact, the formation of these states along mutually identifiable lines through categories such as nation and artifices such as precise state boundaries is a critical aspect of the creation of a global society, where the only really effective boundary to societal processes is the physical globe.

Under the regime of perceived and progressive secularization – meaning the rational institutional state's superior legitimacy and power to assure the basis for a good national society – the issues of religion more generally and religious diversity more specifically could be fairly well contained and thought to be situated within the boundaries of individual states; states had to regulate religion as a matter of the common good in order to ensure that it remained safely confined and that it was allowed to operate "freely" in its "privatized" domain, either indefinitely or until such time as it withered away. This arrangement began to take solid hold in many states in the later part of the nineteenth and first decades of the twentieth century, reaching its apogee in the 1950s and probably peaking in the 1960s in most places around the world – from North America to Europe, from China to the United Arab Republic, and from the Soviet Union to India. Since then, however, the world has changed – or at least our perception of the world has changed – in response to a real or perceived transformation that observers have sought to capture in various new concepts, especially those of globalization and the postmodern. It is to a consideration of this contemporary circumstance that I now turn.

The "Resurgence" of Religion, Challenge to the State, and the Problem of Religious Diversity

The perceived secularization of national societies from the later nineteenth to the mid-twentieth century probably reflected the greater differentiation and comparatively accelerated power upgrading of nonreligious systems more than a real decline in institutional and differentiated religion; indeed, it is arguable that in many regions religion increased its distinctiveness and societal presence over this period. In much the same way, the contemporary situation is also a matter of a change in perception regarding the relative power of these same institutions, most particularly the state and religion. With hindsight, we can see many of the developments responsible for bringing this change about.

The year 1979 can serve as a convenient symbolic starting point, as this was the year of the Iranian Revolution, the founding of Jerry Falwell's Moral Majority Inc. in the United States, the Nicaraguan Revolution with its liberation-theology priests and their mobilization, and the accession to the papal throne of John Paul II (see Beyer 1994). The former two especially were greeted with what can only be called shock by a great many observers accustomed to seeing the world as secularized or secularizing. Here expressly religious and institutionally religious people and movements exerted what seemed to be direct and effective political power, breaking forth from their privatized domains into an arena deemed essentially secular in the sense already described. These events were followed over the next decade and a half by several more: the rise of the Solidarity movement in Poland, with its openly Catholic identity; an increasingly violent situation in the Indian Punjab that eventuated in the partial destruction of the Sikh Golden Temple in Amritsar and years of intense violence between Sikh nationalists and Indian government forces; the deterioration of Tamil-Sinhalese relations in Sri Lanka, leading to a civil war largely defined in terms of Hindu Tamils versus Buddhist Sinhalese; the rise of long-standing Hindu nationalist parties to prominence and eventually government in India, along with continued or increased "communal" violence as represented most graphically in the destruction of the Babri Masjid in Ayodhya in 1992; the sharply increased profile of religious Zionism in Israel, both in terms of presence in government and in terms of the settlement movement in the occupied territories; and accelerated Islamist mobilization in a wide range of countries from Algeria and Egypt (one thinks of the assassination of Anwar Sadat in 1981 by Islamist militants) to Pakistan and the Philippines. Significantly, these politicized religious movements rose out of the "world religions": Christianity, Sikhism, Hinduism, Buddhism, Judaism, and Islam.

If these movements – characteristically, and in a somewhat fearfully pejorative manner, labelled "fundamentalisms" – could be seen as representing the resurgence of religion, the effective transformation or elimination of the most secularist states over the same period had an analogous, if opposite, effect on the perception of the strength of states. The People's Republic of China and the Soviet Union both began significant internal transformations in the 1980s, as the former embarked on the "capitalist road" of Deng Xiaoping and the latter pursued glasnost and perestroika under Mikhail Gorbachev. But it was the fall of the Berlin Wall in 1989, and with it the so-called Iron Curtain, and the dissolution of the Soviet Union itself in 1991 that opened the floodgates for a significant reconceptualization of how the social world was perceived. The concept of globalization dates from the late 1970s and early 1980s and to some extent even before (see Modelski 1968), but it was in the early 1990s that *globalization* became a common buzzword among academics and politicians, in the mass media, and in common debate. In effect, the fall of the Soviet Union ended the Cold War and therewith the basis for the division of nation-states into first, second, and third worlds. Rapid change in China did not exhibit the discontinuity displayed in the Soviet case – although the Tiananmen Square Massacre in 1989 was symptomatic of what was happening in this regard – but it effectively removed this state from the possibility of being seen as the new leading torchbearer of the global socialist option. The upshot was that globally the socialist – and explicitly secularist-atheist – option was dead. In this context, its erstwhile rival, capitalism, was perceived by many to have won the war. The dominant understanding of the now wildly and suddenly popular term *globalization* was that it denoted worldwide dominance of the capitalist economic system, especially in the form of, or in conjunction with, the neoliberal ideology that had apparently been adopted by the vast majority of the powerful and not so powerful states – from the United States and Great Britain to Turkey, China, and even India. As framed by Francis Fukuyama (1992), (capitalist) liberalism had triumphed as the only option! To be sure, there were other significant developments that contributed to such reconsiderations, notably but not exclusively the much more global flux of transnational migration after the 1960s and the invention and spread of the Internet and other electronic communication technologies. One could even argue that the development of computerized technology in the 1970s and 1980s was just as instrumental in the fall of the Soviet empire as any other factor. However that may be, in the early part of the 1990s the world seemed to be much more closely integrated, with capitalist economy as its main integrating force and with the United States as the only undisputed world power. Compared to these now seemingly dominant aspects, the old nation-states were seen by many to have faded (Rudolph and Piscatori 1997; Beck 2000). At the same time, however, the perceived triumph of capitalist liberalism over the state, coupled with the worldwide incidence of apparent religious resurgence, did not go unnoticed, yielding an alternate and, by the beginning of the twenty-first century, just as persuasive conceptualization of the "world order."

Much has been said about Samuel Huntington's (1996) "clash of civilizations" thesis, particularly how it represents a quasi-reactionary defence of the "West against the rest," how it misconstrues and invents the so-called civilizations that are supposedly clashing, and how it has, if anything, taken on the character of a dangerously self-fulfilling prophecy, eagerly taken up by those who would dearly love the world to be this way. Although such criticisms do have their justification (I count myself among those who see his arguments as fundamentally flawed), we must pause to look more closely at the context that makes sense of Huntington's text given that the objections do not seem to have been fatal to his thesis and that certain events arguably illustrate, at least graphically, what he has said – including what has undoubtedly been the most iconic of the current era, the attacks of 11 September 2001. As I have outlined, the series of religiopolitical movements that gave rise both to the idea of a (global) religious resurgence and to the current meaning of the term *fundamentalism* occurred during the same decades that saw the end of the Cold War and the emergence of the idea of globalization, with its neoliberal overtones. Among the many consequences of this simultaneity has been a much heightened awareness that all of us in the world are in fact living in the single social space – the global society – to which the idea of globalization refers (see Robertson 1992). These are not the only factors that have encouraged such an awareness, but they are two very important ones. They also point in opposite directions concerning the internal ordering of the global society: whereas neoliberal globalization is a homogenizing perspective, fundamentalisms point to fundamental differences. Yet the religions out of which fundamentalist movements have emerged are not consistently coterminous with states; they do not express the logic of the Westphalian model of the secular state and national society. It would be more accurate to say that they contradict it. Huntington's categorization for the most part feeds on and reflects this situation; the civilizations, only one of which represents Fukuyama's (1992) liberalism, are all religiously characterized, if not consistently along the lines of the so-called "world religions." From this perspective, the "clash of civilizations" implicitly points to the perceived end of the dominance of the Westphalian model. The secular state is under attack and being undermined in terms of both its secularity and its national statehood. It is no longer the principal delimiter of the encompassing whole – society – in which human beings live out their lives. This attack comes from the side of capitalism, communication technologies, and transnational networks, all of which erode the efficacy of the secular state's boundaries, as well as from the side of religion and civilization, which substitute alternate boundaries. This conclusion leads back to the third notion in the common theme mentioned at the outset of this chapter: that of religious diversity.

Religious diversity, as I tried to show earlier, is not a new issue. Even in its current form, centred as it is on the idea that the singular domain of religion expresses itself predominantly through (world) religions, it is at least a couple of centuries old. What is new, however, is the connotation that very often accompanies reference to religious diversity, namely that there is something inherently problematic about this diversity or at least that what is most significant about religion in today's world is its inherent diversity. This problematic or significant nature of religious diversity, I suggest, is a reflection of the contemporary circumstance that I have just discussed. The secular state as the premier institutional expression of the national society has lost a good portion of its self-evidence. In terms of religion, this has meant an undermining of the basic, and for a long time comfortable, secularization assumption. No longer subordinated in Westphalian fashion to the state and its national society, religion appears to be making a comeback. Instead of upholding secularization as the dominant lens through which religion is observed – or, more often, ignored – it seems imperative to find a substitute because it is now evident that religion is a resurgent or threatening force that cannot be ignored. In this situation, it is not secularization but religion's diversity that appears as the new self-evident and dominant organizing concept when observing religion (see Beyer 2007). Globally, religious diversity manifests its importance through "fundamentalism" (especially the Islamic sort), perhaps to the point of an ineluctable "clash of civilizations." Within the confines of the state-centred society, this powerful alternate form of identification appears to be at best a challenge and at worst an invasion by global forces that could undermine the order and integrity of the national society, the state, and the nation. Religious diversity can appear to threaten chaos.

The form that such a challenge or invasion takes corresponds to the global forms that seem to have undermined the secular state: politicized religion (which wishes to take over the state) and the global ties that allow the easy circulation of religious ideologies, religious ways, and the migratory populations that carry "foreign" religions. The details of the situation vary significantly from state to state and from global region to global region. For the rich Western countries of North America, western Europe, and Australasia, the challenge and the threat have been substantially funnelled through transnational migration and the intensification of the transnational networks in which the migrants participate. The questions that arise are indicative. Will the new migrants practise their different religions, and even the religions that dominate in host countries, in a way that threatens or reinforces national integrity and order? Will they act as conduits for the infection of the national body politic with the actions and orientations of the civilizationally and religiously irreconcilable Other – most poignantly through the "native"-born children of these migrants? What constitutes "reasonable accommodation" of this comparatively "irrational" religious diversity? Interestingly, all of these questions have been posed before, notably in the late nineteenth and early twentieth centuries, albeit substantially funnelled through different or additional categories of difference, most notably "race." Today, however, it is religion that has become the privileged category in this regard. Declaring itself to be "legion," it carries the "strangers at the gates" who may threaten the good and peaceable kingdom within. One irony, of course, is that one of the entirely possible responses to this situation is to seek a kind of reinforcement of the original Westphalian formula, which addressed the problem of religious diversity by insisting on a single religion within – whether a recognized religion or its ersatz in the form of civil religion, both of which are in effect reassertions, with different degrees of explicitness, of the necessity of having a single religion within.

My formulation of the problem that religious diversity presents is deliberately extreme and perhaps overly dramatic. What I want to underscore with this language is the degree to which religion and religious diversity are becoming or threaten to become convenient and identifiable representatives of the unease and uncertainty that come with a fundamentally changing global sociostructural situation or at least with the increasing awareness of this change. The question must then be raised of whether religion, as it has been institutionally reconstructed since the sixteenth century, is the problem and challenge today that it was for Europeans in the sixteenth and seventeenth centuries? Is the shared judgment of various secularization attitudes that religion represents irrationality at all appropriate for the current world-historical circumstances? If we consider the underlying sociostructural issue, with its strong semantic correlates, to be one of differentiation of distinct rationalities that are not reducible to one another – that is, if we regard religious, political, economic, scientific, and other rationalities as simply different and not incommensurate – religious diversity is no more, and is probably significantly less, of a problem than economic singularity.

Summary and Conclusions

My basic argument hinges on the core "sociology of knowledge" idea that what we think we know has everything to do with the social context – the social structures – that we inhabit. The perception that the relationship between the notions and social structures that we call state and religion is problematic and that this problematic relation has found its expression in supposed challenges to the secularity of the state in the face of the diversity of (resurgent) religions is highly contingent on a peculiar confluence of historical circumstances and transformations. In the West, as in most other regions of the world, the modern idea of sovereign states with precise boundaries that express and exist for collective agents called nations is a peculiar historical conception and institutional construction – as is the idea that systematic and institutional religions, mainly but not exclusively the world religions, are the main way that the idea of religion manifests itself. In the context of specific historical developments, the notions and structures of religions and states not only arose, and came to be conceived of as being, in opposition to each other but also arose intimately tied to one another; that is, states, nations, nationalisms, and religions emerged together as categories of understanding and as social structures.

Towards the middle of the nineteenth century, and in several cases well before, the growing independence of the state and religious institutional domains, along with the greater power of the former, seeded the development of the idea and the expectation that states and their national societies should become, or were becoming, more secularized – which is to say, less religious. This development reached its apogee towards the middle of the twentieth century, when a series of transformations that had undoubtedly been going on for some time eventuated in a rising number of events that convinced many an elite observer that we were now living in a different world, namely a postmodern and globalizing one. These events included religious ones that seemed to suggest that we were no longer living in a secularized or increasingly secularizing world and political ones that seemed to suggest that both the state's secular character and its ability to guarantee and carry forward the good national society were weakening. In this context, the religious challenge appears to take the form of religious diversity, sometimes expressed in movements emerging from the so-called world religions and labelled *fundamentalist,* a term that carries heavy intimations of the nonmodern, the irrational, and the dangerous.

The fact that much of the problem is therefore an artifact of the concepts and denotations that we use, and thus largely a problem of perception, does not in the least detract from the fact that there have been real and challenging developments in our world to which these perceptions correspond. The attacks of 11 September 2001 and the fall of the Soviet Union happened, as did so many other momentous events. The recognition of their import, however, not only should lead us to answer the question "now what?" but also should signal the need to question some underlying and taken-for-granted assumptions, including those about the place, form, and importance of religion within society, and in relation to the state, as a still powerful and dominating structure. A start in this direction may be to question whether we ever did live in an increasingly secularizing world, whether what we call religion is really any more irrational – as opposed to differently rational – than any other human endeavour, and therefore whether religious diversity represents any more of a threat or a challenge that needs to be managed and controlled than anything else, be it capitalist enterprise, artistic expression, or high-performance sport. It may be that religion in its diversity becomes far less of an issue to the degree that we simply convince ourselves that it belongs in our world as much as these other things, no more and no less, and that it is normal even in its strong versions.

Works Cited

Beck, Ulrich. 2000. *What Is Globalization?* Translated by P. Camiller. London: Polity.

Berman, Harold J. 1983. *Law and Revolution: The Formation of the Western Legal Tradition.* Cambridge, MA: Harvard University Press.

Beyer, Peter. 1994. *Religion and Globalization.* London: Sage.

–. 2006. *Religions in Global Society.* London: Routledge.

–. 2007. "Globalization and Glocalization." In *The Sage Handbook of the Sociology of Religion,* edited by James A. Beckford and N.J. Demerath III, 98-117. London: Sage.

Byrne, Peter. 1989. *Natural Religion and the Nature of Religion: The Legacy of Deism*. London: Routledge.

Délumeau, Jean. 1983. *Le péche et la peur: La culpibilisation en Occident, XIIIe-XVIIIe siècles*. Paris: Fayard.

Despland, Michel. 1979. *La religion en occident: Evolution des idées ed du vécu*. Montreal: Fides.

Feil, Ernst. 1997. *Religio: Die Geschichte eines neuzeitlichen Grundbegriffs zwischen Reformation und Rationalismus (ca. 1540-1620)*. Vol. 2. Göttingen: Vandenhoeck and Ruprecht.

Fukuyama, Francis. 1992. *The End of History and the Last Man*. New York: Avon Books.

Huntington, Samuel P. 1996. *The Clash of Civilizations and the Remaking of World Order*. New Delhi: Viking/Penguin.

Luhmann, Niklas. 1995. *Social Systems*. Translated by J. Bednarz Jr. and D. Baecker. Stanford, CA: Stanford University Press.

–. 1997. *Die Gesellschaft der Gesellschaft*. Frankfurt am Main: Suhrkamp.

Masuzawa, Tomoko. 2005. *The Invention of World Religions*. Chicago: University of Chicago Press.

Modelski, George. 1968. "Communism and the Globalization of Politics." *International Studies Quarterly* 12 (4): 380-93.

Poggi, Gianfranco. 1987. *The Development of the Modern State: A Sociological Introduction*. Stanford, CA: Stanford University Press.

Robertson, Roland. 1992. *Globalization: Social Theory and Global Culture*. London: Sage.

Rudolph, Susanne Hoeber, and James Piscatori, eds. 1997. *Transnational Religion and Fading States*. Boulder, CO: Westview.

Smith, Wilfred Cantwell. 1991. *The Meaning and End of Religion*. Minneapolis: Fortress.

Secular Modernity, Religion, and the Politics of Knowledge

Bruce J. Berman

Chapter 2

In the 1960s social scientists in America predominantly taught that religion was a declining force in human life and was increasingly being supplanted by a humanistic secular modernity based on scientific knowledge. Indeed, it was as a systematic and verifiable way of knowing and acting on the world that secular science was replacing belief in the supernatural and the "superstition" of religious faith. The era was the apogee of the Keynesian regimes of state-managed capitalism and social-democratic welfare, which offered citizens of western Europe and North America both social stability and increasing affluence. The only serious threat to liberal democracy was the Cold War rivalry of the even more extreme secular modernity of Soviet communism. Internally, sociologists like Daniel Bell (1960) and Daniel Lerner (1951) could proclaim the "end of ideology" in the obsolescence of class struggle through the collaboration of labour, capital, and the state guided by the instrumental reason of the "policy sciences." In Western intellectual life it was an era of belief in the power of expert knowledge to limitlessly expand the horizons of human agency. Liberation movements in the colonial world were driven by secular ideologies of nationalism and diverse strains of socialism. It was widely believed that the problems of poverty and development in the newly named and emergent third world nations would be solved within a generation.

I need hardly point out that almost none of these expectations have come to pass, not least the demise of religion as a force in human societies. Indeed, the world seems to have become more religiously inclined than ever, with "faith-based" politics increasingly pursued by strident and aggressive religious institutions and movements. The battle over secularism and the separation of religion and politics has re-emerged in the West, particularly in the United States, and rapidly developed within ethnocultural communities in the non-Western world since 1980, replacing the modernist movements of anticolonial mobilization of the 1940s to the 1970s and giving ethnic conflicts an increasingly violent edge through "fundamentalist" religious movements and intensified battles over "authenticity" (Fox 2004, 718-19, 721, 724-28). Secularism appears to be an ever more beleaguered doctrine in the face of a worldwide religious revival and ethnoreligious conflicts in increasingly multicultural and religiously diverse societies.

Or is this really the case? The intrusion of religion into national and international political arenas appears to come largely from a few very specific sources: evangelical Protestantism centred in the United States; radical Islam emanating from Saudi Arabia, Iran, and Pakistan, with global penetration in both the Western and non-Western worlds; and immigrant ethnoreligious communities in Europe and North America that command substantial attention in their political arenas and the media. On the other hand, during the past forty years in three of the most religiously grounded national communities in the West – Spain, Quebec, and Ireland – the influence of the Catholic Church has dramatically declined in the face of secular modernity. Moreover, continuing sensational revelations about sexual abuse of children by Catholic clergy and cover-ups by the church's hierarchy have deeply undermined its moral authority, especially in North America and Europe. Even in the United States, as indicated by the Pew Foundation surveys published early in 2008, the most rapidly growing religious category was those who had no religious affiliation, reaching an unprecedented 16 percent of the population, as high as in Canada, and even evangelical churches had experienced slight declines in their membership (Pew Forum 2008). Nonetheless, the place of religious institutions in political life is certainly an issue everywhere, but I would suggest that it reflects less a growing religiosity than a response to a social crisis and a perceived threat to religious institutions from secular modernity.

In this chapter I sketch out an argument about the relationship between religious communities and institutions and the growing social crisis of globalization, noting how this relationship is expressed through what I call the "politics of knowledge" and through the growth of both religious and secular millennial and utopian movements that challenge the secular state.

This analysis focuses on the political, economic, and cultural factors that shape institutions rather than on the specific aspects of religious belief systems, except in so far as these systems mould the political presence or actions of the institution and its adherents. Such belief systems encroach on the secular political arena as a combination of both interest and faith, particularly in the rejection of the moral grounding of both secular institutions and other faith communities by the most extreme religious movements.

Religion and Politics in the Premodern World

The unique Western historical and cultural experience of the development of secular modernity created "religion" (i.e., Judaism, Christianity, and Islam) as a distinct and separate sphere of human knowledge and practice in a way that would be largely unknown to the rest of the world until it arrived with European colonization and global hegemony. For most peoples and cultures the natural and supernatural were united dimensions of a single understanding of the world; the profane and sacred worlds were two intimately linked dimensions of a single reality. There was no sense, in particular, of the political as a distinct sphere into which religious belief and practice could intrude. Instead, the sacred and supernatural worlds provided an immediate and ritualized legitimation of the temporal distributions of power, wealth, and social honour. In what was likely the earliest cultural conception of the unity of the natural and supernatural, and in what is still probably one of the most universal conceptions even within the context of modern religions, ancestor worship both honoured forebears, whose spirits continued to affect the well-being of their living descendants, and sanctioned the patriarchal and matriarchal authority of living elders, soon to be ancestors themselves, in extended multigenerational kin groups.

The development of larger and more complex communities brought the development of distinct supernatural beings – gods – who shaped the destiny of the living community and were addressed directly by temporal rulers on behalf of the whole society. As Karl Marx noted, the hierarchies of the gods closely corresponded to the secular hierarchies of power. The most common epithet for "God" in ancient Israel was "Melech ha Gadol," the "high king," the typical title for rulers of states in the region. The supernatural world, however, was a crowded one, with each state, and even each local community, having its own god or gods, and people often worshiped several. Polytheism was common even in ancient Israel up to the construction of modern Judaism in the last centuries BCE. (Why choose between Yahweh or Baal, and risk offending one, when you could prudently honour both?)

Ancient imperial states did not destroy the gods of the states they conquered but absorbed them into a sacred and secular hierarchy that preserved local elites in the pattern of indirect rule that has typified imperial states down to the twentieth century. Religious beliefs and institutions, including the development of specialized practitioners, served to legitimate the moral economy of the unequal distribution of political power, material wealth, and social honour. This included the reciprocal obligations of rulers and subjects, with the loyalty and obedience of the latter balanced by the obligation of rulers to provide protection and stability for their subjects against outside attack and natural disaster, including the redistribution of material goods to meet the needs of survival. Rulers, with their direct and intimate relationship to the gods, had to do their duty to even the poor and powerless; to fail was to lose the "mandate of heaven" – a loss that brought down the dynasties of ancient China.[1]

The ancient Middle East also saw the development of an insurgent religious tradition that challenged the intertwined structures of sacred and profane power and its legitimating moral economy. This included the development of diverse sects and cults outside of the official hierarchies in response to imperial conquest and domination. Christianity emerged as part of the Jewish response to Roman rule, building on a prophetic tradition that "spoke truth to power" in the name of the poor and powerless and on belief in messianic redemption, as well incorporating widespread contemporary beliefs in the apocalyptic and millennial transformation of the world. As an oppositional movement that threatened the hegemonic moral economy and sacred-secular hierarchy of the Roman Empire, it was initially ruthlessly suppressed. When, with Constantine's conversion, Christianity became the official religion of the empire, inextricably intertwined with the secular institutions of power and with the central ideological basis for the legitimacy of the empire's moral economy, a crucial contradiction was introduced into Western institutions and culture. On the one hand, the developing institutions of the church maintained an intimate and mutually supportive, if often strained, relationship with the secular institutions of political power while, on the other hand, harbouring a tradition of apocalyptic millennialism that challenged both temporal and spiritual power.

The Western Development of Church and State:
Separating Secular and Sacred Power

After the decline of the Roman Empire western Europe broke into a variety of polities, including feudal baronies, self-governing towns and city-states, often vaguely defined kingdoms, an increasingly shadowy Holy Roman Empire, and even self-governing peasant communes in Switzerland and Spain – some 400 units of varying degrees of size and autonomy by 1500. Through a period of more than a thousand years, the only "universal" institution was the Catholic Church, which developed as a hierarchy of power parallel to and in competition with secular political units and exercised direct temporal political power in the rule of episcopal city-states and the papal realms of Italy and France. Church institutions generally supported the positions and power of the dominant class, despite increasing tension over competition for supremacy, but this close association with temporal power and wealth "corrupted" them. During periods of acute social crisis the millennial tradition emerged in mass movements that challenged the concentrated political power and wealth of princes and the church and drew, in turn, savage repression from political and ecclesiastic authorities.

The Reformation marked a deep cleavage as Protestant sects rejected the corrupt material wealth and secular power of the Catholic Church and the princes it supported, articulating a truth sanctioned "by faith alone." The princes of Europe, however, were divided between those who became Protestants and those who remained Catholic, and Lutherans sought mutual support from Protestant princes. The resulting religious wars, with both temporal and spiritual power at stake, produced an extraordinary "exterminating" violence, as well as the consolidation of larger and more powerful monarchic states. From the sixteenth to the eighteenth century the developing states gradually subjugated ecclesiastic institutions to secular power in return for state recognition and ideological support of the dominant position of these institutions within the realm. The Peace of Augsburg in 1555 established the doctrine *cuius regio, eius religio* (whose reign, that religion; or in the prince's land, the prince's religion), thereby permitting the German princes to be either Catholic or Lutheran and to establish either religion as the faith of their realm, and the Treaty of Westphalia in 1648 extended recognition to Calvinist churches and to a European system of sovereign and ostensibly equal states after thirty years of sanguinary religiopolitical warfare. By the seventeenth century Europe had developed a unique system of states based on politically sustained "established" churches that were clearly tied to the legitimation and support of monarchic power in developing modern states through the doctrine of the "divine right of kings."

The Christian countertradition of messianic and millenarian movements also produced in the intense upheavals of the early-modern era numerous more radical movements that challenged the developing hierarchies of churches and states and were repressed by both Catholic and Protestant princes and churches. In Norman Cohn's classic study *The Pursuit of the Millenium* (1970), these movements are described as having an idea of salvation with five distinctive characteristics: it was *collective,* in that it was enjoyed by the community of the faithful; *terrestrial,* in that it was realized on earth rather than in heaven or in an afterlife; *immanent,* in that it was bound to come soon and suddenly; *total,* in that it would not only improve life on earth but also transform and perfect it; and *miraculous,* in that its coming would be achieved or assisted by divine agency. The English Civil War in the mid-seventeenth century is widely recognized as a crucial starting point for the transition from medieval millennialism to modern secular revolution with a focus on bringing into being a utopia of perfect social order and harmony without oppression, poverty, or human conflict. Radical sects like the Levellers and Fifth Monarchy Men challenged the Puritan parliamentary elite from within the Parliamentary Army itself and looked to the establishment of divine rule on earth (Walzer 1965). The millenarian tradition carried with it as well a sanctioning of violence to destroy the corrupt old world and nonbelievers who opposed it in a cleansing and therapeutic process that brought the new world into being by blood and fire. Again, state and religious authorities moved to crush such threatening heresies and threats to the established social order.

Western Secularism and Anti-Clericalism

If the establishment of the discrete but linked temporal and spiritual hierarchies of state and church was a unique aspect of Western historical experience, so too were the later efforts to sever the link and to place a wall of separation between church and state. The basis of Western secularism is an anticlericalism focused on eliminating the earthly power of religious institutions. Anticlericalism was directed at the power of established churches and its use to prop up the secular power of the absolutist state, as well as at their oppression of minority religious communities, both Christian and non-Christian. At one crucial level the issue was not the particulars of religious belief but the direct exercise of secular power by religious institutions and clerical authorities. Religious belief and adherence to one or another religious community became instead a matter of private belief and choice. The anticlericalism of the eighteenth-century revolutions began a process of separating church and state as part of the overthrow of the *anciens régimes* of the absolutist monarchies. It did not necessarily eliminate the political expression of religious belief as much as gradually introduce and legitimate religious pluralism as a central component of the rights of citizenship. This process, however, was particularly protracted in those developing constitutional monarchies of Europe that maintained an established church and where the adherents of other religions acquired their citizen rights by leaving the public expression of their faith behind. As I note below, in the United States the separation of church and state, in striking contrast, actually promoted the development of a powerful but increasingly diverse religious presence in the public arena.

For European states the particular focus of religious freedom and pluralism was the extension of full citizenship rights to Jews in both the state and civil society that came as a consequence of the secular revolutions of the eighteenth century. Although the civic nation welcomed the Jews as citizens, antimodernist conservatism, increasingly obsessed with the "volkskultur" of the "real" people as the basis of the nation, had by the end of the nineteenth century proclaimed increasingly ethnicized conceptions of citizenship and had expelled Jews from the national community, condemning them as evil agents of the most hated aspects of secular modernity: science, capitalism, and socialism. At that time the central arena of the confrontation between the forces of secular modernity and clerical conservatism, and between civic and ethnic nationalism, came in France with the Dreyfus affair, which still divides French political and intellectual life into the twenty-first century. Most European states removed the civil restrictions on and exclusions of Jews, both legal and customary, piecemeal during the nineteenth century, although they were reimposed with a murderous rigour with the rise of fascism and Nazism. Jews did not, in fact, achieve full civic citizenship and the ability to publicly express their religious life and institutions throughout Europe until the end of the twentieth century and the fall of communism. And it is worth remembering that the stigmatization and oppression of the Jews are unique to Western Christian experience, in contrast to their far more benign experience of subordination in the Islamic world and in the areas of Asia and Sub-Saharan Africa that had no awareness of them until being subjected to European imperialism.

The more difficult dimension of the relationship between religion and politics is derived from the secular culture of modernity, which undermines and delegitimizes the expression of religious belief in the political arena.

Religion and the Culture of Modernity: The "Disenchantment of the World"

The culture of modernity derives from the Enlightenment project of applying "reason," or an instrumental rationality, to understanding and controlling the natural and social worlds. The key was the use of "practical reason" to extend human agency and free humanity from the uncontrolled power of forces beyond human understanding. For Max Weber (1948, 129-56), this was the "disenchantment of the world," in which human understanding and agency were freed from the unseen power of the supernatural. Modernity radically separated the sacred and the secular and denied any causal effect of the former on the latter. This was a radical secularization of the world through the systematic development of rational knowledge and its instrumental application. The world is the contingent outcome of scientific laws whose understanding permits purposeful intervention to control both social and natural reality. Secular modernity is, literally, a-theistic. Rather than the result of divinely ordained necessity or fate or the work of magical or supernatural forces, events were now the deliberate, although often unforeseen and unintended, outcome of human agency and choice. For Marx, this was the movement from the realm of necessity to the realm of freedom, the advent of humanity being able to choose and create its future.

Valid knowledge in modern culture is grounded in our theoretical and conceptual understanding of verifiable empirical knowledge about the temporal world, not based on faith in the unseen and supernatural. From the eighteenth century, proponents of secular modernity, especially among Western natural and social scientists, assumed and repeatedly declared the ultimate demise of religion and other forms of irrational superstition and their replacement by rational science (Fox 2004, 715-17). At the same time, from the very beginnings of the scientific revolution, new knowledge about nature was readily and enthusiastically applied to our understanding of real-world problems of production, engineering, and commerce (Jacob 1997). Furthermore, the development of human agency and instrumental reality was based increasingly on our understanding of probability and risk in a contingent world. This latter change remains one of the most challenging cultural expressions of secularization, as suggested by the title of Peter Bernstein's history of probability and risk, *Against the Gods* (1998).

Anthony Giddens (1991) famously described the culture of modernity as being based on "surveillance and reflexive self-monitoring," namely the systematic surveillance of nature and society and the reflexive self-monitoring of actions and consequences through the application of increasingly diverse systems of specialized knowledge, all grounded in claims to apply scientific methods in the production of valid knowledge that permits the rational management of risk. Such "expert systems" provide the basis for the expansion of the agency and control of capitalist enterprises and the state and are a central characteristic of formal bureaucratic organizations. For organization theorists like James March and Herbert Simon (1958), expert knowledge combining surveillance and self-monitoring is the basis for the "control of uncertainty" in bureaucracies, whether in the manufacture of cars, the marketing of fast food, the delivery of public health systems, or the defence of the nation. The evolution of secular modernity has thus involved a radical change both in the kind of knowledge accorded an authoritative position within its dominant institutions and in the kind of social roles accorded interpretive authority in the management of risk and uncertainty.

At the cultural and epistemological levels, secular modernity not only radically separated the sacred and profane worlds but also denied the worldly agency of the supernatural. The content of religious belief or faith does not constitute verifiable or falsifiable knowledge and thus cannot meet the criteria of truth that are supposed to be met by scientific knowledge and technical expertise. Religious "knowledge" has thus steadily lost its hegemony in pluralistic secular societies in the face of the authority of science and other forms of expert knowledge. One was free to believe what one wished about the supernatural and even free to pray for divine intervention, but when seeking guidance, one was never to rely on the supernatural as a replacement for expert knowledge of material reality: "Praise the Lord *but* pass the ammunition." Secular modernity not only separated church and state institutionally but also rejected religious belief as the basis for action in the public arenas of state and market. Scientific secularism has been identified largely with the liberal and left-wing traditions in Western politics since the eighteenth century, whereas antimodernism has been the primary underlying factor of right-wing politics, whether in the movements of religious revival, romantic reaction, or conservative nationalism in the nineteenth and twentieth centuries. What the political right in the West reacted against was the profound threat that secular modernity posed to the legitimacy of traditional political and religious elites by undermining – indeed, destroying – the hegemonic moral economy on which their power and wealth rested, the relations of power and dependence embedded in the ontological frameworks of religious cosmologies, and the meaningful routines of social tradition.

The victory of science in the politics of knowledge in the West was based on the stereotypical notion, actively promoted by scientists, that science provided knowledge that was undistorted by values or subjective judgments and thus true, confirmed, universal, and objective. What is interesting is that contemporary studies of the history and sociology of science reveal an actual process that is highly political in practice, where theories and empirical findings are often contested and where intense negotiations are involved in the acceptance or rejection of claimed major innovations. The "proof" of even so profoundly important a scientific development as the theory of relativity turns out to be based on ambiguous evidence accepted on the basis of subjective judgments by the scientists involved and "confirmed" by the success of future research built on acceptance of the premise of its truth.[2] For this reason, scientific knowledge is increasingly spoken of as "constructed" rather than discovered. Nevertheless, the hegemony of science and the diverse forms of expert knowledge that have emulated its methods and claims to objective reason and truth probably reached their apogee in the first half of the twentieth century, before being increasingly undermined by catastrophic moral and political failures like the Holocaust and the American attempt in Vietnam to fight a "technically perfect war."[3]

Secular modernity thus excludes religion from the public arena both institutionally and culturally. Of these, the latter is more politically problematic and contested, especially in increasingly religiously pluralistic contemporary societies and in response to the developing crisis of the moral economy in global capitalism. I would like to look first at the politics of knowledge in the relationship between religion and the state in secular liberal democracies and then at the major dimensions of the contemporary confrontation between religion and politics in the United States.

Religion, the State, and the Politics of Knowledge

Kalman Silvert (1963) and Robert Dahl (1956) have defined secular, democratic nation-states in complementary ways. For Silvert, the state is the ultimate and impersonal arbiter of secular disputes in societies of formally free and equal citizens. Its policies proclaim an interim and provisional "truth" regarding only temporal issues; all laws and policies are in principle revisable in light of changed circumstances. For Dahl, the secular state takes no position and makes no decisions with regard to "ultimate values"; instead, democratic politics have forged "cross-cutting ties" among diverse competing interests in pluralistic societies with regard to alliances on specific issues and policies dealing only with the secular natural and social worlds.

Underlying both perspectives is a belief in democracy as contained in procedural rules for the peaceful resolution of conflicts occasioned only by issues of mundane reality. In religiously pluralistic societies, governments make no judgment on the "truth" of one religion versus another. At the same time, although religious belief or faith cannot be excluded as the basis for an individual's or a group's position on secular political issues, religious knowledge or faith can claim no special authoritative status and, as noted above, is politically castigated not only because it is based on nonverifiable superstition but also because conflicting claims of faith by different religious groups cannot be resolved by reference to verifiable empirical evidence.

This emphasis on democracy as grounded in procedural rules of conflict resolution reflects the actual history of democratic development from the eighteenth century – a deeply contested process of fragmented and piecemeal development of the institutions of liberal democracy through conservative and radical reforms against the threats of revolutionary upheaval from both the political left and right. Liberal democracy did not secure hegemony in North America and western Europe until after the Second World War, and its quest for global hegemony was challenged by Soviet communism until 1990. Both Silvert and Dahl are also sensitive to issues of the internal conditions of democracy, including elite domination and cleavages of class and race, as well as the broadening development of notions of the rights and responsibilities of citizenship, particularly as they initially shaped the possibilities of effective participation in the political process. Here, too, the development was piecemeal and extended further into the twentieth century than most of us realize, particularly with regard to the effective achievement of the bedrock condition of liberal democracy, the universal franchise, which was granted to women in Canada, the United States, and Britain in the early twentieth century and to African Americans only in 1964 with passage of the Civil Rights Act (Therborn 1977).

The underlying logic and direction of the fragmented and piecemeal construction of institutions and policies in liberal democracies are abstracted and rationalized by Dahl's colleague and collaborator Charles Lindblom in the concept of "disjointed incrementalism," which refers to advancement in successive small steps towards the goals of social cohesion, stability, and civic order. He recognizes the key role of social science in the policy process as providing "argument with evidence" (Lindblom 1979, 1990). Although often criticized and rejected by more radical analysts on the left in the 1960s and 1970s as a wishy-washy and elitist liberal reformism, Dahl's and Lindblom's analyses of what they call "pluralist democracy" show that it actually framed the goals and methods of the reconstruction of the moral economy of industrial capitalism after the catastrophes of depression and war. Pluralist democracy combines Keynesian macroeconomic management of markets and full-employment policies – framed by the notion of a tripartite collaboration between labour, capital, and the state – with social-democratic welfare and social engineering. The procedural dimension of this development, as important as its substantive achievements, was a process of contest and negotiation in which the politics of knowledge – the demand for "argument with evidence" – played a crucial role.

What, then, is the role of religious belief and institutions in secular liberal democracies that protect freedom of religion as a fundamental right of citizenship? Religion certainly plays an active role in the political arena in liberal democracies, particularly in the United States, where politics are saturated with references to God and appeals to faith and where no professed atheist has much hope of being elected to public office except in a small number of large urban areas.[4] In early 2006 cartoons in a Danish newspaper that supposedly insulted Muslims by caricaturing their faith raised the issue of what constitutes fair criticism of a religious institution's or community's ostensibly faith-based position on issues in the political arena as opposed to a bigoted attack on its core values and beliefs and a threat to its members – an interesting question in Western societies where anti-Semitic images and the defamation of Judaism were common in mass media and the political arena until muffled in the embarrassed aftermath of the Holocaust, only to resurface in the first decade of the twenty-first century under the flimsy cloak of "anti-Zionism" (Julius 2010). The line is crossed, I argue, when criticism of the political position at issue, and even of the moral principles or beliefs behind it, turns into a denial of the religious community's and its members' right to enter the political arena in the first place, as in the traditional exclusions of the Jews and in the dismissal of Islam as a "terrorist" religion, which was notably present in the images of several of the Danish cartoons.

There are two further dimensions to this issue. The first concerns the limits of faith or "sincere belief" with regard to the practices or treatment of members of a religious community itself and the right of the state and civil society to intervene to end practices regarded as oppressive and contrary to fundamental human rights. At what point is this line drawn, especially with regard to religious sects or communities that attempt to isolate themselves from contact with the wider society, whether the Branch Davidians, polygamist Mormons, or the Satmar Hasidim of the town of Kiryat Joel? As I discuss below, this has become a crucial contemporary political issue in increasingly religiously diverse societies.

The other dimension is the role of religious institutions in the democratic political process. Institutional separation of church and state prohibits the exercise of secular power and appropriation of areas of public policy by religious institutions, but it does not prohibit the participation of adherents in the political process or curtail their ability to form explicitly political organizations, including pressure groups and nongovernmental organizations, mass media outlets, and "confessional" political parties led by lay members of the community, and in the United States it does not even prevent individual members of the clergy from seeking and serving in electoral office. Through such groups the political participation of diverse religions is substantial both in the United States and elsewhere. The underlying concepts in which this participation is grounded are perceptively analyzed by Rajeev Bhargava in his chapter as "principled distance" and "contextual secularism." Under principled distance religious institutions and individuals may seek to influence policy only through their access to the political resources of the democratic process available to other interests and individuals in society. In this participation in the democratic process they cannot claim access to a higher or exclusive "truth" vis-à-vis other, potentially conflicting interests but solely belief as the basis for secular policy choices consonant with liberal-democratic values and processes. This is the basis for Dahl's notion of cross-cutting ties that link different interests and ideologies, religious and secular, in alliances on secular principles and policies to be implemented in a nonsectarian fashion. Thus in Canada the Co-operative Commonwealth Federation (CCF), later replaced by the New Democratic Party, combined the leadership of Protestant ministers from western Canada who were motivated by the Social Gospel – namely J.S. Woodsworth, Stanley Knowles, and Tommy Douglas – with the work of labour leaders from urban centres whose views were grounded in secular socialism and Marxism.

Contextual secularism recognizes that both the process of secularization and the meaning of secularism can vary over time and in different sociocultural settings; moral reasoning and political conflict are contextually grounded. There are three crucial consequences: constitutive values are always potentially in conflict, a level of internal discord and instability is inevitable in the democratic process, and issues are settled on a case-by-case basis, where the outcomes are not wholly satisfactory to either party but are reasonable to both. What is pursued is a mutually agreeable middle way that combines elements from more than one approach or interest, and decisions are made on a provisional rather than a final basis. The goal of contextual secularism is to reach ethically sensitive negotiated settlements. But this goal is really a synthesis of the outcomes that the democratic process is supposed to achieve in secular states.

The key characteristics of secular liberal democracy – the exclusion from the political arena of "ultimate" questions about the end and purpose of human existence, a focus on proximate temporal goals in secular reality, and an emphasis on issues of process and political means as much as on goals – turn out to be both its greatest strengths and its greatest weaknesses. The underlying ethos is that human conflict is an inevitable condition of life, that history is a series of contingent events with no ultimate end or purpose beyond what humans attribute to them and construct in the material world, and that because our goals can rarely, if ever, be fully or purely realized in secular reality, we live through our means more than our ends. Rather than certainty, this ethos espouses existential doubt, of which Max Weber is a striking example. Bureaucracy for Weber (1948, 196-244) is an "iron cage" that threatens to envelop the conditions of human life, whereas the modern state is ideally a neutral instrument of democratic governance that implements the policies of democratically elected governments with impartial professional efficiency. He did not live to see the instrument of the modern state turned to realize the ends of Nazism and Stalinist communism.

The Contemporary Confrontation between Religion and the Secular State

The contemporary religious "revival" is a response to the past thirty years of economic globalization and rapidly developing environmental and social crises. These disruptive and threatening changes have resulted in increasingly aggressive attempts by religious institutions and communities to directly intervene in secular states and to appropriate control of important areas of public policy. This revival is taking place on two levels. The first involves the unprecedented movement to North America and western Europe of peoples from "developing" countries in Asia, Latin America, the Middle East, and Africa, creating a dramatic increase in ethnic and religious pluralism in western Europe. The second involves the development on a wider global plane of powerful millennial movements grounded in both secular and religious ideologies.

During the past thirty years immigration has brought into western Europe and North America ethnically diverse religious communities, particularly

Muslim, from societies where the Western experience of the separation of church and state has not occurred and has no cultural or political meaning, and where the culture of secular modernity remains deeply contested. In these societies the sacred and the secular were intimately intertwined in the traditional moral economy that was undermined and threatened by the secular state and market of European colonialism. In Islamic societies this intertwining has brought almost two centuries of internal struggle over how to respond to both the threat of European political hegemony and the challenge of secular modernity, with responses ranging from complete rejection to enthusiastic acceptance of the secular state and capitalism through attempts to retain fundamental Islamic values in the context of "Islamic socialism" and "Islamic capitalism."[5] A generation of neoliberal globalization has brought these issues to intense ferment in both Islamic and other ethnoreligious communities by generating unprecedented extremities of wealth and poverty and the internal social and political crises of the Arab Spring. Much of the local turmoil in Islamic societies and throughout Africa has focused on the control of women and younger men within patriarchal families as mandated by traditional religious law and customary practice. These crises have driven the immigration to the West, both on political and economic grounds. Immigrants to western Europe and North America carry the internal conflicts of their societies with them, especially when the communities grow large and diverse enough to reproduce a range of religious and social institutions. When immigrants who are entering societies that demand assimilation and integration into the national culture and "values" erect barriers of racism and ethnocentrism, they struggle to deal with both individual access to the wider society and the internal politics of their own communities. In December 2006 during one of the first workshops of the Ethnicity and Democratic Governance project, Tariq Modood noted that the politics of ethnoreligious communities in Britain have involved both demands for access to the economic, educational, and political institutions of the society and, more recently, demands for certain communal rights and forms of autonomy. Reflecting the internal politics of communities, these demands have involved both claims for special treatment ("affirmative action") to overcome discrimination and claims for exemption from secular state laws, especially with regard to control over family, gender, and generation. Such claims have brought confrontation with civil authorities, most seriously in cases of "honour" killings of young women in Muslim and Sikh families in Britain and more recently in Canada, and they have included communal demands for the right to administer Sharia (Islamic law) within the community. In the United States these claims have also involved the case of Kiryat Joel, a town populated almost entirely by Hasidic Jews, which attempts to run itself entirely separately from the civil authorities.[6] In these cases, religious institutions claim authority to administer for their community significant portions of the policies and laws of secular civic institutions through the application of codified religious knowledge.

A much wider attack on the separation of religious and political institutions, as well as on the authority of secular scientific knowledge, has come from the so-called "religious right" in the United States, which is composed of evangelical Protestant groups. Too denominationally and organizationally fragmented to be called a coherent social movement, evangelical Protestants have had a major impact on American politics as a voting bloc and through several powerful interest groups, culminating in the presence of the self-professed "born-again Christian" George W. Bush in the White House. Focused on "moral issues" and "family values," many of the most public aspects of the religious right's attack have been directed at supposedly decadent and corrupt American popular culture. The government has compromised the traditional American institutional separation of church and state by giving public funding to "faith-based" programs in welfare and social services and by relaxing antidiscrimination rules that prevent religious agencies from hiring staff only from their own denomination (Savage 2008).

More serious politically, however, has been the religious right's involvement in contests of knowledge over key secular issues of public policy, including environmental crises and global warming, evolution versus creationism or "intelligent design," human genetics and stem cell research, and of course medical abortion. In all of these areas, knowledge based on faith and grounded in the "inerrant truth" of the Bible has been framed as absolute and superior to secular scientific knowledge, which is only "theoretical." These attacks have taken advantage of the actual practice of science, where scientists remain skeptical about declaring anything true, except in a tentative and revisable way, and where there is always some degree of disagreement over empirical evidence and its interpretation. The Bush administration systematically denigrated scientific knowledge in key policy areas like global warming as "junk science," and its officials suppressed or politically distorted the evidence provided by scientists in the government's own research institutions. Disastrously, this extended to the denigration and dismissal of empirical evidence in the government's political-intelligence operations. In 2002 a senior White House aide criticized *New York Times* reporter Ron Suskind (2004), explaining to him "that guys like me were 'in what we call the reality-based community,' which he defined as people who 'believe that solutions emerge from your judicious study of discernible reality.' I nodded and murmured something about enlightenment principles and empiricism. He cut me off. 'That's not the way the world really works anymore,' he continued. 'We're an empire now, and when we act, we create our own reality.'"[7]

Even more compelling is the evidence of Christian millenarianism and absolutism in the president's understanding of the "war on terror" against the "axis of evil" and his reliance on "instinct" and "faith" in making decisions contrary to known facts. Suskind (2004) uncovered repeated evidence of this "faith-based" approach to making important decisions with absolute certainty and a "with us or against us" understanding of opposition. Many evangelicals in his support base apparently believed that he was a messenger from God, and the president himself apparently believed that through prayer he received messages from God to guide his decisions (ibid.). Several churches in the evangelical community – including the Pentecostal church attended by the 2008 Republican nominee for vice-president – promote versions of an apocalyptic millennial theology that envisions the coming "End Time" of secular history as proceeding through a climactic battle of good against evil in Armageddon, the second coming of Christ, and the Rapture, when the elect will be transported to heaven in an earth-destroying nuclear holocaust.

Since the election of Ronald Reagan in 1980, Republican hegemony in American politics has been grounded in the striking ideological marriage of Christian fundamentalism's "family values" and advocacy of the "culture wars" with extreme free-market ideology. What appears to have been forgotten by members of the contemporary evangelical movement is that a century ago their forebears were actively engaged in radical populist religious and Christian Socialist movements among the rural poor in the American South and West (Craig 1995). Indeed, this was part of the Social Gospel movement, from which the leaders of the Canadian CCF emerged. The rightward movement of evangelical churches was propelled by the political and cultural unease of the anti–Vietnam War movement and the counterculture of the 1960s, as well as by the increasing prosperity and changing class position of their congregations in the 1970s with the shift of the focus of American capitalist expansion to the Sun Belt states. At the same time, the free-market ideology with which Christian fundamentalism bonded in the Republican Party, called neoconservatism in the United

States and neoliberalism elsewhere, was a secular millennial movement bearing many of the intellectual and political characteristics of Christian millennialism.

The incorporation of apocalyptic and millennial beliefs into secular political movements in the twentieth century has been understood for some time. The point was impressed upon me as a student in the 1960s through the pointedly titled book *The God That Failed* (1950), a widely read collection of essays written by former communists and edited by British Labour Party leader Richard Crossman. Nazism and communism rejected liberal democracy and democratic socialism precisely because of their inability – indeed, their refusal – to deal with issues of ultimate meaning and to achieve historically "necessary and inevitable" goals. With "science" – "racial science" in the case of Nazism and "dialectical materialism" in the case of communism – replacing God as the source of guidance and absolute truth, both movements claimed to understand and move towards the ultimate end and purpose, the telos, of human history in the form of either a "thousand-year Reich" or a utopia of communist freedom and equality. Both were able to attract fervent mass followings during periods of social upheaval. Both also acted with extreme and genocidal violence that made full use of the technical and organizational achievements of modernity to purify society of "class enemies" or "racially inferior" elements and to attain the utopia promised at the end of history (Gray 2008, Chap. 2).

Neoliberalism, based on the work of Friedrich Hayek and Milton Friedman (both treated as prophets by their followers), reproduces many of the same characteristics. One is the claim that science informs free-market neoclassical economic theory, or "positive economics," as its proponents call it. This approach to economics is based on deductively derived, abstract mathematical models of how markets should behave under ideal conditions. Such free markets, if allowed to run without hindrance from state intervention, are said to produce ideal allocations of goods and services under the natural laws of supply and demand. The underlying utopian moral economy is grounded in the view that these allocations are just and proper and will produce a society without conflict, rancour, or politics that meets everyone's needs. Thus markets will produce a frictionless world without the upheavals and conflicts of earlier history. Free markets are the necessary condition of liberal democracy's quest to produce a minimally intrusive state that maximizes individual freedom. This outcome, as Francis Fukuyama (1992) has proclaimed, is envisioned as the "end of history," the highest and final stage of human development.

Neoliberalism from the 1960s was championed by an ideological pressure group centred in the University of Chicago's Department of Economics that attacked the prevailing Keynesian social-democratic hegemony and aggressively sold its message to politicians and economic elites all over the world. Neoliberalism's sectarianism was quickly recognized by other social scientists who labelled it "market fundamentalism or idolatry." Its claims to being based on objective science, however, were used to forcefully attack its critics as being themselves "unscientific" and "ideological." Although the empirical content of the abstract theoretical models was limited, the mathematical theorems were used almost as ritual incantations to prove the scientific character of free-market economics and its ability to understand the "laws" of the market. Indeed, the market was depicted as a naturally occurring entity, and the laws of its optimal functioning could not be resisted without dire consequences to society. It is well known in political philosophy that labelling any feature of human society and culture as "natural" is an attempt to place it beyond political challenge or opposition. This tactic was employed in neoliberalism's insistence that there were "no alternatives" to its policy prescriptions, something repeated often by political leaders like Ronald Reagan and Margaret Thatcher.

Neoliberalism has been the most potent and forceful attempt to create self-regulating markets since the first half of the nineteenth century. Like the earlier movement, it has actually relied upon active state intervention to create its market utopia through deregulation and privatization of public services. In the West it has been most successful in the United States, where the Keynesian moral economy was weakest and least defended. In other liberal democracies, with stronger social-democratic politics, there has been greater resistance to dismantling the welfare state and macroeconomic management of national economies. In the non-Western world, however, starting with Chile in 1973 under what Naomi Klein (2007) has called the "shock doctrine," it has relied upon coercion and violence directed by authoritarian dictatorships and international financial institutions to take advantage of, and in some instances deliberately provoke, social and economic crises in order to impose the neoliberal "reforms" of the Washington Consensus.[8] For the past twenty years these reforms have also been tied to "democratization" in developing countries, as though the free market were the condition for the development of democracy rather than the cause of the social crises and conflicts from which democracy emerged.

Faced with the repeated failure of such reforms in the developing world, particularly with regard to growing poverty and the dramatic declines in many countries of the United Nations' basic human-development indicators, neoliberalism has responded in typical cult fashion to protect the tenets of the faith. First, there has been denial of the empirical evidence of failure, particularly claims that the measurements were not "scientific," along with an almost wilful historical ignorance of the catastrophic effects of the earlier efforts in the nineteenth-century era of laissez-faire to create a self-regulating market, something that has led to an international revival of interest in Karl Polanyi's (2001) sixty-five-year-old account of this period.[9] Where empirical evidence cannot be denied, the typical response is to denigrate the government involved for not having properly carried out the reforms, thus putting the onus on human and governmental failure, not on the failure of the theory or, horrors, of the system itself.[10]

The current global crisis of capitalism and governance, which began in 2007-08, is a direct challenge to the hegemony of neoliberalism, which bears significant responsibility for it. The response to the crisis from free-market true believers has typically been to protect the theory and shift the blame to the corrupt behaviour of Wall Street executives. Appearing before a Congressional committee, Alan Greenspan, former head of the US Federal Reserve and one of the high priests of neoliberalism, admitted that he had had too much faith in the self-correcting power of free markets and had failed to anticipate the destructive power of predatory and irresponsible mortgage lending: "Those of us who have looked to the self-interest of lending institutions to protect shareholders' equity, myself included, are in a state of shocked disbelief." This shock was inevitable because neoliberalism does not study real economic behaviour but simply assumes that it is determined by the discipline of the market (i.e., "invisible hands" or the "magic of the market place"). Pressed to say whether he had been misled by his "ideology," Greenspan conceded, "Yes, I've found a flaw. I don't know how significant or permanent it is. But I've been very distressed by that fact." So it is not clear whether the flaw is inherent in the theory or whether the crisis occurred because the theory was not implemented correctly. Greenspan was further pressed by the committee's chairman, Henry Waxman, to explain whether his policies were wrong: "'Partially,' the former Fed chairman reluctantly answered, before trying to parse his concession as thinly as possible" (Andrews 2008).

Neoliberalism has never provided an effectively legitimate moral economy in the globalized world not only because of its unrealizable utopian fantasy but also because of its callous indifference to the enormous suffering imposed by the political repression and economic distress involved in the attempt to bring it into being (Gray 1998; Klein 2007). It will now be challenged by the efforts of leading liberal-democratic states to redefine a workable moral economy and international institutions – building on the earlier Keynesian social-democratic model – and, in particular, to bring finance capital back under effective regulation. In the United States every month brings sharp critiques of free-market economic "science," including from the conservative *New York Times* columnist David Brooks (2010), from a former fervent proponent like Richard Posner (2010), and from the philosopher Michael Sandel (2012). The administration of President Barack Obama, meanwhile, as secular and modernist as any in recent American history, struggles to free itself from the thrall of neoliberalism and its Wall Street advocates. However, the instability and insecurity of the global crisis are producing precisely the social conditions that will spawn new millennial movements, religiously based as well as secular, with characteristic tendencies towards scapegoating and violence, including attacks on ethnic and religious minorities. Such movements will mount serious challenges to secular states and their political and religious pluralism; whether they will overwhelm them is an open question.

Notes

1 The Axial Age of the first millennium BCE saw the emergence of what would become the great world religions in ancient Judea, Greece, Persia, imperial China, and the Indian subcontinent. As Shmuel Eisenstadt (1982) points out, the revolutionary import of the Axial Age involved the institutionalization of a basic tension between the transcendental and mundane orders. However, most of these institutionalized religions began, with the crucial exception of Christianity, as "court religions" of the political elites in which clerical roles were intimately connected to the state under a divine or semidivine ruler, and sacred knowledge of the official religion coexisted with the beliefs of local cults and the ancestor worship of scattered agrarian communities, who paid homage to it as part of their subservience to the state. Most state religions became mass faiths or disappeared after the collapse or destruction of the state and the survival of the clerics among the "people." The unique experience of post-Roman spiritual unity and political fragmentation over a millennium in western Europe brought about a divergence of religious and political institutions, of church and state, and of sacred and secular knowledge that culminated in a revolution of modernity as significant as that of the Axial Age.
2 The theory of relativity is revealingly discussed, along with several other important case studies, by Harry Collins and Trevor Pinch (1998).
3 As Zygmunt Bauman (1989) has argued, it was precisely the most distinctive and valued characteristics of modernity – scientific and technical expertise, the organization and management of large-scale systems, and precise and disciplined action –

that made the Holocaust possible. The American attempt to fight a technically perfect war, conceived and executed under the consummate modern corporate manager Robert McNamara, is analyzed by James William Gibson (1986).

4 Notice the questions to candidates in the 2008 presidential election about their "faith" in the televised "debates" and the appearance of the presidential candidates for an "interview" with a leader of the Protestant evangelical movement, with the clear message that claiming adherence to no faith was an unacceptable answer. The question was actually a violation of the constitutional separation of church and state insofar as it implied a religious test of the candidates' eligibility for public office.

5 This history is brilliantly analyzed by Charles Tripp (2007).

6 Kiryat Joel raises the issue of special exemption and treatment in a manner very different from Muslim communities' desire to implement Sharia. In the Rosen Lecture in Jewish Studies at Queen's University in January 2008, Samuel Heilman of the City University of New York described the desire of "ultra"-orthodox Jews to withdraw from as much contact as possible with civil society as an effort to "reconstruct the walls of the ghetto and lock them from inside." Kiryat Joel is an incorporated village of more than seven thousand people, almost all of whom are from the Satmar Hasidic community via Brooklyn and previously Hungary, who moved to the town at the behest of the Satmar rebbe. The community runs all of the village's government functions and services, but it is also linked to the local county government and New York State. Since the village has no local economy to speak of and the principal male occupation is study of the Talmud, more than 50 percent of its families have incomes under the poverty line and are eligible to draw welfare payments from the state.

7 The evangelical and neoconservative dismissal of empirical reality, especially among the former students and followers in the government of the conservative political theorist Leo Strauss, is explored more fully by John Gray (2008, 189-205).

8 This tactic is analyzed by Klein (2007) in relentless detail for cases around the world.

9 Polanyi's (2001) book is rapidly becoming one of the most widely used university texts for the study of the early development of capitalist modernity.

10 This practice of protecting core tenets of faith from empirical evidence of failure by blaming the practitioners for incorrectly carrying out the required rituals is identified by British anthropologist E.E. Evans-Pritchard as the underlying logic of African witchcraft beliefs in his classic study *Witchcraft, Oracles and Magic among the Azande* (1937).

Works Cited

Andrews, Edmund L. 2008. "Greenspan Concedes Error on Regulation." *New York Times,* 24 October.

Bauman, Zygmunt. 1989. *Modernity and the Holocaust.* Cambridge, UK: Polity.

Bell, Daniel. 1960. *The End of Ideology: On the Exhaustion of Political Ideas in the Fifties.* Glencoe, IL: Free Press.

Bernstein, Peter. 1998. *Against the Gods: The Remarkable Story of Risk.* New York: Wiley.

Brooks, David. 2010. "The Return of History." *New York Times*, 26 March.

Cohn, Norman. 1970. *The Pursuit of the Millennium*. Rev. ed. London: Paladin.

Collins, Harry, and Trevor Pinch. 1998. *The Golem: What You Should Know about Science*. 2nd ed. Cambridge, UK: Cambridge University Press.

Craig, Robert H. 1995. *Religion and Radical Politics: An Alternative Christian Tradition in the United States*. Philadelphia: Temple University Press.

Crossman, R.H.S. 1950. *The God That Failed: Six Studies in Communism*. London: Hamish Hamilton.

Dahl, Robert A. 1956. *A Preface to Democratic Theory*. Chicago: University of Chicago Press.

Eisenstadt, Shmuel. 1982. "The Axial Age: The Emergence of Transcendental Visions and the Rise of Clerics." *European Journal of Sociology* 23 (2): 294-314.

Evans-Pritchard, E.E. 1937. *Witchcraft, Oracles and Magic among the Azande*. Oxford, UK: Clarendon.

Fox, Jonathan. 2004. "The Rise of Religious Nationalism and Conflict: Ethnic Conflict and Revolutionary Wars, 1945-2001." *Journal of Peace Research* 41 (6): 715-31.

Fukuyama, Francis. 1992. *The End of History and the Last Man*. New York: Free Press.

Gibson, James William. 1986. *The Perfect War: Technowar in Vietnam*. Boston: Atlantic Monthly.

Giddens, Anthony. 1991. *The Consequences of Modernity*. Cambridge, UK: Polity.

Gray, John. 1998. *False Dawn: The Delusions of Global Capitalism*. London: Granta.

–. 2008. *Black Mass: Apocalyptic Religion and the Death of Utopia*. London: Penguin.

Jacob, Margaret. 1997. *Scientific Culture and the Making of the Industrial West*. New York: Oxford University Press.

Julius, Anthony. 2010. *Trials of the Diaspora: A History of Anti-Semitism in England*. New York: Oxford University Press.

Klein, Naomi. 2007. *The Shock Doctrine: The Rise of Disaster Capitalism*. Toronto: Knopf Canada.

Lerner, Daniel. 1951. *The Policy Sciences*. Stanford, CA: Stanford University Press, 1951.

Lindblom, Charles. 1979. *Usable Knowledge: Social Science and Social Problem Solving*. New Haven, CT: Yale University Press.

–. 1990. *Inquiry and Change: The Troubled Attempt to Understand and Shape Society*. New Haven, CT: Yale University Press.

March, James, and Herbert Simon. 1958. *Organizations*. New York: Wiley.

Pew Forum on Religion and Public Life. 2008. "U.S. Religious Landscape Survey." http://religions.pewforum.org/comparisons.

Polanyi, Karl. 2001. *The Great Transformation*. 1944. Reprint, Boston: Beacon.

Posner, Richard. 2010. *The Crisis of Capitalist Democracy*. Cambridge, MA: Harvard University Press.

Sandel, Michael. 2012. *What Money Can't Buy: The Moral Limits of Markets*. New York: Farrar, Strauss and Giroux.

Savage, Charlie. 2008. "Bush Aides Say Religious Hiring Doesn't Bar Aid." *New York Times*, 18 October.

Silvert, Kalman. 1963. "The Strategy of the Study of Nationalism." In *Expectant Peoples*, edited by Kalman Silvert, 1-32. New York: Random House.

Suskind, Ron. 2004. "Without a Doubt." *New York Times*, 17 October.

Therborn, Goran. 1977. "The Rule of Capital and the Rise of Democracy." *New Left Review* 1 (103).

Tripp, Charles. 2007. *Islam and the Moral Economy.* Cambridge, UK: Cambridge University Press.

Walzer, Michael. 1965. *The Revolution of the Saints: A Study in the Origins of Radical Politics.* Cambridge, MA: Harvard University Press.

Weber, Max. 1948. *From Max Weber: Essays in Sociology.* Edited by H.H. Gerth and C. Wright Mills. London: Routledge/Kegan Paul.

Can Secularism Be Rehabilitated?

Rajeev Bhargava

Chapter **3**

Over the past three decades, secular states virtually everywhere have come under severe strain. It is hardly surprising, then, that political secularism, the doctrine that defends them, has also come under heavy criticism. Some scholars have concluded that these critiques are so profound and justified that political secularism cannot be rehabilitated. In this chapter I reject this conclusion, although I do not deny that the crisis of secularism is real. However, the criticism of secularism looks indefeasible only because it has focused on one or two doctrinal versions of Western secularism. I argue that it is time we shifted focus away from doctrines and towards the normative practices of a wide variety of states, including the best practices of non-Western states such as India. Once we do so, we will begin to see secularism differently, as a critical perspective that is not against religion but against religious homogenization and institutionalized religious domination. We might seek, then, not an alternative to secularism but rather an alternative conception of it.

Identifying a defensible alternative conception is not always easy. To do so, it is crucial to keep in mind a set of distinctions. First, we need to distinguish between the entire complex of practices and institutional arrangements that either connect religion to or disconnect religion from the state and a subset of these practices and arrangements that embody norms – that is, an implicit sense of how states and religions *should* relate to one another. Whereas the former include the normative and the non-normative and operate at the entire *practical* level, the latter operate only at the *normative* level. Second, these norms are then articulated in representations and ad hoc, unstable reflections found in statements of politicians, laws enacted by legislators, executive decisions, judicial pronouncements, and constitutional articles. These articulations operate at the *discursive* level. Finally, the normative conceptions implicit in these practices and either subtly or explicitly articulated in the legal and political discourse are then posited as a normative ideal that is sometimes expressed as ideology and doctrine and that occasionally becomes an object of theoretical enquiry, thus operating at both the *doctrinal* and the *theoretical* levels. The distinction between a comprehensive practical level and the exclusively normative level is important because identifying secularism with any particular practice or institutional arrangement that relates religion and the state will not do. True, secularism needs to be institutionally grounded, but to distinguish secular from religion-centred states and, even more important, to articulate a critical, normative secularism, the distinction between the normative and the non-normative is crucial.

More to the point, I argue that secular norms conceived at the doctrinal and the theoretical levels have become part of the problem. This has happened because these levels are colonized by mainstream, Western doctrines and theories of secularism. Once we shift away from these currently dominant models and focus on the normative practices of both Western and non-Western states, we shall see that better forms of secular state and much more defensible versions of secularism are available.

Crisis of Two Models of Secularism

In 1979 secularism was severely jolted with the establishment in Iran of the first modern theocracy, having been rejected in that country partly because of the perception that it was a Western idea. By the late 1980s similar Islamic political movements had emerged in Egypt, Sudan, Algeria, Tunisia, Ethiopia, Nigeria, Chad, Senegal, Turkey, Afghanistan, Pakistan, and even Bangladesh (Ahmed 1987; Kepel 1994; Mohsin 1999; Westerlund 1996). Movements challenging secular states were hardly restricted to Muslim societies. Protestant movements decrying secularism emerged in Kenya, Guatemala, and the Philippines. Protestant fundamentalism became a force in American politics. Singhalese Buddhist nationalists in Sri Lanka, Hindu nationalists in India, practitioners of religious ultra-orthodoxy in Israel, Sikh nationalists in the Indian state of Punjab, and diasporic communities in Canada and Britain all began to question the separation of state and religion (Juergensmeyer 1994).

In short, Western conceptions of political secularism do not appear to have travelled all that well in other societies. What is surprising is that such conceptions and the secular states they underpin are coming under strain even in Europe, where, until recently, they were believed to be firmly entrenched and secure. Why so? It is true that the substantive secularization of European societies has brought about the extensive secularization of European states; regardless of their religious affiliation, citizens have a large basket of civil and political rights unheard of in religion-centred states, past or present. Nevertheless, two problems remain.

First, migration from former colonies and intensified globalization have thrown together in Western public spaces Christian, Islamic, and pre-Christian faiths such as Hinduism (Turner 2001). The cumulative result is unprecedented religious diversity, the weakening of the public monopoly of single religions, and the generation of mutual suspicion, distrust, hostility, and conflict. This is evident in Germany and Britain but was dramatically highlighted by the headscarf issue in France, the cartoon affair in Denmark, and the murder of filmmaker Theo Van Gogh in the Netherlands shortly after the release of his controversial film about Islamic culture (Barker 2004; Bowen 2007; Buruma 2006; Freedman 2004; Modood, Triandafyllidou, and Zapata-Barrero 2006).

Second, despite substantial secularization, in some European states inequities resulting from the formal establishment of the dominant religion have done little to bolster better intercommunity relations or to reduce religious discrimination. With the deepening of religious diversity, the religious biases of European states have become increasingly visible. European states have continued to privilege Christianity in one form or another. They have publicly funded religious schools, maintained clerical salaries and real estate holdings of Christian churches, facilitated the control by churches of cemeteries, and trained the clergy. In short, there has been no impartiality within the domain of religion, and despite formal "equality" this privileging of Christianity continues to have a far-reaching impact on the rest of society (Klausen 2005). Even the widespread belief regarding the existence of a secular European public sphere is based largely on a myth. As a result, the formal or informal establishment of a single religion, even the weaker variety of establishment, continues to be part of the problem.

Why so? The short answer is that theocratic states and states with established religions perpetuate intra- and interreligious domination. Historically, they have recognized as the "official" religion a version of the religion enunciated by a particular church or denomination and have compelled individuals to congregate for only one church, punished them for failing to profess a particular set of religious beliefs, levied taxes in support of one particular church, and made mandatory the instruction of the favoured interpretation of this religion in educational institutions (Levy 1994). In such cases, there has been inequality not only between two or more religions – say, Christianity and Judaism – but also among churches or denominations of the same religion. Societies with such states have been either wracked by interreligious or interdenominational wars or characterized by persecution of minority religious groups.

States with substantive establishments have not changed with time. The most obvious example is Saudi Arabia (Ruthven 2002). Or consider Pakistan, where the virtual establishment of the dominant Sunni sect has proven disastrous, even to Muslim minorities. For example, Ahmedis have been deemed a non-Muslim minority and therefore persecuted for calling themselves Muslims (Malik 2002; Bhargava 2004). The "democratic" state of Israel suffers from the same problem. Once it was declared a Jewish state, it had to exclude from its full scheme of rights and benefits its own Arab citizens, not to mention Palestinians. The result would be the same if a Hindu state was established in India.

What, in the face of this imbroglio, should weakly or strongly religion-centred states do? Those reflecting on this crisis have at least four conceptions of secularism staring back at them. The four conceptions flow from the different ways that the metaphor of separation is unpacked, the levels at which separation is sought, and the manner in which ends are conceived. The first of these conceptions is thoroughly amoral and unethical because it separates religion from the state precisely because of the ethical or moral restrictions that religions can place on ends of the state such as wealth and power. These amoral secular states are inconsistent with the moral self-organization and self-understanding of most European states as liberal-democratic, and the amorality of this conception tarnishes the overall image of secularism as practised in non-Western societies.

Mainstream Western Secularisms: Part of the Problem

What, then, of the other three conceptions? The dominant self-understanding of Western secularism is that it is a *universal* doctrine requiring the strict separation of church and state for the sake of individualistically conceived moral or ethical values. This dominant self-understanding is constructed out of two highly idealized forms, one being an idealized French model of separation and the other an equally idealized version of the American model.

Can states be morally reinvigorated by these two forms of Western secularism? Can these forms help states to better deal with the new reality of the vibrant presence of multiple religions in public life and the accompanying social tensions? In what follows, I argue that the available mainstream *conceptions* of Western secularism are unlikely to meet the challenge presented by the vibrant public presence of religion, by increasing religious diversity, or by intra- and interreligious domination.

The Idealized French Model

The idealized French conception holds that the state must be separate from religion while retaining the power to interfere in it. However, religion is divested of any power to intervene in matters of the state. In short, separation means *one-sided exclusion*. The state may interfere to hinder and suppress or even to help religion, but in all cases this must be done only to ensure its control over religion. Religion becomes an object of law and public policy but only according to terms specified by the state. This conception, which arose in response to the excessive domination of the church, encourages an active disrespect for religion and is concerned solely with preventing the religious order from dominating the secular. It hopes to deal with institutionalized religious domination by taming and marginalizing religion. States governed by this conception typically have a single, robust conception of the good life that translates into deep skepticism about the truth claims and value of religion and about its public role and capacity to ever prevent forms of oppression and domination. Over time, states that follow this conception also develop a hierarchy between the secular and the religious and may perpetuate the nonreligious domination of the religious. This happens even more so when, to promote more rigorous nonreligious conceptions of positive freedoms and substantive equalities, states cross minimal thresholds of morality, formal equality, and decency. To be sure, this stance may help states to deal with cases of intrareligious domination where some members of a religious community dominate members of their own religion, as occurs with anticlericalism in France. But often their relative blindness to religion makes states driven by such conceptions insensitive to religious freedoms, particularly to the religious freedoms of minorities. As a result, states may even, wittingly or unwittingly, perpetuate interreligious domination. This blindness to interreligious domination has other deeper sources, which I mention below. Here it suffices to point out that this secularism does not understand the believer's life as it is lived from the inside. It misses out on perhaps the most significant feature of most religions: that they encourage their members to choose to live a disciplined, restricted, rule-bound, and desire-abnegating life. A religious life is not just a life of personal and whimsical attachment to a personal God but one in which the individual submits to His commands and lives obediently by them. This feature may be a nightmare for secularists, but it captures the constitution of most religions better than this conception of secularism does.

Many segments in virtually every society, on the right but particularly on the left, are tempted to follow the anti-multicultural French model, largely because they have bought into the view that religion – in Europe, more specifically Islam – is a "problem" and that its solution requires the coercive power of the state. Such an approach would be detrimental to interfaith relations because while strongly interfering with non-Christian faiths, it leaves the formal or informal establishment of a single Christian religion untouched. Moreover, every attempt to further intervene in religions is likely to meet with resistance not only from Muslims but from non-Muslims as well. Any reliance on the heavy-handed and one-sided French model is likely to exacerbate problems. In addition, a remedy normatively unsuitable for European states will be rejected outright elsewhere. Indeed, states that have drawn inspiration from this model – for example, communist states such as China and the Kemalist state in Turkey – have a very poor record of protecting religious freedoms or sustaining intra- and interreligious equality.

The Idealized American Model

Can states turn, then, to the American model? The idealized American self-understanding interprets separation to mean *mutual exclusion.* Neither the state nor religion is meant to interfere in the domain of the other. This mutual exclusion is held to be necessary to resolve conflicts between different Christian denominations, to grant some measure of equality between them, and – most crucially – to provide individuals the freedom to set up and maintain their own religious associations. Mutual exclusion is believed necessary for religious liberty and for the more general liberties of individuals. This strict or "perfect separation," as James Madison has termed it, must take place at each of the three distinct levels of ends, institutions and personnel, and law and public policy. The first two levels make the state nontheocratic and disestablish religion. The third level ensures that the state has neither a positive nor a negative relationship with religion. On the positive side, for example, there should be no policy of granting aid, even nonpreferentially, to religious institutions. On the negative side, it is not within the scope of state activity to interfere in religious matters even when some of the values professed by the state, such as equality, are violated within the religious domain. Consider President Barack Obama's helplessness in the face of the recent threat in America to publicly burn the Quran. As Leonard W. Levy (1994) puts it, Congress simply has no power to legislate on any matter pertaining to religion (see also Hamburger 2002).

This noninterference is justified on the grounds that religion is a privileged, private (i.e., nonstate) matter, and if something is amiss within this private domain, it can be mended only by those who have a right to do so within this sphere. This view, according to its proponents, is what religious freedom means. Thus the freedom that justifies mutual exclusion is negative liberty and is closely enmeshed with the privatization of religion.

In my view this model of secularism encourages the state to passively respect religion. In this model any intervention is tantamount to control; the only way to respect religion is to leave it alone. Idealized American secularism, then, has some resources to fight interreligious domination (e.g., it necessitates the disestablishment of the dominant religion) but no resources to wage a struggle against other aspects of this domination or against intrareligious dominations. The state is unable to facilitate freedoms or equality *within* religions, and this inability forces members to exit from their religion rather than to press for intrareligious equality. The American state may have worked out other strategies to minimize such dominations. However, states that lack its more conciliatory history or that possess religions that do not easily allow the option to exit would perpetuate religion-related domination in following the American model. Moreover, by interpreting separation as exclusion, this model of secularism betrays its own sectarianism; it can live comfortably with liberal, Protestantized, individualized, and privatized religions, but it has few resources to cope with religions that mandate greater public or political presence or that have a strong communal orientation. This group insensitivity makes it virtually impossible to accommodate community-specific rights, such as the right of religious communities to set up and maintain their own educational institutions, and therefore virtually impossible to more robustly protect the rights of religious minorities. In short, although this secularism copes with interreligious domination, it does not possess adequate resources to deal fully with intrareligious domination. It cannot get the state to act in ways that might check those less apparent forms of intrareligious domination that are deeply but sometimes less visibly inscribed in structures of society.

Furthermore, as a product of the Protestant ethic, American secularism's greatest drawback is its universal pretension. It presupposes a Christian civilization, something easily forgotten because over time this civilization has silently slid into the background. Christianity allows this self-limitation, and much of the world innocently mistakes this somewhat cunning self-denial for Christianity's disappearance (Connolly 1999, 24). But if this is so, this "inherently dogmatic" secularism cannot coexist innocently with other religions (Keane 2000, 14; Madan 1998, 298). Given the enormous power of the state, it must try to shape and transform other religions – a clear instance of illegitimate influence, if not outright violence. Thus, despite all its claims of leaving religions alone and granting religions liberty, this secularism is hostile to nonliberal, non-Protestant believers (Hamburger 2002, 193-251).

The current theoretical formulations of this model – represented, for example, by philosophical liberalism – only exacerbate these problems. Thus liberal secularist theories enjoin the citizen to support only those coercive state laws for which there is public justification. If others are expected to follow a law based on terms that they do not understand and for reasons they cannot endorse, the principle of equal respect is violated – so the reasoning goes (Audi 1993, 701; Macedo 1990, 249; Rawls 1971, 337-38; Solum 1990, 1065; Weithman 1997, 6). Coercive principles must be as justifiable to others as they are to us and therefore must be based on terms that all citizens can accept on the grounds of their common reason (Larmore 1996, 137).

Because a religious rationale is a paradigmatic case of a basis for conduct that other citizens have good reasons to reject, it does not count as public justification; thus a law grounded solely in a religious rationale must never be enacted. In short, purely religious convictions or commitments have no role to play in democratic and pluralist polities. This requirement that religious reasons be excluded from liberal-democratic politics is offensive to religious persons who, like others, wish to support their favoured political commitments according to their conscience (Sandel 1993). If people believe that their politics must be consistent with their morality as derived from religion, why should they be discouraged or stigmatized for grounding their politics in religious convictions? By asking the religious to exercise restraint and exclude theological reasons from their justification for a coercive law, liberal secularism forces them to act against their conscience and, in so doing, violates its own principle of equal respect. Indeed, the demand that restraint be exercised is counterproductive because exclusion from the larger public sphere forces the religious to form their own narrow public where resentment and prejudice will flourish (Spinner-Halev 2000, 150-56). This response would lead not only to the freezing of identities but also to the building of unbreachable walls between religious and nonreligious citizens. Therefore, "engagement with religious people is typically better than shunning them" (ibid., 155).

Furthermore, these theories of secularism rely excessively on a rationalist conception of reason that imposes unfair limits on the manner in which issues are to be brought into the public domain. Some issues are constitutively emotive; others become emotive because they are articulated by people who are not always trained to be rational in the way that secularists mandate (Connolly 1999, 27). Overall, the model of moral reasoning typical of such secularisms is context-insensitive, theoreticist, and absolutist (or noncomparative), enjoining us to think in terms of this or that since it is too heavily reliant on monolithic ideas or values considered to be true, superior, or wholly non-negotiable.

In sum, mainstream Western conceptions of secularism developed in the context of a single-religion society and as a way to solve the problems of one religion, namely Christianity. They were not designed to deal with deep religious diversity. Both the idealized French and American versions of secularism understand separation as exclusion and make individualistically conceived values – individual liberty, or equality between individuals, or both – the grounds for separation. Overall, it would not be wrong to say that they force upon followers of Western conceptions of secularism a choice between active hostility and benign indifference to religion. Because of its diversity-resistant and individualistic character, the mainstream Western secularism constructed out of these two models has become part of the problem.

Western Secularism in European Societies

Neither of these two models adequately captures the models of secularism actually in play in European societies. Most European states follow neither the French nor the American model. Virtually all European states have a stable regime of individual rights that includes the right to religious liberty. None could have managed to install this regime without having attacked the power and privilege of their churches in the past, a stridency that would not have been possible without some degree of state-church separation. Yet, unlike in France, there is no lingering hostility towards religion in other European state structures.

In Europe initial hostility was followed by active support. Virtually all European states have developed an institutional arrangement that grants some privilege or public recognition to their church. Indeed, some still have an established church, a privileged arrangement that goes well beyond recognition. Tariq Modood (2011) finds the combination of separation of church and state and support for religion compatible with secularism; he calls it "moderate secularism." Such is the context in which non-Christian migrants to Europe, the majority of whom are Muslims, have been arriving, settling, and making claims that relate to the place of religious identity in the public sphere. But it is precisely here that a sense of a crisis of secularism can be found. Since the advent of large-scale non-Christian migration, moderate secularism has had a precarious life in Europe.

Europe's political secularism is currently destabilized. Europe cannot just go on with the same moderate secularism and properly face this destabilization. Modood (2011) hopes that the historical compromises between church and state will be extended to other religions, particularly to Islam. However, the multiculturalization of this secularism is neither easy nor sufficient. It is not easy because it presupposes massive change in the cultural background. Institutional adjustment is bound to be difficult because an internal link exists between the collective secular self-understanding of European societies and deeply problematic institutional arrangements. Quite plainly, current European institutions are deeply biased. They have accommodated Christians but will not be able to accommodate Muslims. They are not sufficient because simple accommodation without some accompanying "hostility" may not work for all Muslim citizens, such as many Muslim women who might welcome hostility to some customs that have come to be associated with their religion.

Why are institutional adjustments difficult to achieve? Using a broad brush, we might say that European secularisms arose in predominantly single-religion societies. Issues of radical individual freedom and citizenship equality arose in European societies *after* religious homogenization. The birth of confessional states was accompanied by the massive expulsion of subject communities whose faith differed from the religion of the ruler. Such states eventually found some place for toleration in their moral space, but as is well known, toleration was consistent with deep inequalities and with a humiliating, marginalized, and virtually invisible existence. For instance, the church buildings of minority religious groups could not look like churches and had to be tucked away in lanes far from the church of the dominant group.

The liberal democratization and the consequent secularization of many European states has helped citizens with non-Christian faiths to acquire most formal rights. But such a scheme of rights neither embodies a regime of interreligious equality nor effectively prevents religion-based discrimination and exclusion. Indeed, it masks majoritarian, ethnoreligious biases.

The new reality of deepening religious diversity has brought the religious biases of European states into increasingly sharper relief (Klausen 2005). Despite all changes, European states have continued to privilege Christianity in one form or another. They have publicly funded religious schools, maintained the real estate of churches and clerical salaries, facilitated church control of cemeteries, and trained the clergy. In short, there has been no impartiality within the domain of religion, and despite formal equality, this lack of impartiality continues to have a far-reaching impact on the rest of society.

Thus these biases are evident in different kinds of difficulties faced by Muslims. For example, in Britain one-third of all primary school students are educated by religious communities, yet applications for state funding by Muslims are frequently turned down. Veit Bader (2007) informs us that there are currently only 5 Muslim schools, compared to 2,000 run by Roman Catholics and 4,700 run by the Church of England. Similar problems persist in other European countries. In both France and Germany not a single school run by Muslims is subsidized by the state. This bias is also manifest in the failure of many western European states to deal with the issue of headscarves (most notably France), in unheeded demands by Muslims to build mosques and therefore to properly practise their own faith (Germany and Italy), in discrimination against practices of ritual slaughter (Germany), and in unheeded demands by Muslims for proper burial grounds of their own (Denmark, among others). Given that in recent times Islamophobia has gripped the imagination of several Western societies – as exemplified by the cartoon controversy in Denmark and by the minarets issue in Switzerland – it is very likely that their Muslim citizens will continue to face disadvantages due only to membership in their religious community.

Removing the biases of European states will not be easy because of resistance from the right, institutional resilience, and differences between Christianity and Islam, not to mention between Christianity and non-Semitic religions such as Hinduism. Moderate secularism will be severely tested. Indeed, the test has already begun, which is why talk of strain or even crisis is justified.

So far I have been talking as though the initiative lies squarely with only one agent, the European state (and its supporters), and as though Muslims will respond enthusiastically to any initiative from this reformed (i.e., multi-culturalized) state. But this view is too sanguine about the self-understanding of Muslims and about their current condition in Europe. It underestimates their alienation and ghettoization. Only with a better and deeper under-standing of Muslims in different parts of Europe can we learn about what should and should not be accommodated and about what currently can and cannot be accommodated. Indeed, only in a more relaxed atmosphere can a plurality of voices – the more vulnerable voices – emerge and be better heard, a change that will have a huge bearing on our collective judgment of what should and should not be accommodated. (As of now, we hear two domin-ant voices: that of the ultra-orthodox Muslim and that of the lapsed Muslim, a convert to radical secularism.) These voices may necessitate not just ac-commodation but also more active state intervention either to foster or to suppress some hitherto unnoticed beliefs and practices of Muslims. It is en-tirely possible that the state may not only have to support some religious practices but also have to inhibit others. European states may be only too happy to abort some Muslim practices, but such intervention would entail a massive shift in their conception of secularism: from first separate and then only support religion to first separate and then sometimes support, some-times inhibit religion, what I call *principled distance.* In short, they may have to set aside their moderate stance of accommodating, rather than being hos-tile to, religion. Currently, the practice of most European states is to offer little official support, to provide no accommodation, and with few excep-tions, to stay indifferent to massive societal intolerance. What might be re-quired is more support of some religions, less support of others, and active interference in societal intolerance – that is, an attempt by the state to tackle both inter- and intrareligious domination.

In sum, extending moderate (i.e., accommodative) secularism to Muslims, under existing conditions, will be very difficult, for it presupposes massive shifts in background cultural conditions for which Europe may not yet be prepared. It would not be too off the mark to say that not appreciating deep religious and cultural diversity is one of the central failures of modern Europe. To my knowledge, overcoming this issue is a bigger challenge than any other. Even the conceptual resources for such change appear to be missing. In any case, moderate secularism's accommodation will not be sufficient because the modern (i.e., democratic) state must have the legit-imacy to also negatively intervene in some socioreligious practices, if only to protect the interests of vulnerable internal minorities. This in part en-tails abandoning moderate secularism. To respond to the challenge of deep diversity, Europe might be better off with an altogether different conception of secularism.

What I have said above needs some qualification, for it ignores two facts. First, it neglects the informal politics of state and nonstate actors where interesting changes might be occurring. Second, it does not take into account the existence of the European Constitution, which is very different from the constitutions of individual European states. I acknowledge the importance of both. These factors could make a substantial difference. But two difficulties block progress here too. The first difficulty is that nothing prevents individual states from ignoring the European Constitution. Would France, Belgium, or Italy listen to the European Union if it declared banning the burka to be unconstitutional? The second difficulty, even more noteworthy, is the need to make distinctions between (1) norms of secularism embedded in the informal politics of both states and nonstate actors; (2) norms of secularism embedded in formal, institutional politics and articulated in representations and reflections found in laws enacted by legislatures, executive decisions, judicial pronouncements, and constitutional articles; and (3) normative ideals governing the relationship between state and religion expressed in doctrines, ideologies, and political theories.

I believe, then, that the doctrinal, ideological, and theoretical formulations of Western secularism have become highly restricted and inadequate, as too have the formal politics and laws inspired by these doctrines and ideologies. The rehabilitation of secularism is virtually impossible unless we reduce our reliance on these formal practices and formulations. These doctrines and theories have become part of the problem, hurdles to properly examining the issues at stake. These include the French and the American models of exclusionary separation of church and state as well as the formal, institutional political practices of most European states. If we continue to remain in the grip of these formulations and practices, we will simply not notice other conceptions that have probably been pushed into the background. Once we shift away from these alternate perspectives and start to focus on the normative informal practices of a broader range of Western and non-Western states, we shall see that better forms of secular state and much more defensible versions of secularism are available.

The Indian Model of Secularism

Are we caught, then, between ideologies that legitimate religious domination of the secular and forms of secularism that are unable to prevent instances of intra- or interreligious domination? Or can a version of secularism be found that is sensitive simultaneously to the moral integrity of both liberal and nonliberal religious ways of living, as well as able to address religious or religion-based oppression and exclusions – one that goes beyond liberal, libertarian, and republican theories? Although theoretically less developed, another model of secularism exists, one not generated exclusively in the West, that meets the needs of societies with deep religious diversity and also complies with the principles of freedom and equality. This model meets the secularist objection to nonsecular states and the religious objection to some forms of secular state. To identify it, we must consider the *normative* and *discursive* levels and look at some of the developing normative practices of the French, British, and even American states. Take the example of the public funding of faith-based schools. Officially, American secularism does not sanction public financing of religion. Yet public funding of religion exists – albeit without proper assessment of the dilemmas of recognition and cooperation. Likewise, in practice, the French state not only directly and indirectly funds Roman Catholic schools but also tries to accommodate even Muslim minorities. In the Netherlands, at least until recently, forty-six Muslim schools were directly funded by the state. However, the best place to find this version of secularism is within the best intercommunal practice in the subcontinent of India and in the country's Constitution appropriately interpreted. In India the existence of deep religious diversity has ensured a conceptual response to problems not only within religions but also between them. Without taking it as a blueprint, the West must examine the Indian conception in the hopes of learning from it.

Several features of Indian secularism can be identified that distinguish it from other variants. First, multiple religions are not extras added on as an afterthought but were present at Indian secularism's starting point as part of its foundation. Indian secularism is inextricably tied to deep religious diversity. Second, this form of secularism has a commitment to multiple values, namely liberty, equality, and fraternity – not conceived narrowly as pertaining to individuals but interpreted broadly to cover the relative autonomy of religious communities and their equality of status in society – as well as other more basic values such as peace, toleration, and mutual respect among communities. It has a place not only for the right of individuals to profess their religious beliefs but also for the right of religious communities to establish and maintain educational institutions crucial for the survival and sustenance of their distinctive religious traditions.

The acceptance of community-specific rights brings me to the third feature of Indian secularism. Because it was born in a deeply multireligious society, it is concerned as much with interreligious domination as it is with intrareligious domination. Whereas the two Western conceptions of secularism have provided benefits to minorities only incidentally (Jews benefited in some European countries such as France not because their special needs and demands were met but because of a change in the general climate of the society), under the Indian conception even community-specific political rights (through political reservations for religious minorities) were almost granted during the drafting of the Constitution but were withheld in the last instance only for contextual reasons. In fact, it is arguable that a conceptual space is still available for these rights within the Indian Constitution.

Fourth, Indian secularism does not erect a wall of separation between religion and state. There are boundaries, of course, but they are porous. This situation allows the state to intervene in religions in order to help or hinder them without the impulse to control or destroy them. This intervention can include granting aid to educational institutions of religious communities on a nonpreferential basis and interfering in socioreligious institutions that deny equal dignity and status to members of their own religion or to those of others – for example, the ban on untouchability and the obligation to allow everyone, irrespective of their caste, to enter Hindu temples, as well as, potentially, other actions to correct gender inequalities. In short, Indian secularism interprets separation to mean not strict exclusion or strict neutrality but what I call *principled distance*, which is poles apart from one-sided exclusion, mutual exclusion, strict neutrality, and equidistance.

Fifth, Indian secularism is not entirely averse to the public character of religions. Although the state is not identified with a particular religion or with religion more generally, official and therefore public recognition is granted to religious communities. Sixth, this model shows that in responding to religion, we do not have to choose between active hostility and passive indifference or between disrespectful hostility and respectful indifference. We can combine the two, permitting the necessary hostility as long as there is also active respect. The state may intervene to inhibit some practices as long as it shows respect for other practices of the religious community and does so by publicly lending support to them.

Seventh, by not fixing its commitment from the start exclusively to individual or community values and by not marking rigid boundaries between the public and the private, India's constitutional secularism allows decisions on these matters to be made either within the open dynamics of democratic politics or by contextual reasoning in the courts. Finally, the commitment to multiple values and principled distance means that the state tries to balance different, ambiguous, but equally important values. This makes its secular ideal more like a contextual, ethically sensitive, politically negotiated arrangement – which it really is – rather than a scientific doctrine conjured by ideologues and merely implemented by political agents.

A somewhat forced, formulaic articulation of Indian secularism goes something like this. The state must keep a principled distance from all public or private and individual-oriented or community-oriented religious institutions for the sake of the equally significant – and sometimes conflicting – values of peace, worldly goods, dignity, liberty, equality, and fraternity in all of its complicated individualistic and nonindividualistic versions. Indian secularism, then, is an ethically sensitive, negotiated settlement between diverse groups and divergent values. This model thus embodies what I call *contextual secularism*. Allow me to elaborate on two features of the Indian model: principled distance and contextual secularism.

Principled Distance

As seen above, for mainstream Western secularism, separation of church and state means mutual exclusion. The idea of principled distance unpacks the metaphor of separation differently. It accepts a disconnection between state and religion at the level of ends and institutions but does not make a fetish of it at the level of policy and law; this distinguishes it from all other models of secularism, moral and amoral, that disconnect state and religion at this level. No other arrangement would be possible in a society where religion frames some of the people's deepest interests. Recall that political secularism is an ethic whose concerns relating to religion are similar to theories that oppose unjust restrictions on freedom, morally indefensible inequalities, intercommunal domination, and exploitation. Yet a secularism based on principled distance is not committed to the mainstream Enlightenment idea of religion. It accepts that humans have an interest in relating to something beyond themselves, including gods or God, and that this manifests itself as individual belief and feeling as well as social practice in the public domain. It also accepts that religion is a cumulative tradition (Smith 1991, 154-69) as well as a source of people's identities. But it insists that even if it turns out that God exists and that one religion is true and others false, this will not give the "true" doctrine or religion the right to force itself down the throats of others who do not believe it. The moral obligation to ensure the equal distribution of liberties and other valuable resources would prevent discrimination.

Similarly, a secularism based on principled distance accepts that although religion may not have special public significance antecedently written into and defining the very character of the state or the nation, it does not follow that religion has no public significance at all. Some versions of the "wall of separation" thesis make precisely this assumption. However, as long as religion is publicly significant, a democratic state simply has to take it into account. Indeed, institutions of religion may influence individuals as long as they do so through the same processes and resources as anyone else and without undue advantage or unduly exploiting the fears and vulnerabilities that frequently accompany people in their experience of the religious.

But what precisely is principled distance? The policy of principled distance entails a flexible approach to the issue of the state's inclusion or exclusion of religion and to the issue of its engagement with or disengagement from religion, which at the level of law and policy depends on the context, nature, and current state of relevant religions. Inclusion or engagement must be governed by principles undergirding a secular state that flow from a commitment to the values mentioned above. This requirement means that religion may intervene in the affairs of the state if such intervention promotes freedom, equality, or any other value integral to secularism.[1] For example, citizens may support a coercive state law by including a purely religious rationale as ground if this law is compatible with freedom, fraternity, or equality. Principled distance rejects the standard liberal idea that the principle of equal respect is best realized only when people come into the public domain by leaving their religious reasoning behind.

Engaging positively or negatively, depending entirely on whether the above-mentioned values are promoted or undermined, is one constitutive idea of principled distance. A second idea distinguishes it from strict neutrality, which dictates that the state must help or hinder all religions to an equal degree and in the same manner; if it intervenes in one religion, it must also do so in others. This makes principled distance rest upon a distinction explicitly drawn by the American philosopher Ronald Dworkin (1978, 125) between equal treatment and treating everyone as an equal. The principle of equal treatment in the relevant political sense requires that the state treat all citizens equally in the relevant respect – for example, in the distribution of a resource of opportunity. In contrast, the principle of treating people as equals entails that every person or group is treated with equal concern and respect. This second principle may sometimes require equal treatment – say, equal distribution of resources – but it may also occasionally dictate unequal preferential treatment. Treating people or groups as equals is entirely consistent with differential treatment. This idea is the second ingredient in what I have called principled distance.

When I say that principled distance allows for differential treatment, what kind of treatment do I have in mind? First, religious groups have sought exemptions when states have intervened in religious practices by promulgating laws designed to apply neutrally across society. This demand for non-interference is made on the grounds either that the law requires them to do things not permitted by their religion or that it prevents them from doing things mandated by their religion. For example, Sikhs demand exemptions from mandatory helmet laws and from police dress codes to accommodate religiously required turbans. Muslim women and girls demand that the state not interfere in the religious requirement that they wear the chador. Jews and Muslims seek exemptions from Sunday closing laws on the grounds that such closing is not required by their religion. Principled distance allows a practice that is banned or regulated in the majority culture to be permitted in the minority culture because of the distinctive status and meaning it has for the minority culture's members. For the mainstream conception of secularism, this variability is a problem because of a simple and somewhat absolutist morality that attributes overwhelming importance to one value – particularly to equal treatment, equal liberty, or equality of individual citizenship. Religious groups may demand that the state refrain from interference in their practices, but they may equally demand that the state interfere in such a way as to give them special assistance so that they are able to secure what other groups are routinely able to acquire by virtue of their social dominance in the political community. The state may grant authority to religious officials to perform legally binding marriages or to have their own rules for or methods of obtaining a divorce. Principled distance allows the possibility of such policies on the grounds that holding people accountable to a law to which they have not consented might be unfair. Furthermore, it does not discourage public justification – that is, justification based on reasons endorsable by all. Indeed, it encourages people to pursue public justification. However, if the attempt to arrive at public justification fails, it enjoins religiously minded citizens to support coercive laws that, although based purely on religious reasons, are consistent with freedom and equality (Eberle 2002).

However, principled distance is not just a recipe for differential treatment in the form of special exemptions. It may even require state intervention in some religions more than others, considering the historical and social conditions of all relevant religions. To ensure the promotion of a particular value constitutive of secularism, some religions may require more interference from the state. For example, suppose that the value to be advanced is social equality; pursuing this value requires in part undermining caste hierarchies. If this is the state's aim it may have to interfere in caste-ridden Hinduism much more than, say, in Islam or Christianity. However, if diversity-driven religious liberty is the value to be advanced by the state, it may be necessary to intervene in Christianity and Islam more than in Hinduism. In responding to a variety of values, the state can neither strictly exclude considerations emanating from religion nor keep strict neutrality with respect to religion. It cannot antecedently decide that it will always refrain from interfering in religions or that it will interfere in each equally; it may not relate to every religion in exactly the same way or intervene in each to the same degree or in the same manner. Wanting to do so would plainly be absurd. All the state must ensure is that its relationship with all religions is guided by nonsectarian motives consistent with some secular values and principles.

Contextual Secularism

A context-sensitive secularism, one based on the idea of principled distance, is what I term contextual secularism. It is contextual not only because the precise form and content of secularism will vary from one context to another and from place to place but also because it embodies a certain model of contextual moral reasoning. It is a multivalue doctrine. To accept its multivalue nature is to acknowledge that its constitutive values do not always sit easily with one another. On the contrary, they are frequently in conflict.

Some degree of internal discord, and therefore a fair amount of instability, is an integral part of contextual secularism. For this reason, it forever requires fresh interpretations, contextual judgments, and attempts at reconciliation and compromise. No general a priori rule of resolving these conflicts exists, no easy lexical order, no pre-existing hierarchy among values or laws that enables us to decide that, no matter what the context, a particular value must override everything else. Almost everything, then, is a matter of situational thinking and contextual reasoning. Whether one value will override or be reconcilable with another cannot be decided beforehand. Each time the matter will present itself differently and will be differently resolved. If this is true, the practice of secularism requires a different model of moral reasoning than the one that straitjackets our moral understanding in the form of well-delineated and explicitly stated rules (Taylor 1994). This contextual secularism recognizes that conflicts between individual rights and group rights, or between equality and liberty, or between liberty and the satisfaction of basic needs cannot always be adjudicated by recourse to some general and abstract principle. Rather, they can be settled only case by case and may require a fine balancing of competing claims. The eventual outcome may not be wholly satisfactory to either claimant but may still be reasonably satisfactory to both. Multivalue doctrines such as secularism encourage accommodation – not the giving-up of one value for the sake of another but their reconciliation and possible harmonization so that apparently incompatible concepts and values may operate without changes to their basic content.

This endeavour to make concepts, viewpoints, and values work simultaneously does not amount to a morally objectionable compromise. This is so because nothing of importance is being given up for the sake of something less significant, something without value or even with negative value. Rather, what is pursued is a mutually agreed-upon middle way that combines elements from two or more equally valuable entities. The roots of such attempts at reconciliation and accommodation lie in a lack of dogmatism, in a willingness to experiment – to think at different levels and in separate spheres – and in a readiness to make and accept decisions on a provisional basis. The pursuit of this middle way captures a way of thinking characterized by the following dictum: "Why look at things in terms of this or that, why not try to have both this and that?" (Austin 1972, 318). This way of thinking recognizes that, although we may currently be unable to secure the best of both values and may therefore be forced to settle for a watered-down version of each, we must continue to have an abiding commitment to searching for a transcendence of this second-best condition.

It is frequently argued that Indian secularism is contradictory because it tries to bring together individual and community rights and that those articles in the Indian Constitution that have a bearing on the secular nature of the Indian state are deeply conflictual and at best ambiguous (Tambiah 1998, 445-53). This characterization, however, misrecognizes a virtue as a vice. In my view, the attempt to bring together seemingly incompatible values is a great strength of Indian secularism. Indian secularism is an ethically sensitive negotiated settlement between diverse groups and divergent values. When it is not treated as such it turns either into a dead formula or into a facade for political manoeuvres.

Secularism – Not Only a Christian and Western Doctrine

The Indian version of secularism shows that claims of a necessary link between secularism and Christianity are exaggerated. It is true that the institutional separation of church and state is an internal feature of Christianity and an integral part of Western secularisms. But, as we have seen, this church-state disconnection is an insufficient condition for the development of secularism, even in societies with church-based religions. Absolute separation is clearly not a necessary condition for the development of all forms of secularism. Moreover, as I have argued, the state's mutual exclusion of religion is not the defining feature of secularism. The idea of separation can be interpreted differently. Nor are religious integrity, peace, and toleration – interpreted broadly to mean "live and let live" – unique to Christian societies. Most non-Christian civilizations give significant space to each. It follows that even though we find in Christian writings some of the clearest and most systematic articulations of the Western conception of secularism, this doctrine is not exclusively Christian.

All right, one might say, secularism is not just a Christian doctrine, but is it not Western? The answer to this question is both *yes* and *no*. Up to a point, it is certainly a Western idea. More specifically, as a clearly articulated doctrine, it has distinct Western origins. Although elements that constitute secularism assume different cultural forms and are found in several civilizations, one cannot deny that the idea of the secular first achieved self-consciousness and was properly theorized in the West. One might say, then, that the early and middle history of secularism is almost entirely dominated by Western societies. However, the same cannot be said of its later history. Nationalism and democracy arrived in the West after the settlement of religious conflicts had made societies religiously homogeneous or had almost done so – except with regard to Jews, of course, who continued to face persistent persecution. The absence of deep religious diversity and conflict meant that issues of citizenship could be addressed almost entirely without taking religious context into account; the important issue of the community-specific rights of religious groups could be wholly ignored. This had a decisive bearing on the Western conception of secularism. However, for non-Western societies such as India, the case is different. Both national and democratic agendas in countries such as India had to face issues raised by deep religious difference and diversity. In India nationalism had to choose between the religious and the secular. Similarly, the distribution of active citizenship rights could not be conceived or accomplished by ignoring religion. It was done by actively disregarding religion in the case of all political rights and by developing a complex attitude towards it in the case of cultural rights, which required the state to balance claims of individual autonomy with those of community obligations as well as claims of the necessity of keeping religions "private" with their inescapable, often valuable, presence in the public. By achieving this balance, Indian secularism never completely annulled particular religious identities.

In addressing these complex issues, India took the idea of political secularism further than it had evolved in the West. Mainstream theories or ideologies of secularism in modern, Western societies take little notice of these features. As a result, they are struggling to deal with their postcolonial religious diversity. The later history of secularism is more non-Western than Western. Elsewhere I have suggested that to discover its own rich and complex structure, Western secularism can either look backward at its own past or look sideways at Indian secularism, which mirrors not only the past of secularism but in some aspects also its future (Bhargava, 2007). Doing the latter would certainly benefit the secularisms of many Western societies. For example, French secularism needs to look beyond its own conceptions of *läicité* in order to take into account its own relatively recent multicultural and multireligious reality. It cannot continue to take refuge in claims of exceptionalism. A good hard look at Indian secularism could also change the self-understanding of other Western secularisms, including a very individualistic, American liberal secularism. These models can also be altered and reinvigorated at least partly by unearthing their own best contemporary practices. An articulation of these practices would show that these models are closer to the Indian variant and quite far removed from their theoretical and doctrinal self-understandings.

Let me sum up. How can secularism be rehabilitated? For a start, we must loosen the hold of mainstream Western conceptions. Second, secularism should sever its ties with amoral secular states. This means coming to realize that, somewhat paradoxically, secularism is against some secular states. Third, the disconnection or separation of church and state needs rethinking, and the two hitherto paradigmatic models of exclusion – the French and the American – must be jettisoned; instead, there must be discussion of principled distance. Fourth, the ends in question should be a mixture of the moral and the mildly ethical. Put differently, the focus should be on ending religion-related domination. Fifth, political secularism must be viewed as part of a critical social secularism – indeed, as a self-critical social perspective against four types of domination: interreligious, intrareligious, secular domination of the religious, and religious domination of the secular. We need to conceive secularism anew as not against religion but against institutionalized religious domination of the secular. Sixth, secularism must not be seen exclusively as a Christian and Western doctrine that needs to be imported to other societies. Instead, as the Indian case shows, it can develop its own path in other societies. Finally, we need to give up the binary opposition between the secular and the religious. A new, refashioned conception of secularism must not see a necessary opposition between the secular and the religious. On the contrary, it must encourage a way to conceive of a world inhabited by both religious and nonreligious people where the four religion-related dominations – in particular, intra- and interreligious dominations – are minimized, if not altogether eliminated.

Note

1 The Christian Council of Kenya played this role with great honour and distinction during the most repressive phase of the government of President Daniel arap Moi, circa 1984-92. At least one Anglican bishop and one Catholic priest were murdered by Moi's thugs.

Works Cited

Ahmed, I. 1987. *The Concept of an Islamic State: An Analysis of the Ideological Controversy in Pakistan*. London: Frances Pinter.

Audi, Robert. 1993. "The Place of Religious Argument in a Free and Democratic Society." *San Diego Law Review* 30 (4): 677-702.

Austin, Granville. 1972. *The Indian Constitution: Cornerstone of a Nation*. New Delhi: Oxford University Press.

Bader, Veit. 2007. *Secularism or Democracy? Associational Governance of Religious Diversity*. Amsterdam: Amsterdam University Press.

Barker, Christine R. 2004. "Church and State: Lessons from Germany?" *Political Quarterly* 75 (2): 168-76.

Bhargava, Rajeev. 2004. "Inclusion and Exclusion in South Asia: The Role of Religion." Background paper for the United Nations Development Programme, New York.

–. 2007. "The Distinctiveness of Indian Secularism." In *The Future of Secularism*, edited by T.N. Srinivasan, 20-63. Delhi: Oxford University Press.

Bowen, John. 2007. *Why the French Don't Like Headscarves: Islam, the State and Public Space*. Princeton, NJ: Princeton University Press.

Buruma, Ian. 2006. *Murder in Amsterdam: The Death of Theo van Gogh and the Limits of Tolerance*. London: Penguin.

Connolly, William E. 1999. *Why I Am Not a Secularist*. Minneapolis: University of Minnesota Press.

Dworkin, Ronald. 1978. "Liberalism." In *Public and Private Morality*, edited by Stuart Hampshire, 113-43. Cambridge, UK: Cambridge University Press.

Eberle, Christopher J. 2002. *Religious Conviction in Liberal Politics*. Cambridge, UK: Cambridge University Press.

Freedman, Jane. 2004. "Secularism as a Barrier to Integration? The French Dilemma." *International Migration* 42 (3): 5-27.

Hamburger, Philip. 2002. *Separation of Church and State.* Cambridge, MA: Harvard University Press.

Juergensmeyer, Mark. 1994. *New Cold War? Religious Nationalism Confronts the Secular State.* Berkeley: University of California Press.

Keane, John. 2000. *The Political Quarterly – Secularism?* Oxford: Blackwell.

Kepel, Gilles. 1994. *The Revenge of God: The Resurgence of Islam, Christianity, and Judaism in the Modern World.* University Park: Pennsylvania State University Press.

Klausen, Jytte, ed. 2005. *The Islamic Challenge: Politics and Religion in Western Europe.* Oxford: Oxford University Press.

Larmore, Charles. 1996. *The Morals of Modernity.* Cambridge, UK: Cambridge University Press.

Levy, Leonard W. 1994. *The Establishment Clause: Religion and the First Amendment.* Chapel Hill: University of North Carolina Press.

Macedo, Stephen. 1990. *Liberal Virtues: Citizenship, Virtue and Community in Liberal Constitutionalism.* Oxford: Clarendon.

Madan, T.N. 1998. "Secularism in Its Place." In *Secularism and its Critics,* edited by Rajeev Bhargava, 297-320. New Delhi: Oxford University Press.

Malik, Iftikhar. 2002. *Religious Minorities in Pakistan.* London: Minorities Rights Group International.

Modood, Tariq. 2011. "Moderate Secularism: A European Conception." *Open Democracy* 7:1-8.

Modood, Tariq, Anna Triandafyllidou, and Ricard Zapata-Barrero, eds. 2006. *Multiculturalism, Muslims and Citizenship: A European Approach.* London: Routledge.

Mohsin, Amena. 1999. "National Security and the Minorities: The Bangladesh Case." In *Minority Identities and the Nation-State,* edited by D.L. Sheth and Gurpreet Mahajan, 312-32. New Delhi: Oxford University Press.

Rawls, John. 1971. *A Theory of Justice.* Cambridge, MA: Belknap.

Ruthven, Malise. 2002. *A Fury for God: The Islamist Attack on America.* London: Granta.

Sandel, Michael J. 1993. "Freedom of Conscience or Freedom of Choice." In *Religious Liberty in the Supreme Court: The Cases That Define the Debate over Church and State,* edited by Terry Eastland, 483-96. Cambridge, MA, and Grand Rapids, MI: Eerdmans.

Smith, Wilfred Cantwell. 1991. *The Meaning and End of Religion.* Minneapolis: Fortress.

Solum, Lawrence. 1990. "Faith and Justice." *DePaul Law Review* 39:1047-81.

Spinner-Halev, Jeff. 2000. *Surviving Diversity: Religion and Democratic Citizenship.* Baltimore, MD: Johns Hopkins University Press.

Tambiah, Stanley J. 1998. "The Crisis of Secularism in India." In *Secularism and Its Critics,* edited by Rajeev Bhargava, 418-53. New Delhi: Oxford University Press.

Taylor, Charles. 1994. "Justice after Virtue." In *After MacIntyre: A Critical Perspective on the Work of Alasdair MacIntyre,* edited by John Horton and Susan Mendus, 16-43. Cambridge, UK: Polity.

Turner, Bryan S. 2001. "Cosmopolitan Virtue: On Religion in a Global Age." *European Journal of Social Theory* 4 (2): 131-52.

Weithman, Paul. 1997. "Religion and the Liberalism of Reasoned Respect." In *Religion and Contemporary Liberalism,* edited by Paul Weithman, 1-37. Notre Dame, IN: University of Notre Dame Press.

Westerlund, David. 1996. *Questioning the Secular State.* London: Hurst.

Part 2
Secularisms in the West

Between Secularism and Postsecularism
A Canadian Interregnum

Paul Bramadat and David Seljak

In Ontario a provincial election is decided on the issue of whether the state should extend funding to religiously based independent schools in the same way it funds Roman Catholic schools alongside the public system. In British Columbia politicians boycott the Sikh community's Vaisakhi Parade because of the presence of a float celebrating Sikh "martyrs" and because the safety of certain moderate Canadian Sikh politicians cannot be guaranteed. In Quebec, two years after the report of a government commission meant to defuse the controversy over what accommodations secular institutions, including the state, should make for the religious needs of religious and ethnic minorities, the government proposes a law banning the *niqab* (or face-covering worn by some Muslim women) in public institutions – and receives the support of 95 percent of the population. The return of religious issues to the public arena has caught politicians, pundits, and political theorists off guard. Canada – they thought – had settled the issue of the relation between church and state, and the secularization of public life had resolved the injustice of Christian privilege. The adoption of policies of multiculturalism, human rights charters, and labour codes forbidding discrimination on the basis of, among other things, religion was supposed to have meant that religion would cease to be a significant concern in a multicultural, democratic, and prosperous Canada. However, even a cursory glance at the news in the past five years indicates that these expectations have not been realized.

The current arrangement of liberal secular multiculturalism – which emerged as a solution to the dual problem of Christian privilege and Anglo-Franco cultural hegemony – helped to constrain Christianity. Nevertheless, we argue that this solution has its own contradictions and ambiguities. Clearly, Canadian society has changed: church membership and attendance have declined, and secular institutions perform many functions formerly accomplished by church organizations. Christianity no longer has the cultural power it once enjoyed. One cannot deny, however, that the shape and texture of this secularity have been created by Canada's unique ethnoreligious history. In this sense, we agree with Roger O'Toole (2000, 45) that, despite secularization, Canada remains an essentially Christian society in terms of cultural values, institutional topography, and habits of the heart. Although we argue that the current arrangements with regard to state power and religious pluralism are residually Christian, we base this claim not on the actual or remaining power of the major Christian churches, many of which are, in fact, in decline (Bramadat and Seljak 2008, 11-15, 420-22). Rather, one can make such an assertion based on the influence of Christianity on the historical definition of the Canadian state and society – including the distinctive form of Canadian secularism. The current arrangement is the product of a history in which Christianity has played a very significant role.

We argue that the particular – here one might add "closed" – secularist solution to the Christian privilege of the late twentieth century does not allow us to respond to the new challenges associated with, among other things, the need to recognize and accommodate large numbers of members of non-Christian religious communities as well as non-European Christian groups. Indeed, it is possible that Canada may well have outgrown the current "secular" – or more accurately, "secularist" – arrangement.[1] If we delve into the key tensions evident in political and public discourse, we will see that Canadians today face a choice between reverting to an openly Christian national identity (common-sensical in the nineteenth century), maintaining a supposedly neutral secular multiculturalism (popular since the 1960s), or adopting a new model of what we call a "postsecular" society where the ground rules for the appropriate interaction between religion and society remain rooted in the principles enshrined in the Charter of Rights and Freedoms (1982) and the Multiculturalism Act (1988) – but nonetheless seek to enable religious individuals and communities to operate in the public sphere in ways that are meaningful to them. In truth, we do not know what exactly a postsecular society looks like because we are in the midst of what we describe as an ideological interregnum between past solutions to religious intolerance and discrimination that no longer work and new solutions that have yet to be found. There are obvious parallels between the notion of a postsecular society as it has emerged from European discourse on religion and the state and the notion of a society based on "open secularism," as broadly sketched out by Gérard Bouchard and Charles Taylor (2008) in the hearings of Quebec's Consultation Commission on Accommodation Practices Related to Cultural Differences.[2] Nonetheless, both concepts are quite new and remain provisional; moreover, the introduction of recent laws such as those banning the wearing of religious face-coverings in both Europe and Canada demonstrates how far we are from adopting these ideals. In any event, before we can address the ambiguities and contradictions that might move Canadians to embrace some notion of a postsecular society, an overview of the development and nature of Canadian secularism is in order.

The Social Construction of a Christian Canada

Some thirty years ago John Webster Grant, Canada's pre-eminent church historian, attempted to trace the religious development of Canada by examining the relationship of the Christian churches to the state. He divided his brief history into three separate periods. The first era, which he called the "transplanting of Christendom," grouped together the truncated experiment that was New France with the earliest period of British North America because both societies shared the project of reproducing European-style religious establishment, where the state guaranteed the church a religious monopoly and the church worked to ensure the legitimacy of the state and the cooperation of the population (Grant 1977, 9). This project unravelled in Canada only in the 1840s and early 1850s. After the 1854 liquidation of the "clergy reserves," lands set aside for the Church of England, the Canadian state and society understood the nation to be Christian, but no single denomination would enjoy a religious monopoly. This second era, however, did not mark the beginning of an American-style "separation of church and state" since in Canada there emerged an oligopoly of Christian communities that clearly enjoyed special status, received government support, and provided government-sponsored services (e.g., healthcare and education). The contradictions and inequalities inherent in this arrangement led to a third and final period of secularization, which Grant identified with the massive immigration of the late nineteenth and early twentieth centuries, large-scale industrialization and urbanization, as well as the development of mass communication. Although these processes began roughly a hundred years ago, they culminated in a rapid secularization of Canadian society – especially of the public and institutional expressions of this society – in the 1960s when the state took over many of the social-service, healthcare, and educational duties of the churches and when the mainline churches began to experience declines in membership and attendance. Some further reflections on the historical arc underneath these three phases are worthwhile at this point.

The British North America Act (1867), which brought together the original four colonies (to which would be added six more provinces and three territories), gave to the provinces power over education, healthcare, and social services. In most cases this arrangement meant ceding control to the churches since they were in a far better position to dominate these sectors than were the small provincial state bureaucracies (Guindon 1988a, 104). For example, in Quebec the Roman Catholic Church had enough power to block the government's attempt to create a provincial Ministry of Education until 1964. The period between Confederation and the First World War was one of remarkable religious revival. Churches grew along with the unprecedented numbers of immigrants pouring into Canada. As immigrants arrived in Canada's West they were greeted both by an organized police force (i.e., the Royal Canadian Mounted Police) and by established churches – especially Presbyterian and Methodist but later Roman Catholic, Lutheran, Mennonite, and Baptist – that provided newcomers with familiar structures and thus helped to ease the trauma of international migration (Grant 1972, 46-52).

Sociologists have often used the terms *shadow establishment* or *social establishment* to describe this second period of Christian privilege, in which a limited number of denominations – namely Anglican, Presbyterian, Methodist (later folded into the United Church of Canada), Roman Catholic, Lutheran, and Baptist – acted as an oligarchy that performed the functions and enjoyed most of the legal, administrative, cultural, and direct political privileges of an established church, without the formal constitutional articulation of this arrangement (Martin 2000, 26-27).[3] The cultural power of the churches was also great. From Confederation until the 1960s Christianity was the "essential wellspring of societal virtue (and thus central to the goals of a spiritually uplifting society) and a means of inculcating ethics of duty and countering any lax moral standards among the citizenry" (Davies 1999, 3).

Secularization: The Canadian Version

Even this period of general consensus on the building of a Christian Canada, or "God's Dominion" (the former formal name of the country was the Dominion of Canada, a reference to Psalm 72), was not without its ambiguities and contradictions. Confederation facilitated the emergence of the structures of a liberal-democratic state and capitalist economy, and by the end of the First World War institutions in political and economic society would challenge the role of the churches in defining Canadian culture and providing essential services to Canadians. For example, daily newspapers, often run by political parties, quickly dwarfed the circulation numbers of the religious press. Despite their power and prestige, many in the churches of the early 1900s understood that they were losing ground in modern society. Industrialization and urbanization meant that many workers in crowded city dwellings escaped their influence, sometimes falling into drink and criminality. Catholic bishops in Quebec, for example, railed helplessly against new entertainments such as movies and distractions such as shopping. The Temperance Movement and the Social Gospel, often pointed to as examples of the strength of the churches, were in fact signs of their weakness. Other forces – not always understood at the time – were shaping the structure of Canadian society, and these two "moral crusades" (to use their own term) were rearguard actions to protect the Christian nature of Canada. Even the francophone Roman Catholics in Quebec, long thought to be the most intransigent opponents of modernization, enthusiastically embraced these emerging social forces in the wake of the First World War.[4]

In Quebec, and elsewhere, "during that period of transition when the poor, the sick, and the ignorant, as Everett C. Hughes once put it, no longer belonged to their kin and did not yet belong to the state" (Guindon 1988b, 133), the dynamism of the churches in providing social services hid the fact that the state and the market were becoming the real spheres of power, wealth, and prestige in Canadian society. For example, Quebec's Public Charities Act (1921), which transferred much responsibility for funding important social services from the churches to the provincial and municipal governments, announced that, even in this province, only the state – and no longer the religious communities – had the resources to provide social security for a modern, industrial, urban society (Hamelin and Gagnon 1984, 252-58). The churches remained in control of these sectors until the 1960s because permitting them to do so served the needs of the Quebec state and business interests. Similarly, in English Canada the state left most of the provision of social services and healthcare to the Christian churches, giving them enormous cultural power and influence (Christie and Gauvreau 1996). In retrospect, however, historians have concluded that in the first half of the twentieth century the churches had increasingly become junior partners with government and business in defining Canadian social reality.

After the Second World War the baby boom, along with rapid economic expansion, accelerated the growth of the state and business to the detriment of the churches. Moreover, the evolution of the welfare state in response to the Great Depression meant that the state assumed control more or less successfully – depending on local needs, regional policies, political exigencies, and economic realities – of those areas previously left to the church. Even so, prior to the 1960s the secularization of the Canadian public sphere was something of an unconscious process, largely set in motion by church-going liberal Christians. Few Canadians openly challenged the legitimacy of the power and prestige of the churches. This cultural consensus on the Christian nature of Canadian society, however, often hid the fact that the power of the churches had always been circumscribed by that of more robust actors – namely the state and economic institutions – and that this power was being further circumscribed by new social phenomena such as consumerism and mass communication, including new forms of entertainment, all of which competed successfully with the churches to define Canadian culture.

Secularization as a Social Project

Although the forces that undermined the project of a Christian Canada can be traced back to its very origins in Confederation, there was a significant cultural shift after 1960. The rapid secularization of Quebec has been called the Quiet Revolution, but the "social" disestablishment of the churches in the rest of Canada was no less momentous. Public schools were increasingly de-Christianized from roughly the 1960s, and indeed court challenges under the 1982 Canadian Charter of Rights and Freedoms led to the dramatic and rapid eclipse of the explicitly Christian dimension of education. Through changes in regulation and funding arrangements, governments took control of healthcare and social services, although religious organizations could retain ownership of their institutions. Where governments still wanted religious involvement (e.g., in hospital, military, and prison chaplaincy, as well as at official events such as Remembrance Day ceremonies), such involvement became multifaith, more inclusive, and subject to human rights legislation. Public culture became decidedly less Christian – indeed, some conservative Christians felt that public discourse was becoming decidedly anti-Christian (Bibby 1990, 71; Bramadat 2000; Noll 2006).

Although obviously a product of the same series of social changes that began even before Confederation, secularization after 1960 had some unique features. First, secularization was now concomitant with secular*ism*, the normative claim that Christian privilege had to be eliminated for *moral,* not just pragmatic, reasons. Whereas secularization had been largely a process occurring in the substratum of Canadian society – part of the structural differentiation of Canadian society as it modernized – it now became a conscious program positively identified with "progress." If the state was to be fair to all citizens, it had to be religiously neutral; if all citizens were to receive equal consideration for leadership positions, the churches needed to be stripped of their privileges; if institutions were going to offer the most effective services, they needed to be guided by science, not religion.

Second, this relatively new ideology of secularism was soon identified with multiculturalism, a liberal discourse and public policy identified with human rights and progress. The introduction of multiculturalism in 1971 cannot be separated – in the public imagination or the historical trajectory of Canadian society – from the liberalization of immigration laws in the late 1960s. Although the policy of multiculturalism was initially driven by well-established white and Christian ethnic minorities (especially Ukrainian Canadians), beginning in the 1970s it was employed alongside a host of human rights policies and labour legislation to protect the religious free-dom of the increasingly significant numbers of non-Christians (e.g., Hindus, Buddhists, Sikhs, Jews, Muslims, and practitioners of Chinese religion) who began to settle in Canada in the early 1970s.[5] The adoption of the Charter added new legal grounds, not to mention cultural legitimacy, for these pro-tections. Through these liberal policy measures many Canadians thought they had finally assured the neutrality of the Canadian state with regard to religion and, in so doing, had finally protected religious pluralism in Canada.

However, a new chapter was being written in Canadian history. Just as Canadian society was becoming more and more secular – that is, post-Christian – it was becoming more and more religiously diverse. It is now increasingly apparent that the broader social and ideological structures that were erected to manage Christianity do not necessarily effectively ad-dress the changes that have unfolded since the late 1970s and especially since the late 1990s. Canada now sees new and largely unforeseen forms of diversity: increasing numbers of non-Christians (likely to reach roughly 10 percent of the population by 2017 and 14 percent by 2031); increases in the racial and ethnic diversity *within* generally and historically Christian denominations of white, European origin (Bramadat and Seljak 2008); and large "visible minority" populations in Toronto, Vancouver, and Mont-real that by 2031 are likely to reach 63 percent, 59 percent, and 31 percent respectively.[6]

Naive Secularism and Postsecularism

In each of the three major periods discussed in this chapter (establishment, plural establishment, and secularization), social actors operated according not only to a more or less common vision of the ideal type of church-state relationship but also to quite specific views of the political, social, and moral dilemmas that their solution would address. In hindsight we can see that although the solutions they promulgated resolved a certain number of identifiable problems, new problems quickly arose to replace the old ones.

Proponents of each relatively novel solution were eager to resolve the contradictions associated with the proverbial *ancien régime*; they were later surprised when the world changed, leading to the emergence of entirely new and perhaps unpredictable challenges. In retrospect, of course, one can see that with regard to the third phase of our development – the phase that arguably passed its high-water mark in the early years of the twenty-first century – a naive and frequently triumphalist secularism was bound to alienate religious minorities, new and old; but this is simply retrospective wisdom since ardent secularists had some good reasons in the 1960s and before to expect that the rest of the world, and their own societies, would continue the disenchantment process that German sociologist Max Weber outlined so well roughly a century ago. Although it is always difficult to generalize about such broad historical shifts, we suggest that this emerging naive secularism created a public culture founded on a number of linked assumptions, most of which are discussed in this chapter:

1 that this new ideology represented the forces of enlightenment, reason, democracy, egalitarianism, and progress;
2 that religion was inherently divisive (especially evident in the enduring tensions in Canada between Roman Catholics and Protestants as well as the persistence of anti-Semitism);
3 that a move towards the formal separation of church and state would solve the problems of Christian privilege;
4 that religions should be defined according to and protected inasmuch as they were consistent with Christian categories (especially the focus on "faith," "creeds," and "beliefs");
5 that we could promote multiculturalism, as a policy or a discourse, without taking religion (especially its connection with ethnicity, its internal heterogeneity, and its role in transnationalism) into account.

These assumptions were widely accepted and largely invisible as long as the Canadian population remained almost uniformly or even nominally Christian. The emergence of the new cultural, religious, and ethnic pluralism – alongside the problematic persistence of religion in the public arena – has highlighted the shortcomings of this form of secularism.

The elite proponents of this naive secularism could not foresee the underlying contradictions, new developments, local and global conflicts, and religious transformations that would lead to a fundamentally different kind of society, one that would problematize their often rigid conceptualization of a public sphere without religion. As mentioned, the form and content of *Christian Canada,* although a rejection of the formal and legal establishment of a single religion, clearly bore the influence of the project of transplanting European Christendom. Similarly, secular Canada today is strongly marked by the legacy of the shadow establishment; witness our educational, healthcare, and social-service systems, not to mention our legal, administrative, and cultural topography.[7] Today religious pluralism, postcolonialism, dramatic changes in immigration policies, industrialization, and democratization are presenting Canadians with entirely new challenges and options. One option, a postsecular Canada, would be neither a return to Christian privilege nor a complete repudiation of naive or "closed" secularism. After all, by most accounts, Canadians continue to be committed to both the centrality of diversity in Canada as well as the key claims of secularism identified by Bouchard and Taylor (2008, 14-137), including the moral equality of persons, freedom of conscience and religion, state neutrality towards religions, and the separation of church and state. Although there is some common ground on which Canadians can meet to discuss these matters, during roughly the past decade in Canada and abroad, the fraught relationship between religious individuals and communities on the one hand and the secular public sphere on the other hand has demonstrated that these points of political and legal consensus may not be able to manage forms and degrees of cultural and religious diversity that would have been nearly unimaginable to people in the first two phases of Canadian history (i.e., the transplanting of Christendom and the shadow establishment) and unpalatable to those in the third (i.e., the secularist) phase.

Although Canadians still support diversity, they have begun to ask how much diversity is or might be too much. Are there limits to accommodation? If so, how should these limits be defined? Are the state's laws sufficient or efficient means to adjudicate these matters? Which requests for accommodation are "unreasonable" – and whose definition of *reason* is presupposed here? For example, should the state – founded as it is on gender equality – countenance religious organizations and accommodations that severely circumscribe the life-worlds of its female members? What kind of citizen loyalty do we have a right to expect in a world where more and more people define themselves as "transnational," move frequently from place to place, and sustain deep affective, not to mention political and economic, ties to other national, religious, and ethnic communities? What role ought the state have in governing matters such as marriage between two – or indeed more – consenting adults? Should religion be considered a matter of individual rational and unassailable choice or a more complex feature of – or even a kind of – culture?

Of course, there are many more questions and quandaries that might be listed here. Many of these issues arise out of the shortcomings of the approaches to religious diversity fashioned in the wake of the Second World War and especially after the 1960s and 1970s. In the current phase of liberal secular multiculturalism the strategy of solving the problem of Christian privilege by creating a putatively neutral, liberal, and secular framework finds itself wanting for three reasons. First, it approaches the relationship of religion and ethnicity in a naive fashion so that the supporters of this dominant sensibility believe they can support ethnic diversity and multiculturalism while often espousing an exclusive secularism as the basic ground rule of the public sphere. Second, inasmuch as the dominant approach deals with religion at all, it tends to overlook the heterogeneity both within and between religious communities, organizations, and individuals. Finally, the current arrangement ignores the fact that globalization, transnationalism, and consumerism have changed the ability of the nation-state, not to mention the religious community, to provide a total horizon of meaning for its members. A postsecular outlook will have to take at least these three factors into account as it attempts to integrate religion into Canadian public life.

Religion and Ethnicity

Canadian multicultural policy and theory have, until recently, generally ignored the question of religion, focusing instead on the promotion of ethnic diversity and antiracism (Biles and Ibrahim 2009; Bramadat 2008).[8] This neglect grows out of both a certain political resistance to any involvement with complex and perhaps controversial religious issues and an overattachment to an American-style conceptualization of the "separation of church and state" that is foreign to Canadian law and history. The tendency to assume the widespread intelligibility of the distinction between religion and ethnicity represents an obstacle to a more nuanced account of the relationship between religion and society (in either a secular or a postsecular era). In fact, although the categories of "religious" and "ethnic" are distinct in theory, they are exceptionally blurry in practice. However, scholars, policy makers, religious insiders, and many others still employ definitions of *religion* and *ethnicity* that presuppose clear distinctions, in which the former commonly refers to a set of well-defined beliefs, values, practices, and forms of community related to matters of ultimate significance – although beliefs are almost always privileged – and in which the latter usually refers to a form of identity and solidarity usually associated with a putatively common genetic or "blood" filiation.[9]

If you ask a Manitoba Mennonite, an Israeli Jew, a Punjabi Sikh, or a Saudi Arabian Muslim about the difference between their religious and their ethnic identities, you will likely hear a number of minimally prepared formal ways of delineating between these two dimensions. The habit of speaking as though these two concepts are cleanly distinguishable and as though these distinctions make sense to most people in the group is quite practical. However, it is worth noting that these initial conceptual distinctions are based upon abstractions or ideal types that do not really stand up very well when juxtaposed against the realities of people's lives. If you ask another question or two of the imagined individuals just mentioned, the conversation will likely break down, leaving people confused about which of their claims are "ethnic" and which are "religious" in origin or content.

The most obvious examples of the muddiness of these concepts are evident in the cases of Canadian Jews (Ravvin 2009) and Mennonites (Loewen 2008). Again, in each case individual community members will often speak as though there is an intelligible distinction between their religious and their ethnic identities. However, the contrived nature of these juxtaposed categories – the religious and the ethnic – is revealed within moments of engaging in conversations with many Jews and Mennonites about the religious origins of cultural and ethnic practices or about the ethnic and cultural origins of religious practices. Such conversations devolve very quickly into "chicken or egg" puzzles, with some people arguing that a social phenomenon predates the articulation of this sensibility in a religious vernacular and others arguing that so-called religious attitudes shape and even determine cultural or ethnic sensibilities. The artificial distinctions made between these concepts are not just problematic but also idiosyncratic, as we see when two Jews or two Mennonites disagree with one another about which elements of their lives ought to be considered religious and which ought to be considered ethnic – and perhaps which ought to be considered both.

The fluidity of the Jewish and Mennonite ethnic and religious identities is typically contrasted with the clarity of the way the distinction is expressed in Muslim communities. For example, it is certainly common for Muslims to claim that there is a tidy distinction between their religious convictions – understood as derived from an ideal and pure Islam – and the minor local ethnic and cultural accretions that have attached themselves to the tradition (McDonough and Hoodfar 2009). In Canada, Sheila McDonough and Homa Hoodfar (2009) argue, Muslims have, with significant success, sought to transcend the cultural and ethnic features of their forms of Islam and have created mosques that cater to and represent a more broadly based Islam. However, others argue that most, and perhaps all, "Islams" reflect local renditions of a broader ideal type of the tradition, which exists nowhere in a pure and noncontroversial form (Asad 1993; Cesari 2009; Rosen 1984; Tripp 2009). In fact, what McDonough and Hoodfar (2009) may be cataloguing is not the emergence on Canadian soil of a universal Islam but a Canadian Islam. Nonetheless, the commonly made formal distinction between a Muslim's religious identity (e.g., as a Sunni) and his or her ethnic identity (e.g., as a Pashtun) does function in Muslim and Canadian discourse to organize both social and religious phenomena as well as human identities. However, it will be necessary in the future to problematize this conceptual binary, to trace out the limitations of its application, and to make its imprecision apparent.

Equally vexing is that, since journalists, pundits, and policy makers are usually outsiders to these groups, they commonly assume that a given group's beliefs and practices are internally homogeneous, consistent, and unchanging. Many of the controversial items about religion that appear in local and national news and on the task lists of policy makers deal with claims related to explicit religious signs and symbols (e.g., hijabs, niqabs, kirpans, and turbans) and with explicit demands related to religiously sanctioned violence or ritual requirements, events, and schedules (Bramadat 2008). These religious signs and claims never reach the public arena without being inflected, or often even encompassed, by ethnic markers and meanings. That is, these signs and claims are often described as features of timeless religious traditions but are usually bound up with the very real and practical politics of particular contemporary ethnic communities.

Nonetheless, once these matters appear in the public arena the interpenetration of religion and ethnicity – and indeed politics – is often obscured. Instead, the issue is typically framed in terms of a conflict between a putatively pure religious symbol or claim, on the one hand (e.g., some one-dimensional normative insider account of the hijab, kirpan, or jihad), and an inherently political reality, on the other hand (e.g., the practical effort to achieve "social cohesion" or "security" in a multicultural state). The question, then, becomes: How will the dominant society, understood as complex, negotiable, and dynamic, respond to religious symbols and claims, understood as simple, non-negotiable, and eternal? However, this mischaracterizes the matter considerably. Scholars of Islam, Hinduism, Sikhism, and Judaism remind us that within these communities religious claims about articles of clothing and other religious requirements are the topic of much debate and disagreement. As such, the religious symbols and claims in question are usually a good deal more fluid and internally contested than either outsiders might assume or insider advocates of the positions might publicly admit. Moreover, the dominant society is itself often rooted more in ideological principles than in simply pragmatic ones (as the example of France demonstrates most clearly).

The point is that when religious issues do enter the public sphere, the symbols and claims involved tend to be flattened out, depluralized, de-historicized, de-ethnicized, and decontextualized. It is difficult to determine whether the reluctance to consider the intersection of religious and ethnic forms of identity reflects the reticence of commentators (e.g., lawyers, judges, journalists, and professors) to discuss issues with which they are unfamiliar, the capacity of the dominant secular ideology to manage and minimize all difficult topics, or the social deference that is usually – although clearly not always – shown to religion in Canada under the aegis of both the principle of "reasonable accommodation" (Milot 2009; Moon 2008) and good manners.

Missing from the broader conversation in the public arena is awareness of the ambiguity and historicity of these claims about pieces of fabric, millinery, rules governing the acceptable use of force, women's rights, dietary restrictions, and days of rest around which so many public debates occur. Claims originating from within the minority communities and also from within the dominant society arise at specific points in time; they change, they mean many things, and they are contested within the groups. They change in response to local and global forces, and there is no simple way to predict the direction of changes within communities. Consider, as examples, the multiple meanings attributed by Muslim and Sikh insiders and by outsiders to the meanings of the hijab and turban. These lengths of cloth are variously

- expressions of resistance to or rejection of secularism;
- expressions of deep familial pressures or casually inherited familial traditions;
- ways to resist an intra-ethnic peer group perceived as debauched;
- ways to aggravate parents who might be perceived as overly controlling;
- ways to aggravate parents who might be perceived as insufficiently learned in religious matters;
- expressions of a personal commitment to an independent spiritual conviction;
- expressions (in the case of the turban) of an identification with a particular national liberation struggle;
- expressions (in the case of the hijab) of progressive feminism or regressive androcentrism.

The diversity of motivations and meanings evident in this list does not imply that all claims advanced about, for example, the hijab and turban are mysterious or idiosyncratic. Rather, it suggests that neither political nor philosophical responses to such claims will be effective without sincere and informed efforts to engage religious interlocutors in honest and meaningful discussions about the place of a particular claim within the broader and often remarkably heterogeneous tradition. To put it another way, Canadian multiculturalism will achieve only a portion of its objectives if it focuses almost exclusively on ethnicity and race and systematically excludes religion from the matrix of identity and community.

The third reason that the dominant approach to religion and secularism is flawed is that it assumes that the borders of Canadian religious communities are coterminous with the borders of Canada. Globalization means that the "world religions" can become truly *global* religions (Casanova 2008, 116-17). Moreover, transnational identities tied to these globalized religions mean that newcomers and their children – and others as well – identify with multiple places (Bramadat and Seljak 2008, 2009; Ebaugh and Chaftez 2000; Levitt 2007; McLellan 1999; Warner and Wittner 1998). Thus it should not surprise anyone that many Canadians feel tied to Canada and to some other place – usually a place that is both religiously and ethnically salient to them. These ties are affirmed by travel, of course, but also by involvement in virtual communities and Canadian-based communities devoted to some other place. Although Canadian scholars of religion and diversity are becoming increasingly attentive to the transnational forces at work in the ways Hindu, Sikh, Jewish, and Muslim Canadians identify themselves, much work remains to be done to enable us to adequately understand what emerging deterritorialized and denationalized modes of identification mean or will mean for ethnic and religious minorities, much less what they mean and will mean for the broader society.

Many are troubled by this emerging transnationalism because they see it as a rejection of Canadian citizenship. Many worry about the harmful effects of these multiple identifications on "social cohesion" or "Canadian identity" (Bibby 1990; Bissoondath 1994; Gwyn 1995; Reitz and Banerjee 2007). These concerns seem to us to be misplaced. The proponents of this critique assume either that Canadian society is religiously and culturally neutral (making newcomer or non-Christian discomfort illegitimate) or that Canadian society embodies an unchanging and monolithic identity or set of values. Neither assumption seems warranted by our brief overview of the development of Canadian secularism. Moreover, the evidence does not necessarily justify an equation between cosmopolitanism and transnationalism among religious and ethnic minorities, on the one hand, and an erosion of their attachment to the broader project of Canada, on the other hand (Adams 2007; Jedwab and Berns-McGown 2007). Other social forces – most notably racism, religious discrimination, and experiences of economic frustration – are far more likely to have a greater negative effect on the attachment of ethnic and religious minorities to Canada.

It is almost a truism that people are related to the communities into which they are born and also – at least potentially – to other places. Indeed, these "intersections of identity" – the here and the elsewhere – are not new in Canadian history. Early waves of immigrants similarly identified with (at least) two places: they combined the culture of the "old country" with what they discovered in the broader society upon arrival. What is arguably new, however, is the breadth of options available now that immigrants from not just Europe but virtually the entire world have footholds in Canadian society. Moreover, modern communications technology, the Internet, and relatively inexpensive international travel have made physical distance less of an obstacle to transnational forms of identification. As a result, scholars interested in religion and ethnicity need to attend to the ways that both phenomena interact against a highly globalized backdrop that enables hybridized, mixed, and complicated ethnoreligious identities to emerge that would have been nearly inconceivable in previous decades. Many ethnic and religious new-comers – especially those comfortable with the Internet – do not wring their hands over the false choice others feel they must make between Canada and elsewhere, nor do they fret about how to be both ardently, conserva-tively religious Christians, Muslims, or Sikhs, and members of the secular Canadian public sphere. Many newcomers are in fact quite comfortable with complex forms of identity that scholars would describe as postmodern and postsecular. It is not just that they *can* have it both ways or that we *must* let them have it both ways: they simply *do* have it both ways. Taking religion – especially its connection to ethnicity – seriously is a key component of both understanding this relatively new reality and reshaping our public sphere to affirm and recognize these new forms of civic and personal identity.

Conclusion: The Interregnum

It is increasingly difficult to espouse a unidirectional or "vulgar" version of the secularization hypothesis. The world simply has not moved uniformly or seamlessly in the direction predicted by the advocates of this kind of naive secularism (Casanova 1994, 2006, 2007). Around the world for roughly the past two decades scholars and politicians have been struggling to come to terms with the fact that religion – a cultural force they thought was spent or at least would recede wherever education and modernization advanced – has burst back onto the national and international stages. In innumerable liberal-democratic countries in the West, political leaders, aca-demics, bureaucrats, teachers, and members of security services regularly grapple with the challenges posed by the resurgence of religion in public arenas (Bramadat and Koenig 2009). In Canada, and in many other places, public debates no longer concern the ways we might rein in an expansionist or established Christianity but rather how and to what extent we might ac-commodate the non-Christian religions associated with ethnic minorities that now form increasingly large and sometimes restive components of these societies.

In each liberal democracy the current relationship between religion(s) and the state has been determined by distinctive political and historical factors. So the approach or approaches adopted in France, Canada, Great Britain, and Germany reflect the unique historical circumstances of these countries as well as the nature of claims made by the specific religious and ethnic groups upon which these countries have relied in the modern period to expand their labour force and population (Casanova 2006; Eisenstadt 2000; Koenig 2009). In some sense, therefore, specific challenges evident in these societies – for example, the regulation of religious clothing in France, the emergence of "homegrown" terrorism in Britain, the niqab debates in Canada, and the citizenship debates in Germany – are simply reflections of local forces linked to particular historical sets of conditions, such as a given pre-election political movement, a particular no longer docile immigrant population, or a specific act of violence.[10]

However, we suggest that these specific challenges actually point to a far more profound fault line running through most liberal democracies. It now appears incontrovertible that we are living in the middle of a transition, an "ideological interregnum" (Bramadat 2007), in which we see more clearly the flaws in the often imperious naive secularism that appears to be more and more attractive to Western societies as they try to come to terms with religious diversity and to shore up the ramparts of secularism. The reign of the most recent political narrative has not ended abruptly or entirely, although of course its end has been captured in dramatic episodes that have been political, philosophical, or religious – such as, respectively, 11 September 2001, Jürgen Habermas's (2005) intellectual aporia towards the entry of religious discourses into the public arena, and a rash of religious entrenchments in India, the United States, and the Muslim world. In response, vociferous protests have been raised by the "new atheists," such as Richard Dawkins (2006), Christopher Hitchens (2007), and Sam Harris (2004), over the declining likelihood that we will ever see the fruition of the closed-secularist hopes of progress towards a world (or at least a public sphere) free from and of religion. Moreover, we have seen in recent years in the West a number of rearguard actions to articulate the clear limits of religious pluralism, constrain multiculturalism, limit immigration (mostly from predominantly Muslim societies), and promote the norm of assimilation (Bramadat and Koenig 2009).

In this interregnum we no longer have easy access to the comforting and broadly plausible narratives that guided the political and intellectual leaders of the twentieth century. Here it is important to observe that the claim that religion would inevitably recede or act as a mere epiphenomenon of social or economic forces was *not* a minor feature of the regnant metanarrative of Enlightenment secularism; on the contrary, the retreat of religion (into oblivion or the "private sphere") was central to the whole structure of the modern liberal project. As a result, the current national and international anxieties associated with the resurgence of religion in the Western public sphere reflect an arguably fundamental challenge to the dominant understanding of the Enlightenment project.

However, we lack any consensus that a new postsecular paradigm exists that would be acceptable to the Canadian public in general or to the ethnic and religious minorities that are increasingly significant components of our societies. What is clear, however, is that the central issue is no longer how to tame those we wish to control, tolerate those who now live next to us, and manage the conflicts that occur when "our" (capitalist, predominantly Christian, ideologically secularist, multicultural, rational, liberal, democratic, egalitarian, etc.) cultures chafe against "their" (Muslim, Hindu, Sikh, developing, illiberal, gender-segregated, etc.) cultures. Such an approach to the problem can lead only to further conflict. The challenge is how – or whether – to reconfigure our societies in a way that enables us to engage religious individuals, communities, and claims in a more meaningful, reciprocal, and equitable manner.

As mentioned earlier, a complicating feature of this interregnum is the fact that members of most of the religious communities mentioned in this chapter – indeed, in this book – enter or re-enter the public arena as members of religious as well as ethnic, and in some cases national, minorities. Thus it is no longer sufficient to devise a formal means of grappling with a particular religious claim or with religious claims in general (whatever that might mean); rather, we need to develop an approach to social life that enables us simultaneously to engage both the religious and the ethnic features of the communities and claims that have now fundamentally called into question the very telos and meaning of our societies. The ways we respond to these challenges will define the kinds of society – postsecular, opensecular, closed-secular, or what have you – we build and the kinds of future we have.

Notes

1 The term *secularist* is used here to denote a normative ideological assertion of the positive moral value of those secularization processes associated with the diminishment of religion in all social spheres. In this sense, the term *secularist* is synonymous with what Gérard Bouchard and Charles Taylor (2008, 139-54) describe as "closed secularism," which they contrast with "open secularism," the latter being a relationship between religion and society where there is not a rigid exclusion of religion from the public arena.

2 On the European context, see Jürgen Habermas (2008); on the Canadian context, especially the Quebec debate, see Bouchard and Taylor (2008).

3 Veit Bader (2003, 61-67) demonstrates that the concept of "establishment" need not be confined to constitutional arrangements. A religious community can enjoy legal, administrative, cultural, or political power without being given any special constitutional privileges.

4 More than twenty-five years before Fernande Roy (1993) illustrated that the French Canadian middle class (all good Roman Catholics) embraced the liberal vision of material progress, personal liberty, and social harmony, William F. Ryan (1966) demonstrated that even the conservative clergy had adopted elements of the project of modernization by promoting electrification of the province as well as technological advances in agriculture and other industries.

5 Obviously, there were non-Christians in Canada for almost a century before the liberalization of the Canadian immigration regime, but it is clearly the case that non-Christians began to make up a far greater proportion of the overall immigrant population following these policy changes in the 1970s (Bramadat and Seljak 2009).

6 A 2005 Statistics Canada population projection predicted that members of non-Christian religious groups will represent some 9.2 to 11.2 percent of the Canadian population by 2017. By 2017, Canada's 150th year, membership in the Muslim, Hindu, and Sikh communities, the report stated, will have increased by 145 percent, 92 percent, and 72 percent respectively, compared to their 2001 census totals (Bélanger and Malenfant 2005). According to a 2010 study by Statistics Canada roughly 14 percent of Canadians will be non-Christian by 2031, and approximately one-half of these non-Christians will be Muslims (Statistics Canada 2010). In fact, these projections may be too low because they do not include practitioners of Chinese religion, something the census questions do not allow us to measure. On the other hand, they may be too high because they assume that the children of members of minority religious groups will retain the faith of their parents.

7 José Casanova (2008, 111-13) argues the same for Europe after the Second World War. Most European democracies (other than France) have maintained the constitutional arrangements of the past. For example, England and Scotland in the United Kingdom as well as the Scandinavian Lutheran countries (except for Sweden after 2000) maintain established churches. Only Catholicism has eschewed establishment since 1974. He writes, "What is clear is that no European state can be said to meet the criteria of a secular neutral state, which is supposed to offer equal access, equal distance, equal respect, or equal support to all the religions within its territory" (ibid., 113).

8 Paul Bramadat (2008) demonstrates that of the 546 research projects funded by the Multiculturalism Program from 2000 to 2004, only 3.4 percent related directly to religion.

9 Naturally, scholars have disagreed on definitions of both *religion* and *ethnicity* for some time. For a discussion of the debates on religion, see William Arnal (2000), Talal Asad (1993), and Russell T. McCutcheon (1997). For parallel debates on ethnicity, see Himani Bannerji (2000) and Mark Moberg (1997).

10 Matthias Koenig (2009, 305-10) offers a concise description of the factors that influence the policies of Western democracies towards the new religious pluralism.
Koenig identifies these as (1) demographic characteristics of the host society and
immigrants (e.g., types of immigrant populations, types of claims being made,
socioeconomic status of immigrants, degree of religious diversity, and geographic
concentration); (2) structural factors (e.g., access to the political process, historically entrenched church-state relations, and government involvement in religion
generally); and (3) cultural factors (e.g., the cultural legacy of a religious past and
attitudes towards immigrants). Among cultural factors, one could highlight the legacy of xenophobia, racism, and religious intolerance and their interaction in
Canada's past.

Works Cited

Adams, Michael. 2007. *Unlikely Utopia*. Toronto: Viking Canada.
Arnal, William. 2000. "Definition." In *Guide to the Study of Religion,* edited by Willi
    Braun and Russell T. McCutcheon, 21-35. London: Cassell.
Asad, Talal. 1993. *Geneaologies of Religion: Discipline and Reasons of Power in
    Christianity and Islam*. Baltimore, MD: Johns Hopkins University Press.
Bader, Veit. 2003. "Religions and States: A New Typology and a Plea for Non-
    Constitutional Pluralism." *Ethical Theory and Moral Practice* 6 (1): 55-91.
Bannerji, Himani. 2000. *The Dark Side of the Nation: Essays on Multiculturalism,
    Nationalism and Gender*. Toronto: Canadian Scholars' Press.
Bélanger, Alain, and Éric Caron Malenfant. 2005. *Population Projections of Visible
    Minority Groups, Canada, Provinces and Regions, 2001-2017*. Ottawa: Ministry of
    Industry, Government of Canada.
Bibby, Reginald. 1990. *Mosaic Madness: Pluralism without a Cause*. Toronto: Stoddart.
Biles, John, and Humera Ibrahim. 2009. "Religion and Public Policy: Immigration,
    Citizenship and Multiculturalism – Guess Who's Coming to Dinner?" In *Religion
    and Ethnicity in Canada,* edited by Paul Bramadat and David Seljak, 154-77.
    2005. Reprint, Toronto: University of Toronto Press.
Bissoondath, Neil. 1994. *Selling Illusions: The Cult of Multiculturalism in Canada*.
    Toronto: Penguin.
Bouchard, Gérard, and Charles Taylor. 2008. *Building the Future: A Time for
    Reconciliation*. Quebec City: Government of Quebec.
Bramadat, Paul. 2000. *The Church on the World's Turf: An Evangelical Student
    Group at a Secular University*. New York: Oxford University Press.
–. 2007. "Our Current Interregnum and the Decline of Secular Modernity." http://
    canada.metropolis.net/pdfs/Bramadat_e.pdf.
–. 2008. "Religion and Public Policy in Canada: An Itinerary." *Studies in Religion*
    37 (1): 121-43.
Bramadat, Paul, and Matthias Koenig, eds. 2009. *International Migration and the
    Governance of Religious Diversity*. Montreal and Kingston: McGill-Queen's Uni-
    versity Press.
Bramadat, Paul, and David Seljak, eds. 2008. *Christianity and Ethnicity in Canada*.
    Toronto: University of Toronto Press.

–. 2009. *Religion and Ethnicity in Canada.* 2005. Reprint, Toronto: University of Toronto Press.

Casanova, José. 1994. *Public Religions in the Modern World.* Chicago: University of Chicago Press.

–. 2006. "Rethinking Secularization: A Global Comparative Perspective." *Hedgehog Review* 8 (1-2): 7-22.

–. 2007. "Immigration and the New Religious Pluralism: A EU/US Comparison." In *Democracy and the New Religious Pluralism,* edited by Thomas Banchoff, 59-83. New York: Oxford University Press.

–. 2008. "Public Religions Revisited." In *Religion: Beyond a Concept,* edited by Hent de Vries, 101-19. New York: Fordham University Press.

Cesari, Jocelyne. 2009. "Islam, Integration and France." In *International Migration and the Governance of Religious Diversity,* edited by Paul Bramadat and Matthias Koenig, 195-224. Montreal and Kingston: McGill-Queen's University Press.

Christie, Nancy, and Michael Gauvreau. 1996. *A Full-Orbed Christianity: The Protestant Churches and Social Welfare in Canada, 1900-40.* Montreal and Kingston: McGill-Queen's University Press.

Davies, Scott. 1999. "From Moral Duty to Cultural Rights: A Case Study of Political Framing in Education." *Sociology of Education* 72 (1): 1-21.

Dawkins, Richard. 2006. *The God Delusion.* Boston: Houghton Mifflin.

Ebaugh, Helen Rose, and Janet Saltzman Chaftez. 2000. *Religion and the New Immigrants: Continuities and Adaptations in Immigrant Congregations.* Walnut Creek, CA: Alta Mira.

Eisenstadt, Shmuel Noah. 2000. "Multiple Modernities." *Daedalus* 129 (1): 1-29.

Grant, John Webster. 1972. *The Church in the Canadian Era: The First Century of Confederation.* Toronto: McGraw-Hill Ryerson.

–. 1977. "Religion and the Quest for a National Identity: The Background in Canadian History." In *Religion and Culture in Canada,* edited by Peter Slater, 7-21. Waterloo, ON: Canadian Corporation for Studies in Religion.

Guindon, Hubert. 1988a. "The Crown, the Catholic Church, and the French-Canadian People: The Historical Roots of Quebec Nationalism." In *Quebec Society: Tradition, Modernity, and Nationhood,* edited by Roberta Hamilton and John H. McMullan, 94-111. Toronto: University of Toronto Press.

–. 1988b. "Quebec and the Canadian Question." In *Quebec Society: Tradition, Modernity, and Nationhood,* edited by Roberta Hamilton and John H. McMullan, 125-46. Toronto: University of Toronto Press.

Gwyn, Richard. 1995. *Nationalism without Walls: The Unbearable Lightness of Being Canadian.* Toronto: McClelland and Stewart.

Habermas, Jürgen. 2005. "Religion in the Public Sphere." Lecture presented at the Holberg Prize Seminar, Bergen, Norway, 29 November. http://www.holbergprisen.no/.

–. 2008. "Notes on a Post-Secular Society." 18 June. http://www.signandsight.com/features/.

Hamelin, Jean, and Nicole Gagnon. 1984. *Histoire du catholicisme québécois: Le XXe siècle.* Vol. 1, *1898-1940.* Montreal: Boréal.

Harris, Sam. 2004. *The End of Faith: Religion, Terror, and the Future of Reason*. New York: W.W. Norton.

Hitchens, Christopher. 2007. *God Is Not Great: How Religion Poisons Everything*. New York: Twelve/Hachette Book Group USA/Warner Books.

Jedwab, Jack, and Rima Berns-McGown, eds. 2007. *Diasporas: What It Now Means to Be Canadian*. Special issue of *International Journal* 63 (1).

Koenig, Matthias. 2009. "How Nation-States Respond to Religious Diversity." In *International Migration and the Governance of Religious Diversity*, edited by Paul Bramadat and Matthias Koenig, 293-322. Montreal and Kingston: McGill-Queen's University Press.

Levitt, Peggy. 2007. *God Needs No Passport: Immigrants and the Changing American Religious Landscape*. New York: New Press.

Loewen, Roy. 2008. "The Poetics of Peoplehood: Ethnicity and Religion among Canada's Mennonites." In *Christianity and Ethnicity in Canada*, edited by Paul Bramadat and David Seljak, 330-64. Toronto: University of Toronto Press.

Martin, David. 2000. "Canada in Comparative Perspective." In *Rethinking Church, State, and Modernity: Canada between Europe and America*, edited by David Lyon and Marguerite Van Die, 23-33. Toronto: University of Toronto Press.

McCutcheon, Russell T. 1997. *Manufacturing Religion: The Discourse on Sui Generis Religion and the Politics of Nostalgia*. New York: Oxford University Press.

McDonough, Sheila, and Homa Hoodfar. 2009. "Muslims in Canada: From Ethnic Groups to Religious Community." In *Religion and Ethnicity in Canada*, edited by Paul Bramadat and David Seljak, 133-53. 2005. Reprint, Toronto: University of Toronto Press.

McLellan, Janet. 1999. *Many Petals of the Lotus: Five Asian Buddhist Communities in Toronto*. Toronto: University of Toronto Press.

Milot, Micheline. 2009. "Modus Co-vivendi: Religious Diversity in Canada." In *International Migration and the Governance of Religious Diversity*, edited by Paul Bramadat and Matthias Koenig, 105-30. Montreal and Kingston: McGill-Queen's University Press.

Moberg, Mark. 1997. *Myths of Ethnicity and Nation: Immigration, Work and Identity in the Belize Banana Industry*. Knoxville: University of Tennessee Press.

Moon, Richard, ed. 2008. *Law and Religious Pluralism in Canada*. Vancouver: UBC Press.

Noll, Mark. 2006. "What Happened to Christian Canada?" *Church History* 75: 245-73.

O'Toole, Roger. 2000. "Canadian Religion: Heritage and Project." In *Rethinking Church, State, and Modernity: Canada between Europe and America*, edited by David Lyon and Marguerite Van Die, 34-51. Toronto: University of Toronto Press.

Ravvin, Norman. 2009. "Jews in Canada: A Travelling Cantor on the Prairie, and Other Pictures of Canadian Jewish Life." In *Religion and Ethnicity in Canada*, edited by Paul Bramadat and David Seljak, 111-32. 2005. Reprint, Toronto: University of Toronto Press.

Reitz, Jeffrey G., and Rupa Banerjee. 2007. "Racial Inequality, Social Cohesion, and Policy Issues in Canada." In *Belonging? Diversity, Recognition and Shared*

Citizenship in Canada, edited by Keith G. Banting, Thomas J. Courchene, and F. Leslie Seidle, 489-545. Montreal: Institute for Research on Public Policy.

Rosen, Lawrence. 1984. *Bargaining for Reality: The Construction of Social Reality in a Muslim Community.* Chicago: University of Chicago Press.

Roy, Fernande. 1993. *Histoire des idéologies au Québec aux XIXe et XXe siècle.* Montreal: Boréal.

Ryan, William F. 1966. *The Clergy and Economic Growth in Quebec, 1896-1914.* Quebec City: Laval University Press.

Statistics Canada. 2010. "Study: Projections of the Diversity of the Canadian Population." *The Daily,* 9 March. http://www.statcan.gc.ca/daily-quotidien/100309/dq100309a-eng.htm.

Tripp, Charles. 2009. "All (Muslim) Politics Is Local: How Context Shapes Islam in Power." *Foreign Affairs,* September/October. http://www.foreignaffairs.com/articles/.

Warner, R. Stephen, and Judith Wittner, eds. 1998. *Gatherings in Diaspora: Religious Communities and the New Immigration.* Philadelphia: Temple University Press.

Tolerance and Accommodation as Vestiges of the Empire

Lori G. Beaman

Chapter 5

The language of tolerance and accommodation infiltrates academic, legal, public-policy, and public discourses in discussions of the management of diversity. Recently, for example, the Supreme Court of Canada has solidified its reliance on the concept of accommodation by drawing from what had previously been an analytical framework relegated to labour law. The Bouchard-Taylor Commission brought the notion of reasonable accommodation into a much broader public forum.[1] Even in critical academic analyses of diversity, difference, and multiculturalism the words *tolerance* and *accommodation* are used without much reflection on the work that this language does (e.g., see Bader 2007; Connolly 2005; Gutmann and Thompson 2004; Jakobsen and Pellegrini 2004; Kymlicka 2007; and Shachar 2001).

Religion is at the core of these discussions; for example, should Muslims who want prayer space be "accommodated"? A just and peaceful society "tolerates" religious minorities who might ask to carry a kirpan, be exempt from photographs on drivers' licences, or wear a headscarf on the soccer field. Tolerance is the mark of a civilized society, or so goes the rhetoric encompassing a wide range of discursive frames that includes liberalism and interfaith dialogue. Accommodation is the act that operationalizes this tolerance in tangible terms. So what, then, is wrong with tolerance and accommodation?

In this chapter I argue that the notions of tolerance and accommodation are vestiges of the empire that conceptually anchor a hierarchy of privilege that works to maintain a boundary of *otherness*. I explore the ways that accommodation and its close relative tolerance tap into discursive constructs such as diversity, equality, identity, and social cohesion. First, I talk about tolerance, accommodation, and the notion of diversity in a general way. I then turn to the use of accommodation in the context of the Supreme Court of Canada. Finally, I propose an alternative – albeit rather roughly formed at present – to the concepts of tolerance and accommodation.

Accommodation relies on the idea that there exists a "we" who can accommodate a "them" in the name of a diverse Canada. My central argument is that the very use of the term *accommodation* invokes a way of thinking about religious freedom that is necessarily embedded in inequality, cultural imperialism, and an assumption that the religious other is inherently "unenlightened."

The peril of making this argument about accommodation is that one may be (carelessly) read as supporting a "melting pot" ideology that seeks to replace the dichotomy between "we" and "them" with a monolithic "us" by imposing a uniform texture on society. This is not my intention, nor should it be the effect of challenging the use of the language of accommodation. Rather, the assumption underlying this argument is that the vested interests of the empire, or colonial hegemony, remain embedded in the language of accommodation.[2] The purpose of interrogating the language of accommodation is to explore the discursive processes by which hegemony is preserved but also the possibilities for subversion, resistance, and a shift from the language of giving to an understanding of reciprocity.

In his piece "Reluctant Hosts," Howard Palmer (1994, 300) reminds us that in Canada "there has been a long history of racism and discrimination against ethnic minorities" and that it is against this backdrop that "current attitudes must be understood. No matter how one understands the notions of 'diversity' and 'multiculturalism' they must be situated in the context of stages of 'Anglo-conformity' and 'melting pot assimilation' in Canadian history, the residue of which is not lightly shaken off" (ibid., 297). Implicit in this residue is an understanding that the host and the guest are not on equal footing.

For the purposes of this chapter I draw on the literature of diversity and multiculturalism to frame some of my arguments, but there is no implication here that religion can be reduced to ethnicity or race.[3] Religious diversity is intertwined with immigration, but it is a complex picture made up, for example, of multiple generations of Sikhs, of First Nations spiritual practices that are, or at least should be, impossible to reduce to "religion," of new religious movements, and of variations on themes of Christianity that bring Mormon fundamentalists and Jehovah's Witnesses into the picture of religious diversity. To be sure, religion is an identity marker that may coincide with race or ethnicity, but the intention here is to be broad in scope in terms of the definition of religion.[4]

Further, although religion is the central focus, it is employed in broad and inclusive terms and with the understanding that singling it out as an identity point is an exercise in partiality that places in the background the complexities of both individual and group identity. Moreover, the social panic du jour is subject to change, and therefore accommodation as a strategy for "dealing with diversity" is reflective of a current social location. In other words, social and historical locations position the "religious" citizen differently. For example, Latter-Day Saints in the late 1800s and early 1900s experienced discrimination that was intertwined with nation building; First Nations spiritualities were dismissed as either nonexistent or pagan and dangerous; and Scientologists were criminally prosecuted in the "cult" scare of the 1970s and 1980s. The fluidity of individual, group, and social location renders a single-point identity marker like religion amorphous at best. This being said, religion is an important conduit for designations of difference and diversity.

The fluidity of social context is illustrated by the events beginning in 2007-08 that have witnessed a global economic meltdown of epic proportions. There was early public commentary and speculation about the inevitable effect on immigration policy – at the very least, a narrowing of possibilities in terms of both entry and opportunity. Managing diversity within the framework of tolerance and accommodation increases the possibility for exclusion and inequality. Religion is one point of identity or reference that provides a basis on which this narrowing can occur in a seemingly "reasonable" manner within a framework of accommodation.

The language of diversity has become code for "what to do with the immigrant other," one who is conceptualized as a guest to be accommodated. In the popular imaginary, there is a notion that guests will be accommodated; at the same time, there is the expectation that they are present only temporarily or that if they do not comply with the rules of the host – or if they question the rules! – they can be asked to leave.

Sherene Razack (2008, 122) develops the idea of the guest-host relationship in some detail, arguing that "immigrants are scripted in this story as guests whose first obligation is gratitude to the hosts." She argues that this narrative in part depends on an imagined shared history that in turn depends on the silence of counternarratives: "The story of immigration, told as one of guests and hosts (the former duplicitous, the latter generous), depends upon a profound disavowal of the interconnectedness of the past with the present, of the spaces of wealth and poverty, and of the prosperity of original citizens and the poverty of newcomers" (ibid., 123). Part and parcel of this story is the Christian basis of Canadian society, which has now also morphed into a story of secularism that obscures the ways that, institutionally and interpersonally, Canadians are still bound by a Christian hegemony. This too has become part of the silence that allows for a presentation of a "secular" society as the civilized alternative in the face of those who are ruled by the irrationality of religion.

The guest-host frame is preserved by way of a number of discursive tricks that have been considered in detail by Wendy Brown (2006), Sherene Razack (2008), Sarah Song (2007), and Anne Phillips (2007), who have all explored the contours of multiculturalism. Each of these theorists critiques the ways that culture has been framed as something that is largely absent in the West. By this I mean (as do they) that the emphasis on individual autonomy, born largely of liberalism, has meant a denial of culture – or anything that would interfere with individual agency – by those who seek to juxtapose Western society (i.e., empire, civilization, and so on) against "culture." A narrative of a civilized "us" is juxtaposed with that of an uncivilized "other" that looks something like this:

Hosts – Western society	*Guests – Oriental society*
Culturally advanced (acultural)	Culturally primitive
Modern	Primitive or premodern
Rational, reasonable, logical, law-abiding	Passionate, superstitious, custom-abiding
Tolerant	Dogmatic
Generous	Duplicitous
Secular	Religious
Individualistic	Communal
Values-centred[5]	Culture-centred

Razack (2008, 8) identifies the homogeneous community – "us" – as being "made up of subjects who imagine themselves as raceless individuals, consumers, and agents without defining links to community – in other words, as citizens who have the freedom to make their own choices." Thus diversity is framed as the "problem of diversity," which refers to the question of what to do about those unruly, or potentially unruly, guests and how to treat them with kindness. The idea of limits emerges in this context as a way to acknowledge that kindness is not boundless.

Gerald Kernerman (2005, 92) has described this response to diversity as the "but clause" problem, identifying the tendency of Canadians to celebrate diversity but always to keep a veto, or "but clause," "as if to neutralize diversity's dangers." Such veto power is integrally linked to legal and policy provisions that tame the wildness of diversity. Thus limits form an important mechanism for curbing diversity's "dangers":

> The discourse of the limit acts like a safety net for Canadians, so that they can celebrate diversity – despite its dangers – knowing that there is a limit to minority behaviours that threaten to move beyond what is deemed acceptable. It constructs "Canadians" as not only liberal but also as the guardians of liberal values in the face of the illiberal potential of the other. The continual strenuous assertion of the limit implies a latent desire on the part of the minority to behave illiberally, generating multiple cases of misrecognition. (Ibid., 96)

The obscured "us" – made up of white, European colonial stock, the empire's representatives – participates in the limit-setting process. Accommodation is a strand of the "problem"-solving process that smoothes out the wrinkles of otherness and reifies a hegemonic mode of organizing. Limits are most visibly articulated in law, which frames the discussion as one of rights and freedoms that are bounded by section 1 of the Charter of Rights and Freedoms (1982).[6] Although rights are guaranteed to all citizens, some groups find themselves before the courts requesting clarification of their rights.

Within this discourse of limits is the notion that diversity must somehow be managed or that it is a problem to be solved. Richard Day (2000) challenges this idea in relation to diversity's most important champion: multiculturalism. Rather than singing the praises of multiculturalism, Day identifies it as a rational-bureaucratic strategy for controlling diversity. Although Day's criticism of multiculturalism goes further than I would like to go here, the language of accommodation and tolerance can be located in precisely this space between the "problem" of diversity and the "solution" of multiculturalism. Day (ibid., 104) takes on the issue of tolerance, arguing that "selves, of course, do not need to be tolerated: no special provisions need to be made for them, they are not even noticed. It is only when one is in the presence of what appears to be intolerable difference that tolerance becomes necessary and, in many cases, manifests itself as a gloss on hidden resentments." To Day's comment should be added "hidden fears," for it seems that some of what motivates the determined entrenchment of language that preserves the dichotomy between the "other" and "us" is a fear of losing privilege. Other critics of multiculturalism as a homogenizing discourse have made similar points. Himani Bannerji (2000, 115), for example, notes that "the multi-culturalism stance may support a degree of tolerance, but beyond a certain point, on the far edge of equality, it asserts a 'Canadianness' and warns off 'others' from making claims on 'Canada.'" Those who dare to ask are discursively framed in the language of special interests and accommodation.

One of the conceptual tools used to shore up the binary walls between guest and host is the framing of rights claims by marginal or minority groups as originating among "special interest groups." Although this language is not typically used by the courts, it is reconstituted in law as "accommodation." This translates into arguments such as that made by F.L. Morton and Rainer Knopff (2000, 68), who are critical of the equality protections offered to all Canadians:

> The list of equality-seeking groups includes the "charter" members of the section 15 club: women, visible and religious minorities, the mentally and physically disabled, and the elderly. Also included are the so-called "analogous" section 15 groups added by the courts via interpretation: homosexuals and non-citizens. Official language minorities (sections 16-23), the multicultural communities (section 27), and aboriginals (sections 25 and 35) round out the equality-seekers.

The sentiments expressed by those who frame requests for recognition and equality as "special interests" are somewhat pervasive in public discourse, where they are advanced through position papers released by groups such as the Fraser Institute and expressed in everyday conversation in comments such as "I am tired of them shoving their beliefs down my throat," or "they shouldn't be promoting their lifestyle," or "shouldn't they be fitting in?" Miriam Smith (2005, 13) notes the tendency of right-wing groups to label activist collectivities as special interest groups, especially when they do not like the goals of the group.

The transposition of rights claims into a discourse of special interests is not so far removed from the language of tolerance and accommodation. Both rely on a binary that separates "normal" citizens from everybody else.

The latter are framed as promoting "their" interests, which are often framed as being in opposition to those of "normal" citizens and as tolerable only at a cost to society – hence the idea of limits and the perception that accommodation and tolerance need only go so far,[7] with the boundary of the limits shifting according to the fears of, or perceived threat to, majority groups. Can we dismiss the identification of all such costs as imagined or trivial? Some citizens may have interests that oppose and conflict with interests of the majority or other groups. These interests may involve costs, either in terms of use of state resources, a shifting of familiar terrain, or inconvenience. The negotiation of these issues must take place in a fair, public process that recognizes power inequities, challenges preconceived notions, and strives for justice and, ultimately, a substantive notion of equality. Framing such interests as "special" shifts the burden to the disadvantaged groups who make identity-based claims.[8] Recasting the dialogue or discourse as one of differing interests allows for an entry point with more even footing.

Framing a legal equality claim as a demand by a special interest group depends on an assumption that the group is asking for more than what everybody else has – something to which its members are not entitled. The assumption underlying both accommodation and special interests presumes the existence of a gatekeeper who decides whether a group is worthy of receiving the special dispensation requested. Often there is a critical failure to recognize one's own privilege in the process of identifying the desire of the "other" for equality, which is often described as "special treatment." Further, there is a tendency to attribute malice and greed to the requesting group and generosity, goodwill, and kindness to the dispensing group. There is a hierarchy of dispensation within which worthiness for accommodation is assessed.[9]

The Slippery Slope to Accommodation

Curiously, the language of reasonable accommodation was, until very recently, limited to labour-law cases where employers were called upon, as the jurisprudence developed, to ensure reasonable accommodation of employees whose religious beliefs and practices came into conflict with the habits and schedules of the workplace. In this context, the language of reasonable accommodation was perhaps more appropriate, although even there Shelagh Day and Gwen Brodsky (1996) have made a convincing argument that it established a problematic basis on which to evaluate cases. The challenge I present in this chapter was originally inspired by Day and Brodsky's article "The Duty to Accommodate: Who Will Benefit?" Written in the early days of the emergence of the reasonable accommodation framework in law, it expresses serious concerns about the use of this framework in cases involving claims to religious freedom in employment contexts:

> The developing reasonable accommodation framework lacks the capacity to effectively address inequality and foster truly inclusive institutions. It is flawed by its implicit acceptance that social norms should be determined by more powerful groups in the society, with manageable concessions being made to those who are "different." As long as this is the framework for accommodation, less powerful groups cannot expect much from it, since accommodation discourse will serve primarily as a means of limiting how much difference "the powerful and the majority" must absorb. (Ibid., 435)

Although Day and Brodsky see some possibility of reconstituting accommodation to facilitate equality, I argue that the reasonable accommodation framework is inherently flawed and cannot be resurrected in a manner that will facilitate or achieve equality for religious minorities. Accommodation always preserves the power of the majority or hegemonic group to deny equality or recognition.

I turn now to the Supreme Court of Canada decision in *Multani v. Commission scolaire Marguerite-Bourgeoys* (2006),[10] a case that represents a critical moment in the turn towards a more entrenched legal reliance on reasonable accommodation. The *Multani* case involved a Sikh school boy who was forbidden to carry his kirpan to school. Despite the fact that his parents and the school board had reached an agreement, it was overridden by the school board's council of commissioners, and the matter made its way through the courts. The Supreme Court upheld his right to carry the kirpan at school under the conditions that had been agreed upon (i.e., the kirpan had to be concealed, its sheath sewn shut, and so on).

Accommodation played a central role in the reasoning of the Supreme Court:

> A total prohibition against wearing a kirpan to school undermines the value of this religious symbol and sends students the message that some religious practices do not merit the same protection as others. *Accommodating* G and allowing him to wear his kirpan under certain conditions demonstrates the importance that our society attaches to protecting freedom of religion and to showing respect for its minorities. (*Multani v. Commission scolaire,* 7, emphasis by author)

And further:

> The analogy with the duty of reasonable accommodation is helpful to explain the burden resulting from the minimal impairment test with respect to an individual. In the circumstances of the instant case, the decision to establish an absolute prohibition against wearing a kirpan does not fall within a range of reasonable alternatives. (Ibid., 6)

The *Multani* case seemed to solidify the direction of the Supreme Court on religious freedom, especially in the post-Charter cases. Importantly for our purposes, the *Multani* decision intertwined the balancing of "rights and freedoms" and "reasonable limits" called for in section 1 of the Charter and the idea of accommodation of religious minorities. Justice Louise Charron cited law professor José Woehrling as correctly explaining "the relationship between the duty to accommodate or adapt and the *Oakes* analysis." Woehrling states:

> Anyone seeking to disregard the duty to accommodate must show that it is necessary, in order to achieve a legitimate and important legislative objective, to apply the standard in its entirety, *without the exceptions* sought by the claimant. More specifically, in the context of s. 1 of the *Canadian Charter*, it is necessary, in applying the test from *R. v. Oakes*, to show, in succession, that applying the standard in its entirety constitutes a rational means of achieving the legislative objective, that no other means are available that would be less intrusive in relation to the rights in question (minimal impairment test), and that there is proportionality between the measure's salutary and limiting effects. At a conceptual level, the minimal impairment test, which is central to the section 1 analysis, corresponds in large part with the undue hardship defence against the duty of reasonable accommodation in the context of human rights legislation. (*Multani v. Commission scolaire*, 286, para. 53, emphasis by author)

The effect of this proposition is to expand the language of accommodation to the terrain of balancing found in section 1 of the Charter, which "guarantees the rights and freedoms set out in it subject only to such reasonable limits prescribed by law as can be demonstrably justified in a free and democratic society." In a sense, such an expansion recalibrates the discussion except with respect to legal questions of evidentiary burden and so on, which are not of interest for our purposes. It is this discursive framing that imposes the shift from a negotiation between equals to a situation where one party is in a position to grant and to act as gatekeeper, and the other is in a "less than" position. Such a shift reflects and reifies a disparity between "we" and "them."

Justice Charron stated that "religious tolerance is a very important value in Canadian society." Tolerance performs the same discursive framing as does accommodation, opening the possibility for arguments such as the ridiculous rejoinder, actually attempted in *Multani*, "but if he can bring his knife to school, why can't I?" Indeed, the idea of special treatment was embedded in the arguments presented to the Supreme Court. One of the major lines of argument of the school board was based on the premise that Gurbaj Singh requested special treatment: "The respondents also contend that allowing Gurbaj Singh to wear his kirpan to school could have a ripple effect. They submit that other students who learn that orthodox Sikhs may wear their kirpans will feel the need to arm themselves so that they can defend themselves if attacked by a student wearing a kirpan" (*Multani v. Commission scolaire*, 293, para. 68). Fortunately, the court made short work of this special treatment argument, displacing it with a focus on freedom of religion. Unfortunately, it did this by retaining the language of "tolerance":

> Religious tolerance is a very important value of Canadian society. If some students consider it unfair that Gurbaj Singh may wear his kirpan to school while they are not allowed to have knives in their possession, it is incumbent on the schools to discharge their obligation to instil in their students this value that is, as I will explain in the next section, at the very foundation of our democracy. (Ibid., 296, para. 76)

Even though the court rejected the argument based on formal equality, the language of tolerance opened the space for such arguments in the first place by positioning the claimant/applicant as someone to be tolerated, to be accommodated, and/or for whom to make exceptions. Religious freedom (or any other freedom) should not be positioned as an "exception" or as an accommodation granted to a special interest group.

Justices Marie Deschamps and Rosalie Abella attempted to put the brakes on the enthusiastic merging of accommodation and minimal impairment (section 1 of the Charter), noting that although there are similarities between the two, they "belong to two different analytical categories." Their differing opinion in *Multani* was based primarily on a concern about this categorical merging, which they defined as problematic. Although they did not articulate the concerns about the use of accommodation that I discuss here, it is heartening to note the desire of the justices to contain the analytical purview of the idea of reasonable accommodation.[11] Although their reasons may have been rooted in the legal messiness of accommodation, their objection offered a glimmer of hope that the Supreme Court would in the future rethink a widespread application of accommodation as an appropriate conceptual framework for rights. How might the court proceed?

Deep Equality: Moving Away from Tolerance and Accommodation

Before moving too hastily away from tolerance and accommodation it is perhaps necessary to consider two common objections to my argument: first, that accommodation can be considered simply as a negotiated solution reached between free and equal citizens with deep differences; and second, that accommodation and tolerance might be seen as interim values in a process of new settlements among old and new citizens in a developing political community.[12] The first argument essentially holds that these concepts can be reconstituted so as to work for minority groups.[13] The response to the first objection is really to restate the arguments made in the previous sections. My position is that these concepts are so imbued with meaning – that disadvantages minority groups and that privileges majority or hegemonic groups – that they cannot be recovered or reconstituted. Use of the concepts necessarily invokes an inequality. The second argument places the emphasis on a slightly different matter that brings into the conversation the recognition of the contributions that tolerance and accommodation have made. This argument has been presented by both academic colleagues[14] and members of faith communities in conversation when I have presented my position about tolerance and accommodation in public talks. Their worry is that abandoning tolerance and accommodation would create a void that risked a regression or narrowing of interpretations of minority rights and that it would create a high-risk situation for religious minorities. Although tolerance and accommodation have been an important interim step (it is a matter of debate whether the costs of this path have outweighed the benefits), my argument is that it is time to move on to a new framework that would begin with the premise of equality.

In thinking about the problems of reasonable accommodation and tolerance I have reflected on the ways that we might dismantle this hierarchical discourse. Dismantling tolerance and accommodation would have a number of effects, including reorganization of the discursive production of groups and individuals who assert their rights. There is a risk that dismantling these concepts would render minority religious groups more vulnerable. For this reason, an alternate discursive framing is needed that would move us in a positive direction. There are no guarantees in this move, but an obvious beginning point in thinking about new strategies is the concept of equality. A point often missed is that those who come before the courts or human rights tribunals *are* equal, not asking to be declared equal. They are not, therefore, seeking accommodation, tolerance, or special rights or interests. That their claims necessitate a recognition of equality is part of the process.

Are there limits? There is a "yes, but" here. All of the rights and freedoms to which we are entitled are subject to the limits, to paraphrase section 1 of the Charter, that are demonstrably justified in a free and democratic society. What we need to attend to most carefully is that the default in interpretation is the status quo. Put another way, equality as conceptualized in this chapter is not formal equality but substantive equality; inspired by William Connolly's (2005) notion of "deep pluralism," I have begun to refer to this as "deep equality."

Day and Brodsky (1996, 462) link the use of accommodation to formal equality, which, they argue, concerns itself with "like treatment of individuals" and does little to address inequality:

Accommodation does not go to the heart of the equality question, to the goal of transformation, to an examination of the way institutions and relations must be changed in order to make them available, accessible, meaningful and rewarding for the many diverse groups of which our society is composed. Accommodation seems to mean that we do not change procedures or services, we simply "accommodate" those who do not quite fit. We make some concessions to those who are "different," rather than abandoning the idea of "normal" and working for genuine inclusiveness.

Day and Brodsky (1996) touch on the structural problems inherent in the use of accommodation without naming the hegemonic power of a colonial presence that is at the heart of the fear of the "other" that works to shore up the boundaries (limitations) of equality. Their cautionary wisdom about the use of the idea of reasonable accommodation was meant to flag an emerging problem in the realm of employment law. Unfortunately, accommodation discourse has expanded rather than receded in cases of religious freedom, many of which do not involve conditions of employment.

Equality, of course, raises its own set of problems that have been well documented by feminist legal theorists. Equality here does not mean sameness. In other words, I am not advocating or proposing a *laïcité* approach such as that of France or Turkey, where citizenship is publicly displayed through a whitewash of identity (at least in theory) and where religion is pushed to the realm of the private.[15] Rather, equality here is more robust. The language of difference invokes problems that have been identified by a number of scholars and that echo the concerns raised by second-wave feminists who worried that building claims for substantive equality on the foundation of difference meant that women were forever destined to be contrasted to men and, inevitably, constructed as being inferior. If difference in the case of religious diversity is imagined as difference among pluralities, or many groups and constituencies, this problem may be partially avoided. In other words, the language of difference can be used to identify differences between many religious groups without one group – as in the case of women's difference – being the "baseline," as it were. This may be optimistic at best given that Canada is a nation shaped by Christianity, but the multiplicity of religious groups renders this reading of difference at least a possibility. Although writing specifically about women and difference, Audre Lorde (2007, 111) best articulates the optimistic version of difference inextricably bound to notions of deep equality that I am espousing here:

> Advocating the mere tolerance of difference between women is the grossest reformism. It is a total denial of the creative function of difference in our lives. Difference must be not merely tolerated, but seen as a fund of necessary polarities between which our creativity can spark like a dialectic. Only then does the necessity for interdependency become unthreatening. Only within that interdependency of different strengths, acknowledged and equal, can the power to seek new ways of being in the world generate, as well as the courage and sustenance to act where there are no charters.

If a positive layering of difference infiltrates equality at a profound level, we may arrive in a place of deep equality and leave behind, forever, "tolerance" and "accommodation."

Notes
Thank you to the Social Sciences and Humanities Research Council of Canada for its financial support of this research. Thank you to Morgan Hunter and Heather Shipley for editorial assistance.

1 In early 2007 a commission was struck by the Quebec government whose purpose was to hold public hearings and to explore the accommodation of diversity in this province. The reasons for the implementation of the commission, known as the Bouchard-Taylor Commission (2008), are the subject of some debate – see, for example, Solange Lefebvre (2008) and Pauline Côté (2008). Nonetheless, the impetus for the commission was in part a rising sense of panic and fear within Quebec society (and arguably beyond) related to the perception that accommodation of minority groups, especially Muslims, Sikhs, and Jews, was out of control.

2 The terms *empire* and *colonial hegemony* are not unproblematic, and like any structural concept, they are based on somewhat tenuous and essentialist assumptions that largely gloss over differences respecting gender, class, and country of origin. However, there is a currency to the notion of empire. See, for example, Anne McClintock (1995), whose analysis brings race, class, and gender into critical tension with empire. For the purposes of this chapter, *empire* is used primarily in reference to the British Empire as an imperial player in the Canadian context. The other relevant empire for Canadian purposes, of course, is France.

3 For some authors the relationship between religion and race is inextricable. See, for example, Sherene Razack (2008).

4 The definition of *religion* is a site of great debate and intellectual inquiry. For an especially cogent treatment of this subject, see Talal Asad (1993). Benson Saler (2000) has also contributed important nuance to the critical conceptualization of the concept of religion.

5 Values might seem out of place here, but they belong more to hosts than to guests if we think about the recent rise of values talk in the Canadian public sphere. For example, state representatives have talked about polygamy as being contrary to Canadian values. So too is the reaction to the *niqab* – which concerns the ability to see one's fellow citizens' faces – constructed around Canadian values and the values attending liberal democracy. These values are portrayed as having been carefully worked through by democratic processes and as somehow being representative of the recipe for social cohesion. In contrast, culture is framed as a monolithic weight that eviscerates or obscures agentic capacity. The "other" is thus driven by primal, unthought, cultural structures that are imagined almost as biological imperatives and that prevent proper assimilation.

6 *Canadian Charter of Rights and Freedoms,* Part 1 of the *Constitution Act, 1982,* being Schedule B to the *Canada Act 1982* (UK), 1982, c.11.

7 Think here of the debates on same-sex marriage and how frequently those in opposition expressed objections to gays and lesbians "promoting" their "lifestyle" at a cost to the "traditional family."

8 For a detailed discussion of what a fair process might look like, see Avigail Eisenberg (2009).

9 One of the central strategies of those who make the argument that special interest groups are too readily accommodated is to frame the decisions of the courts, particularly the Supreme Court of Canada, as "activist." This rhetoric draws primarily from debates among conservatives in the United States and is inappropriately used in the Canadian context to stir popular belief that somehow the "other" is getting

more than his or her fair share, taking away from the resources of hardworking, average Canadians (see Kelly 2005).

10 *Multani v. Commission scolaire Marguerite-Bourgeoys*, 2006 SCC 6, [2006] 1 S.C.R. 256.

11 This objection was picked up in the majority decision in *Alberta v. Hutterian Brethren of Wilson Colony*, 2009 SCC 37, where the court, despite not completely abandoning the idea that the standard of reasonable accommodation might have a role to play in future decisions, clearly reasserted the *Oakes* test's interpretation of the balancing of "rights and freedoms" and "reasonable limits" called for in section 1 of the Charter.

12 Thank you to Rajeev Bhargava for posing these common objections so eloquently.

13 Tariq Modood (2005) uses these concepts in this way. His pragmatic approach attempts to reconstitute the concepts by bypassing their traditional connotations.

14 See especially the work of Natasha Bakht (2012), who worries that abandoning these principles leaves open the possibility of a regression in the protection of minority rights.

15 This, of course, is an extremely simplistic version of the ways that policies are experienced in these countries. Moreover, Robert Orsi's (2003) insistence that religion, especially lived religion, is never "private" is a reminder of the necessarily holistic and imminently public nature of identity.

Works Cited

Asad, Talal. 1993. *Genealogies of Religion: Discipline and Reasons of Power in Christianity and Islam*. Baltimore: John Hopkins University Press.

Bader, Veit. 2007. *Secularism or Democracy? Associational Governance of Religious Diversity*. Amsterdam: Amsterdam University Press.

Bakht, Natasha. 2012. "Veiled Objections: Facing Public Opposition to the Niqab." In *Reasonable Accommodation: Managing Religious Diversity*, edited by Lori G. Beaman, 70-108. Vancouver: UBC Press.

Bannerji, Himani, ed. 2000. *The Dark Side of the Nation: Essays on Multiculturalism, Nationalism and Gender*. Toronto: Canadian Scholars' Press.

Bouchard, Gérard, and Charles Taylor. 2008. *Building the Future: A Time for Reconciliation*. Quebec City: Government of Quebec.

Brown, Wendy. 2006. *Regulating Aversion: Tolerance in the Age of Identity and Empire*. Princeton, NJ: Princeton University Press.

Connolly, William. 2005. *Pluralism*. Durham, NC: Duke University Press.

Côté, Pauline. 2008. "Québec and Reasonable Accommodation: Uses and Misuses of Public Consultation." In *Religion and Diversity in Canada*, edited by Lori G. Beaman and Peter Beyer, 41-65. Leiden: Brill.

Day, Richard J.F. 2000. *Multiculturalism and the History of Canadian Diversity*. Toronto: University of Toronto Press.

Day, Shelagh, and Gwen Brodsky. 1996. "The Duty to Accommodate: Who Will Benefit?" *Canadian Bar Review* 75 (3): 433-73.

Eisenberg, Avigail. 2009. *Reasons of Identity: A Normative Guide to the Political and Legal Assessment of Identity Claims*. Oxford: Oxford University Press.

Gutmann, Amy, and Dennis Thompson. 2004. *Why Deliberative Democracy?* Princeton, NJ: Princeton University Press.

Jakobsen, Janet R., and Ann Pellegrini. 2004. *Love the Sin: Sexual Regulation and the Limits of Religious Tolerance.* New York: Beacon.

Kelly, James B. 2005. *Governing with the Charter: Legislative and Judicial Activism and Framers' Intent.* Vancouver: UBC Press.

Kernerman, Gerald P. 2005. *Multicultural Nationalism: Civilizing Difference, Constituting Community.* Vancouver: UBC Press.

Kymlicka, Will. 2007. *Multicultural Odyssey: Navigating the New International Politics of Diversity.* Oxford: Oxford University Press.

Lefebvre, Solange. 2008. "Between Law and Public Opinion: The Case of Québec." In *Religion and Diversity in Canada,* edited by Lori G. Beaman and Peter Beyer, 175-98. Leiden: Brill.

Lorde, Audre. 2007. "The Master's Tools Will Never Dismantle the Master's House." In *Sister Outsider: Essays and Speeches by Audre Lorde,* 110-13. Berkeley, CA: Crossing.

McClintock, Anne. 1995. *Imperial Leather: Race, Gender, and Sexuality in the Colonial Context.* New York: Routledge.

Modood, Tariq. 2005. *Multicultural Politics: Racism, Ethnicity, and Muslims in Britain.* Minneapolis: University of Minnesota Press.

Morton, F.L., and Rainer Knopff. 2000. *The Charter Revolution and the Court Party.* Peterborough, ON: Broadview.

Orsi, Robert. 2003. "Is the Study of Lived Religion Irrelevant to the World We Live In?" *Journal for the Scientific Study of Religion* 42 (2): 169-74.

Palmer, Howard. 1994. "Reluctant Hosts: Anglo-Canadian Views of Multiculturalism in the Twentieth Century." In *Century Immigration in Canada: Historical Perspectives,* edited by G. Tulchinsky, 297-333. Toronto: Copp Clark Longman.

Phillips, Anne. 2007. *Multiculturalism without Culture.* Princeton, NJ: Princeton University Press.

Razack, Sherene. 2008. *Casting Out: Race and the Eviction of Muslims from Western Law and Politics.* Toronto: University of Toronto Press.

Saler, Benson. 2000. *Conceptualizing Religion: Immanent Anthropologists, Transcendent Natives, and Unbounded Categories.* New York: Berghahn.

Shachar, Ayelet. 2001. *Multicultural Jurisdictions: Cultural Differences and Women's Rights.* Cambridge, UK: Cambridge University Press.

Smith, Miriam. 2005. *A Civil Society? Collective Actors in Canadian Political Life.* Peterborough, ON: Broadview.

Song, Sarah. 2007. *Justice, Gender and the Politics of Multiculturalism.* Cambridge, UK: Cambridge University Press.

In God We Trust?
Secular States, Diversity, and the "Clash" within North America

Yasmeen Abu-Laban and Claude Couture

Chapter 6

Although a newly emerging body of work dealing with history and public opinion is beginning to explicitly compare what appears as a "religious America" versus a "secular Europe" (Berger, Davie, and Fokas 2008; Norris and Inglehart 2004, 94-95), in this chapter we attend to key scholarly interventions that have sought to differentiate between two important countries of North America: Canada and the United States. This focus is useful for illustrating long-standing assumptions that have characterized, and still reverberate in, scholarly work across a number of disciplines. As we will illustrate, these assumptions concern the idea that Western states are characterized by secularism, that modernity is connected to secularism, and that anomalies in the case of America can be explained by reference to the strength of individualism. It should be noted that these assumptions have – even before 11 September 2001 – inspired considerable theoretical work on the experience of Muslim minorities, portrayed as religious and communal, in European states (Carens 2000, 141). Since 11 September 2001 there has been an increase in academic and policy interest in the impact of international migration from the developing world on Western liberal-democratic states. Thus as Paul Bramadat and Matthias Koenig (2009, ix) note, "While a decade ago religion was almost absent in academic and policy debates about international migration and integration, there is now a steadily increasing stream of symposia and workshops, papers, journals, and books devoted to this topic."

Similarly, as the editors note in the introduction to this volume, despite the widely held assumption in the decades following World War Two that "secular modernity" was an unstoppable force, in actual fact religion has not faded away. Thus religion continues to inspire many people irrespective of observable varied expressions between or among religions (see Bhargava, this volume) as well as irrespective of varied forms of secularism.[1] What might also be noted is that in many accounts, including some chapters in this volume (e.g, see those by Bruce J. Berman, Peter Beyer, and Lori G. Beaman), secularism – defined as the separation of church and state – is seen to have originated in the West and in many cases to have been imposed on non-Western societies through colonialism.

In this chapter we propose a slightly different exploration and analysis by mobilizing a distinct, but important, understanding of secularism that carries implications for how we understand "secularism" as originating in the West. In our view the term *secularism* is often wrongly conflated with the harder approach to religion – specifically the idea of no religion or the absence of faith in public life (Kosmin 2007, 3). In what follows we use the definition of George J. Holyoake, who is widely considered to be one of the first authors to write on secularism. For Holyoake (1896, 3) the secular "is distinct from theology" and "secularism does not conflict with theology." The idea of secularism in Holyoake's vision, one that we also stress, is to make possible the *peaceful* cohabitation of all religions as well as religious believers and nonbelievers in the same society. As Holyoake (ibid., 52) argued, "By its nature, Secularism is tolerant with regard to religions. I once drew up a code of rules for an Atheistic school. One rule was that the children should be taught the tenets of the Christian, Catholic, Moslem, Jewish, and the leading theological systems of the world, as well as Secularistic and Atheistic forms of thought." If secularism is associated with the idea of the cohabitation of religions, it cannot be said to have come uniquely from the Western world. For example, prior to European colonization there were periods, some longer and more successful than others, of tolerant religious cohabitation in Islamic, Indic, and Sinitic "civilizations" (e.g., see Bhargava 1998, 2004; and Basan 2010).

Conversely, it seems to us that Western colonialism was frequently marked by a deep religious intolerance, manifested especially by consistent conversion attempts by missionaries (Tyrrel 2010; Neil 1966). It was only after declonization in the 1950s, which was closely followed by the growth in immigration to the West from parts of the developing world, that a more peaceful cohabitation of the kind that Holoyoake envisioned became more evident in Western polities. For this reason, a secularism of peaceful co-habitation is inseparable from multiculturalism, insofar as the growing presence of immigrants of different faiths in countries of the West – often coming from non-Western societies and world regions where religious co-habitation was part of the historical experience – may even be seen to have pressured Western states and societies to become more secular (see Seljak 2007 for the case of Canada). Moreover, if secularism did not emanate uniquely from the West, it also follows that the West cannot be considered the unique centre of modernity.

To further illustrate our argument that the West is neither the unique centre of secularism nor the unique centre of modernity, we take on six key themes of the post–World War Two social-sciences and history literature that impact discussions of the United States and North America. These themes are (1) multiculturalism and the "clash of civilizations," (2) ideological-fragment theory, (3) religion and civil religion, (4) individualism versus local communities, (5) Canada as seen from the vantage of American liberalism, and (6) Quebec as seen from the vantage of American liberalism. These six themes are all interconnected by way of our argument challenging the centrality of the West in relation to secularism and modernity. Hence in what follows we are not concerned primarily with enumerating social forms of religion, public policies on religion, or the constitutional frameworks of "church and state." Rather, we are concerned with destabilizing a metanarrative on the Western world that is deeply entrenched in a variety of literature concerning America and North America. Before discussing the six themes, we consider the relevance of considering the United States in this context.

In God We Trust: Narrative, Conflict, and Metanarrative

As a matter of intellectual interest and as a symbolic point for analysis of the role of religion, we might go back to 1956, when President Dwight D. Eisenhower signed a joint resolution with the American Congress declaring "In God We Trust" the national motto of the United States. As a result of this declaration, in 1957 this motto appeared for the first time on paper currency, as opposed to only on coin. Writing in 2007, on the occasion of the fiftieth anniversary of the motto's presence on the back of the dollar bill, David Masci (2007, 1), a senior research fellow at the Pew Research Center, observed that the expression was also at the heart of an ongoing domestic debate:

Many people see the "In God We Trust" motto and other official evocations of a creator as a reflection and acknowledgement of America's rich religious heritage. Supporters also contend that the motto is simply recognition of the fact that the people of the United States have always relied on "divine providence." But others argue that the government's evocation of God in any official capacity amounts to the establishment of a state religion, which is prohibited by the First Amendment to the United States Constitution. Critics also say that "in God We Trust" is divisive because it excludes those who do not believe in God, as well as Buddhists, Hindus, and others who follow non-monotheistic faiths.

As the constitutionality of this motto has never been ruled to violate First Amendment rights, specifically religious freedom, it might be easy to dismiss this discussion as a nonissue. However, as we will further establish, the discussion itself is indicative of a deep and significant divide in America that should not be dismissed in any serious consideration of secularism. It is precisely this broader divide behind the motto debate that should alert us to important questions regarding the nature and basis of "secularism" and "secular states" from a comparative perspective. As more scholars and policy makers address themes of diversity and religion, we think it is relevant to reflect on the assumptions that have influenced thinking about America, on the nature of its "secularism," and on America in the context of North America. Specifically, we suggest that America's uniqueness, as represented by the six themes we cover in the extant literature, is based on a problematic reliance on individualism as an explanation, with individualism presented in a confusing manner. In addition to individualism being used frequently in the sense developed by French sociologist Émile Durkheim (1893), who viewed individualism as the absence and encumbrance posed by traditional norms, it is also used in the sense elaborated by Alexis de Tocqueville (2012) in the mid-1800s. Tocqueville defined individualism in the American context in terms of voluntary association with religious groups. We hold that rather than individualism (whether in its Durkheimian or Tocquevillian uses), what is most important in the United States is the power of local communities.

The relevance of local communities is frequently overlooked because of the emphasis on individualism. But it is the power of local communities that, in the case of the United States, has uniquely challenged the process of establishing secularism in the sense articulated by Holyoake, with implications for the nature of the state and politics. This challenge may be symbolically captured in America's motto "In God We Trust" (supported long past the Cold War days of President Eisenhower), but it is more concretely captured in the domestic tension that this motto still taps into: tension between those who believe that the American Creed is fundamentally religious and those who believe that it is secular. If secularism is understood in its original articulation as being about the *peaceful* cohabitation of the two great options of believing or not believing, then this is arguably more the case in some states than others. Peaceableness is not only about the absence of violence but also about the relative degree of harmony. As we will show, such peaceful cohabitation is more observable in Canada than in the United States, and this also warrants attention to the thematic of individualism and other key themes that are frequently considered in comparisons between the United States and Canada, as well as between Quebec and the United States and between Quebec and the rest of Canada. As we will detail, it appears that the "continental divide" (one could say "clash") between the United States and Canada, as described by Seymour Martin Lipset (1990) and more recently by Jason Kaufman (2009), bears striking similarities to the same alleged "clash" (one could say "divide") between "the West" and "the rest" articulated by Samuel Huntington (1997a). Such similarities may give us pause to consider the narratives used in past decades – and still influential today – to guide comparative social science, particularly as it concerns culture. Specifically – and this is the position we take – American culture, like all cultures, might more fruitfully be examined from the vantage point of hybridity instead of the paradigm of the American Creed and its attendant themes, like individualism as defined in the literature presented here. This is a vision also advanced by, among others, African American studies expert Henry Louis Gates (Kiros 1998, 177). Similarly, many contemporary anthropologists see all cultures as "creolized." Still, because such a considerable amount of influential work refers to a singular "American" creed, set of values, or culture, in our discussion of the six key themes that emerge in the literature on the United States, we pay close attention to the tenets of this formulation and advance a critique from within the terms set in this formulation of the American Creed. This critique of America also lays the basis for further decentring the metanarrative where secularism and modernity are unique to the West.

The United States, Multiculturalism, and the "Clash of Civilizations"

Noted Canadian philosopher Charles Taylor (1991) describes and analyzes the "malaise of modernity" as the more or less perverse effect of the successes of modernity: the triumph of individualism over other forms of solidarity has created an existential malaise and a quest for new forms of solidarity; the success of science and rational answers to problems have created a deep anxiety about finding solutions for all problems. Taylor (2004) explains that in traditional societies people were embedded in their community and had no ability to imagine themselves outside a certain matrix. The process of modernization was consequently in large part a process of disembedding: among other things, modernization worked to sever links with the community and religion, fostered a process of substituting one moral order for another, and fostered new forms of solidarity. According to Taylor (2007) the intensity of modernity is particularly obvious in the Western world and is most pronounced among predominantly anglophone Protestant societies. Taylor (ibid., 448) writes,

> But the United States' path to modernity, although considered paradigmatic by many Americans, is in fact rather exceptional. All Western societies have trodden the path out of ancien régime form into the Age of Mobilization, and beyond to our present predicament ... But the ride was much bumpier and more conflictual in old Europe. This was particularly the case in Catholic societies ... where the old model of presence lasted much longer.

Although the idea of interpreting the conditions of secularism is an important contribution, the general consideration of secularism as a modern Western consequence of the erosion of traditional norms is hardly novel. A century ago several authors focused on the erosion of traditional norms (see Camic 1997), and Durkheim (1893), among others, expressed a conclusion similar to Taylor's regarding the modern world leaving the individual isolated and without the security provided by mechanical forms of solidarity such as family, religion, communities, and tradition – even if the individual had options (see also Tönnies 1887). Since Durkheim, the dominant paradigm, arguably repeated by Taylor, has been that the modern world has been characterized by the erosion of traditional norms, the "disembedding process," and that the rise of individualism is a distinctly Western, particularly American, phenomenon.

At the same time that the Western world saw the rise of individualism, it also witnessed the rise of immigration. Thus the disembedding process that began at the end of the nineteenth century and continued through the twentieth happened at a time of high immigration, which contributed to the malaise of modernity. Today this malaise creates fierce debates on multi-culturalism. To answer this challenge, a country like the United States, according to David Hollinger (1995), should be able to manage ethnic and religious diversity by transcending both in a transcultural and transracial society based on new affiliations in a postethnic America. This postethnic America should be beyond multiculturalism. He writes, "Multiculturalism is a prodigious movement, but its limitations are increasingly apparent" (ibid., 1). He further explains,

> This book argues that defenders of cultural diversity need to take a step beyond multiculturalism, toward a perspective I call "postethnic." This perspective pulls together and defends certain elements of multiculturalism and criticizes others. A postethnic perspective favors voluntary over involuntary affiliations, balances an appreciation for communities of descent with a determination to make room for new communities, and promotes solidarities of wide scope that incorporate people with different ethnic and racial backgrounds. (Ibid., 3)

Only a cosmopolitan and postethnic America will be able, according to Hollinger, to manage the conflict between the three main affiliations of the American nation-state: the business elite, diasporic communities, and the social right, which claims religious and family values as the core of the American nation.

The same year that Hollinger's book was published, Michael Lind (1995) presented a similar vision of a postethnic America, although from a radically different starting point. Lind defines three phases in American history, each corresponding to an opposite pole outside of America: the first is *Anglo*-America, referring to opposition to the United Kingdom; the second is *Euro*-America, referring to the opposition of the United States to a corrupt Europe; and the third is multicultural America, referring to the erosion of American values in a multicultural world. For Lind, America is a nation-state built on a single culture, *not* a multicultural one. Consequently, he holds that the Government of the United States must do everything to preserve this single culture by favouring interracial, interethnic, and interfaith marriages. He envisions the advent of a fourth era of American history characterized by a return to a solid recognition of America as a nation-state based on a single unique culture. This America will be postethnic and fully active in preventing further erosion of the American culture as a result of its soft acceptance of multiculturalism. It should be noted that both Hollinger and Lind are hostile to multiculturalism from a liberal point of view.

Samuel Huntington (1996, 1997a, 1997b) has also developed a thesis about the assault on the two components of America's identity: its culture and the American Creed. This assault has come from the legions of immigrant minorities and hostile civilizations opposed to the West and to American identity specifically. He too stresses the importance of defending America's fundamental values of individualism, democracy, and religious tolerance. Regarding the American Creed, Huntington (1997b, 29) writes,

> The second component of American identity has been a set of universal ideas and principles articulated in the founding documents by American leaders: liberty, equality, democracy, constitutionalism, liberalism, limited government, private enterprise. These constitute what Gunnar Myrdal termed the American Creed, and the popular consensus on them has been commented on by foreign observers from Crevecoeur and Tocqueville down to the present. This identity was neatly summed up by Richard Hofstadter: "It has been our fate as a nation not to have ideologies but to be one."
>
> These dual sources are, of course, closely related. The creed was a product of the culture. Now, however, the end of the Cold War and social, intellectual, and demographic changes in American society have brought into question the validity and relevance of both traditional components of American identity. Without a sure sense of national identity, Americans have become unable to define their national interests, and as a result subnational commercial interests and transnational and non-national ethnic interests have come to dominate foreign policy.

Regarding multiculturalism, Huntington (ibid., 33) also points out,

> The ideologies of multiculturalism and diversity reinforce and legitimate these trends. They deny the existence of a common culture in the United States, denounce assimilation, and promote the primacy of racial, ethnic, and other subnational cultural identities and groupings. They also question a central element in the American Creed by substituting for the rights of individuals the rights of groups."

He concludes, "Reviving a stronger sense of national identity would also require countering the cults of diversity and multiculturalism within the United States" (ibid., 48).

Interestingly, in similar fashion and just a few years before the publications by Hollinger, Lind, and Huntington, Seymour Martin Lipset (1990) also tried to explain the unique characteristics of America by contrasting America with Canada. Whereas America is, according to Lipset, based on an individualistic culture, Canada is based on a purported conservative and community-oriented culture. The dichotomy developed by Huntington between the individualistic West (dominated by the United States) and the religious-communal rest of the world (the Other) bears a striking resemblance to Lipset's paradigm of the "continental divide" between an individualistic America and a conservative Canada. According to Lipset, the individualism of America – its culture based on voluntary association and religion, as opposed to adherence to an established structure or religion – prevented the rise of a large-scale secular-oriented left/socialist opposition in America. For example, the traditional structures of European and, to a lesser degree, Canadian culture provoked an important countermovement and introduced distinct binary oppositions between conservatism and socialism and between religiosity and secularism. For Lipset, these same forms of binary opposition are missing in the United States because of its unique culture based on individualism and voluntary adherence – the largely accepted American Creed.

Thus, if we combine Lipset's vision with Lind, Huntington, and Hollinger's vision, we start to see that the United States is said to confront a number of external and internal challenges, including opposition between an individualistic and exceptional America and the Others around the world who confront it, a multicultural/immigrant Other inside of the country but outside of the American Creed, and a multicultural Canada. Indeed, it is notable that Lind frequently refers to Canada's official multiculturalism policy as an example not to emulate. In our assessment, these writings showcase how, over the past two decades, influential American intellectuals have defined the nation. The American nation is viewed as representing a unique stage of individualistic modernity always challenged by communitarian Others. These Others are both inside and, although with more contrasting intensity, outside of the Western world.[2]

The Old Theory of the Ideological Fragment, Liberalism, Religion, and Nationalism

A generation before the elaboration of the paradigm of the 1990s regarding the clash of civilizations and the alleged danger of multiculturalism, the theory of the "ideological fragment," developed by Louis Hartz (1955), was vibrant in Canadian and American historiographies (see Grabb and Curtis 2005). In the 1950s Hartz, of Harvard University, argued that as a result of historic migration patterns and the views held by migrants, the absence of feudalism was a basic factor that accounted for the unique liberalism of the US political culture. According to Hartz, the absence of feudalism meant the absence of a static social order and, equally, the absence of a profound social passion to destroy such an order. It deprived the United States of the traditions both of conservatism and of true revolution. The American Revolution was aimed only at national independence, not at social change in the sense of a revolution for all social classes. As argued by Lipset (1990), since 1783 political conflict in the United States has been congealed in an atmosphere of consensus on "American exceptionalism" and individualism. For both Hartz and Lipset, individualism is defined as the shift of political predominance from the traditional structure of power deeply embedded in local communities to a structure of power dominated by individual owners vehemently opposed to a central state but also opposed to any sense of local communitarian moral responsibility. With time, this form of individualism has been conflated with the sociological-Durkheimian definition of *modern individualism,* meaning the erosion of the local and traditional norms of structures such as family, religion, and community and the rise of the modern individual without any of these traditional attachments. Thus it seems to us that American exceptionalism, based on this conflation, has helped to fuel the idea that the United States is at the epicentre of modernity and that many other countries/civilizations are at the periphery and therefore either not modern or not as modern as the United States.

In addition to the important 1990s literature against multiculturalism reviewed in the previous section, at the international level the literature on nationalism has predominantly established a link between liberalism, nationalism, culture, and geographical location. Illustrating this requires some examination of the long-standing distinction between "civic" and "ethnic" nationalism. This distinction has been widely used in the literature on modernity and nationalism as developed in the 1990s by authors like Michael Ignatieff (1994, 6), who upholds Great Britain as the birthplace of civic nationalism, and Liah Greenfeld (1992), who says civic nationalism first appeared and is strongest in the United Kingdom and the United States.

It is also noteworthy that this implicit endorsement of the British and/or American experience reflects a broader tendency in the literature on democratic culture going back at least to the 1960s to uphold the British and American experiences, particularly the American, as an ideal (e.g., see Almond and

Verba 1963). Until now the dominant point of view in the study of nationalism (Smith 2000), which we refer to as the "modernist paradigm," has clearly identified zones of modernity, where a "civic culture" flourishes, and zones of backwardness, where the "collective" is still the norm. It is also widely assumed that "backward" societies will try to impose a particular religion as a norm, whereas civic societies will instead present religion as an option. Today this dichotomy usually emerges as a distinguishing point between the West and the rest of the world, with the West, of course, being characterized as distinctly civic. Notably, however, *inside* the Western world the same dichotomy is easily identifiable in narratives in which the British-American world is portrayed as modern and civic in opposition to the non-English-speaking and non-Protestant societies of the West. Hartz's (1955) ideological-fragment theory is a perfect example of how this dichotomy emerged in a major historical narrative that influenced the social sciences. In Canada statements about the backwardness of "French Canada" in contrast to the more modern "English Canada" employed stunningly similar discursive strategies and almost identical vocabulary and echoed constructions of the backwardness of other groups of non-Western origins (Abu-Laban and Couture 2010, 437-40).

Religion, Contradictions, and Civil Religion

At this juncture it is worth asking some central questions about the modernity paradigm utilized by the authors discussed above. Is "the West" at the centre of all modernity? Is the United States at the centre of the Western centre? Is there actually a geographical centre to modernity? To begin to address the issue of anomalies and the other questions that we identify, it is relevant to examine the impact of religion on these discussions and, more important, the treatment of religion in modern states, especially the United States.

A logical consequence of modernist theories of nationalism that uphold America as the place of civic nationalism – exemplified by Liah Greenfeld's (1992) approach – is the expectation that slowly and gradually modernity will erode the basis of conservatism and tradition in the United States. Yet the dominant expression of nationalism in the United States in the past decade, articulated by the conservative movement, posits the United States as a religious nation where religion is one essential part of the American Creed. Additionally, the American public at large appears more deeply attached to religious identity than do other parts of North America. One important survey has found that a whopping 60 percent of Americans define religion as the most important dimension of their life – in contrast to only

30 percent of Canadians and a mere 10 percent of Quebeckers (Pew Research Center 2002; see also Statistics Canada 1993, Tables 1, 3, and 6). Perhaps an indicator of this fierce attachment to religion is the comparatively strong opposition expressed in the United States to science and the theory of evolution. Consider that out of thirty-five countries surveyed in 2006 regarding the acceptance of the theory of evolution, the United States was second to last – just ahead of predominantly Muslim Turkey – with only 39 percent of Americans who were questioned accepting the principle of the theory of evolution (Miller, Scott, and Okamoto 2006, 765-66).

In the case of the United States it seems that liberal intellectuals working on nationalism have tended to exclude the enduring relevance of conservative and religious elements from their understanding of the "modern and civic nation." At the same time, inside the United States a significant number of conservative and religious groups have continually tried – not always successfully – to impose religion as the main dimension of the nation. This may be viewed as a very real "clash," and it is the insecurity that this internal clash creates within the United States – perhaps more so than Huntington's (1997a) alleged clash of civilizations involving the global community – that has arguably helped to fuel ongoing debates about American foreign policy in the past decade(s). At the very least, one must acknowledge that even if the state is secular in terms of the clear separation of church and state, there is extraordinary pressure in the United States by religious elements to impose a religious agenda in the political sphere. Put differently, even if judges have tended to see the motto "In God We Trust" as signifying merely a kind of "ceremonial deism," there remains ongoing tension about the public sponsorship of religious practices such as Bible reading and prayer in schools (Masci 2007, 1). This tension speaks to the fact that the sentiment expressed by "In God We Trust" may be a much more profound characteristic of America than acknowledged in the literature that makes use of the idea of the American Creed.

If religion is indeed an important part of the American Creed – or at least important for portions of America – how can one explain this presence of religion and its opposition to the modern, secular America? To explain the importance of religion in America, Taylor (2007) and Lipset (1990) both use the concept of "civil religion" developed in the 1960s by Robert Bellah. According to Bellah (1967), Americans embraced a set of institutionalized practices, rituals, fundamental beliefs, holidays, and values that created a national religion – a type of national self-worship used periodically to attack nonconformist and liberal ideas or groups. Bellah (1992) argues that there were three periods in American history during which the American Creed faced some skepticism: the War of Independence, the Civil War, and the social and political upheaval of the 1960s. On each occasion this adversity was overcome, and the "civil religion" was reinforced. Lipset (1990, 76-77) quotes Bellah:

> The American Protestant ethos has assumed, in practice if not in theology, the perfectibility of humanity and an obligation to avoid sin, while the churches whose followers have predominated in Europe, Canada and Australia have accepted the inherent weakness of people, their inability to escape sin and error, and the need for the church to be forgiving and protecting ... They tend to view social and political dramas as morality plays, as battles between God and the devil, so that compromise is virtually unthinkable. As Samuel Huntington notes, Americans give to their nation and its creed "many of the attributes and functions of a church."

As for Taylor (2007, 448-50), he sees a resemblance and reciprocity between the phenomenon of civil religion and denominationalism in the United States, with denominationalism understood to be an important feature of American modernity emerging from voluntarism and mobilization. After acknowledging that, in "taking the United States as a paradigm case of this new idea of order, I am following Robert Bellah's tremendously fertile idea of an American 'civil religion'" (ibid., 447), Taylor (ibid., 454) avers,

> So it is a feature of denominationalism that, just because one's own church does not include all the faithful, there is a sense of belonging to a wider, less structured whole which does. And this can find at least partial expression in the state. That is, the members of mutually recognizing denominations can form a people "under God," with the sense of acting according to the demands of God in forming and maintaining their state, as in the case of the American "civil religion" alluded to above. Indeed, insofar as the divine Design includes freedom, this can be interpreted as calling for openness to a plurality of denominations.

In other words, for Taylor, the dominant presence of religion in the United States is not an obstacle to secularism since it is based on a voluntary participation as opposed to an inherited culture. In reference to premodern societies and the US case, Taylor (ibid., 447) also writes,

But in the earlier days, when the plan was understood as Providential, and the order seen as Natural Law, which is the same as the law of God, building a society which fulfills these requirements was seen as fulfilling the design of God. To live in such a society was to live in one where God was present, not at all in the way that belonged to the enchanted world, through the sacred, but because we are following His design. God is present as the designer of the way we live. We see ourselves, to quote a famous phrase, as "one people under God."

Finally, linking the religious factor to nationalism, Taylor (ibid., 456) states,

> The point I want to make about the British and later American patriotism, based as it was at first on the sense of fulfilling God's design, is that national identity was based on a self-described pre-eminence in realizing a certain civilizational superiority. The superiority may have ultimately been understood as that of "Christendom" over infidel religions, but within Christendom, Britain/America stood at the cutting edge.
>
> This sense of superiority, originally religious in essence, can and does undergo "secularization," as the sense of civilizational superiority becomes detached from Providence.

In contrast to Taylor, we do not think this is a sufficient justification for seeing the United States as secular or even as secularizing.

Here it is useful to review the discussion – as contained in the works of many key intellectuals and social scientists – that we have presented thus far:

- Among the different authors of different affiliations (conservative, liberal, or even communitarian) discussed above, there is a clear consensus that the United States forms an *exceptional* society at the very centre of modernity;
- This exceptionality is characterized by a greater reliance on individualism and voluntarism;
- This exceptionality was articulated at the very beginning of the American nation, so the process of disembedding – of replacing old norms with new ones – was quickly accomplished at the outset of the nation's development and is still mostly uncontested, despite the occasional rise of new challenges, such as contemporary multiculturalism.

In marked contrast to this view, we hold that it is in fact not individualism but the powerful insertion of local communities that has been most central from the start of American settler colonization. We also suggest that the process of disembedding was never completed in the United States, thus making permanent an extreme and marked tension between different "affiliations." This tension is not favourable to a secular state, where, according to Holyoake (1896), a certain harmonious cohabitation is necessary; in fact, this tension does not exist as strongly in other parts of North America. To make this argument, we will address the relevance of local communities in America and the different experience of another part of historic North America, namely Canada.

Individualism versus (the Tyranny of?) Local Communities

In *The Myth of American Individualism* Barry Shain (1994, xvl) convincingly demonstrates that

> based on live testimony as well, most 18th-century Americans cannot be accurately characterized as predominantly individualistic or, for that matter, classically republican. The vast majority of Americans lived voluntarily in morally demanding agricultural communities shaped by reformed-Protestant social and moral norms. These communities were defined by overlapping circles of family- and community-assisted self-regulation and even self-denial, rather than by individual autonomy.

In other words, the core of the American Creed was in fact fragmented local communities, not individuals free of traditional norms as portrayed in Durkheim's understanding. This fascination with local communities also seems to have influenced governance. Historian Elizabeth Mancke (2005, 162) observes, "As the imperial crisis deepened in the 1760s and 1770s, many elite Loyalists fruitlessly tried to convince their fellow colonists to consider a more federal imperial system, although it is not clear that metropolitan authorities would have accepted such a plan"; however, "many of these Loyalists, like the Assembly in Nova Scotia when it drafted its 1775 petition on imperial reform, were far from obsequious sycophants to metropolitan dictates." In fact,

> what often distinguished them from revolutionaries was that they had a different vision of how the linkages of power within the British Atlantic world might be configured and they were ideologically committed to

working within a system with greater vertical linkages. The revolutionaries, however, were more ideologically opposed to such a structure of power, and more committed to preserving and protecting local expressions of power. (Ibid.)

In sum, it seems that the most powerful core of the American Creed was local communities, where belonging was defined in terms of interpersonal relations (i.e., everyone knew each other personally), not in terms of autonomous individual ownership or free agency. When individuals "voluntarily" joined the local community, they perhaps did so for the simple reason that the only other viable option was to be an outcast. Thus the American "exceptional" culture seems to have been based on a constant rejection of some Other by groups of people who knew each other personally, and in most cases this rejection was typically religious because the ceremonial practice of religion was the best way to achieve it. This basis for American exceptionalism is obvious when one looks at the history of immigration in the United States since the eighteenth century. In a remarkable book on the topic political scientist Aristide R. Zolberg (2006, 434) observes a constant tension in American society over immigration, which in turn reflects a broader religious tension:

The confrontation between a sanctimonious mid-nineteenth-century Anglo-American Protestantism and a demonized Roman Catholicism strikingly evoke the late twentieth-century construct of a "clash of civilizations" between the West and Islam, and more particularly European reactions to Muslim immigrants. Beyond this, the massively up-rooted poor were perceived as "paupers" who wilfully resisted the imperative of the nascent market economy and hence were not suitable for membership in American society, much as the "welfare" abusers of the later period.

Of course, the socioeconomic characteristics of migrants who return to their country of origin and their reason(s) for doing so may be varied and warrant serious study both today and historically. Still, it is worth mentioning that the demonization of religious minorities and immigrants in "progressive-era" America may have influenced the decision of migrants to leave. For example, more than half of the 4 million Italians who came to the United States between 1899 and 1924 went back to Italy, and 40 percent of the 1.5 million Poles who came to the United States during the same period also returned (Hollinger 1995, 152-53). As well, Zolberg (2006) observes

that when it comes to immigration a variety of authors from different political perspectives, even polarized ones, seem to agree on the danger of fragmentation represented by multiculturalism. We believe that this striking
convergence of visions proceeds in fact from a religious culture of rejection
deeply embedded in local communities and that this culture may be seen as
a main characteristic of the United States. Zolberg (ibid., 452) very astutely
observes,

> For example, "communitarians" argue that since it is well established that
> cultural heterogeneity is a source of acute political conflict, a democracy is
> justified in restricting the immigration of very large numbers of people who
> are very different because of the difficulty of integrating them. Such argu-
> ments are made today not only by extreme nationalist fringes such as Le
> Pen in France or David Duke, Pat Buchanan, and Samuel Huntington in
> the United States, but also by respectable traditionalists such as the late
> George Kennan and even socially minded liberals such as Michael Walzer.

In other words, if we accept Shain's (1994) analysis of the "myth of American
individualism," we start to see the foundational paradigm very differently
and even to identify its contemporary reverberations very differently. Instead
of being individualistic, the initial paradigm was very much communitarian.

In today's America conservatives and the religious right may still refer to
the mythic individualistic paradigm, but in advancing their position (often
with vitriol), they foster and use a deeply traditional form of interpersonal
relations apparent especially in small states and nonurban centres (Couture
2008b). The contemporary impact of the communitarian paradigm may
also be seen to have shaped the electoral battles of the past decade between
the famously counterintuitively labelled "Red" (Republican) smaller states,
particularly in the Southeast and Midwest, and the "Blue" (Democrat)
states, as well as battles involving a religious right committed to the supremacy of local, religious, traditional communities over large urban centres.
Thus it seems to us erroneous to declare the disembedding process complete in the United States. On the contrary, despite the assumptions made in
the paradigm of American exceptionalism, the United States is a country
where the clash between modern individualism and the deep need for interpersonal and more traditional connections remains particularly vehement.
This observation may help to account for the commitment of a significant
part of the American population to living on the periphery of big cities,
where suburbs and smaller areas mushroom at the expense of these cities

(Perry 2006). This internal migratory movement, although not explained by one factor, connects with other quests for more interpersonal and less anonymous forms of connection. The lack of attention to the intensity of the clash between individualism and community in America carries profound implications when it comes to assessing secularism and the secular state in comparative perspective. Arguably, this inattention diverts analysts away from a serious consideration of whether the clash between individualism and community may actually be stronger in the United States than in other Western countries.

American Liberalism versus Canada

As we have seen, Hartz (1955) characterized the United States as a pre-eminently liberal society. In Europe, he wrote, liberalism was a bourgeois political movement of opposition to the old feudal order, but in the United States, where there had never been a feudal order, liberalism was associated with no particular class. Judged against this standard, Canada was often, but not always, stigmatized as a more "conservative" place. Hartz held that a variety of historical factors accounted for this difference, some of which have been debated (see Ajzenstat and Smith 1995). The most important factors were the failure of the American Revolution to advance northward either in 1776 or during the War of 1812, as well as the crushing of the liberal-democratic rebellions in Upper and Lower Canada in 1837. Both events are seen to have further entrenched the forces of conservatism in British North America, with the consequence that Canada's core values were thus set by the middle of the nineteenth century. Whereas the political culture of the United States was purely liberal, that of Canada contained a significant admixture of Toryism.

Lipset (1990) goes further with these same generalizations. Canada is, according to him, more elitist than the United States in the sense that Canadians show more deference to authority and less opposition to class differences. Lipset views Canadians as less individualistic and entrepreneurial or achievement-oriented than Americans, accounting for why the welfare state (especially as measured in terms of access to universal healthcare) is better developed in Canada. Although the overall access of Canadians to healthcare may remain greater than that of their American counterparts – even in the face of healthcare reform undertaken by the administration of President Barack Obama – Lipset's view of the deferential Canadian attitude is challenged by more recent popular accounts of Canadian and American characteristics based on public-opinion data. The work of pollster Michael Adams

(2003), for instance, suggests that stereotyped "polite" Canadians are actually more likely to question authority than their American neighbours to the south, which accounts in his view for greater Canadian opposition to the war in Iraq. Edward Grabb and James Curtis (2005) also question Lipset's theory of the "continental divide" as well as the Hartzian paradigm that Canadians are more state-oriented and less liberal than Americans, or conversely that Americans have a fundamental "creed" based on individualism and voluntarism. Grabb and Curtis use survey evidence to show that those in the northern United States and English-speaking Canadians are, in terms of their ideological centrism, actually deeply similar on most issues. The two other regions that Grabb and Curtis study are the southern United States, which is clearly conservative, and Quebec, which is clearly on the centre-left of the political spectrum. In fact, the real divide in the United States seems to be not so much between the North and South as between the New England, West Coast, and Great Lakes regions and the rest – that is, the Southeast and the massive Midwest. The US electoral results for 2000, 2004, and even 2008 clearly indicate the country's deep divisions, which also correspond to the regional scheme just discussed (Couture 2008b, 56-57). This internal regional division will likely remain for the foreseeable future, regardless of ebbs and flows in partisan control of the House and the Senate.

Thus, more than ever, it seems that the United States, rather than being a cultural monolith, is most deeply characterized by the absence of consensus on cultural issues: on one side there are liberals and their vision of an epicentre of modernity in which select elements of the American Creed are not seen as a fundamental part of the nation; on the other side there is a social right fully mobilized to claim – as a fundamental national component, if not the essential one – the America of earlier centuries characterized by the supremacy of local, religious, and traditional communities over perilous modern cities. If this is the case, and we believe it is, the United States cannot be characterized as being in opposition to *conservative* Canada.

American Liberalism versus Quebec

The case of Quebec is even more fascinating when placed in this North American context. Although Grabb and Curtis (2005, 149) do not see any major difference between the northern United States and English-speaking Canada, they situate contemporary Quebec clearly more on the left of the North American political spectrum. They also note their findings corroborate other attitudinal studies that show that "Quebecers are the most liberal or least traditional population in the two nations, followed by English Canadians, northern Americans, and southern Americans." This is in sharp contrast with the way that Quebec is often portrayed in much scholarly literature (and in much popular commentary too) as having deep "traditional" roots.

Interestingly, the image of a traditional Quebec was first articulated in the work of 1930s American anthropologists and sociologists associated with the Chicago School (e.g., Horace Miner and Everett Hughes). Work done in the Chicago School also influenced Quebec sociologists of the mid-twentieth century (Couture 1996). These Quebec sociologists, particularly Hubert Guindon, Jean-Charles Falardeau, and Marcel Rioux, interpreted the province as being a fundamentally traditional society. In this view, Quebec was essentially propelled into modernity during the Quiet Revolution in the 1960s – that is, only in the latter part of the twentieth century. The objective of these authors was to capture the elements of French Canadian society from a synchronic angle at the moment of its dissolution due to the effects of industrialization and urbanization. In combination, these works presented an evolutionary schema of Quebec society that was generally narrated in the following way:

- During the period of New France, French Canada reproduced to a large degree the structures of pre-revolutionary France, mainly centred on community, parish, and a precapitalist mentality;
- Following the Conquest of 1760 French Canadians, deprived of privileged contact with the English metropolis, turned to self-subsistence agriculture, which stressed a tendency to prioritize pre-revolutionary, precapitalist values;
- After 1791 and the Constitutional Act a French Canadian nationalism emerged with responsible government as its main theme, but this vision came to an end with the failure of the Patriot movement of 1837-38;
- This failure precipitated the marginalization of French Canadians in the area of trade and reinforced the power of the dominant Catholic bureaucracy at the end of the 1860s, just a few years after Confederation in 1867;
- The Catholic bureaucracy emerged as responsible for the preservation of a conservative ideology centred on faith, tradition, agriculture, and anti-materialism just at the moment of the development of modern capitalism characterized by urbanization and, obviously, industrialization;
- Upset by these phenomena, the dominant values of French Canadian society were eroded little by little until they collapsed during the Quiet Revolution in the 1960s (Couture 1996).

In fact, in most of the literature on Canadian politics, Quebec's nationalism (i.e., the nationalism of French Canadians living in Quebec) is described as "ethnic" (see Hobsbawm 1990). As a result, it is portrayed as essentially racist, being comparable, for example, to Afrikaner nationalism in South Africa as described in the *Concise Oxford Dictionary of Politics* (Allison 2003, 336) or even to Zulu ethnic nationalism (Taras 2002). It should be noted that Quebec's ethnic nationalism is frequently seen as operating in distinction to the civic nationalism of the rest of Canada, thus obliterating the need for attention to the very real racism and processes of racialization that may operate in the rest of Canada (Abu-Laban and Couture 2010) and underscoring the limitations of the dichotomy between ethnic and civic nationalism.

This particular labelling of Quebec nationalism as "ethnic" is generally based on the following narrative, very similar to the traditional one just described in the Hartz-Lipset paradigm:

- Quebec is the result of the white settler colonization that took place in the seventeenth century;
- It is derived from an *ancien régime* society based on rural and religious values;
- The Conquest of 1760 stigmatized these values in what became a very religious and rural French Canada in the nineteenth century, whereas the British embraced the project of modernity, secularism, and urbanization, as Lord Durham pointed out in 1839;
- Quebec remained a premodern society until the Quiet Revolution of the 1960s, although it is still haunted by the ghosts of its past. Consequently, its nationalism remains in the twenty-first century essentially "ethnic" (i.e., "racist") in a fragile secular society. Quebec's 2007 Bouchard-Taylor Commission hearings – debates on the so-called "reasonable accommodation" of non-Catholic religious minorities led by historian Gérard Bouchard and philosopher Charles Taylor, two prominent scholars at the international level – were, in the eyes of many, a perfect illustration of this alleged malaise and distinction from the rest of Canada (see Macpherson 2007).

As we have seen, although the survey findings of Grabb and Curtis (2005) have much to offer, their treatment of Quebec raises some interesting questions. They explain Quebec's own exceptionalism as a deep reaction against the traditional, conservative Catholic culture that characterized the province before the 1960s. Suddenly, with the Quiet Revolution of the 1960s, Quebec went from being an anachronistic nonmodern society upon which religion was imposed to being extremely individualistic and hostile to traditional forms of social solidarity such as local communities, families, and religion. There seems to be a contradiction, which even the postcolonial literature is unable to explain, between the common view that Quebec's nationalism is based on an attachment to tradition and culture, as fuelled by its economic backwardness, and the sociological reality of twenty-first-century Quebec (Couture 2008a, 5). The Quebec case is still key to understanding Canada, particularly when it comes to situating Canada and the United States in reference to modernity. Also, since Quebec is in an unequal relationship with English-speaking Canada and must therefore be placed in a sphere of colonial dominance, it is important to revisit this case in light of a new historiography that has emerged in the past three decades.

Since the 1980s certain historians have rightly challenged the characterization of Quebec modernity as a sudden post-1960s eruption – a literature not mentioned by Grabb and Curtis (2005). Although saddled with the unfortunate term *revisionist,* the new historiography challenges the notion of a traditional, Catholic, and monolithic society prior to the Quiet Revolution. Offering a new and different historical narrative, it suggests that there was no discrepancy between the popular classes and the elites in Quebec before 1960, that liberalism was well distributed across the province, and that the French Canadian bourgeoisie were prosperous and influential in Canada. These historians also insist that within Quebec history there are numerous examples of the modern "normalcy" of the province (Linteau, Durocher, and Robert 1979).

One of these examples includes the issues of migration and immigration. During the nineteenth century large numbers of French Canadians moved to urban centres throughout North America. Despite the Catholic Church's official but sometimes ambiguous opposition to migration, Quebeckers left their rural homes as early as 1840 and moved to urban centres in New England or to cities in the province of Quebec. From 1850 to 1930 the province's urban population grew steadily. In 1871 only 15 percent of the people lived in cities. Two decades later the number had doubled, and by 1921 the urban population had reached 52 percent. This figure was above the Canadian average and comparable to that of Ontario (Linteau, Durocher, and Robert 1979, 42-43). By 2001 Quebec's population was 80 percent urban, the second-highest proportion in Canada, just behind Ontario with 83 percent (Rural Secretariat 2007, 1-3). In other words, the population was not appropriately seen as a rural community oriented towards conservative values. Additionally, throughout the nineteenth and twentieth centuries Quebec attracted waves of immigrants from increasingly diverse countries and regions (Linteau, Durocher, and Robert 1979, 61-62), although this reality is frequently overlooked in the literature that treats Quebec as a historically monolithic society (Couture 1992).

Grabb and Curtis's (2005, 143) data suggest that even if many Quebeckers still identify with the dominant religion of origin, Catholicism, they still have the lowest rate of practice in North America. But even in the 1970s and 1980s, according to Lipset's (1990) numbers, Quebeckers were already trailing the rest of North America when it came to religiosity, although the gap was less evident compared to English-speaking Canada. For example, according to a Kettering-Gallup survey from 1975 cited by Lipset (ibid., 85), there was a gap of 20 percent between Americans (56 percent) and Canadians (36 percent) who deemed their religious beliefs to be important. Asked about the Ten Commandments, 83 percent of Americans said these commandments applied to them, compared to 76 percent of English Canadians and 67 percent of French Canadians. When asked whether the commandments should fully apply to others, 36 percent of Americans agreed, compared to 28 percent of English Canadians and 23 percent of French Canadians. When asked in 1975 whether they believed in the devil, 66 percent of Americans said they did, whereas 45 percent of English Canadians and 22 percent of French Canadians said they did. As noted in our discussion of the relative ranking of the United States internationally in terms of the population's support for the theory of evolution, the 1970s results showed significant differences from other industrialized countries – differences similar to those found in the 2000s. This finding suggests a very intense American opposition to science and to the "option" of not believing. This is not to say that there is no tension between the two options of belief and nonbelief in Quebec or the rest of Canada; rather, the difference between the American context and the Quebec and wider Canadian contexts is one of degree.

Moreover, the theory that it is the power of local communities and their denominations rather than individualism that is the foundation of the United States also stands out more sharply when we make comparisons to Canada and particularly to Quebec. In Canada and specifically Quebec, the religious bureaucracies of the nineteenth century paradoxically led in the twentieth century to the form of Durkheimian individualism that Taylor mistakenly seems to attribute to the United States (Heintzman 1983). This evolution in Canada is perhaps most powerfully exemplified by the individual auton- omy that veil-wearing nuns achieved as a result of their avoidance of marriage and motherhood in the nineteenth and early twentieth centuries (Danylewycz 1987). Thus we suggest once again that the process of disem- bedding in the United States is not a fait accompli and that this situation creates tension, with no sign of a more peaceful or harmonious cohabitation between believers and nonbelievers on the immediate horizon. In the case of Quebec the 2007 Bouchard-Taylor Commission on reasonable accom- modation of religious minorities and the accompanying 2008 report might be interpreted as representing a deep clash between regional, even rural, Quebec and cosmopolitan Montreal, similar to the clash between urban and regional America. But the debate in Quebec – both in Montreal and outside – has never featured an aggressive defence of a still very Christian Quebec. In fact, it was *secularism* that emerged as the dominant theme in the com- mission's discussions (Bouchard and Taylor 2008, 133). As a result, the terms of the clash are different and less inflammatory than those of the clash in the United States, suggesting a more peaceful cohabitation of the options of belief and nonbelief in Quebec.

Conclusion

It seems that since the mid-twentieth century the social-sciences literature in the Western world has been obsessed with the location of an epicentre of modernity. Indeed, today secularism is often attributed to "the West" and portrayed as an ideal that stands at the epicentre of the West's recent mod- ernity (Abu-Laban and Couture 2010, 438-39). However, this kind of por- trayal ignores the secularism and state neutrality towards religion that were in fact observed outside of the West as far back as the eleventh through the thirteenth centuries in the Great Seljuk Empire (Basan 2010). Here it should be noted that the Seljuk Empire incorporated most of the former Abbasid Caliphate, notably including the territories of modern-day Turkey, Iran, Iraq, Syria, Saudi Arabia, and Azerbaijan, and stretched to the northwest of India.

Likewise, although it is widely assumed, particularly among American writers of the past few decades, that the United States occupies this centre where individualism flourishes in a secular age and where religion is treated as an option in a secular state, there is more to this assumption than meets the eye. Conflicting visions of the nation have been clashing with perhaps more intensity in the United States than in many (any?) other Western countries, and the place of religion as an option – or on the contrary as an imposed norm – is still much debated. This process continues to generate a lot of insecurity in the United States.

As for the representation of America as the epicentre of modernity, it is extremely interesting to note that evidence, including the results of surveys analyzed by Grabb and Curtis (2005), points more strongly to Canada and even more so to Quebec as locales of much greater peaceful cohabitation between the general options of belief and nonbelief than is seen in the United States. Some would say that the 2007 hearings on reasonable accommodation are evidence of Quebec's ethnic and nonmodern impulses towards immigration and multiculturalism. The still ongoing discussion of reasonable accommodation may indeed be seen as capturing some very real public sentiments – not confined to Quebec – that reflect racism (specifically Islamophobia and anti-Semitism). However, it is nonetheless very interesting that there was a *public* debate on religion in Quebec, arguably made possible by the strong degree of secularity that exists there. It may be possible to envision similar debates in other parts of Canada, but it is difficult to imagine any federal or state government in the United States even daring to create a public forum on issues of multiculturalism and religious cohabitation. Thus any lingering challenges to the motto "In God We Trust" will remain where they have been for over five decades: in the hands of the US judiciary.

We are living in a period when religion – and its connection to the state, secularism, and diversity – has become a dominant question on the agenda of both social scientists and policy makers. In a context where immigrants from non-Western states have become a popular (and well-funded) object of study since 11 September 2001, it is especially useful to review the assumptions about Western states and societies that guided earlier generations of scholars. As we have illustrated here, much of this debate captures themes on the agenda of study in the global South (and its differences from or similarities with the North) including religiosity, liberal democracy, and individualism. For good or for bad, earlier assumptions about particular states and societies in the West may still echo in what appears to be new and contemporary research studies about non-Western societies compared to the West. As we have attempted to highlight, in the case of the global superpower – the United States – scholarship might be more sharply assessed when placed in the context of North America, with prevailing assumptions being tested rather than repeated.

Notes

Our thanks to the editors of this volume as well as to Anne Linscott and Anna Drake for helpful and constructive comments on this chapter.

1 For a classification of "passive" secularism as exemplified by the United States and "active" secularism as exemplified by France, see Ahmet T. Kuru (this volume). For a discussion of "contextual" secularism, see Rajeev Bhargava (this volume).

2 Historically, this intense focus on the threat of the outsider, in the form of the immigrant, may also account for the highly varied responses to British playwright Israel Zangwill's 1908 play *The Melting Pot,* which was central to the popularization of the metaphor of America as a melting pot. Although Zangwill himself saw America as a nation of immigrants and as a haven for those fleeing persecution – particularly Jews facing virulent anti-Semitism in Europe – and although his play was endorsed by President Theodore Roosevelt, critics countered that this proved presidents could be wrong. These varied responses need to be placed in relation to this era's restrictionist backlash surrounding America's "new immigrants" (i.e., non-Protestant, non-Catholic, and non-Jewish immigrants from southern and eastern Europe). Notably, however inclusionary the vision of Zangwill was for its time, his imagined melting pot did not accommodate African Americans (see Abu-Laban and Lamont 1997).

Works Cited

Abu-Laban, Yasmeen, and Claude Couture. 2010. "Multiple Minorities and Deceptive Dichotomies: The Theoretical and Political Implications of the Struggle for a Public French Education System in Alberta." *Canadian Journal of Political Science* 43 (2): 433-56.

Abu-Laban, Yasmeen, and Victoria Lamont. 1997. "Crossing Borders: Interdisciplinarity, Immigration and the Melting Pot in the American Cultural Imaginary." *Canadian Review of American Studies* 27 (2): 23-43.

Adams, Michael. 2003. *Fire and Ice: The United States, Canada and the Myth of Converging Values.* Toronto: Penguin.

Ajzenstat, Janet, and Peter J. Smith. 1995. *Canada's Origins: Liberal, Tory or Republican?* Ottawa: Carleton University Press.

Allison, Lincoln. 2003. "Nationalism." In *The Concise Oxford Dictionary of Politics,* edited by Iain McClean, 335-36. 1996. Reprint, Oxford and New York: Oxford University Press.

Almond, Gabriel, and Sidney Verba. 1963. *The Civic Culture.* Princeton, NJ: Princeton University Press.

Basan, Aziz. 2010. *The Great Seljuks: A History.* New York: Routledge.

Bellah, Robert. 1967. "Civil Religion in America." *Journal of the American Academy of Arts and Sciences* 96 (1): 1-21.

–. 1992. *Broken Covenant: American Civil Religion in Time of Trial.* Chicago: University of Chicago Press.

Berger, Peter, Grace Davie, and Effie Fokas. 2008. *Religious America, Secular Europe?* London: Ashgate.

Bhargava, Rajeev. 2004. "India's Model: Faith, Secularism and Democracy." *Open Democracy,* 3 November. http://www.openDemocracy.net.

–, ed. 1998. *Secularism and Its Critics*. New Delhi: Oxford University Press.

Bouchard, Gérard, and Charles Taylor. 2008. *Building the Future: A Time for Reconciliation*. Quebec City: Government of Quebec.

Bramadat, Paul, and Matthias Koenig. 2009. Preface to *International Migration and the Governance of Religious Diversity*, edited by Paul Bramadat and Matthias Koenig, ix-x. Montreal and Kingston: McGill-Queen's University Press.

Camic, Charles, ed. 1997. *Reclaiming the Sociological Classics*. Oxford: Blackwell.

Carens, Joseph H. 2000. *Culture, Citizenship and Community: A Contextual Exploration of Justice as Evenhandedness*. Oxford: Oxford University Press.

Couture, Claude. 1992. *Le mythe de la modernisation du Québec*. Montreal: Méridien.

–. 1996. *Paddling with the Current*. Edmonton: University of Alberta Press.

–. 2008a. "Borders, Migration and Managing Diversity: New Mapping." *International Journal of Canadian Studies* 38: 5-14.

–. 2008b. "Nation-Building and Regionalism in the US, Canada and Mexico." In *Politics in North America: Redefining Continental Relations*, edited by Yasmeen Abu-Laban, Radha Jhappan, and François Rocher, 51-69. Toronto: University of Toronto Press.

Danylewycz, Marta. 1987, *Taking the Veil: An Alternative to Marriage, Motherhood and Spinsterhood in Québec, 1840-1920*. Toronto: McClelland and Stewart.

Durkheim, Émile. 1893. *De la division du travail social*. Paris: Presses Universitaires de France.

Grabb, Edward, and James Curtis. 2005. *Regions Apart: The Four Societies of Canada and the United States*. Don Mills, ON: Oxford University Press.

Greenfeld, Liah. 1992. *Nationalism: Five Roads to Modernity*. Cambridge, MA: Harvard University Press.

Hartz, Louis. 1955. *The Liberal Tradition in America*. New York: Harcourt, Brace and World.

Heintzman, Ralph. 1983. "The Political Culture of Québec." *Canadian Journal of Political Science* 16 (1): 3-60.

Hobsbawm, Eric. 1990. *Nations and Nationalism since 1780: Program, Myth, Reality*. Cambridge, UK: Cambridge University Press.

Hollinger, David A. 1995. *Beyond Multiculturalism: Postethnic America*. New York: Basic Books.

Holyoake, George J. 1896. *The Origin and Nature of Secularism: Showing That Where Freethought Commonly Ends Secularism Begins*. London: Watts.

Huntington, Samuel P. 1996. "The West and the World." *Foreign Affairs* 75 (6): 28-47.

–. 1997a. *The Clash of Civilizations and the Remaking of World Order*. New York: Simon and Schuster.

–. 1997b. "The Erosion of American National Interests." *Foreign Affairs* 76 (5): 28-50.

Ignatieff, Michael. 1994. *Blood and Belonging*. Toronto: Penguin.

Kaufman, Jason. 2009. *The Origins of Canadian and American Political Differences*. Cambridge, MA: Harvard University Press.

Kiros, Teodros. 1998. "The Colors of Multiculturalism: An Interview with Henry Louis Gates." In *The Promise of Multiculturalism: Education and Autonomy in the*

21st Century, edited by George Katsiaficas and Teodros Kiros, 166-77. New York: Routledge.

Kosmin, Barry A. 2007. "Contemporary Secularity and Secularism." In *Secularism and Secularity: Contemporary International Perspectives,* edited by Barry A. Kosmin and Ariela Keysar, 1-13. Hartford, CT: Institute for the Study of Secularism in Society and Culture.

Lind, Michael. 1995. *The Next American Nation.* New York: Free Press.

Linteau, Paul-André, René Durocher, and Jean-Claude Robert. 1979. *Histoire du Québec contemporain: De la Confédération à la crise.* Montreal: Boréal.

Lipset, Seymour Martin. 1990. *Continental Divide: The Values and Institutions of the United States and Canada.* New York: Routledge.

Macpherson, Don. 2007. "Racism in Québec." *Montreal Gazette,* 16 January, A-21.

Mancke, Elizabeth. 2005. *The Fault Lines of Empire: Political Differentiation in Massachusetts and Nova Scotia, ca. 1760-1830.* New York: Routledge.

Masci, David. 2007. "A Half Century after It First Appeared on the Dollar Bill, 'In God We Trust' Still Stirs Opposition." *Pew Forum,* 12 September, 1-2. http://pewforum.org/docs/?DocID=247.

Miller, Jon D., Eugenie C. Scott, and Shinji Okamoto. 2006. "Public Acceptance of Evolution." *Science* 313 (5778): 765-66.

Neil, Stephen. 1966. *Colonialism and Missions.* New York: McGraw Hill.

Norris, Pippa, and Ronald Inglehart. 2004. *Sacred and Secular: Religion and Politics Worldwide.* Cambridge, UK: Cambridge University Press.

Perry, Marc J. 2006. "Domestic Net Migration in the United States, 2000-2004." *Population Estimates and Projections,* April. http://www.census.gov/prod/2006 pubs/p25-1135.pdf.

Pew Research Center for the People and the State. 2002. "Among Wealthy Nations ... U.S. Stands Alone in Its Embrace of Religion." 19 December. http://people-press. org/report/167/.

Rural Secretariat. 2007. *Rural Québec, a Profile: A Ten-Year Census Analysis.* Ottawa: Government of Canada.

Seljak, David. 2007. *Religion and Multiculturalism in Canada: The Challenge of Religious Intolerance and Discrimination.* Multiculturalism and Human Rights Research Reports No. 2. Ottawa: Strategic Policy, Research and Planning Directorate, Multiculturalism and Human Rights Program, Department of Canadian Heritage.

Shain, Barry. 1994. *The Myth of American Individualism.* Princeton, NJ: Princeton University Press.

Smith, Anthony D. 2000. *The Nation in History: Historiographical Debates about Ethnicity and Nationalism.* Hanover, NH: University Press of New England.

Statistics Canada. 1993. *Religions in Canada.* 1991 Census of Canada Catalogue No. 93-319. Ottawa: Industry, Science and Technology Canada.

Taras, Ray. 2002. *Liberal and Illiberal Nationalisms.* New York: Palgrave Macmillan.

Taylor, Charles. 1991. *The Malaise of Modernity.* Toronto: Anansi.

–. 2004. *Modern Social Imaginaries.* Durham, NC: Duke University Press.

–. 2007. *A Secular Age.* Cambridge, MA: Belknap/Harvard University Press.

Tocqueville, Alexis. 2012. *Democracy in America.* 1835-40. Reprint, Indianapolis: Liberty Fund.

Tönnies, Ferdinand. 1887. *Gemeinschaft und Gesellschaft.* Leipzig: Fues's Verlag.

Tyrrell, William. 2010. *Reforming the World: The Creation of America's Moral Empire.* Princeton, NJ: Princeton University Press.

Zolberg, Aristide R. 2006. *A Nation by Design: Immigration Policy in the Fashioning of America.* New York and Cambridge, MA: Russell Sage Foundation/Harvard University Press.

Ideologies, Institutions, and Laws
Religious Freedom in Secular States

Ahmet T. Kuru

Chapter 7

Are secular state policies on religious freedom products of value-neutral institutions? This chapter argues that secular state institutions are not value-neutral but are affected by, and generally divided through, ideological views. Therefore, state policies concerning religious freedom are the products of ideological struggles in which courts and parliaments act as carriers of ideological preferences and strategies rather than as value-free representatives of the neutral state or law. Some scholars regard ideology as a mere reflection of the economic structure and a means for the dominant economic class to exert power.[1] In my analysis, however, ideology is neither a superstructure nor a simple instrument of power. Ideology and material conditions are separate but interrelated. I do not deny agents' strategic behaviours but argue that ideas and ideologies come first because they define the identity and preferences of the actors. Based on their ideas, actors evaluate their conditions, use their rationality, and decide strategies.

Although the chapter analyzes ideological struggles, it does not focus on a secular-religious divide. Instead, it examines the polarization between "assertive" and "passive" types of secularism. Assertive secularism requires the state to play an "assertive" role in excluding religion from the public sphere and confining it to the private domain. Passive secularism demands the state play a "passive" role by allowing public visibility of religion. Assertive secularism is a "comprehensive doctrine"[2] since it claims to define the appropriate status of religion in not only political but also socioeconomic life, whereas passive secularism mainly prioritizes state neutrality towards such doctrines and makes limited claims about the public roles of religions. Countries where assertive secularism is dominant include Mexico and Uzbekistan, whereas passive secularism dominates cases such as Canada and India.

The three cases I examine – the United States, France, and Turkey – are secular states because their courts and parliaments are not under institutional religious control and because they lack constitutionally established religions. They differ from *religious states,* which make religious law and courts the bases of their legal and judicial systems, from *states with an established religion,* which recognize an official religion, and from *anti-religious states,* which take a hostile position against religions. Despite their similar secular characteristics, these three states have sharply different policies towards religion due to differing ideological struggles over secularism.

In France the supporters of assertive secularism (*laïcité de combat*) are dominant, whereas those of passive secularism (*laïcité plurielle*) are in opposition. Assertive secularists were dominant in Turkey, starting the foundation of the republic, whereas recently passive secularists have become increasingly influential. The United States is the only case among the three where assertive secularists are marginal and passive secularists are dominant. Yet it experiences a struggle between the opposing conservative and liberal interpretations of passive secularism. As a result, the United States recognizes students' rights to display religious symbols, France bans such symbols only in public schools, and Turkey forbids them in both private and public schools. The following sections explore how ideological clashes pit institutions, especially courts and parliaments, against each other during the process of public policy making concerning religion.

Supreme Court, Congress, and President in the United States

The division between the conservatives and liberals in the United States is so deep that it is generally known as the "culture wars" (Hunter 1991). In debates on issues such as abortion, gay marriage, and euthanasia, liberals support more individualism and multiculturalism, whereas conservatives defend more religious and traditional perspectives. In terms of party affiliation, conservatives are generally Republican, whereas liberals are largely Democrat (Kohut et al. 2000). All three branches of the federal government – the president, Congress, and the Supreme Court – are divided along conservative and liberal lines.

Conservatives and liberals have substantial disagreements on the appro-priate relations between the state and religion as reflected in their conflict-ing interpretations of the First Amendment to the Constitution: "Congress shall make no law respecting an establishment of religion, or prohibiting the free exercise thereof." The first part of this amendment is named the Establishment Clause, and the second part is the Free Exercise Clause. The main disagreements of conservatives and liberals focus on the Establish-ment Clause, which requires the state to avoid favouring a religion. Conserv-atives support closer state-religion relations, arguing that strict state-religion separation has marginalized religion in the public sphere (Carter 1993; Monsma and Soper 1997). Liberals, on the other hand, support the Supreme Court's decision in *Everson v. Board of Education* (1947),[3] which defines the Establishment Clause as seeking a "wall of separation." Thus the mainstream conservative position is called "accommodationism," whereas that of liber-als is named "separationism." Liberals also refer to the court's decision in *Lemon v. Kurtzman* (1971),[4] which specifies three criteria to determine the constitutionality of legislation: "First, the statute must have a secular legis-lative purpose; second, its principal or primary effect must be one that nei-ther advances nor inhibits religion; finally, the statute must not foster 'an excessive government entanglement with religion.'" For conservatives, both *Everson* and *Lemon* are deeply problematic and should be reversed.

In addition to their mainstream groups – accommodationists and separ-ationists – conservatives and liberals also include some more radical factions. The radicals on the conservative side, the Christian right, seek to establish a cultural dominance of Christianity. On the liberal side, the radicals are as-sertive secularists who aim to exclude religion from the American public sphere. Despite opposite policy preferences, the mainstream accommoda-tionists and separationists jointly oppose both a cultural establishment of Christianity and an assertive-secularist exclusion of religion from the public sphere.

In this regard, conservatives and liberals largely agree on the interpreta-tion of the Free Exercise Clause. Both groups attach importance to religious freedom, including students' freedom to display religious symbols. There-fore, they are defenders of two different interpretations of passive secular-ism, both of which allow public visibility of religion. Among the few cases where individuals' displays of religious symbols have been contested in the United States is *Goldman v. Weinberger* (1986).[5] In this case the US Supreme Court decided by a margin of 5 to 4 that the Air Force had the right to prohibit an officer from wearing a religious headgear – the Jewish yarmulke – indoors. The court stressed that the armed forces were different from other institutions because the "purpose of the military and its need to foster cohesiveness were regarded as appropriate justifications to restrict the religious rights of individuals." Nevertheless, in the following year, Congress passed legislation that reversed this decision by allowing members of the armed forces to wear religious apparel inside military buildings.[6]

Recent US policies on the country's Muslim population have not invalidated the predominance of passive secularism. Muslims in the United States faced troubles in the aftermath of the terrorist attacks of 11 September 2001. About a hundred thousand of them were subjected to security measures, including being investigated, interrogated, or arrested, mainly as a result of racial and religious profiling (Cainkar 2008, 53). Yet these mistreatments occurred not because of, but despite, passive secularism. Muslims still enjoy religious freedom in the United States in terms of constructing mosques, opening Islamic schools, and founding organizations (Bilici 2008). Since Bill Clinton, US presidents have made pronouncements celebrating Muslim holidays, in addition to organizing *iftaar* dinners during the month of Ramadan in the White House. Moreover, there is no restriction against Muslim headscarves in the United States. An exceptional case occurred in 2004 due to the dress code of a public school in Oklahoma, which prohibited a sixth-grade Muslim girl from wearing a headscarf. The US Justice Department intervened on the side of the student, who eventually won her case. The assistant attorney general announced the department's intervention and said, "No student should be forced to choose between following her faith and enjoying the benefits of a public education" (quoted in Knowlton 2004).

In the United States religious practices cannot be prohibited by being singled out. The French ban on religious symbols and the Turkish ban on headscarves have no legal basis in the American system. Furthermore, some laws and regulations in the United States explicitly exempt individuals given their religious beliefs. For example, in its online visa guidelines the US Department of State specifies that for photos "you must remove hats or head-coverings that obscure your hair or hairline, *unless worn for a religious purpose*."[7] The controversial issue is whether the US Constitution exempts individuals from neutral, generally applicable laws because of their religious beliefs, even if these laws do not specify such an exemption.

Supporters of constitutional exemption argue that the Free Exercise Clause provides adherents of religious practices with the right to be exempt from general regulations. The rationale for this approach is that religious practices are beyond personal *choice;* believers perceive them as *obligations.* In this regard, freedom of religious expression should be taken more seriously than mere freedom of choice (Sandel 1998). Those who support this position mainly refer to the US Supreme Court's decision in *Sherbert v. Verner* (1963),[8] which resulted in the compelling-interest test. This test demands that states have a compelling interest in restricting particular religious practices by subjecting them to a neutral, generally applicable regulation. According to the test, it is also necessary to show that this interest cannot be served by a less restrictive means.[9] Another case where the court upheld constitutional religious exemption was *Wisconsin v. Yoder* (1972).[10] The court decided that Amish parents had legitimate religious reasons to require that their children be exempt from school attendance beyond the eighth grade because their free exercise of religion outweighed the state's interests in compelling student attendance. The court emphasized that such an exemption was permissible only on religious grounds: "A way of life, however virtuous and admirable, may not be interposed as a barrier to a reasonable state regulation of education if it is based on purely secular considerations; to have the protection of the Religion Clauses, the claims must be rooted in religious belief."

The US Supreme Court rejected constitutional religious exemption in *Oregon v. Smith* (1990).[11] The court upheld Oregon's refusal to pay unemployment compensation to a Native American and his white coworker fired by a private drug-rehabilitation organization for using an illegal mild hallucinogenic – peyote – in a Native American religious ceremony. On issues related to the Establishment Clause, such as organized school prayer and indirect state funding of religious schools, the court has generally been divided between conservative and liberal justices.[12] On the issue of religious exemption, which was primarily about the Free Exercise Clause, justices had a basic agreement that Oregon, like several other states, could legislate to exempt the use of drugs such as peyote for religious purposes. Yet they disagreed on whether the Constitution provided an exemption without such state legislation. Five justices rejected an exemption and voted for the abolishment of the compelling-interest test. The remaining four justices accepted the validity of both the constitutional exemption and the test: one justice voted to affirm the existence of a compelling state interest in *Oregon v. Smith,* and three justices voted to deny its existence. The court members' disagreement was so complex that it did not clearly reflect the conservative-liberal divide because there were multiple ways of reading the case. From a conservative point of view, one could either defend the compelling-interest test for promoting religious freedom or reject the test to oppose stretching the meaning of the Constitution beyond its words, to stress state authority vis-à-vis the federal government, or to ensure a relative disregard for religious minorities (i.e., Native Americans in the case). From a liberal point of view, one could either oppose the test for denying religion a special status or support the test given the liberal mandate to promote individual liberties and protect religious minorities.

Conservative justice Antonin Scalia delivered the court's opinion by quoting *Reynolds v. US* (1878),[13] which claimed that to permit individuals to excuse their practices contrary to laws because of their religious beliefs "would be to make the professed doctrines of religious belief superior to the law of the land, and in effect to permit every citizen to become a law unto himself." Scalia also added that "a private right to ignore generally applicable laws is a constitutional anomaly." The dissenting justices, however, emphasized that "almost half the states, and the federal government, have maintained an exemption for religious peyote use for many years, and apparently have not found themselves overwhelmed by claims to other religious exemptions."

The critics of the decision in *Oregon v. Smith* included both conservatives and liberals. Michael McConnell, a conservative law professor and later a federal judge, wrote a 100-page *Harvard Law Review* article to criticize the decision and to show that constitutional religious exemption was the framers' intent while crafting the Free Exercise Clause. For him, the framers gave "a special, protected status to religious conscience not because religious judgments are better, truer, or more likely to be moral than nonreligious judgments, but because the obligations entailed by religion transcend the individual and are outside the individual's control" (McConnell 1990, 1497). The legislative reaction to the case was also unprecedentedly bipartisan. In 1993 Congress overturned the decision in *Oregon v. Smith* and restored the compelling-interest test. The House unanimously and the Senate overwhelmingly voted to pass the Religious Freedom Restoration Act (RFRA), which President Bill Clinton signed into law. This act states,

(a) In general: Government shall not substantially burden a person's exercise of religion even if the burden results from a rule of general applicability, except as provided in subsection (b) of this section.

(b) Exception: Government may substantially burden a person's exercise of religion only if it demonstrates that application of the burden to the person – (1) is in furtherance of a compelling governmental interest; and (2) is the least restrictive means of furthering that compelling governmental interest.[14]

Based on the RFRA, Clinton issued the Memorandum on Religion in Schools, which stressed that "students may display religious messages on items of clothing to the same extent that they are permitted to display other comparable messages ... When wearing particular attire, such as yarmulkes and headscarves, during the school day is part of students' religious practice ... schools generally may not prohibit the wearing of such items" (*New York Times* 1995). In *City of Boerne v. Flores* (1997),[15] however, the US Supreme Court struck down the RFRA as an unconstitutional restriction on the states' authority. In response, legislatures of thirteen states adopted versions of the RFRA, and "at least another thirteen states – arguably as many as seventeen states – have interpreted their state constitutions" in a manner consistent with the RFRA (Laycock 2006, 537). Clinton also issued a guideline on religious freedom in federal workplaces where he had direct jurisdiction: "An employee must be permitted to wear religious garb, such as a crucifix, a yarmulke, or a head scarf or hijab, if wearing such attire during the work day is part of the employee's religious practice or expression, so long as the wearing of such garb does not unduly interfere with the functioning of the workplace" (United States Government 1997). Recently, in *Gonzales v. O Centro Espirita* (2006),[16] the Supreme Court upheld the constitutionality of the RFRA only for the federal government.

The interaction between judges, legislatures, and executive rulers produces US policies towards religion. The actors' conservative or liberal views and networks have generally shaped their preferences and strategies in policy-making processes. Some issues, such as school prayer and school vouchers, are examples where in-group uniformity is strong and out-group polarization is very deep for both conservatives and liberals. This chapter focuses on the debates on constitutional religious exemption, which exceptionally blur boundaries between the two groups. The distinction between the federal government and the states, which was not an important aspect of controversies over school prayer or school vouchers, played an important role in the exceptional complexity of the debate on constitutional religious exemption. The reason why I chose this American controversy, instead of others, is its ability to reveal the comparative differences between the United States, on the one hand, and France and Turkey, on the other, in terms of the relationship between the secular state and religious freedom.

Council of State, Parliament, and President in France

In France, like Turkey and unlike the United States, there are multiple higher courts, instead of a single supreme court. The French Constitutional Court can review legislative bills only before they become law. It does not have a monopoly to interpret the constitutional principle of secularism. The French Council of State, which reviews executive decisions and regulations, is the highest court for administrative justice. France is similar to Turkey and different from the United States in that it is a unitary state, where there are no subnational parliaments. French parliamentarians and executive politicians are largely divided along the lines of the left and the right. The leftists have generally defended assertive secularism, aiming to exclude religion from the public sphere and to confine it to the private domain, whereas the rightists have supported public visibility of Catholicism.

The growth of the Muslim minority, which has reached 5 million and about 8 percent of French society (Fetzer and Soper 2005; Haut conseil à l'intégration 2001, 37-38), has led to a redefinition of the coalitions on state-religion debates. During the headscarf debate, assertive-secularist leftists cooperated with the anti-immigrant and Islamophobic[17] rightists to ban headscarves in public schools, whereas multiculturalist leftists and rightists opposed such a ban and sought an alternate passive secularism that would tolerate public visibility of religion.

The headscarf debate in France continued for one and a half decades (Amiraux 2009; Asad 2006; Roy 2007; Scott 2007). When the controversy began in 1989, Minister of Education Lionel Jospin leaned towards passive secularism by opposing the expulsion of students from schools for headscarves and by promoting dialogue as an alternate solution. Another important state actor that embraced a passive-secularist position was the Council of State. In its 1989 opinion the council emphasized religious freedom: "In schools, the students' wearing of signs by which they intend to manifest their affiliations with a religion is not by itself incompatible with the principle of secularism as long as it constitutes the exercise of the freedom of expression and manifestation of religious beliefs." The council also added that students' religious symbols should not disturb educational activities by performing as "an act of pressure, provocation, proselytism, or propaganda."[18] During the 1990s, the majority of students wearing headscarves were tolerated by the school administrators; very few cases were taken to the courts, and fewer reached the council. From 1992 to 1999 the council reviewed forty-nine cases and upheld the expulsion of students in only eight cases, those where students wearing headscarves and their parents staged street protests and thus were perceived as harmful to the public order (Debré 2004, 92; Haut conseil à l'intégration 2001, 66).

A clear representative of the coalition between the assertive-secularist left and the Islamophobic right was Christian Democrat François Bayrou, minister of education from 1993 to 1997. Despite substantial disagreement with the assertive secularists on state funding of Catholic schools, Bayrou allied with them to ban headscarves in schools by issuing a circular. Yet the Council of State cancelled Bayrou's circular, noting that a general ban on headscarves in public schools did not have a legal basis (Burdy and Marcou 1995, 27). During the premiership of Jospin from 1997 to 2002, the coalition of assertive secularists and Islamophobes could not overturn the council's accommodating decisions by imposing a new law to ban headscarves.

The 2002 presidential elections, however, demonstrated the rising popularity of the Islamophobic far-right. In the first round Jean-Marie Le Pen, the leader of the far-right National Front, received 17 percent of the votes, whereas centre-rightist Jacques Chirac won only 20 percent and socialist Jospin won only 16 percent. After his re-election President Chirac came out explicitly against students wearing headscarves in public schools (there were 1,465 students wearing headscarves in the 2003-04 academic year) (Ministère de l'éducation 2005). Meanwhile, the supporters of the headscarf ban reached 72 percent of the French population (Debré 2004, 179). Chirac appointed the Stasi Commission, composed mostly of assertive secularists. The commission then proposed a new law to ban students' religious symbols in public schools (Stasi Commission 2003; Zuber 2004, 36).[19]

Nicolas Sarkozy, the centre-right politician and minister of the interior – who would later become president – had initially opposed a general ban. Having realized the rising popular support for the ban, he changed his position. Sarkozy even went to Egypt, met with the grand sheikh of Al-Azhar University, Muhammad Sayyid Tantawy, and received a fatwa declaring France's right to ban headscarves (*Le Monde* 2003). The French Parliament followed the public mood and approved a legislative bill to prohibit students' religious symbols. Both the Chamber of Deputies (494 for, 36 against, and 31 abstentions) and the Senate (276 for and 20 against) passed the bill by a large majority. In March 2004 Chirac signed the bill into law, which stated, "In public primary, secondary, and high schools, the wearing of signs or dress with which the students manifest ostentatiously a religious affiliation is prohibited."[20]

The way Parliament bypassed the Council of State with the new law on secularism fitted French institutional tradition. Parliament had also played the leading role in the establishment of assertive secularism through the secularization laws of the 1880s and the Law of Separation of 1905. Another similarity between the historical establishment and the contemporary implementation of assertive secularism in France is the primary role of ideological concerns in shaping state policies. In the 1990s passive secularists resisted a general ban on headscarves; yet the coalition of assertive secularists and Islamophobes eventually dominated French politics. The new law's prohibition against all religious symbols, which resulted in the expulsion from public schools not only of Muslim students with headscarves but also of some Sikh students with turbans, was a reflection of assertive secularism.[21] Yet it was clear that Islamophobia had also influenced the law given that it banned primarily Muslim students' headscarves,[22] even in the Alsace-Moselle region.[23] This region, which includes the city of Strasbourg, has been exempt from secularization laws and has had four established religions – Catholicism, Lutheranism, Calvinism, and Judaism – whose clergy and buildings have received funding from the French state (Froidevaux-Metterie 2009, 172).

The French state's policies towards the Muslim minority have remained a product of ideological struggles. The recent ban on women's face-coverings and other public debates about Islam are reflections of these struggles. The rising vote share of the National Front indicates that Islamophobia, in addition to assertive secularism, will be a crucial factor in shaping public debates and policies towards the Muslim minority in France.

Constitutional Court, Council of State, Parliament, and President in Turkey

Turkey, like France, has embraced civil law, where judges are perceived to be less powerful than those in the common-law tradition of the United States. Recently, however, Turkish judges became extremely powerful due to their self-imposed mission of protecting assertive secularism, which aimed to exclude Islam and other religions from the public sphere. The Turkish Constitutional Court defined secularism as the "separation of religion and worldly affairs," "Turkey's philosophy of life," a principle prior to all rights and freedoms, and a social-engineering project to civilize society.[24] Formerly, it was the military that had defended assertive secularism in Turkey. Recent transformations, from Turkey's process of seeking membership in the European Union to the strengthening of Turkish civil society, have made staging military coups extremely difficult. The judiciary thus came to fill the military's role as the guardian of assertive secularism against elected politicians. Such a guardianship was perceived to be necessary because the assertive-secularist parties received less than 30 percent of the votes in the previous decade and Parliament was thus dominated by passive secularists.

The judiciary elite regarded two policies as pillars of assertive secularism in Turkey and were eager to protect them. One was the headscarf ban, which encompassed faculty and students of all educational institutions, as well as all civil servants and elected politicians. According to public surveys,[25] 63 percent of women in Turkey wore some sort of headscarf, and 78 percent of the people opposed the headscarf ban (Çarkoğlu and Toprak 2006, 58, 62, 71). The second crucial policy was to marginalize the Islamic public (Imam-Hatip) schools and to discriminate against their graduates in the nationwide university entrance exam by giving them a lower coefficient when calculating the scores. According to surveys 85 percent of the people opposed this discrimination against Imam-Hatip graduates (ibid., 55). Both policies were strictly imposed, particularly during military coup processes. Parliament repeatedly attempted to abolish these highly unpopular restrictions, but assertive-secularist actors, such as the Constitutional Court, Council of State, and presidents, preserved these two policies by blocking the legislations.

Until 2008 the Council for Higher Education (YÖK) was the key institution in excluding students wearing headscarves and Imam-Hatip graduates from the universities. The generals who staged the 1980 coup d'état established the YÖK to control universities. Since then, the YÖK has played a crucial role in the appointment of university presidents and even college deans. The YÖK has reflected the power of the president of the republic over universities because it is the president who appoints the head of the YÖK, in addition to one-third of the YÖK's members. In 1982 the YÖK began to expel students with headscarves from universities. The Council of State confirmed the YÖK's expulsions in all cases.

In 1988, Parliament, led by the passive-secularist Motherland Party (ANAP) majority, passed a law to lift the headscarf ban at universities. Assertive-secularist president Kenan Evren, formerly a general, took the law to the Constitutional Court, which struck it down for contradicting the constitutional principle of secularism. According to the court, the law lifting the ban "abolishes the constitutional boundaries of religious freedom by allowing religion to pass beyond the individual's spiritual life and to cause behaviours that influence social life"; moreover, "the dress issue is limited by the Turkish Revolution and Atatürk's Principles and it is not an issue of free-dom of conscience."[26] In 1990 the ANAP majority led the passing of a new law, which stated, "As long as they do not violate existing laws, dress codes are free at universities."[27] Meanwhile, the ANAP's former leader Turgut Özal was the new president and a supporter of the new law. Nonetheless, the assertive-secularist party in opposition applied to the Constitutional Court. The court did not declare the law unconstitutional but instead interpreted it as disallowing headscarves at universities, defining them as inherently against secularism.[28] Since then, assertive secularists have argued that head-scarves are prohibited by the court's decisions. Passive secularists, however, have claimed that the law that freed students to wear headscarves at univer-sities remains valid and that there is no other law about headscarves. For them, the ban on headscarves is an assertive-secularist practice without any legal basis. The universities, therefore, have not pursued a consistent policy on this issue.

In 1992 Özal appointed Mehmet Sağlam as the head of the YÖK. Sağlam was against the headscarf ban, and under his administration few universi-ties imposed the ban. In 1995, however, President Süleyman Demirel ap-pointed Kemal Gürüz as the head of the YÖK. Particularly following the 1997 "soft" military coup, Gürüz strictly imposed the ban in all universities. He also led the reorganization of the university entrance exam, which dis-criminated against the Imam-Hatip graduates by calculating their scores with a much lower co-efficient. When this policy was challenged in a law-suit, the Council of State upheld it. As another result of the 1997 military coup, the secondary branches (sixth to eighth grades) of the Imam-Hatip schools were closed down.

In 2003 President Necdet Sezer, a leading assertive secularist, appointed Erdoğan Teziç, another keen supporter of the ban, as the head of the YÖK. Under Teziç's leadership the ban was extended to wearing wigs and hats, even in departments of theology (*Zaman* 2006a, 2006b). In May 2004 the ruling passive-secularist Justice and Development (AK) Party majority in Parliament passed a legislative bill that would remove Teziç and reorganize the YÖK to lift the headscarf ban and restrictions on Imam-Hatip gradu-ates. The assertive-secularist media launched a campaign against the bill, and the YÖK organized street protests composed of university professors. President Sezer vetoed the bill. The AK Party could not pass the bill again because if it insisted on challenging assertive-secularist policies, the party would face a closure case. In 2001 the Constitutional Court had closed down its predecessor, the Virtue Party, primarily because the party had defended the right to wear headscarves.

In December 2007 the AK Party and the Nationalist Action Party led constitutional amendments to lift the headscarf ban at universities. Parliament overwhelmingly (411 to 103) voted for two amendments, and President Abdullah Gül, a former AK Party politician, signed them into law. The first amendment, to Article 10, emphasized the principle of equality for university students as receivers of education as a public service, while keeping the ban for professors: "State organs and administrative authorities shall act in compliance with the principle of equality before the law in all their proceedings *and in benefiting from all public services*" (the italicized text was added by the amendment). The second amendment, to Article 42, emphasized the freedom to receive a college education, while keeping the ban for students of primary and secondary schools: "No one can be deprived of his or her right to higher education for reasons not openly mentioned by laws. The limits of the use of this right will be determined by law."

The new president of the YÖK, Yusuf Ziya Özcan, a passive secularist appointed by Gül, issued a circular to declare the freedom of all dress, including headscarves at universities. Nevertheless, the Council of State cancelled the circular. The assertive-secularist parties applied to the Constitutional Court. The court struck down the 2007 amendments, noting that the courts had to be active in banning headscarves because Parliament was unable to "limit religious freedom" given that it was "a political institution" elected by the people and that "the majority of the people were affiliated with a particular religion [i.e., Islam]." The two passive secularists among the eleven members of the court voted against the decision. In his dissenting opinion the president of the court, Haşim Kılıç, stressed that the court had violated Article 148 of the Constitution, which prevents it from reviewing the content of constitutional amendments, that it had diminished the separation of power between judiciary and legislature, and that there was no other democratic country that banned headscarves at universities.[29]

In response to the amendments, the chief prosecutor of the High Court of Appeals filed a closure case against the AK Party with the Constitutional Court asking for a five-year ban from politics for Prime Minister Tayyip Erdoğan and sixty-nine other AK Party politicians, in addition to President Gül. The prosecutor's indictment was based on a collection of AK Party politicians' speeches about religious freedom and about their failed attempts to alleviate the conditions of university students wearing headscarves and the Imam-Hatip graduates. Because of several external and internal factors, this judicial-coup attempt was unsuccessful. In July 2008 the court did not close down the party but charged it with supporting antisecular activities and cut half of its annual public funding for a year.[30]

Since the failure of this judicial-coup attempt, assertive secularists have continuously lost their influence over Turkish politics. Constant media criticisms of the armed forces have led to multiple court cases against coup plans, which have resulted in the detainments of about 300 military officers, including 70 on-duty generals. These detainments have ended the "untouchable" image of the generals and weakened their guardianship of assertive secularism (Kuru 2012). Along the same line, a constitutional referendum in 2010 redesigned the judicial hierarchy, which eventually minimized assertive-secularist control over the high courts (Kuru and Stepan 2012, 9-10).

This changing balance of power was immediately reflected in state policies towards religion. The YÖK decided that professors could report the students wearing headscarves but could not expel them from classrooms. Encouraged by this decision, most university presidents lifted the headscarf ban. The YÖK also ended the discrimination against Imam-Hatip graduates in the nationwide university entrance exam. Parliament passed a law in 2012 that led to the reopening of the Imam-Hatip schools' secondary branches. The law also introduced elective courses on the Quran and the life of the Prophet Muhammad in schools. This gradual transition from assertive to passive secularism has also meant better conditions for Christian and Jewish minorities. For example, in 2011 the AK Party government returned or paid compensation for numerous properties of Christian and Jewish foundations that had been confiscated by the assertive-secularist state since the foundation of the republic. It remains to be seen whether new passive-secularist policies will improve the conditions of non-Sunni Muslims, especially Alevis.

As the headscarf and Imam-Hatip controversies reveal, Turkish state policies towards religion are highly politicized and ideologically driven. Discrimination against students wearing headscarves and graduates of Imam-Hatip schools began to be removed not by justice-oriented courts and neutral laws but as a result of the rising power of passive secularists and the declining authority of assertive secularists. Courts, presidents, and heads of the YÖK, when shaping public policies, have largely followed their ideological preferences more than, if not instead of, institutional constraints such as precedents, norms, and even laws. Ideologies, rather than rules of a neutral state, have mattered in many cases regarding state policies towards religion in Turkey.

Conclusion

I have concentrated upon state institutions in this chapter due to the volume's focus on states and religious diversity; the role of societal actors in state-religion relations is analyzed elsewhere (Kuru 2009; Kuru 2013). The US Supreme Court's abolishment of the constitutional religious exemption, the French Council of State's opinion that headscarves in public schools are compatible with secularism, and the Turkish Council of State's and Constitutional Court's imposition of the headscarf ban ignited legislative responses that led to the biggest contemporary controversies over religious freedom in these three countries. After the legislatures passed laws, court activism ended in France, but it continued in the United States due to the Supreme Court's final authority to interpret the American Constitution, and it continued in Turkey due to the judiciary's self-appointed guardianship of assertive secularism.

In all three cases, state policies towards religion are results of ideological struggles. In other words, judicial, legislative, and executive institutions, as well as legal codes (i.e., constitutional principles, legislations, and regulations), are all affected by ideologies. Therefore, neither institutions nor laws can be regarded as value-free in state-religion controversies. When shaping public policies towards religion, institutions might be divided by ideologies (e.g., the US Supreme Court), unified by ideological coalitions (e.g., the French Parliament), or transformed due to the ideological affiliations of new leadership (e.g., Turkey's YÖK). Considerable changes in an institution's ideological dimensions, including altered balances of power, coalitions, and leadership, have substantial impacts on its policy preferences and strategies.

Both passive- and assertive-secularist ideologies claim to solve the problems around religious diversity. Passive secularism's solution is based on a passive, impartial state and the recognition of religious groups in the public sphere, whereas assertive secularism depends on an assertive state that tries to turn religion into a personal affair. Although its various interpretations disagree on details, passive secularism has been largely successful in combining freedom and religious diversity in the United States. Assertive secularism in France, however, has appeared to be a problem, rather than a solution, concerning the integration of various religious groups, especially

Muslims, into French public life. Among the three, Turkey has been the most dynamic case; it has been experiencing a transformation from assertive to passive secularism that has provided increasingly better conditions for religious groups in the public sphere. Turkey will be an important test case for evaluating the interactions of passive secularism, Islam, and religious diversity.

Notes

Some portions of this chapter were adapted from Kuru (2009) and are reprinted with permission. I analyze the dimension of state-society relations and the roles of societal actors in these three cases in Kuru (2013). I am thankful to André Laliberté for his helpful comments.

1 In the words of Karl Marx and Friedrich Engels (1994, 129), "In every epoch the ideas of the ruling class are the ruling ideas ... [which] are nothing more than the ideal expression of the dominant material relationships."
2 On "comprehensive doctrines," see John Rawls (1996).
3 *Everson v. Board of Education,* 330 US 1 (1947).
4 *Lemon v. Kurtzman,* 403 US 602 (1971).
5 *Goldman v. Weinberger,* 475 US 503 (1986).
6 Public Law 100-180, section 508 [reference (c)].
7 Bureau of Consular Affairs, US Department of State, "Frequently Asked Questions," http://travel.state.gov/visa/visaphotoreq/visaphotofaq/visaphotofaq_5328.html (emphasis by author).
8 *Sherbert v. Verner,* 374 US 398 (1963).
9 In *Sherbert v. Verner* (1963) the court decided that an individual had the right to refuse to work on his or her Sabbath without relinquishing his or her unemployment benefits because the state had no compelling reason to deny this right.
10 *Wisconsin v. Yoder,* 406 US 205 (1972).
11 *Oregon v. Smith,* 494 US 872 (1990).
12 Cases on organized school prayer and public funding of religious schools in which the US Supreme Court was divided between conservative and liberal perspectives include *Lee v. Weisman,* 505 US 577 (1992); *Santa Fe v. Doe,* 530 US 290 (2000); *Mitchell v. Helms,* 530 US 793 (2000); and *Zelman v. Simmons-Harris,* 536 US 639 (2002). On Supreme Court justices' ideological (i.e., conservative versus liberal) affiliations, see Jeffery A. Segal and Albert D. Cover (1989).
13 In *Reynolds v. US,* 98 US 145 (1878) the court decided that Mormons could not be exempted from the federal ban on polygamy on the grounds of their religious belief.
14 RFRA, November 16, 1993, 107 Stat 1488, 42 USC sec. 2000bb-1, http://uscode.house.gov/. See also John Witte Jr. and M. Christian Green (1996, 536-47).
15 *City of Boerne v. Flores,* 521 US 507 (1997).
16 *Gonzales v. O Centro Espirita,* 546 US 418 (2006).

17 The European Monitoring Centre on Racism and Xenophobia (2006, 61), a European Union institution, regards the following perceptions as Islamophobic: "Islam is a monolithic bloc, static and unresponsive to change," "Islam does not have values in common with other cultures," and "Islam is violent, irrational, primitive, and sexist."

18 French Council of State, 27 November 1989, 346, 893.

19 In its public hearings the commission listened to only one student wearing a head-scarf (Bowen 2006, 118, 246).

20 Law 2004-228, 15 March 2004.

21 The comparison between France and Germany also reveals the impact of assertive secularism on the French ban on headscarves. In Germany eight of sixteen regions have banned headscarves for public school teachers, without banning any other religious symbol. Except for in a few cases, such as Berlin, these regions have argued that headscarves are not compatible with "Christian" or "Occidental" values, instead of emphasizing secularism (see Joppke 2009, Chap. 3).

22 The students expelled from French schools due to their religious symbols did not include a single Christian or Jewish student. As T. Jeremy Gunn (2005, 92n48) emphasizes, the new law "applies about as equally to all religions as the law that prohibits all people from sleeping under bridges applies to the homeless and the wealthy."

23 For a critique of French secularism as "*Catho-laïque*," see Cécile Laborde (2008, 56-79).

24 Turkish Constitutional Court, 16 January 1998, 1998/1.

25 See the report on a survey conducted by *Milliyet* and Konda in *Milliyet* (Istanbul), 3-4 December 2007.

26 Turkish Constitutional Court, 7 March 1989, 1989/12.

27 This law, passed by Parliament on 25 October 1990, was added to Law 2547 as Annex 17.

28 Turkish Constitutional Court, 9 April 1991, 1991/8.

29 Turkish Constitutional Court, 5 June 2008, 2008/116.

30 Turkish Constitutional Court, 30 July 2008, 2008/2.

Works Cited

Amiraux, Valerie. 2009. "'L'affaire du foulard' en France." *Sociologie et Sociétés* 41 (2): 273-98.

Asad, Talal. 2006. "Trying to Understand French Secularism." In *Political Theologies: Public Religions in a Post-Secular World*, edited by Hent de Vries and Lawrence E. Sullivan, 494-526. New York: Fordham University.

Bilici, Mücahit. 2008. "Finding Mecca in America: American Muslims and Cultural Citizenship." PhD diss., University of Michigan.

Bowen, John R. 2006. *Why the French Don't Like Headscarves: Islam, the State, and Public Space*. Princeton, NJ: Princeton University Press.

Burdy, Jean-Paul, and Jean Marcou. 1995. "Laïcité/Laiklik: Introduction." *Cahiers d'Études sur la Méditerranée Orientale et le Monde Turco-Iranien* 19: 5-34.

Cainkar, Louise. 2008. "Thinking Outside the Box: Arabs and Race in the United States." In *Race and Arab Americans before and after 9/11: From Invisible Citizens* to *Visible Subjects,* edited by Amaney Jamal and Nadine Naber, 46-80. Syracuse, NY: Syracuse University Press.

Çarkoğlu, Ali, and Binnaz Toprak. 2006. *Değişen Türkiye'de Din, Toplum ve Siyaset.* Istanbul: TESEV.

Carter, Stephen L. 1993. *The Culture of Disbelief: How American Law and Politics Trivialize Religious Devotion.* New York: Basic Books.

Debré, Jean-Louis. 2004. *La laïcité à l'école: Un principe républicain à réaffirmer.* Paris: Odile Jacob.

European Monitoring Centre on Racism and Xenophobia. 2006. "Muslims in the European Union: Discrimination and Islamophobia." http://fra.europa.eu/fra/material/pub/muslim/Manifestations_EN.pdf.

Fetzer, Joel S., and J. Christopher Soper. 2005. *Muslims and the State in Britain, France, and Germany.* New York: Cambridge University Press.

Froidevaux-Metterie, Camille. 2009. "The Ambiguous Position of French Muslim Women: Between Republican Integration and Religious Claims." In *Secularism, Women, and the State,* edited by Barry A. Kosmin and Ariela Keysar, 165-76. Hartford, CT: Institute for the Study of Secularism in Society and Culture.

Gunn, T. Jeremy. 2005. "French Secularism as Utopia and Myth." *Houston Law Review* 42 (1): 81-102.

Haut conseil à l'intégration. 2001. *L'Islam dans la République.* Paris: La documentation Française.

Hunter, James Davison. 1991. *Culture Wars: The Struggle to Define America.* New York: Basic Books.

Joppke, Christian. 2009. *The Veil: Mirror of Identity.* New York: Polity.

Knowlton, Brian. 2004. "US Takes Opposite Tack from France." *International Herald Tribune,* 3 April.

Kohut, Andrew, John C. Green, Scott Keeter, and Robert C. Toth. 2000. *The Diminishing Divide: Religion's Changing Role in American Politics.* Washington, DC: Brookings Institution Press.

Kuru, Ahmet T. 2009. *Secularism and State Policies toward Religion: The United States, France, and Turkey.* New York: Cambridge University Press.

–. 2012. "The Rise and Fall of Military Tutelage in Turkey: Fears of Islamism, Kurdism, and Communism." *Insight Turkey* 14 (2): 37-57.

–. 2013. "State-Society Relations and Religious Freedom: The United States, France, and Turkey." In *The Everyday Life of the State: A State in Society Approach,* edited by Adam White, 46-59. Seattle: University of Washington Press.

Kuru, Ahmet T., and Alfred Stepan. 2012. Introduction to *Democracy, Islam, and Secularism in Turkey,* edited by Ahmet T. Kuru and Alfred Stepan, 1-11. New York: Columbia University Press.

Laborde, Cécile. 2008. *Critical Republicanism: The Hijab Controversy and Political Philosophy.* New York: Oxford University Press.

Laycock, Douglas. 2006. "Church and State in the United States: Competing Conceptions and Historic Changes." *Indiana Journal of Global Legal Studies* 13 (2): 503-41.

Le Monde. 2003. "M. Sarkozy obtient l'appui de la plus haute autorité sunnite sur le voile islamique." 12 December.

Marx, Karl, and Friedrich Engels. 1994. "The Communist Manifesto." In *Karl Marx: Selected Writings*, edited by Lawrence H. Simon, 157-86. Indianapolis, IN: Hackett.

McConnell, Michael W. 1990. "The Origins and Historical Understanding of Free Exercise of Religion." *Harvard Law Review* 103 (7): 1409-1517.

Ministère de l'éducation nationale de l'enseignement supérieur et de la recherche. 2005. "Application de la loi du 15 mars 2004 sur le port des signes religieux ostensibles dans les établissements d'enseignement publics." 2 July. http://lesrapports. ladocumentationfrancaise.fr/BRP/064000177/0000.pdf.

Monsma, Stephen V., and J. Christopher Soper. 1997. *The Challenge of Pluralism: Church and State in Five Democracies.* Lanham, MD: Rowman and Littlefield.

New York Times. 1995. "President Clinton's Memorandum on Religion in Schools." 13 July.

Rawls, John. 1996. *Political Liberalism.* New York: Columbia University Press.

Roy, Olivier. 2007. *Secularism Confronts Islam.* Translated by George Holoch. New York: Columbia University Press.

Sandel, Michael. 1998. "Religious Liberty: Freedom of Choice or Freedom of Conscience?" In *Secularism and Its Critics,* edited by Rajeev Bhargava, 73-93. New Delhi: Oxford University Press.

Scott, Joan Wallach. 2007. *The Politics of the Veil.* Princeton, NJ: Princeton University Press.

Segal, Jeffery A., and Albert D. Cover. 1989. "Ideological Values and the Votes of US Supreme Court Justices." *American Political Science Review* 83 (2): 557-65.

Stasi Commission. 2003. "Rapport au président de la République." 11 December. http://lesrapports.ladocumentationfrancaise.fr/brp/034000725/0000.pdf.

United States Government. 1997. "Guidelines on Religious Exercise and Religious Expression in the Federal Workplace." 14 August. http://clinton2.nara.gov/.

Witte, John, Jr., and M. Christian Green. 1996. "American Constitutional Experiment in Religious Human Rights: The Perennial Search for Principles." In *Religious Human Rights in Global Perspective: Legal Perspectives,* edited by Johan D. van der Vyver and John Witte Jr., 497-558. The Hague: Martinus Nijhoff.

Zaman (Istanbul). 2006a. "Peruklu Diye Okula Kaydını Yaptırmadılar." 6 July.

–. 2006b. "SDÜ İlahiyatta Şimdi de Peruk Yasağı." 11 September.

Zuber, Valentine. 2004. "La Commission Stasi et les paradoxes de la laïcité française." In *La Laïcité à l'épreuve: Religions et libertés dans le monde,* edited by Jean Baubérot, 29-39. N.p.: Universalis.

Part 3
Secularisms beyond the West

State Intervention in the Reform of a "Religion of Rules"

An Analysis of the Views of B.R. Ambedkar

Rinku Lamba

Chapter 8

An oft-disputed feature of secularism in independent India is the constitutional mandate of the state to intervene in religion. Article 25 (2) (b) of the Indian Constitution permits the state to intervene in religious reform for social welfare and to ensure that Hindu religious institutions of a public character are open to all classes and sections of Hindus.[1] Similarly, Article 17 involves direct intervention in religion since it abolishes the practice – in any form – of untouchability, arguably the central feature of the caste system endorsed by Hinduism, and makes the enforcement of any disability arising out of untouchability an offence punishable in accordance with law. Articles 17 and 25 (2) (b) are cited when critics point out the anomalous features of Indian secularism. In their view, such provisions contravene the principle of neutrality undergirding the strict separation of state and religion, which in turn is the core element of the doctrine of secularism (Chatterjee 1998; Smith 1964). The perceived lack of fit between the requirements of neutrality and the Indian practice of state intervention in the reform of Hinduism has even led some theorists to question the feasibility of the doctrine of secularism in modern India (Chatterjee 1998).

Rajeev Bhargava (1998, 2003) has underscored the notion that the doctrine of secularism mandates the observance not of strict separation but of "principled distance" between the state and religion to uphold the core values that constitute the secular doctrine. This chapter highlights aspects of the intellectual history that explain the adoption in independent India of constitutional clauses that allow the state to intervene in matters related to Hinduism for the sake of social welfare and reform through an analysis of the political thought of B.R. Ambedkar.[2]

B.R. Ambedkar (1891-1956) was a key – although sometimes lone – political thinker in colonial India influential in fashioning the political institutional architecture of postcolonial India. He was one of the chief architects of independent India's liberal-democratic Constitution, serving as chairperson of the Drafting Committee of the Indian Constituent Assembly. Born into the lowest group of the Hindu caste order – the Untouchables (called Dalits in contemporary India) – he overcame numerous social and financial obstacles to educate himself, earning his law and doctoral degrees from the London School of Economics and Columbia University and stoutly and systematically resisting the multiple forms of domination inflicted by the caste system in India.

For Ambedkar, religiously sanctioned caste inequalities constituted the chief obstacle to the attainment of democratic freedom in modern India. To address the comprehensive injustices inflicted by the caste order, Ambedkar endorsed a centralized, law-governed order for modern India, characterized by robustly representative political institutions that would not ignore minorities, and he often argued for separate electorates for the Dalits – the "depressed classes," as he called them. He also advocated affirmative-action schemes for Dalits many decades before such schemes were even discussed in Western democratic systems; he promoted publicly owned means of production, including state ownership of agricultural land so that members of the lower castes were not systematically disadvantaged in the ownership of a vital means of production; and he envisioned an interventionist secular state that would regulate the hold of religion on the sociopolitical system. He ardently supported the Indian state's role in reforming religion-based personal laws. For Ambedkar, the above arrangements were required to address injustice and to pursue the values of freedom, equality, and fraternity.[3]

In this chapter I highlight Ambedkar's views on the reform of India's majority religion, Hinduism, which he considered to be a "religion of rules" that authorized oppression of the Untouchables. For Ambedkar, a religion of rules is one that fixes for its adherents "habitual ways of doing things according to prescription," such that they do not need to exercise responsibility or judgment while enacting religious precepts.[4] The key point here is that rules are unlikely to encourage reflexivity since they prescribe ways of doing things in a manner that precludes agents from taking responsibility for their actions. "The rule may be right but the act is mechanical" (Ambedkar 2002, 98).

Ambedkar (2002, 300) advocated a "Religion of Principles, which alone can lay claim to being a true religion." Whereas rules are "practical," principles are "intellectual; they are useful methods of judging things." A rule prescribes a specific course of action; a principle does not. A principle may be wrong, but the acts that flow from its observance could still be classified as "conscious and responsible." Moreover, "a religious act may not be a correct act but must at least be a responsible act" (ibid., 298).

Even more strictly, for Ambedkar (2002, 299), Hinduism's rule-bound nature ultimately disqualified it from being classified as a religion. "What the Hindus call religion is really Law or at best legalized class-ethics. Frankly, I refuse to call this code of ordinances, as religion." If Hinduism were "truly" a religion, it would not deprive its adherents of a "moral life of freedom and spontaneity" and reduce them to a "more or less anxious and servile conformity to externally imposed rules."

But the worst aspect of Hinduism as a religion of rules, for Ambedkar (2002, 299), was that it sanctioned an iniquitous social scheme as the work of "Prophets or Lawgivers" and therefore deemed this scheme final and fixed.[5] The immutability attributed to its sectarian scheme cramped and crippled its adherents, depriving them of their humanity by forcing them to live by codes of conduct unsuited to conditions and circumstances that varied for different people and epochs. As long as a caste-based scheme enjoyed the status of "religion" its adherents would be wary of bringing about any change "because the idea of religion is generally speaking not associated with the idea of change" (ibid., 299).

Ambedkar (2002, 300) did not want his critique of Hinduism to imply that he was against religion per se. He was not coy, however, regarding his preference for a religion of principles and for the reform of rules-based social forms such as the Hinduism of his time. Much of Ambedkar's (ibid., 81) thought may be viewed as a systematic attempt to restrict and reform Hinduism's influence in the domains of the social and the political in order to give all persons a "chance for active and direct participation in the regulation of the terms upon which associated life shall be sustained."

In this chapter I suggest that, given his understanding of the structure of the caste system and its sanction by Hinduism, Ambedkar considered the prospects for internally generated reform to be bleak. His analysis of caste and its ill consequences precluded optimism regarding the possibility of internally generated change *transforming* Hinduism into a religion of principles. Still, Ambedkar did not give up on the task of *altering* Hinduism, and he looked to the agencies of the state to effect this reformist task. His aim – less grandiose than transformation but not a modest task – was to employ the services of the state to at least stall the injustices perpetuated by the caste-ridden religion of rules that he saw Hinduism to be.

Evident in the following analysis is the Ambedkarite perspective that constitutional provisions mandating state intervention in Hinduism – far from being anomalous – should be recognized as key and indispensable features of Indian secularism. The generally accepted explanation that the lack of a central authority within Hinduism necessitated the choice of an interventionist state to reform aspects of this religion (Bhargava 2003) might be replaced by the concept that the very structure and terms of membership within the Hindu social and political order – what Ambedkar (2002, 294) termed a "graded system of sovereignties" – made Hinduism incapable of internally generating the changes necessary for it to become the foundation of a political community committed to liberty, equality, and fraternity. If this is the case, the Indian reliance on the instrumentalities of the secular state to address injustices resulting from the relations of domination sanctioned by caste-ridden Hinduism can be considered well-nigh indispensable.

Ambedkar is one of the most significant Dalit voices in colonial and independent India. This chapter attempts to offer a Dalit perspective on religion and the role of the state in regulating certain kinds of religion. Also, I seek to strengthen the notion that the inclusion in the Indian Constitution of provisions such as Article 25 (2) (b) can be read as an affirmation of his perspective, which endorsed state regulation of religion in the interest of individual freedom and equality.

However, Ambedkar's political views regarding improvement of the plight of the Untouchables, or the "depressed classes," should not be considered predominantly a bid to secure institutional benefits distributable to minorities (see Tejani 2007) but can more profitably be understood as consonant with his broader vision of how a democratic political community must be constituted – a vision irreducible to politics conducted along the axes of majorities and minorities. Ambedkar anticipated difficulties in transforming Hinduism internally because beneficiaries of its hierarchically arranged order, he predicted, would never endorse progressive change and because their religion attached a certain immutability to sanctioned – indeed, required – practices such as untouchability.

For those deemed Untouchables, this was highly problematic, not least because they were denied personhood and subjected to subhuman treatment. But it was also highly problematic within Ambedkar's broader political ideals. He deemed "dhamma" to be a code of moral conduct that ideally should inform state policy (Ambedkar 2002, 57-59), and he hoped to enable a social and political order that observed "right relations between man and man in all spheres of life"; this order reflected his understanding of the notion of "righteousness" (ibid., 58). Untouchability and other abominable practices sanctioned by religions such as Hinduism were, therefore, problematic not only because they denied Dalits personhood but also because such practices had negative implications for the requirements of a robustly associational political order. For Ambedkar, institutions of the state had instrumental value in generating a kind of political community that would require regulation of certain kinds of religion, such as Hinduism.

It is possible to find in Ambedkar's arguments for the annihilation of caste a sophisticated understanding of the relationship between an individual and his or her group membership – one with a concern for individual liberty that neither negates a person's group affiliation nor prioritizes it in a culturally communitarian sense. Arguably, the views of Ambedkar, alongside those of other Indian thinkers such as Jotiba Phule (Deshpande 2002) and Mahadev Govind Ranade (1992), represent a strand of modern Indian political thought deeply committed to individual liberty even while couched in language deeply mindful of individuals' group identities; I will focus on Ambedkar's conception of individual liberty, which provides sufficient grounds to question claims regarding the absence of support for individual liberty in modern Indian thought advanced by scholars such as Pratap Bhanu Mehta (2003)[6] and Sunil Khilnani (2009).[7] Also, focusing on Ambedkar's observations in this regard can sharpen the suggestion that secularists can adopt a balanced view of the importance of group life and individual liberty without exclusively or simple-mindedly valorizing or condemning either of the two values. This would be in keeping with the implications for thinking about the value to be attached to freedom for individuals in the context of a commitment to group-centred ways of being that stem from Rajeev Bhargava's notion of "principled distance."

The remainder of this chapter is divided into two sections. The next section focuses on what Ambedkar anticipated as the problems posed by unreformed Hinduism and its caste structure for the development of a desirable political community. He noted that caste consciousness thwarts any potential for "society" owing to its exclusionary nature. The discussion in this section outlines the kinds of group life that Ambedkar criticized and also highlights that his emphasis on an ideally associative and communicative political community did not neglect the importance of liberty for individuals. Given the problems caste posed for sustaining a robust political community, a question arises: How to annihilate caste? The final section of the chapter directly addresses this question and outlines the reasons for Ambedkar's skepticism regarding an internally generated reform of Hinduism. In addition to the difficulties of internal reform posed by the graded sovereignties of caste, the absence of progressive leadership by the intellectual class in India (i.e., the Brahmins, who were also unfortunately the beneficiaries of caste-based advantage) posed a severe obstacle to changing the hierarchical structure endorsed by Hindu religion. As a result, the institutions of a secular state would be indispensable in putting into place the necessary restriction and reform of Hindu religion.

To be sure, the details of many of Ambedkar's policy measures for state restriction of Hinduism sound dire enough to classify his position on Hindu religion as hostile.[8] Be that as it may, the analytical point that requires acknowledgment and evaluation here is that state institutions were indispensable to the process of chastening Hinduism so that it would not pose an impediment to the development of a democratic political community.

Caste-Based Problems for the Development of a Political Community

Caste and the Problem of Sectarianism

Ambedkar held that one fundamental problem with the caste system was that it destroyed public spirit and any sense of public charity. A narrow sense of belonging to one caste, said Ambedkar (2002, 275), had the consequence of restricting each person's sense of charity and appreciation of merit to those inside of his or her caste group: "Suffering as such calls for no response ... There is sympathy but not for men of other caste." This sectarian disposition of caste, then, precluded the development of fraternity, which Ambedkar posited as a feature of an ideal democratic society. Ambedkar's (ibid., 276) explication of fraternity distinguished between democracy as "a form of government" and as "a mode of associated living": "Democracy is not merely a form of government. It is primarily a mode of associated living, of conjoint communicated experience. It is essentially an attitude of respect and reverence towards fellowmen." The crucial point in this commentary on democracy was his firm belief in the necessity of opportunities for *com-municated* experience – that is, the importance of "points of contact" and "possibilities of interaction between different groups" (ibid., 285).

The plurality of distinctive or diverse groups, even within a particular re-ligion, does not appear to have been of concern to Ambedkar (2002, 285) in his consideration of the requirements of a democratic political community:

> In the world of action, the individual is one limit and society the other. Between them lie all sorts of associative arrangements of lesser and larger scope, families, friendship, cooperative associations, business combines, political parties, bands of thieves and robbers. These small groups are usually firmly welded together and are often as exclusive as castes. They have a narrow and intensive code, which is often anti-social. This is true of every society, in Europe as well as in Asia.

In keeping with these observations about the existence of various types of "exclusive" group, Ambedkar willingly acknowledged the presence of caste-*type* groups within religions as diverse as Islam, Sikhism, and Christianity. Given the factual existence of plural groups within society, what is it that distinguishes his ideal society from a nonideal one? In an-swering this question, especially in the context of distinguishing between caste systems among Hindus and non-Hindus, Ambedkar (2002, 285) out-lined acceptable versus unacceptable forms of group life:

> The questions to be asked in determining whether a given society is an ideal society is not whether there are groups in it, because groups exist in all societies. The question to be asked in determining what is an ideal society are: How numerous and varied are the interests which are consciously shared by the groups? How full and free is the interplay with other forms of associations? Are the forces that separate groups and classes more numer-ous than the forces that unite? What social significance is attached to this group life? *Is its exclusiveness a matter of custom and convenience or is it a matter of religion?* (Emphasis by author)

Ambedkar did not systematically address each of these questions, but they served as a framework for differentiating between caste in Hinduism and caste in Christianity, Islam, and Sikhism and for concluding that the existence of caste groups within other religions did not provide grounds to condone their presence in Hinduism. The groupism spawned by the Hindu caste system went beyond the acceptable limits of group-specific ways of being; Hindu religion sanctioned and thus entrenched group life in a way that yielded undemocratic consequences. Its entrenchment of exclusionary forms of group life eliminated its potential to generate sociality, something other religions appeared not to lack. There "is no integrating force among the Hindus to counteract the disintegration caused by caste while among the non-Hindus there are plenty of these organic filaments which bind them together" (Ambedkar 2002, 285).

Caste within Hinduism provided a basis for identity that fostered jealous guardianship of criteria for group membership. A breach of membership rules would result in excommunication from the caste group, which entailed for the outcast the cessation of social ties with fellow human beings. The absence of communicative ties between the outcast and the group posed a tremendous obstacle to the enactment of a robust political community. Instead of enabling associational life the caste system became the basis for severely demarcating members from nonmembers through unreflexive measures (including excommunication) that yielded undemocratic consequences. Ambedkar (2002, 286) maintained that without these rules that marked members from nonmembers, Hindus could not feel sure of what sort of beings they were.

But the most important difference between caste in Hinduism and caste in the other religions was that

> caste among the non-Hindus has no religious consecration; but among the Hindus most decidedly it has. Among the non-Hindus, caste is only a practice, not a sacred institution ... Religion does not compel the non-Hindus to take the same attitude towards caste. If Hindus wish to break caste, their religion will come in their way. But it will not be so in the case of non-Hindus. (Ambedkar 2002, 286)

This religious sanctioning of caste made it difficult for adherents of Hinduism to generate "points of contact" and "possibilities of interaction between different groups which exist within it" (ibid., 285). A question arises here: What is it about religion's backing that makes caste an insuperable barrier to progressive change? Before addressing this question, however, it is worth getting a fuller sense of why Ambedkar thought caste posed impediments to Hinduism's ability to contribute to the making of "society."

How Caste Thwarts the Possibility of Society within Hinduism

In his deliberations on caste, Ambedkar (2002, 267) advanced the claim that "Hindu society as such does not exist." It was merely a collection of castes. The segregated existence encouraged by caste resulted in Hindus lacking "consciousness of kind." "In every Hindu the consciousness that exists is the consciousness of his caste. That is the reason why the Hindus cannot be said to form a society or a nation." Indians, therefore, did not constitute a nation – or a society (Ambedkar regarded the concepts as interchangeable). The occurrence of similarities in habits and customs across the subcontinent could not fulfill the requirements for qualifying Indians as a "society" or a "nation." "Men do not become a society by living in physical proximity any more than a man ceases to be a member of his society by living so many miles away from other men" (ibid., 268).

Although Ambedkar (2002, 268) believed that culture was spread by diffusion, such that when the habits, customs, beliefs, and thoughts of one group were taken on by another group there could appear to be a similarity between the two, he also believed that

> similarity in certain things is not enough to constitute a society. Men constitute a society because they have things which they possess in common. To have similar things is totally different from possessing things in common. And the only way by which men can come to possess things in common with one another is by being in communication with one another ... For that purpose what is necessary is for a man to share and participate in a common activity so that the same emotions are aroused in him that animate the others. Making the individual a sharer or partner in the associated activity so that he feels its success as his success, its failure as his failure is the real thing that binds men and makes a society of them. The caste system prevents common activity and by preventing common activity it has prevented the Hindus from becoming a society with a unified life and a consciousness of its own being.

However, Ambedkar's rather collectivist disposition, evident in this quotation, must be viewed alongside his unequivocal commitment to providing individuals the power to resist, question, and even transform their group's way of doing things, aspects of which will be addressed later in this chapter.

Ambedkar was not celebrating just any kind of "common activity." Communication and common action – by persons belonging to different groups – were also to be "representative of the interests, aims, and aspirations of all the various groups" involved (Ambedkar 2008, 67). When left to themselves, individual groups created their own distinctive variety of what Ambedkar (ibid.) termed "like-mindedness." Persons came to be like-minded *within* their group by participating in the activities of this group. Like-mindedness *among* or *between* groups – so "essential for a harmonious life, social or political" – depended upon groups allowing "endosmosis." Endosmosis rendered possible "a resocialization" of attitudes that stemmed from isolation of groups (ibid.). In arguing for common action that could generate a citizenry who were "sympathetically like-minded," Ambedkar (ibid., 77) emphasized that such activity would have to reflect the interests of all groups. Furthermore, endosmosis and resocialization obliged groups to permit "outsiders" to participate in the said processes. Religiously backed restrictions on interactions among *all* thus rendered restricted persons unfree to participate in codetermining the course of their political lives.

Moreover, the unrestricted interaction generated through inclusive political participation could also aid in transforming existing divisive and exclusionary "attitudes." In 1919, making a case for communal electorates, Ambedkar (2008, 83-84) said,

> An active participation in an associated life ... will not leave unaffected the dispositions and attitudes of those who participate ... the existing set attitude representing the diverse castes and groups will be dissolved only if the diverse groups meet together and take part in a common activity. Such changes of disposition and attitudes will not be ephemeral but will, in their turn influence associated life outside the Council Hall ... Thus those who condemn communal representation on the score of perpetuating the existing divisions will welcome it, on reflection, as a potent solvent for dissolving them.

Resocialization was necessary to offset the worst feature of the Hindu caste system: its "anti-social spirit." "An anti-social spirit is found wherever one group has 'interests of its own' which shut it out from full interaction with other groups, so that its prevailing purpose is protection of what it has got." The antisocial spirit among castes was manifest even within a caste and among subcastes; these were all just "so many warring groups each living for itself and its selfish ideal" (Ambedkar 2002, 269). This antisocial bias curbed the ability of those outside of one's group to freely participate in negotiating the terms of collective life.

Ambedkar, then, clearly perceived serious defects in the ability of the Hindu social order to contribute to an associative and communicative political community where members would be motivated to consider matters of general interest. To the extent that the caste system prevented individuals from thinking outside of their narrow group-based interest, Hinduism required a transformation consistent with its prior commitment to fostering a social and political order that bound persons into society: at the most, a change radical enough to make it a religion of principles; at the least, a change progressive enough to keep it from yielding the ill consequences of a religion of rules.

Caste and the Problems for Individual Liberty

Alongside his commitment to themes such as public spirit and society, Ambedkar was mindful of the importance of the kind of freedom otherwise termed *individual liberty* that would characterize persons participating in creating society. In fact, one can go so far as to say that his notions of public-spiritedness and like-mindedness presupposed individuals who were free from restrictions – such as those perpetuated by caste – in drawing up the terms of their collective lives.

Indeed, for Ambedkar (2002, 274), the beginning of all reform of institutions such as caste was "the assertion by the individual of his own opinions and beliefs, his own independence and interest as over against group standards, group authority and group interests." However, he importantly added that "whether the reform will continue depends upon what scope the group affords for such individual assertion." If groups are "tolerant" and "fair-minded" towards individuals seeking to bring about progressive reform, these individuals might then transform the perspectives of fellow members. But if groups stifle individuals who think differently, by either restricting their efforts or seeking to reduce their efforts to naught, "reform will die out."

Ambedkar held that Hinduism restricted the efforts of individuals to break barriers of caste. Excommunication was the tool used to deal with any person guilty of breaking the rules of caste. And excommunication, for Ambedkar (2002, 274), was a form of punishment akin to death: "There is really little to choose between excommunication and death" because excommunication "involves a complete cesser of social intercourse." He added that although it could be the case that an individual did not "get on with his fellows" it was also true "that he cannot do without them." "He would like to have the society of his fellows on his terms. If he cannot get it on his terms then he will be ready to have it on any terms even amounting to complete surrender. This is because he cannot do without society." The need for human society could compel persons willingly to become unequal partners in relationships drawn on terms they did not accept. If caste could impose its fiat on dissenting individuals, and on those it excluded, it facilitated the adoption of subordinate positions by the nonhegemonic groups involved.

Ambedkar pushed for a quality of freedom that would allow individuals not only to resist the diktat of their group but even to seek to transform the habits of their group. The liberty to do so was vital for effecting reform via protest against the imposition of an external will either through customs or by any dominant subgroup within the group. For Ambedkar, the powerful caste tool of excommunication stifled individual liberty and precluded the possibility of reform or dissent from *within* caste groups. Reducing the power of such rules of caste required that they be invalidated through the intervention of nonsectarian law (Ambedkar 2002, 274-75). He endorsed active laws against such rules of caste.

Ambedkar, then, demonstrably adopted an instrumentalist affirmation of individual liberty. The notion of freedom evident in his bid to annihilate caste was one that allowed a single person holding a minority perspective to challenge the power of custom and dominant group sentiment on a particular issue. But did Ambedkar prioritize liberty for persons only when such was necessary for reform? Did his conception of freedom also contain space for the conventional understanding of negative liberty, where the individual is to be free from external interference in his or her life pursuits, with the caveat that those acts that impinge upon a like freedom for others must be circumscribed?

Unmistakably, Ambedkar was mindful of the importance of liberty for individuals even outside of reform projects. Ambedkar (2002, 276), for example, referred to the "effective and competent use of a person's powers," which translated into the liberty to choose one's profession. Ambedkar contrasted such freedom to choose a profession with its absence, a state he labelled "slavery." To object to this liberty in choosing one's profession would be to perpetuate slavery:

> Slavery does not merely mean a legalized form of subjection. It means a state of society in which some men are forced to accept from others the purposes which control their conduct. This condition obtains even where there is no slavery in the legal sense. It is found where, as in the caste system, some persons are compelled to carry on certain prescribed callings which are not of their choice. (Ibid.)

But an approach that searches for "negative liberty" may not be the best way of capturing the sense in which Ambedkar sought to pursue freedom for the individual. Crucially and fortunately, his statement above contains a notion of freedom that robustly connects individuals' liberty to their social and political context. In seeking to secure persons from conditions akin to slavery Ambedkar was making a statement against the imposition of external will and social power on them; this should be viewed as a key component of reasoning in favour of state intervention in the regulation of religiously sanctioned power that coerces individuals into a state of slavery. In fact, contrary to Khilnani's (2009) view that "freedom as a dimension of the social and political worlds ... as a quality and principle of relations between human beings free to exercise choice" was not an important strand of modern Indian political thought, I argue that there is here evidence to suggest that intellectual traditions in the subcontinent were properly touched by concern for individual freedom and that this concern even influenced the constitutionally mandated secular framework adopted after independence.

That Ambedkar's ideas for regulating religion are irreducible to a discourse of collectivities and "general interest" can be corroborated by the importance he attached to the granting of "free initiative and opportunity to every individual" as an important societal goal.[9] In the context of writing about engendering democratic government, he stated, "The growth of personality is the highest aim of society. Social arrangement must secure free initiative and opportunity to every individual to assume any role he is capable of assuming provided it is socially desirable" (Ambedkar 2008, 70). One of the most abominable consequences of the practice of untouchability was that it arrested the growth of the personality of those deemed Untouchables. Their very "persona" had been "confiscated" owing to the dehumanizing "socio-religious disabilities" to which they were subjected. Their "primary" interest in securing "that common respect which one man owes to another" was hidden from view because they were "so socialized as never to complain of their low estate" (ibid., 75).

How to Annihilate Caste?

Reform and the Need to Acknowledge the Religious Sanction behind Caste-Based Domination

Ambedkar (2008, 287-88) indubitably held that "progress" required changing the Hindu caste system: "You cannot build anything on the foundations of caste. You cannot build up a nation, you cannot build up a morality.

Anything that you will build on the foundations of caste will crack and will never be a whole." Abolishing the caste-based social order was a goal of supreme importance to him: *"How to bring about the reform of the Hindu social order? How to abolish caste?"* (ibid., 288, emphasis by author). In the course of endorsing the significance of making interdining and inter-marriage matters of common course, Ambedkar (ibid., 289) pondered why these practices would have the consequence of weakening caste. "Why," he asked, "is it that a large majority of Hindus do not inter-dine and do not inter-marry? Why is it that your cause is not popular?" (ibid.). It was the sacredness attached by Hinduism to observance of caste rules in marriage and dining that lay at the root of the problem. Ambedkar further stated that the caste consciousness that so deeply forbade customs such as interdining was a "state of mind" not reducible to physical barriers. Its destruction required the obliteration of "notional" barriers as well (ibid.). Even though caste led to conduct "so gross as to be called man's inhumanity to man," Ambedkar (ibid.) noted that Hindus observed its rulings not because they were "inhuman or wrong-headed" but because they were "deeply religious." "To ask people to give up caste is to ask them to go contrary to their fundamental religious notions" (ibid., 291).

For Ambedkar, reformers such as Mohandas Gandhi who sought to abolish untouchability paid too little attention to persuading people to cease their belief in the sanctity of the Shastras in which they grounded their conduct. It was no use "seeking refuge in quibbles" and telling people that the Shastras, properly (logically or grammatically) understood, did not sanction caste because "what matters is how the *Shastras* have been understood by the people" (Ambedkar 2008, 290). Ambedkar (ibid.) wanted to follow in the footsteps of the Buddha and Guru Nanak, who not only discarded the Shastras but also denied their authority: "You must have the courage to tell the Hindus, that what is wrong with them is their religion – the religion which has produced in them this notion of the sacredness of caste. Will you show that courage?"

Limits on the Possibility of Internally Generated Reform to Annihilate Caste

Ambedkar (2008, 290) classified the task of reforming the Hindu social order as herculean, if not "well-nigh impossible." It necessitated the destruction of a deep-seated sense of sacredness and divinity associated with caste and also of "the authority of the *Shastras* and the *Vedas.*"

Ambedkar identified at least three sources of difficulty for internal reform. First was the anticipated role of the Brahmins, putatively the intellectual class in India. Ambedkar (2008, 293) was of the view that the intellectual class in any political community had a leadership role in determining the destiny of the community: "The intellectual class is the class which can foresee; it is the class which can advise and give lead. In no country does the mass of the people live the life of intelligent thought and action. It is largely imitative and follows the intellectual class." Even as Ambedkar (ibid.) accorded a country's intellectual class such a leadership role, he held that "intellect by itself [is] no virtue" but only a means, and the use of this means depended upon the ends pursued: "An intellectual man can be a good man but he can easily be a rogue. Similarly an intellectual class may be a band of high-souled persons, ready to help, ready to emancipate erring humanity or it may easily be a gang of crooks or a body of advocates of a narrow clique from which it draws its support." Of course, if the intellectual class was "honest, independent and disinterested," it could be trusted to "take the initiative and give a proper lead" when crises arose (ibid.).

What could be expected of the Indian intellectual class, the Brahmins, in bringing about progressive change of the social order? Ambedkar noted that in India, pitifully and regrettably, the existence of the intellectual class was bound up with one single caste and shared its interests and aspirations. Constituted of the Brahmin caste, the intellectual class regarded itself as the "custodian of the interest of that caste, rather than of the interests of the country" (Ambedkar 2008, 293).

Writing in the period of anticolonial struggle, he observed that although Brahmins formed the "vanguard" of the movement for political and economic reform, they were not to be found even as "camp-followers in the army raised to break down the barricades of caste. Is there any hope of the Brahmins ever taking up a lead in the future in this matter?" (Ambedkar 2008, 291). Even as Ambedkar was mindful of the presence of "secular Brahmins" who would take up cudgels on behalf of those seeking to break caste (as opposed to "priestly Brahmins" who did not endorse reform), he was keenly aware that the break-up of the caste system would have adverse consequences for the Brahmin caste: "Is it reasonable to expect that the Brahmins will ever consent to lead a movement the ultimate result of which is to destroy the power and prestige of the Brahmin caste?" (ibid., 292).

Ambedkar's (2008, 292) response to both queries above was negative. Secular and priestly Brahmins were "kith and kin"; they were "two arms of the same body" and were "bound to fight for the existence of the other." Ambedkar appeared to bestow upon Brahmins a natural and inherent inability to become revolutionaries. For him, the Brahminical class possessed a constitutive barrier to revolutionary change that barred it from qualifying as a reliable agent for the annihilation of caste (ibid.).

Brahmins not only formed the intellectual class of the country but were also as a class "held in great reverence by the rest of the Hindus. The Hindus are taught that the Brahmins are *Bhudevas* (Gods on earth) ... The Hindus are taught that Brahmins alone can be their teachers" (Ambedkar 2008, 293). Ambedkar (ibid.; see also 317-18) noted that, "when such an intellectual class, which holds the rest of the community in its grip, is opposed to the reform of caste, the chances of success in a movement for the break-up of the caste system appear to me very, very remote."

The second source of difficulty for internal reform of the Hindu social order was that it would require dismantling the proudly maintained hierarchical structure of the caste system. Not only did the Hindu caste system foster an exclusionary and selfish disposition among and within castes, but it also engendered what Ambedkar (2002, 294) called "a graded system of sovereignties." Caste not only divided persons into separate communities but also

> place[d] these communities in a graded order one above the other in social status. Each caste takes its pride and its consolation in the fact that in the scale of castes it is above some other caste ... The higher the grade of the caste, the greater the number of ... rights and the lower the grade, the lesser their number. Now this gradation ... makes it impossible to organize a common front against the caste system. If a caste claims the right to inter-dine and inter-marry with another caste placed above it, it is frozen, instantly it is told by mischief-mongers ... that it will have to concede inter-dining and inter-caste marriage with castes below it! All are slaves to the caste system. But all the slaves are not equal in status. (Ibid.)

Because some "slaves" would lose greater prestige and power than others, Ambedkar concluded that the prospect of a general mobilization of Hindus against the caste system was bleak.

The third impediment to internal social change was persuading Hindus that the observation of caste was "contrary to reason" (Ambedkar 2002, 294). The inability to act morally, which for Ambedkar (ibid., 297) meant action in accordance with reason, deprived Hindus of the crucial where-withal required for the rejection of caste. Hindus' ability to act in accordance with reason appeared to be hindered, for Ambedkar (ibid., 297-98), by the unreasonable nature of their religious texts: "You must not forget that if you wish to bring about a breach in the system then you have got to apply dynamite to the *Vedas* and the *Shastras,* which deny any part to reason, to *Vedas* and *Shastras,* which deny any part to morality ... Nothing else will avail. This is my considered view of the matter."

The Need for External Regulation of Hinduism's Caste Order

Since the reform of Hinduism through its democratization in consonance with notions of liberty, equality, and fraternity was unlikely to be internally generated, Ambedkar (2008, 301) proposed external regulation. The state and the law would exercise the required regulatory power. Hindu law had for too long dictated the functioning of state power. The *separation* of state machinery from the logical entailments of Hindu law – and the destruction of this law itself – necessitated re-envisioning the constitution and purposes of law and state such that these agencies would serve general "democratic" rather than sectarian interests. Freed from the shackles of religious diktat, these agencies – through institutional designs such as mechanisms of representation and policy measures such as regulation of the Hindu priesthood (Ambedkar 2008, 300-1) – could offset "anti-social" sectarian interests backed by religion. Hinduism's sectarian potential had to be curtailed in order to enable the development of both like-mindedness and the robustly associational partnerships required to enact and sustain a democratic political community. And this curtailment was to be achieved by consolidating a political power not bound to a "religion of rules." This was a crucial element in Ambedkar's program to annihilate Hindu caste power.

Ambedkar's (2008, 301) bid for religious reform through the democratic state related to caste's hierarchical structure. It was not the absence of a central authority within Hinduism but the complex graded system of sovereignties that led him to endorse state intervention in Hindu religion. Even as a verdict on Ambedkar's rather Hobbesian prescriptions for regulating priesthood in Hinduism is pending, scholars must acknowledge and evaluate his underlying analytical point that a religion whose precepts discourage democratic social change requires regulation.

To the extent that one acknowledges the significance of sociological aspects of religion, it becomes difficult to dismiss Ambedkar's predisposition

towards an interventionist secular state. Religion, like law and government, is a means by which society exercises its control over the individual to
maintain social order (Ambedkar 2002, 227). Ambedkar considered it erroneous to view religion as apolitical – as only "individual, private and personal." Viewing religion in this manner could become a source of "positive
mischief" (ibid., 225). He further stated,

> Equally mistaken is the view that religion is the flowering of special reli-
> gious instinct inherent in the nature of the individual. The correct view is
> that religion like language is social for the reason that either is essential for
> social life and the individual has to have it because without it he cannot
> participate in the life of the society. (Ibid.)

Aside from the crucial point that religion, like language, is a social practice,
Ambedkar here underscores religion's capacity to provide *but equally to deny*
its adherents a crucial basis for community and solidarity. The depressed
classes, or Untouchables, would have to exit from the Hindu fold because it
denied them the opportunity for kinship typically expected from religion.
Instead of recognizing all of its members as kindred and as equally entitled
to rights, Hinduism sanctioned untouchability, "the lowest depth to which
the degradation of a human being" could be carried (ibid., 229). To overcome the social isolation spawned by a Hinduism that espoused untouchability and to participate in the community of kinship provided by a religion
that "universalized and equalized all values of life," Ambedkar (ibid., 230)
even endorsed exit from Hinduism and conversion to another more equitable religion.[10]

Notes

1 The codification of Hindu family law via a series of legislative measures enacted by
  the Indian Parliament in the 1950s offers a good example of the Indian state's involvement in the reform of Hinduism in accordance with Article 25 (2) (b). Another
  example of intervention sanctioned by this article is the directive requiring the
  opening of Hindu places of public worship to all Hindus, including those stigmatic-
  ally classified by Hinduism as Untouchables.
2 For this chapter I draw chiefly, although not only, on Ambedkar's important text
  "Annihilation of Caste" (in Ambedkar 2002).
3 Independent India's constitutional politics have clearly been influenced by these
  views of Ambedkar. The adoption of affirmative-action schemes for Dalits, the institution of reserved constituencies for Dalits in electoral processes, the presence of
  constitutionally entrenched social and cultural rights for religious and cultural

minorities in India, and the inclusion of a constitutionally supported mandate for the Indian state to regulate religion are all legacies of Ambedkarite thought. Ambedkar's reliance on the law and the secular state to address the malady of caste and thereby enable the pursuit of a democratic order can be viewed as a contrast to Mohandas Gandhi's approach to rectifying the injustices perpetrated by caste-based social forms. Gandhi fought staunchly against the practice of untouchability, but he was not a strong supporter of dependence on the instrumentalities of the law and state to achieve a morally desirable sociopolitical order. For him, such an order would have to emerge primarily through the moral regeneration of each individual in this order. Self-regulation on the part of individuals through internally generated efforts and internally generated law was his chosen path for moving towards a morally appropriate order. An additional point of difference between Ambedkar and Gandhi was that the latter was able to launch struggles against untouchability without rejecting *varnashrama dharma,* the Vedic system that sanctioned caste, something for which Ambedkar criticized Gandhi (see Ambedkar 2002, 149-72, 306-19). Still, it would not be fruitful to posit Ambedkar and Gandhi as interlocutors who only disagreed. For example, both not only espoused robust notions of freedom but also shared the idea that the achievement of freedom was linked to the presence of law, whether inwardly or externally generated.

4 In stressing the role of reflexivity and judgment Ambedkar expected no less of believers than do contemporary political theorists who consider a disposition of reflection, judgment, and questioning to be compatible with the disposition of a faithful adherent of a religion. For examples, see Charles Taylor (1985) and Shelley Burtt (2003).

5 He called them "iniquitous" because the laws upheld were not the same for one class as for another (Ambedkar 2002, 299).

6 Says Mehta (2003): "One of the more revealing oddities in the Indian debate over secularism is that a defence of individual freedom rarely figures prominently in defences of secularism. While many different conceptions of secularism dot our political landscape, none of them makes individual freedom explicitly a political value."

7 Says Khilnani (2009): "The decades before 1947 produced a rich language of freedom – but ... There were limited efforts to imagine a society in which personal freedoms might have priority."

8 For some of the reforms he endorsed see Ambedkar (2002, 300, 301; 2008, 75-76).

9 Further evidence of the importance Ambedkar attached to conventional liberties is available in his observations about what an Untouchable is deprived of when treated as a noncitizen (see Ambedkar 2008, 75-76).

10 Kinship is "by no means a small value to an individual." Kinship engenders the "sympathetic resentment" that members of a community experience "for a wrong done to their fellow" (Ambedkar 2002, 232).

Works Cited

Ambedkar, B.R. 2002. *The Essential Writings of B.R. Ambedkar.* Edited by Valerian Rodrigues. New Delhi: Oxford University Press.

–. 2008. *B.R. Ambedkar: Perspectives on Social Exclusion and Inclusive Policies.* Edited by S. Thorat and N. Kumar. New Delhi: Oxford University Press.

Something Got Lost in Translation
From "Secularism" to "Separation between Politics and Religion" in Taiwan

André Laliberté

In that part of the global discussion that puts a positive value on the secular state as a model to manage religious diversity or that relates to religions in ways that are respectful of both religious believers and nonbelievers, an increasing number of voices point to the necessity of looking at non-Western models. An abundance of literature points to Turkey, for example, as an Islamic society that has successfully established a secular state (Hurd 2008; Kuru 2006). An even more considerable body of literature discusses the case of India as an experiment in secularism that could serve as an inspiration for the world (Bhargava 2004). Yet there is little on the experience of East Asian societies in the establishment of secular states or in the failure to do so. This oversight is all the more surprising since East Asia stands out as a region of the world where the institution of the secular state has not been significantly challenged, in contrast to what is observed elsewhere in South Asia, among Islamic countries, and arguably in Western societies. This chapter seeks to contribute to correcting this oversight by pointing to some important characteristics of the secular state in East Asia. The argument advanced is that the lack of opposition to the secular state in East Asia may have more to do with the idiosyncratic ways that the principle of secularism has been interpreted and adopted in the region than it does with an acceptance of the liberal norms that tend to underpin the secular state in North America and, to a degree, western Europe.[1]

The Case for Including East Asia in Discussing the Secular State

This absence of East Asia in comparative discussion of the secular state is a serious problem that needs to be addressed. One-quarter of the world's population lives under the direct administration of East Asian governments – a greater percentage of the global population than the total number of citizens in the Americas and western Europe, which stand as the models of secularism for the rest of the world. This absence has been long justified by proponents' belief that Western norms are hegemonic owing to Euro-American economic, political, and military supremacy. Given that the economic dominance of the West is currently being challenged and that East Asia has clearly emerged as the other centre of the world system, the lack of attention to this geographical area has become untenable. Ignoring East Asian secularism is also a weak policy prescription, as many societies might gain by learning about the absence of a substantial opposition to the ways that states interact with religion in the democratic societies of East Asia – Japan, the Republic of Korea (or South Korea), and Taiwan – where this opposition could legally express itself.

As mentioned, the discussion of the secular state is no longer limited to the Western experience but increasingly considers the experience of India as a starting point to discuss the virtues and problems of a secular state in societies experiencing deep religious diversity. Similar remarks can be made about Turkey, a republic routinely presented as an example of a society influenced by a non-Western religious tradition – Islam – that has successfully established a secular state. Together, India and Turkey show that the institutions of the secular state have been adapted to fit very different cultural contexts. But both cases also show that the secular state as a set of institutions cannot be easily exported. Both countries are facing strong movements that want to pull back from processes of institutional secularization under way for decades. Students of Indian politics must take into account the importance of a vocal Hindutva movement that claims to speak out in the name of a Hindu majority and that seeks to put into place a different form of secular state, more compatible with what they construe as the view of the majority. These demands, articulated by the Bharatiya Janata Party, have a major impact on Indian politics at the federal and state levels. In Turkey the Justice and Development Party, the ruling party since 2001, claims inspiration from a moderate version of Islam. Many Turks, rightly or wrongly, see in this party's success a threat to the secular state.

The Indian and Turkish cases, however, are only the tip of the iceberg in a global trend. Opposition to the secular state is occurring in societies influenced by traditions other than Hinduism or Islam. It also extends to societies historically influenced by Christianity. Whether it is the activism of the religious right in the United States as it attempts to impose its agenda, the efforts of the resurgent and nationalist Orthodox Church in Russia to restore previous privileges, or the Catholic Church episcopate's intervention in Latin America to prevent the passing of legislation on private matters contrary to its teachings, many religious believers oppose the secularization of their society. Western Europe and those societies of the New World that have been influenced by the British institutional legacy stand as anomalies in this respect: these societies have experienced few revisionist movements critical of the secular state.

It is within this context that a study of the three East Asian democracies matters for the study of secularization as a process, secularism as an ideology or a normative project, and in particular the secular state as a set of institutions dealing with religious diversity. One striking observation regarding the three East Asian democracies is the absence of political movements questioning the establishment of a secular state in the region. In this respect, the experience of these three East Asian societies appears similar to that of western Europe and the Anglo-Saxon societies of the New World, with the exception of the United States. What factors can explain this absence of religious contestation of secularism in these three East Asian states? Can other societies learn from the resilience of the secular state in this region?

One reason why there has been little resistance to the secular state in this region is the thought-provoking possibility that East Asian societies are not as thoroughly secularized as some of its elites claim. In particular, religion's importance in the public life of East Asia is more pervasive than is generally recognized, and state institutions in the region do not correspond to the liberal blueprint for a secular state as it is understood in North America. To put it differently, religious actors in East Asia do not believe that there is a secular state to oppose. Obviously, another explanation for the lack of opposition is that the state has been strong enough to prevent effective contestation by religious actors. But even though this argument is applicable to the People's Republic of China, the Socialist Republic of Vietnam,[2] and the Democratic People's Republic of Korea (or North Korea), it does not explain the contemporary situation of Japan, South Korea, or Taiwan, where this opposition is permissible.[3]

The incorporation of East Asian perspectives and the practices of its three democracies into discussions of the secular state is necessary to debate this issue within a global perspective, especially when international institutions want to impose norms informed primarily by the Western experience upon non-Western societies. Moreover, the approaches to religious diversity adopted by the East Asian democracies matter for another important reason: because of their shared heritage of Chinese classical culture, they can serve as a source of institutional models for the three other major East Asian states that are not democratic and where religious diversity is tightly controlled: China, Vietnam, and North Korea. Therefore, one caveat must be added: just as there are many institutional differences and forms of secular state within the Western world, there are at least two major orientations in East Asian states' approach to religious diversity, but both have grown out of a single tradition of statecraft inspired by China. These orientations can be described as "neotraditionalist" and "secular with East Asian characteristics." Before these models are described, some context is necessary.

The Secular State in East Asia

The prevalence of the secular state in East Asia is counterintuitive if one believes that the prerequisites for such a state include secularization at the level of society and a long history of relations between states and powerful religious institutions. In fact, and despite the claims made by some of its elites, the secularization of East Asian societies is questionable in many important dimensions. To start with, there is no religion in the region that has been strong enough institutionally to achieve a status comparable to Christianity in Europe or Islam in Muslim countries. Although some religious institutions have achieved important status historically, the state has more often asserted its authority over religion than religious institutions have interfered in politics to promote their interests. In sum, the view that the secular state prevails in East Asia rests on a narrower definition of the secular state as "state control of religion." This definition, however, does not correspond to the liberal and democratic view of what constitutes a secular state, namely noninterference from the state in religious affairs and no control of state affairs by any religion – what Alfred Stepan (2000) calls "twin toleration." China and the other East Asian socialist states are not secular states according to this liberal-democratic criterion; however, Japan, South Korea, and Taiwan have embraced it.

Questioning the Hegemony of Secularization and Secularism in East Asia

The claim that East Asian societies are secularized has been articulated most forcefully, and for decades, at the official level in the People's Republic of China, the Socialist Republic of Vietnam, and the Democratic People's Republic of Korea. This is not surprising since Marxist-Leninist parties of the past viewed religion as the "opiate of the masses" and traditional religious practices as the expression of "feudal society." Marxist-Leninists were not the only ones who held this dismissive view of religion. Liberal thinkers such as Hu Shi also looked at Chinese religions and metaphysics as "a black smoke" that needed to be wiped out and replaced by a science-based philosophy of life (de Bary, Chan, and Tan 1960, 179).

Within political science, discussions about the secular states usually uncritically accept the assumption that East Asian societies are secular – that is, devoid of any presence of religion in public affairs – and therefore that there is no point in discussing relations between the state and something that is deemed to be nonexistent. In their study of cultural change worldwide, Ronald Inglehart and Pippa Norris (2003, 54), for example, have noted that China displays a staggeringly low degree of religiosity (at 12 percent), with Japan, South Korea, and Vietnam (at below 50 percent) being in the same league as France, Scandinavian countries, Russia, and a few other countries previously ruled by a communist party. Taiwan stands slightly higher (at 55 percent). In comparison, Canada stands at 67 percent and the United States at 75 percent.

If one considers some East Asian governments' official statistics on religious practice, however, the picture of religiosity shows much more complexity, with wide discrepancies across the regions in the intensity of religious beliefs. Whereas barely one-third of the Chinese population is religious according to the State Council's own data, there are more religious believers in Japan than there are residents in the whole country, owing to the double religious affiliation of many residents. Yet the most significant finding by far is that religiosity has increased, not declined, in recent decades. Chinese statistics until 2005, for what they are worth, claimed that only 100 million people maintained religious beliefs, but surveys conducted in that year revealed that the number of people who called themselves religious was three times higher (Wu 2007). The same is true for statistics on numbers of religious believers in South Korea and Taiwan, which have increased rather than decreased as these societies have embarked on their "economic miracle."

Inglehart and Norris (2003) point to an index of religiosity in their study, but they do not say much about a decrease or increase in religious belief. Moreover, the situation is more complex than a rough measure of religious beliefs will show if one examines societal differentiation between the spheres of the political, the economic, and the religious and if one takes into account the privatization of religion. For example, the involvement of the Komeito, a political party supported by a major lay Buddhist organization, in many of Japan's previous coalition governments points to an intermingling of the political and the religious spheres in this country, despite its secular Constitution. Moreover, as the involvement of religious institutions in the management of hospitals and institutions of higher education in Taiwan suggests, religion in East Asia remains a very public affair.

In particular, the situation of Taiwan reminds us of the need to clearly distinguish between secular states and secularized societies. It is entirely possible for a state to be effectively secular in its political and bureaucratic culture as well as in its relations with religious institutions – including exercising extensive control over them, as was the case in Taiwan until recently – while important segments of the society remain culturally deeply religious. Although the Taiwanese secular state has moved from a rather assertive variant to a more passive one since commencing the process of democratization, the contrast between a secular state and the continued presence of religious customs and beliefs remains strong. States that are "secular with East Asian characteristics" show how indigenous sociocultural practices are being eclectically combined with borrowed Western political values and forms. However, Asian religious pluralism and noncongregational forms of religious belief and practice make it difficult to implement a clear boundary between state and religion. For example, when politicians in an electoral campaign burn incense at a temple, it is never clear whether they are giving a nod to the adherents of the local religion or to the local community, as both are often intertwined.

It turns out that official assessments according to which East Asian societies are secularized – sentiments prevalent among governments in the region, especially those that claim allegiance to Marxist materialism – may misrepresent the situation. The laments made by Chinese authorities that many citizens still hold onto their "superstitious beliefs" as well as the presence of official campaigns against "cults" and "evil religions" suggest that important segments of Chinese society remain untouched by secularization trends. In her study of faith healers in Vietnam, Monique Sélim (2003) goes further, describing a society where the state even co-opts popular religions. The view that East Asian societies are secularized is also disputed by many East Asian social scientists, particularly anthropologists and historians. Hence sociologist Yang Fenggang (2004, 2006) goes as far as to declare that China may be "one of the *most* religious societies in the world" (Yang 2004, 101). Yang's argument is not that socialism is a form of civil religion in the

People's Republic of China, an argument that has been more convincingly made in relation to another state in the region, North Korea under the Kim dynasty. Yang, Sélim, and other authors are pointing instead to the resilience of more traditional and dominant ideas of religion based on a belief in gods living in a not-so-distant heavenly world – ghosts to propitiate and ancestors to worship – alongside the belief that some ritual practices can empower individuals to influence natural forces and alongside the other forms of congregational religiosity seen in the West.

In sum, sophisticated and cosmopolitan citizens of East Asia, who like to represent their societies as both secularized and skeptical on religious matters, live alongside a large proportion of the population – in the countryside, in the suburbs, and even in the neighbourhoods of major cities – who remain attached to their traditions or partake of new *bricolages religieux,* which can be equally sophisticated and cosmopolitan in their embrace of new worldviews. Moreover, and belying the idea that modernization is accompanied by a decline of religiosity understood in a more narrow sense, China has also experienced a spectacular increase in the number of Christians since accelerating its policy of reform and opening. In Japan and Taiwan, where the number of Christian adherents stagnates, it is new religions or Buddhist associations that are growing.

This misperception that East Asian societies are thoroughly secularized rests on a methodological bias. For example, the index of religiosity constructed by Inglehart and Norris (2003, 55) was built on indicators such as belief in life after death, belief in a unique, transcendent, and omnipotent God, regular attendance at religious service, self-identification as a religious person, and agreement with the statements that "religion is important" and that "religion gives comfort." Although many East Asians would answer *yes* to the first question, arguably many would not reply in this way to the subsequent questions. Many of them do not believe in a single and omniscient God, and since the other questions are premised on this particular belief, they do not qualify as religious believers under the former definitions. In other words, people who go to Taoist temples on an ad hoc basis, for instance, are considered nonreligious. In a major survey on religious practice in Taiwan, only 17 percent professed belief in a supreme being (Zhang 2000, 277) and would qualify as religious believers in a narrow sense; yet as many as 87 percent of respondents said they went to a temple to worship spirits (ibid., 239).

In sum, the boundary is hard to maintain between the state and religion when religion is not defined as a belief in an otherworldly reality – a belief focused on the realm of the sacred and supernatural – but instead as a set of beliefs and practices immanent in the mundane world. This distinction, as Bruce J. Berman suggests in his chapter in this volume, reveals a key difference between Christianity and the religions of East Asia, with their emphasis on filial piety and right behaviour. Like Marcel Gauchet (1985), Berman sees this difference as explaining the idiosyncratic – indeed, singular – Western experience of church-state relations, where anticlericalism has resulted in a specific Western-based approach to secularism. Nonetheless, although East Asian religions have historically emphasized the importance of defining correct behaviour in this world, as have Islam and Judaism with their intense focus on Sharia (Islamic law) and Halakah (Jewish law), East Asian religions differ from Islam and Judaism in that they have not been reified into legal systems subject to the kind of intense political contestation seen in Muslim and Jewish societies. In this sense, East Asia too is idiosyncratic, albeit for different reasons.

In particular, the description of East Asian societies as secularized appears much less robust if one looks beyond official views of government officials inclined to downplay a social phenomenon to which many still attach a stigma. The narrow definition of secularism adopted from the experience of Western societies, in turn, does not help us to properly understand the diverse modalities of relations between state and religion in East Asia. Such lacunae have an impact when discussing the relevance to East Asian polities of secularism as a normative project. This is already difficult to discuss in Western societies because this abstract and ill-defined project promotes a variety of institutional mechanisms ranging from regulation of religious affairs by state bureaucracy to the establishment of separation between church and state.

The existing definitions of *secularism* and the models of the secular state that they have inspired are based on the historical experiences of Western societies, where relations between the state and religion are understood to be determined by a range of possible constitutional mechanisms regulating interactions and delineating boundaries between the respective spheres of responsibility of the state and organized churches. The implementation of secularism, in Western constitutional theory, rests on the establishment of a variety of mechanisms aiming to ensure nonintervention of churches and affiliated associations in politics and noninterference of the state in the affairs of religious associations. This approach, however, is problematic in societies where religiosity does not always express itself via an institutional form. In sum, it is surprising that secularization and the normative ideal of secularism could find a hospitable climate in East Asia because of the particular kind of relations that have historically prevailed between state and religion.

The Institutional Weakness of Religion in East Asia

The different variants of the secular state in the West emerged at the end of long negotiations and conflicts between states and churches, whether through concordats between national churches and governments in countries with a Catholic majority, through the establishment of church protection from the Crown in exchange for its support of the monarchy in the United Kingdom and many Reformed countries, or through the establishment of a constitutional wall of separation in the United States between government and religions. Religions in East Asian societies, in contrast, have seldom constituted powerful institutions similar to the Catholic Church, the Anglican Church, or the established Lutheran churches of continental Europe. Religions have been institutionally weak, and states have easily asserted their authority over them.

To remark on the institutional weakness of religions in East Asia is not to imply that they have been absent or that they have left little legacy of note. On the contrary, religions have exercised a deep influence in the arts, in ethics, and in philosophy. Moreover, although in terms of culture each East Asian society is remarkably homogeneous as long as one uses language as a marker of identity, each is extremely diverse when one uses religion as a marker of identity. In this way, East Asia, in its configuration, mirrors the South Asian situation. It has been home, for much of its history, to a number of religious traditions that lack a single central authority. Moreover, it has also been influenced by monotheistic religions from outside of the region, such as Christianity and Islam,[4] and by a number of new religious movements that emerged in the nineteenth century and that consciously sought either to develop East Asian universal religions, such as Yiguandao (the Way of Pervasive Unity), or to introduce new national religions, such as Xuanyuanjiao (the Religion of the Yellow Emperor).

Confucianism, the dominant school of thought in East Asia, has never inspired a church-like organization that might challenge secular authority; indeed, the situation is rather the opposite. During most of East Asian history, states have at times either persecuted Confucian scholars or sought to use the teachings of this tradition to support their theory of government and justify their rule. The Chinese state since the Song dynasty (960-1126), Korea since the fourteenth century, Vietnam since the fifteenth, and Japan since the Tokugawa period (1603-1868) have all used the classical canon of this tradition to shape the examination system for entrance into the bureaucracies. No group of Confucian scholars, however, has constituted an organization challenging state authorities. During the twentieth century, Confucianism as a tradition was persecuted by the Communist Party in China; everywhere else, it subsisted only as an intellectual influence or as a marginal religion.[5]

The doctrines of Taoism and Buddhism may have at times inspired political opposition to governments, but as institutions they did not represent serious challenges. Numerous uprisings have been led by leaders who claimed to have received a celestial mandate from heaven to overthrow an existing ruler and also claimed affiliation with a Taoist or a Buddhist sect. However, Taoist or Buddhist religious institutions have seldom contributed directly to changes of dynasties. Rather, the opposite has been the norm, with the state either controlling Taoist or Buddhist institutions to monitor their activities or supporting them materially in return for the performance of rituals that provide legitimacy to the rulers. The implementation of this policy has ranged from supportive to suppressive. At one extreme, some East Asian governments have proclaimed Buddhism to be the state religion and have done so for durations of time that have varied considerably;[6] at the other extreme, states have persecuted this religion to limit its economic influence and prevent it from gaining political capital.[7]

In China a number of religious movements claiming to represent more authentic variants of the Taoist and Buddhist traditions, alternatives, or new forms of syncretism, such as the White Lotus teachings and the Eight Trigrams Society, have risen against governments.[8] More recent uprisings inspired by religion but with little relation to Confucianism, Taoism, or Buddhism – such as the Taiping (Great Peace) (1853-64) and the Boxer Rebellion (1900) – were devastating and quite consequential in terms of loss of life, material destruction, and lasting damage to society (Michael and Chang 1972). But none of these movements left any lasting institutional legacy, and all were subsequently crushed into oblivion after their military defeats. Similar remarks can be made about the Tonghak (Eastern Learning) Rebellion (1894-95) in Korea. Although it contributed to the fall of a corrupt government, it failed to establish credible political alternatives and remained a marginal religious actor, otherwise known as Cheondogyo (the Religion of the Heavenly Way).

East Asian states have also been directly involved in the performance of religious rituals. Besides sponsoring Taoist and Buddhist traditions and fighting heterodox religious movements, the Chinese state has promoted local historical personages into deities to ensure the loyalty of communities to the empire. The emperor was also responsible for the performance of propitiatory rites to ensure prosperity and peace throughout the empire. He was therefore understood to be the mediator between heaven and earth, and he acted as the *pontifus maximus* of a state religion that subordinated all other religions to his authority. In Korea and Vietnam local kings had similar attributes. In Japan the status of the emperor became even more exalted under the ideology of Kokutai. In sum, East Asian societies have experienced for centuries the opposite of the institutional pattern seen in Western societies: there has been increasing fusion between religious and state authority instead of a centuries-long process of gradual separation between the two. Hence, far from having nurtured the foundations of secular states, they have encouraged the development of the opposite. As the next section discusses, East Asian states have perpetuated this model up to the present day or they are still struggling to emerge from it. The claim that East Asian states are secular is therefore problematic.

This supremacy of the state in religious matters may help us to understand why, in contrast with other areas of the non-Western world, there is so little critique of the secular state in East Asia. There are no reasons to protest the secular state as being an artificial grafting of a Western mechanism imposed during colonial rule, as is the case in other parts of the world. State control of religion is a central part of traditional statecraft in the region, and checks against religion's interference in affairs of the state have been the norm for centuries. However, these checks against religion's interference represent only half of the foundations of a secular state. The other half – the absence of state intervention in religious affairs – has been missing for centuries. The next section points to an important change affecting the region: the increasing divergence between countries that maintain government control over religious affairs and others that seek to establish liberal secular states based on the normative ideal of the model, including sensitivity to the specific nature of local religions.

State Approaches to the Control of Religion in East Asia

Two different approaches to managing religious affairs have been adopted by modern East Asian states since the beginning of the twentieth century. The first approach, which I have called "neotraditionalist," perpetuates the traditional prerogative of the state in controlling religion but appeals to the new ideology of socialism. The Qing dynasty until 1911 and the Japanese empire until 1945 used the traditional approach to state control of religion. The fall of the Qing dynasty and the birth of the Republic of China led to the first attempt to establish a secular state in East Asia, although the circumstances of internal division, war, and authoritarian rule put a limit on the development of a fully liberal secular state where the state refrained from controlling religion. The failure of this regime in Mainland China was followed by a reassertion of state control of religion in 1949 and by the adoption of the same approach by the governments of North Korea in 1950 and North Vietnam in 1954. In the latter two cases, the transition of these two polities from colonial status to sovereign national states meant that state control of religion ceased to be indirect and mediated by distant rulers in Japan and France.

The second form of secular state, which I have called "secular with East Asian characteristics," moves away from the pattern of state control; it applies mechanisms that could be recognized as liberal and democratic but tries to be mindful of regional cultural traditions and religious values. It was put into an embryonic form in Japan by the Meiji Restoration of 1878, but the constitutional proclamation about freedom of conscience could not prevent authoritarian control of religion, especially when the military asserted control and imposed a national religion with the emperor as its head. Only after defeat and the American occupation did effective freedom of religion and legal protection for religious diversity become substantive. As mentioned above, the Republic of China also attempted to establish a secular state when it controlled Mainland China, but the constitutional provisions of freedom of conscience became a substantive reality much later, when this regime achieved a transition to democracy in the late 1980s, and its control was then reduced to Taiwan. Likewise, the Republic of Korea, established in 1948, proclaimed a secular state, but its liberal nature would emerge only during the process of democratization undertaken in the same period as Taiwan's democratization.

Both approaches have been successful in preventing the rise of religious contestation, but they have exacted very different prices. Neotraditionalist states have prevented the emergence of religiously based contestation through repression. States that are secular with East Asian characteristics have gambled that by permitting the intervention in politics of religious associations, they will minimize the friction that forbidding such intervention might otherwise generate. Neotraditionalist states rigidly determine which religions are legitimate and worthy of government support and which religions are illegitimate and worthy of government harassment. In so doing, they limit the expression of diversity. States that are secular with Asian characteristics, in contrast, have gradually deregulated the sphere of religion and have allowed for an increasing diversity.

The view that the modern state should control religion has been strongly endorsed by East Asian elites in at least two contexts. First, radical modernizers in Japan and China believed that the state should stand above religion to control it and, if required, to mobilize its resources. Religion was required either to serve the nationalist projects of the state or to support socialist development. Second, especially after World War Two, liberal elites in the ascendant enthusiastically embraced the normative project of establishing states that did not base their legitimacy on reference to any religious source of authority.

It is true that no East Asian country has proclaimed a state religion since 1945; all have constitutions that proclaim freedom of conscience, or the right to believe or not to believe, and all profess neutrality in religious affairs. Historically, it is also true that East Asian countries have seldom proclaimed a state religion, at least not as this concept is understood in the West. This may give the impression that there exists robust and time-tested support for the idea of the secular state in this region. East Asian states would appear to have a natural propensity towards the development of secular states in East Asia – or to borrow from the neoinstitutionalist literature, there would appear to be a path dependency favouring this outcome. A closer look, however, invites some important qualifications.

Modern East Asian states have experimented with the idea of a state religion prior to establishing a secular state. Indeed, a few reform-minded intellectuals in the late Qing dynasty thought that China *should* have a state religion if it was to become a modern society able to emulate western Europe; these intellectuals failed in their endeavour. In the absence of a Confucian clergy, the idea of a Confucian state religion was never seriously implemented. Japan was more successful. It crafted a Constitution that proclaimed freedom of conscience early on during the Meiji Restoration but also proclaimed the status of Shinto as a national tradition with the emperor at its head. To maintain the fiction that the state protected freedom of conscience Shinto was not officially a state religion; however, it was granted a status of superiority vis-à-vis Buddhism and other religions.

After the defeat of Japan in 1945 and its adoption of a liberal secular state as imposed under American occupation, the only East Asian attempt to establish the equivalent of a state religion was abandoned. All states in the Chinese cultural area – indeed, in the whole East Asian cultural area – have since been trying out different forms of secular state. Some of these models are clearly absorbing the institutional experiences of the Western model and adapting them to local realities. In the case of Japan this absorption was imposed by a foreign power but has been internalized over decades as a defining feature of the nation's own self-definition. In South Korea and in Taiwan, this adaptation has resulted from a series of borrowings from western Europe and North America.

Although the powerful and pervasive superstructure of Marxist-Leninist institutions in education, government, and public administration could help to account for the ability of China, Vietnam, and North Korea to prevent a critique of secularism, it is remarkable that in the East Asian societies that have avoided this institutional legacy, namely Japan, South Korea, and Taiwan, there has also been little significant expression of revisionist attitudes towards the secular state. Religiously inspired critiques of the state have emerged in East Asia: two examples are the Minjung theology of social justice embraced by South Korean Christians and the support for human rights and the right to self-determination espoused by the Presbyterian Church of Taiwan. These critiques, however, have not attacked the secular state per se but rather the authoritarian nature of the governments in both countries. This relative acceptance of the secular state raises two distinct questions: Is there something to be learned from these societies by other societies facing a similar configuration, or is there a major misunderstanding in the first place about the nature of the secular state in these countries? To answer these questions, it is important to inquire about the reasons for this apparent acceptance of the secular state.

East Asia has not undergone the kind of religious revisionism experienced in other non-Western societies since the Boxer Rebellion of 1900. There have been no major movements of religious fundamentalism rejecting authoritarian governments' ways of regulating religion. What explains this absence? One obvious answer might be the overwhelming power of the state and its ability to curtail any possibility of religious contestation. Militaristic Japan until 1945, China and the other socialist states after 1949, authoritarian South Korea, and Taiwan until the 1980s all had the capacity to prevent the rise of any form of opposition, and over the centuries, as we have seen, all had developed instruments to control religious activities.

Nonetheless, the argument that authoritarian states are strong enough to prevent the emergence of religious contestation is not entirely convincing. The Shia clergy in Iran, Sunni clerics in Pakistan, and the lay militants of the

Muslim Brotherhood in Egypt have all nurtured opposition against the state under authoritarian governments. The nature of the political regime matters very little: large democracies such as India and the United States have important political movements that articulate a discourse hostile to secular values and promote a greater place for religion in public life; others, such as Japan and Germany, have important mainstream parties that promote religious values but don't contest the secular state; many other democracies, such as France, Canada, South Korea, and Taiwan, have no political parties of importance seeking election on the basis of religious values.

If political regimes do not matter, perhaps ideology can explain why governments fail or succeed in preventing the rise of opposition inspired by religion? Can the ideology of nationalism trump the appeal of religion? Nationalism may be an ideology substituting for a failed socialism in China, Vietnam, and North Korea, and it may provide the glue that holds together societies facing serious issues of national security such as South Korea and Taiwan; however, besides the official rhetoric used during periods of tension, appeals to nationalism have their limit. In Japan nationalism is considered anathema; the possibility of a nationalist resurgence there is bound to provoke hostility in the region. In China leaders periodically instigate campaigns for patriotic education but are wary of any excess of nationalist fervour, aware that it could easily turn against them (Gries 2005).

One explanation proposed in this chapter is that East Asian societies, including China and Vietnam, are religiously plural and that any effort by the state to impose a single state religion is therefore bound to fail. In democratic contexts where political contestation is considered legitimate, competition between different religions is seen as natural, and state intervention is limited. In these contexts, religious critique of government is likely to be weak because the state provides religious actors with conditions for their development. In authoritarian states, in contrast, it is the political authorities' concerns regarding public remonstrance from religious associations that make it difficult to relax control over them. However, because of the particular nature of noncongregational religious practice predominant in East Asia, even states that seek to implement the Western model of the secular state find it difficult to implement a clear boundary between state and religion in order to prevent religious interference in politics and political intervention in religious affairs. The remainder of this chapter discusses this type of secular state in East Asia and focuses on Taiwan, which is "secular with East Asian characteristics."

The Taiwanese Experience: *Zhengjiao Fenli*

Like Japan and South Korea, and to a certain extent Hong Kong and Macau, Taiwan is a society where the influence of traditional China on the management of religion has bequeathed the island an institutional tradition favouring state control. Japanese colonialism between 1895 and 1945 and the Leninist orientations of the ruling party on the island after 1945 have only reinforced these trends. However, the influence of epistemic communities educated in liberal values and the normative appeal of democracy within the population have inspired the country to move towards a liberal model of the secular state. The nature of the religious economy in Taiwan, like in Japan and in South Korea, is such that this liberal model has characteristics of its own that differ in some respects from the liberal models in the West.

Taiwan, or the Republic of China (ROC), is governed by a Constitution that proclaims freedom of conscience, and it is considered to have been a democracy (in the Schumpeterian sense) since the late 1980s. Its political parties defend programs that are recognizable within a liberal framework, many of its elites have been educated in North America, western Europe, or Japan, and its institutions emphasize the rule of law. In short, Taiwan is hospitable to the secular state in ways that might invite comparisons with the United States, France, or Canada. Officials in charge of religious affairs are clear about these choices.[9] Taiwan's evolution parallels changes observed by José Casanova (1994) in many western European societies, where religious beliefs, which were assumed to be a private matter, have become in recent decades more openly present in the public sphere. However, there is an important difference between Taiwan and western Europe. In Taiwan the original regulatory framework recognized a number of religions, whereas many European countries have historically recognized only one established church. Once religious practice is taken into account, however, these comparisons become problematic. Taiwanese religiosity is much more diffuse than that of societies with a Christian heritage; its presence in the public sphere is more considerable than in France or Canada, but it does not generate "culture wars" comparable to the controversies surrounding religion in the United States. Finally, the legacy of Chinese culture influences the way that Taiwanese look at the issue conceptually.

Hence the concept of secularization is known as *shisuhua* in Chinese, a compound that is untranslatable but revealing in its implicit meaning; *shisu* is a reference to customs and *hua* is a suffix used to connote a transformation. That is, *shisuhua* could mean something approaching *vulgarization*.

The translation of *secular* is even more revealing: it can be *xianshide* (of this world), *shisude* (customary), or *feizongjiaode* (areligious). The French term *laïcité*, which is often presented as denoting a more radical version of secularism, is also translated as *feizongjiaode*. Government officials in Taiwan do not use this term and talk instead about *zhengjiao fenli* (separation between politics and religion). One may note that the Chinese usage contrasts with the English one, as state comes first and religion second.

Herein lies a first element of originality within the Taiwanese secular state. The principle of "separation between politics and religion" is not used in the West, particularly not in the United States, where religion is so often present in political life. Rather, the secular state in the United States rests on the principle of "state-church separation," an institutional mechanism ensuring that no *particular* religious institution can use the state to prevail against others. In Taiwan, where Christian churches are demographically marginal,[10] this principle is largely irrelevant: its application would mean thinking about church-state separation in a society without church. Religion is understood as a more inclusive category than "church": it includes churches and religious institutions but also a variety of practices previously understood as superstitions that are now perceived more positively as "popular beliefs."

Politicians profess their belief in the principle of zhengjiao fenli, and intellectuals as well affirm it as a core value in Taiwanese society. There is a general perception, as revealed in surveys, that religion should be left out of politics. There is also a view held by the media that religious interference in public affairs can be damaging to society's well-being. The prevalence of this view has at least two causes: Japanese colonial rule and the influence of Euro-American liberal values. The doctrine of state-church separation was adopted by the Japanese in the Meiji era (1868-1912) and imposed on Taiwan when Japan controlled the island (1895-1945). In addition, throughout the twentieth century intellectuals influenced by North American and European thought viewed secularism as a hallmark of a modern society. These views never ceased to exercise a strong impact on Chinese nationalists. But as Taiwan evolved to become a democracy, the idea of separation between church and state emerged as a natural element of a democratic society.

Nonetheless, in many ways, relations between state and religion in Taiwan show less conformity to the principle of separation than its proponents are willing to admit. This is the case in at least three respects. First, the state and political actors seek the support of religion in their own political projects. Second, religious actors, in addition, ask the state to intervene on their behalf. And third, the boundaries between state and religion are themselves less watertight than many assume.

In the first case, the state still maintains a certain form of control over religious affairs. This control, to be sure, is vanishing, and the successive governments of the Guomindang, the Democratic Progressive Party between 2000 and 2008, and the Guomindang again have shown a willingness to refrain from involvement in religious affairs. However, beyond the level of state intervention (i.e., bureaucratic management and police monitoring of religious affairs), politicians often call upon religious actors for support. This can be seen in two instances: during electoral campaigns and in policy implementation. During major electoral campaigns politicians seek support from national or regional religious leaders, most notably leaders of Buddhist associations, and during local campaigns they visit smaller communal temples to show recognition of temple networks and to solicit their support. Outside of religious campaigns, politicians also seek out the support of religious associations to help them implement social policies.

In the second case, religious institutions do get involved in politics, even though this intervention is mostly indirect. Unlike in Japan, there is no Buddhist political party, not even a religious wing or a religious movement comparable in scope and influence to the religious right in the United States. In fact, in recent years when religious leaders have gotten involved in Taiwanese politics their interventions have been largely criticized by the population as unwanted interference. For instance, after the Foguangshan Buddhist association supported a candidate for the presidential election in 1996, some media warned of a war of religion. In the presidential election of 2004 the statement of a Buddhist monk against the incumbent caused so much furor that he had to temporarily close his temple after the election. These forms of intervention are limited and generally shunned by the public.

Religious institutions, however, do lobby the government to defend their interests. Buddhist and Taoist associations, for example, sought – and failed – to obtain a law on religious organizations to protect their corporate interests. It is a measure of the weakness of these organizations that despite their pressure the government did not pass the law, but it is also a testimony to the strength of other religious associations that opposed the law. One other form of intervention in public affairs, which is much more difficult to measure but nevertheless of considerable importance to the government, is the intervention of religious institutions in the delivery of social services.

In the third case, religious institutions also intervene by remonstrating against government when they believe political leaders are behaving in ways contrary to their view of justice, fairness, or the common good. The Presbyterian Church performed this role during the period of martial law, criticizing the Guomindang for abuse of human rights and proclaiming Taiwan's right to self-determination. The Buddha's Light International Association (BLIA) provided its support to a protest against President Lee Teng-hui in 1997 for what it saw as a decline in public morality. The Buddhist nun Zhao Hui spearheaded movements against the construction of a nuclear power plant in the same year.

Yet, overall, the influence of religious institutions on Taiwanese politics tends to be marginal because of three factors. First, despite the potential influence of religious beliefs, their diversity ensures that no particular religion is strong enough to impose its views on the whole society, as was illustrated in the case of the proposed law on religious organizations. In this sense, Taiwanese religious diversity invites comparison with the United States, where the diversity of churches impressed on the founders the necessity to impose state neutrality to prevent either discrimination or favouritism. Second, most Taiwanese practise forms of religion based on customs more than on congregational activities. Instead of regularly participating in public gatherings held in one sacred space, within a single month they might worship ancestors at home, burn incense at a Taoist temple before an important event to bring themselves good luck, give alms to Buddhist charities for the poor, and offer angry ghosts fruit and beer placed on a table in the street.[11] In this sense, the Taiwanese religious economy differs from that of the United States and is too weak organizationally to affect the political agenda at the national level.

Third, the boundaries between religion and state are bound to be difficult to maintain in a society where the religious realm is not conceived of as an otherworldly reality but as immanent in this world. Hence, in the world of Chinese traditional religious practices, there is no sacred space distinct from private space in the sense that a church, a mosque, or a synagogue is a space endowed with special significance. True enough, Buddhist temples and the temples of new religious movements try to create this sense of sacred space, yet even the temples of many new religious movements such as Xuanyuanjiao do not successfully project a sense of revered space. Temples in Taiwan can be noisy places where people gather to play mah-jong and discuss mundane matters, and they are often nested within commercial space, which was the case in traditional China and which remains the case even today in locations such as Shanghai.

Political leaders and religious associations have also mingled in ways that would be frowned upon in western Europe. Although the Guomindang was reluctant to recognize religions other than Buddhism, Taoism, Catholicism, Protestantism, and Islam, after it relocated its government to Taiwan in 1949 it granted recognition to the Religion of the Yellow Emperor in the 1950s and to the Heavenly Virtue Religion in the 1970s because their leaders were well connected with the ruling party. Conversely, the Way of Pervasive Unity did not benefit from the same legal protection until its members helped reformist politicians to win local elections; following electoral victory, these politicians advocated lifting the ban on the Way of Pervasive Unity activities.

Some important and high-profile Taiwanese politicians maintain very close relations with religious organizations. For example, Wu Po-hsiung, mayor of Taipei from 1988 to 1990, interior minister from 1990 to 1996, and chairman of the Guomindang from 2007 to 2009, was also president of the ROC chapter of the BLIA from 1997 until 2004. Religious leaders have also intervened in politics quite openly. Thus, as mentioned previously, the Presbyterian Church of Taiwan supported the right of self-determination for Taiwanese and supported one of the candidates for the 1996 presidential election. Hsing Yun, abbot of the Buddha's Light Mountain monastery, founder of the BLIA, and a member of the Guomindang's Central Committee, openly supported the candidacy of a close lay disciple, Chen Lu-an, against the Guomindang candidate, Lee Teng-hui, in the same presidential election.[12]

Religion also permeates the political sphere in more subtle ways. This is visible in the attention politicians give to numerology, in their selection of candidates for elections, in their practice of burning incense in temples at the start of electoral campaigns, and in their attendance at ceremonies during which religious leaders bless the nation. Although most Taiwanese would dismiss as irrelevant the attribution by lottery of inauspicious numbers to candidates during the multiseat elections, associating any perceived significance with superstitious belief, up until as recently as 2006 politicians tried to avoid receiving the number *four,* whose pronunciation, *si,* is the same as that for *death.* Politicians in electoral campaigns also want to ensure that they will be seen in communal temples, where they hope to bring in votes by appealing to local solidarities and also to receive the blessings of monks. Finally, politicians in government have for years made a point of attending the annual ceremony to protect the nation and its ruler – a ceremony that is performed by the leaders of the Buddhist association of the ROC.

Under martial law Taiwan implemented a system of state control of religion that was no different from the traditional model. During the process of democratization, however, liberal-minded officials have decided to move away from this tradition. They have resisted the temptation to legislate on religious matters despite pressures in this direction from some religious associations. The Ministry of Interior's Department for Civil Affairs still maintains a Bureau for Religious Affairs, but this organ of government acts more as a resource centre for religious associations than as an instrument of control. Public intellectuals and government officials subscribe to the principle of zhengjiao fenli but remain uncertain as to whether doing so means the state should adopt the American model of church-state separation, the French approach of *laïcité,* the German approach of multiple established religions, or other variants. Regardless of the choices made, it is clear that the guiding principle is strengthening freedom of conscience, not relegating religion to the margins of society. More important, and relevant to what is discussed in the other chapters of this volume, this principle appears especially germane for religious diversity.

Herein lies a major difference between China and Taiwan, despite similarities in their cultural background and in their political experience as polities led by Leninist political parties. Whereas China associates secularism with atheism and the teleological belief in the ineluctable withering away of religion from society in the long run, Taiwan associates secularism, more modestly, with the establishment of institutional boundaries between the government and religious institutions. The Chinese state is not secular in this sense, for the state-sponsored ideology, which combines Marxism-Leninism, Mao Zedong Thought, Deng Xiaoping Theory, Jiang Zemin's Triple Representativity, Hu Jintao's Harmonious Society, and Xi Jinping's Chinese Dream, is a civil religion more than a political principle. It has its scriptures in the complete works of the leaders, its faithful in party cadres, and its exegesis in the Central Party School. Although it is a far cry from the fervour of the Mao era, it is still the official ideology of the state, notwithstanding the diversity of interpretations. And as the ferocity of the persecution against the Falun Gong religious movement shows, this civil religion does not like competition.

This difference between China and Taiwan debunks the essentialist claim made by the Chinese government, often uncritically relayed outside of China, that a state-religion relationship premised on state supremacy and moral authority over popular beliefs is more compatible with the Chinese cultural tradition than a state-religion relationship based on respect for diversity among public expressions of beliefs in ultimate reality, no matter how strange they may seem. In sum, the Taiwanese situation is very significant because it touches upon the more considerable problem of secularism and the secular state in the Chinese world as a whole. Taiwan is a small polity, and it would be easy to dismiss it as the exception rather than the rule in the Chinese cultural area, as Chinese leaders routinely do when discussing issues such as human rights and democracy. Yet, in many respects, its political transition from an authoritarian one-party state into a pluralist democracy with robust competition shows that political patterns can change dramatically in a very short period of time even in the seemingly most entrenched regimes. The Taiwanese situation demonstrates that culture is not destiny.

Conclusion

I have argued that a comparison of Western societies with East Asian societies such as Taiwan, Japan, and South Korea can be useful because, although East Asian societies may appear to be monocultural in comparison with multicultural Western societies, they also experience tremendous diversity. This is especially true with respect to religion. East Asian societies are home to national traditions such as Shinto in Japan and Taoism in Taiwan; to world religions such as Buddhism that acclimated to local cultures centuries ago; to more recent world religions, particularly Christianity under churches of the Catholic denomination and a wide variety of Protestant denominations; to new religious movements that have emerged from the confluence of the previous ones; and finally to religions brought by new immigrants, a recent phenomenon in the region. The remarkable feature of the region is that this wide diversity of religions has not translated into intercommunal conflict; some even argue that it has significantly contributed to the consolidation of democracy. As religious pluralism is about the agreement to disagree about the ultimate realities and the limits of the community to which one is supposed to owe some obligation, the acceptance of this agreement to disagree suggests that a society is likely also confident about its ability to accept differences of opinion in relatively more mundane matters like the allocation of the country's wealth to different policies. This acceptance, it can be argued, is most germane to democracy.

In sum, I have argued that there is no justification for overlooking East Asia in discussions about the secular state. Moreover, there are some important characteristics of religion in this part of the world that affect relations between state and religion in distinctive and significant ways. Lessons of the region are not easily transposable because East Asian societies have different historical trajectories than most Western societies, where religious controversies have fuelled political conflicts. In East Asian cases the state has sought to promote various forms of orthodoxy, including religious ones. Nonetheless, it is important to explore these differences and their meaning because many people who migrate to the West from East Asia have an understanding of religious belief and nonbelief – and therefore of institutions such as secularism or separation between church and state – that differs from the mainstream Western understanding. In discussions of secularism in Western societies, particularly in North America and western Europe, where an increasing number of new citizens have an East Asian background, it is important to take into account East Asian views.

North Americans and western Europeans with an East Asian background have a variety of beliefs, and a significant number of them have embraced Christianity with a fervour that compares to that of any of their co-religionists with a different background. Overseas, Chinese, Vietnamese, Korean, and Taiwanese communities outside of East Asia are often at the forefront of the revival of the Catholic and Protestant Churches in the countries where they have settled. These communities, in turn, vary in their orientation, ranging from evangelical to more pietistic. In this respect, they reflect the variety of beliefs of their ancestors and a variety of attitudes towards the appropriate relation between state and religion. As the presence of people with such a background is likely to continue in Western societies such as the United States, Canada, and Australia, and likely to become increasingly visible in public life in the decades to come, it is important to be reminded of this reality.

Notes

1 The experience of *laïcité* in France, for example, is not seen as a by-product of liberal philosophy. The perpetuation of the traditions of established churches in Europe and the United Kingdom also contradicts the tenets of liberalism. This is not to say that liberalism has not influenced Europe but simply that there is more than one approach to relations between church and state.

2 Although Vietnam is geopolitically included in Southeast Asia by virtue of its membership in the Association of Southeast Asian Nations, culturally it belongs to the area influenced by Chinese written tradition.

3 This is also true of the dissidents who oppose the Chinese government. Although an important number among them are Christians, they are not critical of the secular

state. Presumably, like Muslims in India, they support the idea of a secular state because it protects their status as a religious minority.

4 This influence varies from one country to another. Only China has a significant Muslim minority, and although Christianity has affected all countries, the numbers of its adherents range from over 17 percent in South Korea to less than 1 percent in Japan.

5 Confucianism is a religion included in South Korean statistics, and there is a tiny True Confucian Religion in Taiwan that counts fewer than 10,000 adherents (Government Information Office 2012).

6 Buddhism was proclaimed the state religion in China during the short reign of Wu Zetian (690-705), in Japan from the Nara period (710-784) to the Tokugawa period (1603-1868), and in Korea during the Goryeo dynasty (918-1392).

7 Campaigns of persecution were directed against Buddhists in China in 574-77, 845-46, and 955. From 1868 to 1902 the Japanese state persecuted Buddhist institutions and promoted the Shinto belief as a national religion.

8 The White Lotus is not an association per se but a tradition with a variety of associations that are independent from each other (Ter Haar 1992).

9 Officials in the Taiwan Ministry of Interior, interviews by author, summer 2008.

10 The historical significance of the Presbyterian Church and the Catholic Church is another matter.

11 These rituals have been observed repeatedly in the North of Taiwan in locations as diverse as the cosmopolitan neighbourhoods and working-class sections of Taipei and in the South of Taiwan in cities such as Kaohsiung and Tainan.

12 The Guomindang had then "mainstream" and "nonmainstream" factions. Hsing Yun identified with the latter.

Works Cited

Bhargava, Rajeev. 2004. "India's Model: Faith, Secularism, and Democracy." *Open Democracy*, 3 November.

Casanova, José. 1994. *Public Religions in the Modern World*. Chicago: University of Chicago Press.

de Bary, William Theodore, Chan Wing-tsit, and Chester Tan, eds. 1960. *Sources of Chinese Tradition*. Vol. 2. New York: Columbia University Press.

Gauchet, Marcel. 1985. *Le désenchantement du monde: Une histoire politique de la religion*. Paris: Gallimard.

Government Information Office, Republic of China. 2012. "Taiwan Yearbook 2012." http://www.ey.gov.tw/en/cp.aspx?n=4ADC064334D460FA.

Gries, Peter Hays. 2005. "Popular Nationalism and State Legitimation in China." In *State and Society in 21st-century China*, edited by Peter Greys and Stanley Rosen, 25-43. London: Routledge.

Hurd, Elizabeth Shakman. 2008. *The Politics of Secularism in International Relations*. Princeton, NJ: Princeton University Press.

Inglehart, Ronald, and Pippa Norris. 2003. *Rising Tide: Gender Equality and Cultural Change around the World*. Cambridge, UK: Cambridge University Press.

Kuru, Ahmet T. 2006. "Reinterpretation of Secularism in Turkey: The Case of the Justice and Development Party." In *The Emergence of a New Turkey: Democracy and the AK Parti,* edited by M. Hakan Yavuz, 136-59. Salt Lake City: University of Utah Press.

Michael, Franz, and Chang Chung-li. 1972. *The Taiping Rebellion.* Vol. 1, *History.* 1966. Reprint, Seattle: University of Washington Press.

Sélim, Monique. 2003. "Marché des croyances et socialisme de marché au Vietnam." *Revue Tiers Monde* 64 (173): 81-97.

Stepan, Alfred. 2000. "Religion, Democracy, and the 'Twin Toleration.'" *Journal of Democracy* 11 (4): 37-57.

Ter Haar, B.J. 1992. *The White Lotus Teachings in Chinese Religious History.* Honolulu: University of Hawaii Press.

Wu Jiao. 2007. "Religious Believers Thrice the Estimate." *China Daily,* 7 February. http://www.chinadaily.com.cn/china/.

Yang Fenggang. 2004. "Between Secularist Ideology and Desecularizing Reality: The Birth and Growth of Religious Research in Communist China." *Sociology of Religion* 65 (2): 101-19.

–. 2006. "The Red, Black, and Gray Markets of Religion in China." *Sociological Quarterly* 47 (1): 93-122.

Zhang Yinghua. 2000. *Taiwan diqu shehui bianqian jiben diaocha jihua: Disanqi diwuci diaocha jihua zhixing baogao* [Basic plan to survey social change in the Taiwan area: Report on the fifth survey]. Nangang: Zhongyuang yanjiuyuan shehuixue yanjiusuo.

The Changing State Monopoly on Religion and Secular Views in Thailand

Manuel Litalien

Chapter 10

Thailand, September 2006: A democratically elected government is forced out of power by an admittedly peaceful coup d'état. King Bhumibol Adulyadej, considered to be a semidivine Buddhist figure, as well as the ultimate moral authority of the nation, endorses the coup, thus assuring social stability in the divided kingdom. The king shows, once again, that the monarchy has checks and balances in a political system dominated by money politics and charismatic leaders. In Thailand many, but not all, revere the monarchy as a symbol and a principal element of national identity. The divine aura attributed to King Bhumibol by his people allows him to seemingly "stand above all politics" while also being intimately involved in affairs of the state (McCargo 2005, 502).

The political sphere in the kingdom is known as the secular domain where worldly matters – in contrast to otherworldly, religious matters – are attended to by the secular political authority of the Parliament (Jackson 1997, 75). Politics corrupt individuals and therefore serve as obstacles to those devoted to studying religion, such as monks. Nevertheless, the king's perceived high-Buddhist moral virtue allows him to avoid being contaminated by all worldly affairs, enabling him to participate in them without becoming tainted.

While writing the 2007 Constitution,[1] the Constitution Drafting Assembly and the Constitution Drafting Committee refused to enshrine Buddhism as the state religion despite the mobilization of pressure groups, even though a Buddhist king must symbolically remain the head of state. The state – understood as the Parliament – shall provide patronage and protection to Buddhism as well as other religious faiths in the kingdom. Buddhism is thus underlined as the established religion in the kingdom and is protected by the monarchy. However, both the king and the state are also theoretically patrons of all faiths – hence the ambiguity over the rapport between the religious and the political spheres in the kingdom. Both of these constitutional committees opted to emphasize the kingdom's religious pluralism and religious freedom instead. Government officials believe the state to be secular with an established national Buddhist *sangha* (clergy). Legally, the state is the final arbiter of interreligious relations and of its control over religious affairs. The Thai case underlines the complexity of secularism in non-Western societies, where the idea of separation between church and state is not viewed in terms of mutual exclusion – as underlined in Rajeev Bhargava's and Ahmet T. Kuru's chapters in this volume. In Thailand established religion coexists with freedom of conscience – at least constitutionally. The political influence of the Thai Buddhist clergy is conceived of as being nearly absent from politics. Thailand can legally be understood as a moderate secular state that embraces toleration and accommodation of religious diversity.

Overall, although the Thai state is seen as dominating religious institutions, the intervention of the king in politics in 2006 demonstrated the deep connection between the state and religion in Thailand. The common assumption that religious institutions would not interfere with government affairs was challenged. In a time of political crisis Buddhism no longer appeared to be an appendage of the state. Religion assumed a prominent role, with the king acting as a moral Buddhist leader capable of saving the nation. However, the political and religious legitimacy of the monarch is no longer assured. At age eighty-two the ailing monarch, as well as the structure of the Thai polity in a post-Bhumibol era, are sources of concern for authorities who support the monarchy.

In Thailand the monarchy, the royalists, and the Buddhist clergy are mutually interdependent. Their political powers rest on the conception of a traditionalist style of democracy, where King Bhumibol's personal achievements as a moral leader are vital to social cohesion. For the conservative royalists, secular influences are highly problematic,[2] as they have the potential to undermine royalist legitimacy within the polity. Royalists view the Thai monarchy as a bulwark protecting the democratic system's well-being (Suwannathat-Pian 2004, 23). In this theologico-political setting, the distinctive social, political, and religious qualities associated with the monarch can be at least partly transferred to his royalist supporters, conferring on them political legitimacy (Fong 2009, 680).

Currently at the centre of political life, royalist advocates are not without their challengers. As the process of democratization has progressed in the country, so have secular views regarding political moral authority. The major source of concern for the royalists is the possible desacralization of the monarchy and the Buddhist clergy. The secularization process has also meant that the monolithic ethnoreligious ideology of Thainess, which is strictly associated with ethnic homogeneity and with Buddhism, is being progressively brought into question by secular forces, both within and outside of government institutions (Connors 2003, 336; Toyota 2005). Moreover, new religious and political niches are being created.

The conflict between the coalition of the royalists, the military, and the Democrat Party, on the one hand, and the supporters of the political party Thai Rak Thai (Thai Love Thai), the People's Power Party, and the Puea Thai Party, on the other hand, has escalated into one of the country's worst cases of political unrest in recent history. In a time of institutional uncertainty the old royalist elites' actions reflect their will to maintain a traditional hold on power networks and institutional benefits.[3] The link between the Privy Council, the military, and the Democrat Party of former prime minister Abhisit Vejjajiva illustrates the continuing political ties of prior royalist elites. During the 2006 coup, for instance, social groups summarized the event as an attempt by the old elites to maintain royalist traditional power networks and to maintain the association of power with a morality centred on the monarchy. The new elites, meanwhile, were accused of promoting a new type of Buddhist morality in politics (Keyes 2006).[4] The situation led to an abusive use, by both camps, of the charge of *lèse-majesté*.

The fundamental difference between old and new elites lies in their opposing views on the kingdom's political system. The new elites are understood to be proponents of electoral politics and participatory civil society, whereas the traditional elites are regarded as advocates of a hereditary, or "appointed," political system (Suwannathat-Pian 2004, 20-29; Thomson 1993, 402). However, the dichotomy between electoral and hereditary politics is overly simplistic, and both the new and the traditional elites have demonstrated struggles with the principle of the people's sovereignty. Thai history shows that extraconstitutional sources of power, such as intervention by the military or by powerful individuals, have been the norm (Suwannathat-Pian 2004, 29).

In his bid for popular support, former prime minister Thaksin Shina-watra's populist leadership challenged the monarchy as the focus of political loyalty and religious orthodoxy. Support from the new elites led to Thaksin's success, in turn stimulating religious pluralism through electoral and wel-fare politics – a strategy intended to undermine the monarchists' monopo-listic stronghold on religion and morality in the kingdom. My objective in this chapter is to analyze social changes and to present the ways that reli-gious institutions and communities are responding both to the progress of pluralism and to the increasing centrality of individual rights within Thai society. The chapter considers the role of Buddhism as a de facto state reli-gion, while discussing the place of religion in the new 2007 Constitution. To analyze the behaviour of religious institutions in the face of secular politics' growing influence in Thailand, the chapter provides a historical perspective on religious diversity and the place of the king in Thai society.

The chapter focuses on the idea that the democratic processes accentu-ated by events of the early 1970s and 1980s, as well as by the economic crisis of the late 1990s, facilitated greater self-determination of minority groups. The increasing presence and autonomy of minority groups, in turn, encouraged the new elites to utilize the state as an instrument for promo-ting religious pluralism, and this trend encouraged opposition from the pro-monarchists, as well as a form of religious revivalism (Evers and Siddique 1993, 1-3; Norris and Inglehart 2004, 229). To analyze how Thailand man-ages its growing secular forces and religious diversity, this chapter covers Buddhism's role in nation-state formation; communism's impact on reli-gious diversity; the democratization and the role of the monarchy; religious pluralism and the process of democratization; secularization, religious plur-alism, and Buddhism as a de facto state religion; and finally religious rep-resentation in modern Thailand. An overview of historical and recent events provides important background to explain the current complexity of the relationship between religious diversity, religious freedom, and politics.

Buddhism's Role in Nation-State Formation

To grasp the nuances in the relationship between state and religion in Thai-land, a brief historical summary of the construction of the modern nation-state is necessary. In Thailand religion and the monarchy were perceived to be society's moral and normative foundations (Taylor 1993, 65). Since the late nineteenth century the formation of the modern Thai nation-state has been marked by the adaptation of a traditional Buddhist cosmography to bolster the image of a strong state amid invading European colonial powers within Asia – the objective being to maintain Thailand's autonomy (Baker and Phongpaichit 2005, 265).[5] Various monarchs adopted the nation-state institution not only to stand equal in their fight against Western intrusions but also to promote the process of modernization. In the early twentieth century, as part of a process of centralization, the state institutionalized a Buddhist clergy and integrated it into its political institutions. The united Buddhist clergy was structured in such a way as to promote an ideological expression of an absolutist state. When the country was facing revolution in 1932 the last absolute monarchs constructed the "Thai nation" by relying on a national religion (Buddhism), a common language (Thai), and a common lineage (Tai[6] ethnicity and a monarchy).[7] These elements made it possible to promote a sense of belonging to a mutual Thai identity.[8] Two decades earlier, in 1911, King Wachirawut (Vajiravudh) had identified three pillars of society: the nation, religion, and the monarch. Since that time political authorities have used these pillars to promote various interpretations of what constitutes the essence of Thai identity (Thai Constitution 2007, Chap. 4, section 70, 29). This trinity was set up in opposition to the "amoral influence" of the West, when the process of modernization and economic liberalization intensified in the twenty-first century (Anderson 1991, 101; Vella 1978, 33).[9] The sacred trinity also reflected the authorities' will to promote a sense of unity while controlling heterogeneity.

Historically, the various non-Buddhist and unorthodox Buddhist groups in Thailand – often associated with minorities – were seen by the authorities as obstacles to the formation of a strong, modern state. In the kingdom the close relationship between the nation-state and Buddhism was adopted by the central government as a strategy to promote homogeneity and a common identity. This rhetoric proved to be useful for the government while fighting communism in the 1950s. The authorities then actively utilized the Buddhist clergy to promote national integration and development programs in the country's poor and underdeveloped areas through the clergy-promoted spread of orthodox Buddhism, the Thai language, and Thai customs among the ethnic minorities in the North, Northeast, and South (Suksamran 1993, 62-67).[10] The terminology of a *civilized core* and *backward peripheries* used at that time came from the traditional ideology of Buddhist polities in Southeast Asia (Toyota 2005, 113). This terminology changed in 1959, when the term *hill tribes* was adopted to classify people living in the kingdom's uplands. The term designated people located at the periphery who needed to be assimilated into the Thai nation-state. At times, the hill tribes were deemed to be people who required the king's personal benevolent protection; recently, they have also been portrayed as "noble savages" with distinct cultural and religious practices (Glassman 2010, 1302). In the 1990s the hill tribes made an effort to define themselves as culturally distinctive and as promoters of a lifestyle harmonious with nature. This strategy was aimed at securing alliances with international environmental movements in order to fight discriminatory state control (Toyota 2005, 116-35).

In Thailand approximately 80 percent of the population is related to Tai-speaking groups (Keyes 1987, 15). If you include the Sino-Thai people this percentage rises to more than 90 percent (de Koninck 1994, 223). From this data, one could gain the impression that Thailand is a largely homogeneous society, but the Tai-speaking group comprises six distinct ethnic groups: Siamese (central Thai), Northeastern Thai (Isaan, Thai-Lao), Northern Thai (Khon Muang, Yuan), Southern Thai, Thai Muslims, and others (Phu Thai, Yo, Lue, Shan, Lao Song, Lao Phuan) (Keyes 1987, 16; de Koninck 1994, 222-23). In fact, the majority of these groups consider their languages to be unique or a variation of the standard Thai language, which comes from the central ethnic Siamese group. The latter community counts for roughly 30 percent of the country's population.

Knowing the potential force of destabilization that ethnic minority groups represented, Siamese monarchs during the Rattanakosin period (1782-present) avoided direct confrontation until the fall of the absolute monarchy in 1932 and instead established a policy of tolerance for minority groups. Currently, the central government, as with previous Thai kingdoms, has opted to rely on widely practised Theravada Buddhism and a national language to promote its strategy of integration and assimilation. Censuses still deliberately avoid questions of ethnic identification to focus specifically on "religious" (i.e., Buddhism, Muslim, Christian) categories (National Statistical Office 2004, 121).

Successive governments up to the present have relied on a common notion of identity founded on Buddhism as the majority's religion (94.2 percent). The 2004 national census promotes "religion" as the core value of the whole population (National Statistical Office 2004, 100). In this environment, use of the term *religion* outwardly subsumes cultural variability and illustrates cultural unification. Religious, rather than ethnic, identification is the authorities' preferred identity marker. Ethnicity is clearly a sensitive issue in the kingdom (Gilquin 2005, 38; Toyota 2005, 125-26). Buddhism is again perceived to play a role in nation building and subsuming ethnic differences.[11]

During the early twentieth century rising elite nationalists found in Buddhism a potential common denominator that they hoped would help them to avoid the complex reality of ethnic diversity. It was agreed that the project of the modern state should rely on the idea of a civic religion infused by a Thai ethnic nationalism. At this time the creation of a Thai civic religion meant harmonizing religion and politics to provide a national commitment and collective moral purpose for the population (Taylor 1993, 70). Following this strategy, the Buddhist Clergy Act of 1902 (Sangha Act) was adopted so that the state could administer and control the unhegemonized community in the religious hierarchy (ibid., 71-72). The act manifested the state's intolerance towards Buddhist pluralism in the kingdom.[12] Religion became a matter of national security and national stability for the central Bangkokian government. Monks who failed to register at a particular monastery were prosecuted and disrobed. Thai civic religion became an instrument by which the state could extend its influence over Buddhist religiosity itself. Being a Thai citizen had become synonymous with being Buddhist (Ishii 1968, 865; Keyes 1993, 262).[13] In the early stages of modern-state elaboration, Buddhism was used as a means to legitimize the state's existence. The newly formed Buddhist clergy was expected to interpret religious doctrine as justifying key government policies (Jackson 1989, 63). Shifts in the political system were then automatically reflected by modifications in the religious domain. Political authorities rapidly promoted Buddhism's socialization function for ethnic and religious minority groups. Such a strategy was also implemented during the Cold War years as a way to fight communism.

Communism's Impact on Religious Diversity

Thai elites had been promoting regional and domestic anticommunist politics as early as the 1920s, when the first anticommunist law was adopted. The elites of the time were concerned with the destabilization effect of a radical economic and social redistributive agenda (Glassman 2004, 40). However, as China witnessed its cultural revolution in the 1960s and through part of the 1970s, Thailand intensified its war against communism – an effort that translated into policies of control over the freedom of ethnic and religious minorities in the kingdom. The Thai military leaders were increasingly worried about political instabilities in neighbouring countries, as well as in the region. By the end of the 1940s and throughout the 1950s, French Indochina, Burma, Malaya, Indonesia, and the Philippines had all became scenes of anticolonial and antigovernment insurgencies (Wyatt 2003, 257). Thai authorities took seriously the threat of civilian radicals and the possible developments they might inspire; this concern led to varying government stances towards religious freedoms and modification of the Sangha Act governing the Buddhist clergy. For example, the political turmoil of Thailand's neighbours had resulted in mass refugee groups along the Thai borders. They brought new religious practices into the kingdom and invoked new concern regarding possible communist incursion (Ishii 1986, 126-27). The government focused on assimilation policies and gradual integration for ethnic minorities on the borders of Laos and Cambodia. Buddhist missionaries, under the auspices of national development, were sent into these regions from Bangkok to provide surveillance. The objective was to fight antagonists by raising their living standard through regional development and religious integration. As part of the program, the Buddhist clergy had to foster a sense of belonging and national loyalty among the hill tribes in order to convince them to assist with and maintain security (ibid., 140-42).

Just as the government acted diligently to assimilate the religious and ethnic minorities at its borders, it adopted similar policies towards the Muslim religious minority in the South. A Royal Decree on the Patronage of Islam was enacted in 1945 (Ishii 1986, 127). This royal decree expressed the central government's intention to bring the Muslim community under its control: it was literally copied from the previously mentioned 1902 Sangha Act. Prime Minister Plaek Phibunsongkhram's administration (1938-44, 1948-57) was notorious for its efforts to eliminate the Malay Muslim identity for the sake of a monoethnic and monoreligious state (Croissant 2007, 2). His government launched a forced assimilation policy aimed at the various minority cultures in the kingdom. The centralization of religious affairs in Bangkok at this time reflected the imposition of the military government's authoritarian policies. In the case of the Thai Muslims, who represented the second-largest minority group, Plaek's policies set off a wave of secessionist violence. By 1959 clashes between insurgents and security forces had become the norm. The country had to wait until the election of Prime Minister Prem Tinsulanonda's pro-royalist government (1980-88) to see a real commitment from the central government to cultural rights and religious freedom in the kingdom. Under Prem's leadership, insurgents were offered amnesty, as well as a new economic plan for developing the South. It was not until 2004, under Prime Minister Thaksin Shinawatra's government, that the southern regions hosted new separatist activities (ibid., 12).

In light of the possible encroachment of communism, it was in the royalists' interest to keep communist influences outside of the Thai border, as they were associated with the abolition of traditional Buddhist values and

the possible demise of the monarchy. For the authorities, fighting communism was not only a matter of maintaining the country's sovereignty but also
a way to legitimize the newly formed nation-state in the eyes of its diverse
ethnic and religious minorities. With the country's public institutions dominated by the military, there was limited space for religious groups to claim
any repression associated with assimilation policies. In this political environment, the Buddhist clergy held a monopoly over Buddhism's expression in the kingdom. The Buddhist clergy also reflected the state's narrow
notion of religious tolerance. The clergy's apparent support of religious
pluralism was shaped by the state's nationalist interest. However, in the
1970s, the clergy's attitude changed as its monopoly was progressively
threatened by the state's increasing focus on distancing itself from its civic
religion. This increasing dissociation had three causes: first, the modern
state's institutional legitimacy (e.g., consolidation of parliamentary institutions, expanding bureaucracy, and competing political parties), which no
longer required a Buddhist ideology to sustain itself; second, the growth
since the 1970s of the pluralization of religious space in Thai society (e.g.,
the Dhammakaya Foundation, Santi Asoke, Bhikkhuni movement, Soka
Gakkai,[14] Tzu Chi, Jemaah Islamiyah, and Unification Church); and third,
political leaders, who could look to other sources of moral authority to govern (e.g., democratic principles and the division of power between the legislative, the executive, and the judiciary) (Keyes 1999, 37).

Historically, communism's impact demonstrates that in the name of national security defending religious pluralism has not been a state priority.
The state, however, has intervened on multiple occasions on behalf of the
clergy to protect Buddhist orthodoxy. At stake has been the connection between Buddhism and Thai national identity. The end of the communist
threat in the late 1980s and in the 1990s did not change the state's inclina-
tion to preserve Buddhist orthodoxy.[15] At this time, however, the state did
initiate the clergy's slow decentralizing process. Encouraged by the ongoing
democratization process in society, the clergy's decentralization favoured
the pluralization of religious space in the country during these two decades.
In turn, the political and economic environment allowed for the growing
influence of the new elites and enabled the new spiritual needs of the middle
class to impact the traditional form of authority held by the royalists (Taylor
1999, 168-71). The construction of a legitimate Thai modern state resting on
a nationalized geobody connected through blood, race, language, land, and
Buddhism, of which the monarchy is the supreme ambassador, has been

progressively debated (Fong 2009, 679). The very definition of the Thai nation, its political identity, and its inevitable link to the religious paternalism promoted by the old elites now face a new challenge as the new elites confront the traditional elites' conception of democracy – one that rests on a constitutional monarchy with a different vision of democratic and religious values.

Democratization and the Role of the Monarchy

In the early 1970s, following a democratic impulse, the political system had embarked on what appeared to be a progressive separation between the government and centralized religious institutions (Keyes 1999, 36). However, the Buddhist monarchy, still part of the existing state apparatus, gained new legitimacy nationally and internationally when it decided to side with the students' democratic demands in the October 1973 rebellion against the military government (Reynolds 1978, 138-39). Consequently, the military, which had been in control of the state, lost the support of the elites and the "middle class."[16] This new, educated middle class, exposed to Western political life and liberal values, had become increasingly uncomfortable with authoritarian military rule and was also becoming more critical of cultural traditions that were regarded as superstitions (Wyatt 2003, 285). The 1973 revolution ended one-man authoritarian rule and brought about a new consciousness regarding the need to share political power. This led to the renewed commitment of the middle class to a loosened public order, although still one structured around the "nation, religion, and monarchy" (ibid., 292). More power rested in the hands of the Buddhist monarch and in Parliament. The military was expected to stay out of politics. Also, following the 1973 revolution, the king began to be depicted as a "democratic" Buddhist king. The Buddhist clergy, however, did not follow this democratic momentum and remained a highly conservative and authoritarian institution.

The 1970s saw a whole generation of Buddhist monks and Buddhist religious movements united in their dissatisfaction with the authoritarian Buddhist clergy as well as with governmental projects. For example, liberal and "development" monks[17] openly challenged the central authority and exposed the state's failures to develop rural Thailand. The religious and conservative clergy, in turn, accused the liberal monks of being communist supporters, thereby creating growing tension over the issue of multiple Buddhisms within Thai society. The homogeneous Buddhist identity and the institutionally centralized structure previously required to build the modern nation-state were openly questioned by the middle class and the new pro-democratic elites (Taylor 1999, 169-71). In spite of the tension between liberal and conservative monks, both parties' royal allegiance remained intact. In addition, the king retained his position as the symbol of the universal Buddhist moral figure embodying the heart and soul of the nation. The concept of nation was imbued with an otherworldly essence. In this religio-political environment the country's well-being and wealth depended on the virtuous father of the nation (Taylor 2001, 133-34). It became clear that monks from one end of the political spectrum to the other could not afford to lose their Buddhist social contract with their rightful ruler.

The democratic ideals of the 1970s and the 1980s isolated the conservative clergy even more; the institution itself was a reflection of the centralized and authoritarian military government of the past. The pluralization of the Buddhist space saw new Buddhist movements emerge in Thai society, marked by the debut of the now state-supportive Dhammakaya Foundation and state-resistant Santi Asoke movements, among others. In the literature, some of these religious movements are referred to as Engaged Buddhism (Swearer 1995; Queen 2003; Sivaraksa and Ip 2004; Hershock 2006). This movement towards engagement, although not homogeneous, was perceived to be centred on promoting a society based on the well-being of its citizens. The movement criticized the state's strategy of heavy reliance on economic development and the open market to look after the welfare of its citizens. It advocated a Thai society based on a bottom-up, citizen-focused structure rather than on the traditional top-down hierarchy. By the 1990s, with the end of the communist threat, Buddhist movements appeared to be somewhat more plural since they had become more and more globally interconnected with business and intellectuals (McDaniel 2006, 101).

Although the monarchy, as an identity marker in the kingdom, could not directly endorse these new Buddhist movements because of its commitment to Buddhist orthodoxy, numerous royal projects conducted in rural areas adopted similar trends and ideologies. However, in 1992 the country faced another political crisis between the military and pro-democratic groups seeking political power. The king's intervention and attempt to resolve this political dead-end demonstrated Bhumibol's capacity to use an efficient system of checks and balances in the kingdom – a feat that would more or less be repeated in 2006. In the earlier case, this intervention put the country back on track in terms of its democratization process. The new democratic will was later enshrined in the country's first People's Constitution in 1997.[18] Like the previous 1991 Constitution, the legal document reiterated the role of the king as a Buddhist and also as the upholder of all religion in the kingdom (Thai Constitution 1997, Chap. 2, section 9). Freedom of religion was then enshrined in the document (Chap. 3, sections 30 and 38). In addition to the king's obligation to practise Buddhism, the Constitution specifically indicated the state's duty to respect and patronize Buddhism and other religions (Chap. 5, section 73). It reiterated the dual responsibility of both institutions towards Buddhism and the protection of all religions. Overall, in the 1990s the monarchy successfully established itself as an institution capable of resolving political conflict and national crisis. The royal version of the Thai constitutional monarchy became the sociopolitical norm of Thai life (Suwannathat-Pian 2004, 65).

Thai official discourse, as endorsed in Thai constitutions, advocates the king's commitment to protect all faiths within the kingdom. However, it is difficult to assess the true position of the monarchy in its commitment to promoting religious pluralism. The monarch's responsibility to nominate the supreme patriarch, the head of the order of Buddhist monks, and to ensure Buddhism's purity in the country reveals that the monarchical institution rests on a conservative notion of Buddhist orthodoxy.[19] Consequently, the monarchy cannot endorse or promote any new Buddhist movements without losing credibility in the eyes of the supreme patriarch, the Buddhist clergy, a section of the Thai population, and the old elites. Traditionally, the clergy supports the monarchy's moral legitimacy and promotes the relevance of traditional values in the kingdom, such as the law of karma.[20] This law of karma itself directly supports the king's prestigious position in society, as he is the only one who has accumulated sufficient merit to hold such a prestigious position. Nonetheless, at least during Thaksin's administration, the growing corruption within the Buddhist clergy, as revealed by the media, led the government to question the social relevance of the clergy and to indirectly attack the moral ground of the monarch.[21]

Early emphasis on a Buddhist state did not translate directly into religious intolerance on the part of the political authorities. The more recent promotion of the state, along with the king as a key political actor in accommodating all religions in the kingdom, testifies, at least legally, to political leaders' commitment to religious pluralism (Thai Constitution 2007, Chap. 4, part 4, section 79). This monarchical approach to religious pluralism, although seemingly new, has deep historical roots in the country. Indeed, royal policies towards religious and ethnic diversity can be traced back to Ayutthaya (1350-1767), the second kingdom of Thailand (Tambiah 1976, 89; Wyatt 2003, 118; Keyes 1993, 269-70). At this time, when the first Christian missionaries visited the kingdom, they were given land to establish themselves. The first legal document on religious freedom and acceptance of religious pluralism was the Treaty of Friendships and Commerce that Siam concluded with Great Britain in 1855. It was meant to encourage trade and commerce as well as diplomatic strategy (Ishii 1994, 455). Nowadays, the narrative construction around tolerance promotes the view that through their behaviours Thai monarchs were already promoting values compatible with a system of democratic governance. The Thai feudal system, for example, has been described by traditional elites, including former prime minister Abhisit Vejjajiva, as a historical institution consistent with an egalitarian form of government. Additionally, the same group advocated Buddhism as a religion compatible, in essence, with democracy (Puntarigvivat 1998, 352).[22] The king's role in this political environment is to produce modern citizens and a political order compatible with Thai traditionalism, a role that lends legitimacy to his position as a supreme Buddhist leader (Connors 2007, 129). In reality, the absolutist nature generally associated with monarchies is eluded to in the monarch's title of "righteous leader," whether he has been elected or not. In light of this, the likelihood of a traditionally elite, democratic royalist or monarchy committed to pluralism becomes somewhat questionable and rests on the political will of a group or individual rather than on the institution's structure itself. As the traditional central authorities are pro-Buddhist, the country is unlikely, for instance, to see a Muslim become prime minister in the near future. As well, there are only timid policies of equal representation for ethnic and religious minorities within state institutions. To this day, data on the religious allegiances of government officials have not been published (McCargo 2008, 17). Moreover, ethnic and religious groups rarely have access to key decision-making positions in the country. These factors undermine the representative policies of the Thai state and its commitment to religious pluralism.

Religious Pluralism and the Process of Democratization

In Thailand the opening of the public space in 1972-73 is associated with the fall of the military government. The space, however, was partially closed down later in 1976 after the bloody repression of the student protest and opposition by a pro-royalist coup regime. (It was gradually reopened in the late 1980s, and the mid-1990s saw a period of great expansion.) In the 1970s the country had nevertheless witnessed a growing demand for religious and ethnic minority rights as authorities initiated a slow decentralization process and began to tolerate group protest, freedom of speech, and the right to associate, join organizations, assemble freely, and conduct strikes. Buddhist communities that were not a part of the state-sponsored Buddhist clergy and ethnic minorities located at the periphery of state territory reaffirmed their right to exist outside of the homogeneous identity prescribed by the state. Growing popular protest in the 1970s had reached the Buddhist clergy (Phongpaichit and Baker 2002, 317).

The 1980s, 1990s, and 2000s saw exponential mobilization against policies of the state and of traditional institutions. Public protests grew from 42 in 1978 to 754 in 1995 to 1,200 in 1997 (Foran 2006, 108). Groups protested against corruption, labour abuses, land policies, and unfulfilled political promises regarding wealth redistribution and economic development. Development policies of past decades had left rural areas generally lagging behind the level of development and industrialization seen in the cities (Puntarigvivat 1998, 348-49). The adoption of a free-market economy caused increasing protests and desperate poverty that threatened traditional values (ibid., 351). Additionally, the majority of monks in the clergy – seeking to gain prestige by cooperating with state policies – endorsed economic development policies that did not benefit the general population. This clergy-state cooperation made the population highly critical of the clergy's morality and spiritual motivations. During this period right-wing monks against communist militants were required to cooperate with an amnesty given to communist fighters and had to adopt a more neutral stance in favour of religious pluralism. To a large extent, the state agreed to encourage religious competition between Buddhist movements located at the periphery of the clergy. Later, in 2001, the process of competition reached its zenith under Thaksin's government when his administration sought to undermine the traditional Buddhist authority of the old elites – one that rested on a vertical conception of welfare.

As the process of democratization became further institutionalized in the 1990s, new religious movements challenged the hegemony of traditional institutions in welfare activities. The growing economic power of the middle class and the progressive industrialization of the country meant religious organizations could further sell their services and gain religious, as well as political, legitimacy. Enlightenment (or nirvana) and Buddhism had become new commodities in the age of open markets and Asian economic miracles (Jacobs 2002). But the Asian economic crisis of 1997 brought an end to this apparently peaceful cohabitation between the state, the monarchy, and the Buddhist clergy. The crisis questioned the failure of the traditional social safety net and reintroduced the idea of extending the state's welfare regime.

Consequently, the traditional elites and the monarchy had to accept a new vision of the state as a provider of welfare services. The previous social contract between a minimal state, the old elites, and the clergy had been profitable and had also reinforced orthodox Buddhist values in the polity. The concept of a state directly involved in the welfare of its citizens, however, was in opposition to a hereditary, or appointed, political system and institutions (such as the monarchy and the Buddhist clergy). New Buddhist organizations could now compete with these institutions in offering welfare services and could also hope to be included in the new welfare regime (Litalien 2010). It was an opportunity for new religious groups to be formally recognized as institutions by the state and to benefit from a new form of political patronage.

Secularization, Religious Pluralism, and Buddhism as a De Facto State Religion?

There have been numerous attempts to approach the challenges of religious pluralism in Thailand. Religious pluralism has received legal recognition in numerous Thai constitutions since 1932, when the country made the shift from an absolute monarchy to a constitutional monarchy. In practice, however, religious minorities had been kept under tight control by the state for the purpose of unity (Reynolds 1994, 435). In fact, the creation of the modern Thai state and the establishment of a civic religion, in an effort to underpin the unity of the state, took place at the same time as the revolutionary authorities engaged in a process of secularization. The process was aimed at key areas such as law, education, social structures, and the economy, all of which have been susceptible to increased tensions between religious minorities and the state.

The state's establishment of secular law[23] has been especially difficult on the hill tribe communities, as their way of life was religiously oriented until recently, with communal religion and communal law being interwoven (Reynolds 1994, 450). Legal issues inevitably became entangled with religious issues. The failure of the secular and legal political systems to recognize these minority groups and their religious practices exacerbated their peripheral position in Thai society. Development projects, still in progress with the help of the united Buddhist clergy, have contributed to the isolation of these groups, stimulating a desire within hill tribe communities to be fully recognized for distinct ethnic and religious identities. Other groups affected by centralized state promotion of secular laws are the Thai Muslim communities, who have also presented obstacles to the secularization of the legal system; Muslim communities insist that "Muslim 'secular' law"[24] ought to take precedence over state secular law. Needless to say, in the case of Muslim communities, insistence on secular laws advocated by the authorities has met with some resistance. To date, the issue remains an area of contention between the central government and Muslim communities (ibid., 449). Freedom in the kingdom has been largely permitted so long as the central government feels capable of normalizing and controlling heterogeneity. There are signs, however, that tensions have been growing; some religious traditionalists promote the superiority of religious law over secular law – vying, for example, for the law of karma to precede the secular law of the nation. This resistance illustrates that specific religious and ethnic groups are not likely to accept secular law. Since it promotes secular law as a core democratic value and the most efficient system of rule, the government has met with opposition.

Another secular legal process in Thailand involves the elaboration of the kingdom's Constitution. Drafted by a committee selected by the military leadership following the 2006 coup, the 2007 Thai Constitution recognizes the king as head of state and acknowledges his obligation to profess the Buddhist faith. Within the same legal document the king is also identified as the supreme defender of religion within the kingdom. These two provisions on religion have been enshrined in almost all of the kingdom's eighteen constitutions dating back to 1932 (Ishii 1986, 38). Like the 1997 Constitution, the 2007 Constitution also stipulates that freedom of thought and freedom of religious association are acceptable as long as they do not run contrary to civic duties, public order, or good morals (Thai Constitution 2007, Chap. 3, part 3, section 37, 14). Good morals are vaguely defined and refer to the king as the "centre of national morality" and to the citizen's adherence to a democratic regime with the king as the head of state. The equation between good morals, the *Buddhist* king, the king as the "centre of national morality," and the exercise of freedom of religion has led to an interpretation of freedom of religion that is beneficial to Buddhism. In other words, freedom of religion is tolerated as long as Buddhism benefits from it (Thai Constitution 2007, 2). As well, with a king on the throne for more than six decades, it seems only natural that recognition of the king was enshrined in the 2007 Constitution, as it had been in previous constitutions.

Currently, most of the public have never known any king other than King Bhumibol. However, the endorsement of the 2006 coup by the Privy Council led some groups to doubt the palace's political neutrality. Additionally, certain social groups claim that there is a lack of judicial will to condemn key actors in the Yellow Shirt movement.[25] Other social groups interpret this lack of judicial will as evidence of the pro-royalists' desire to keep their traditional benefits. Historically, these advantages were attained through political patronage rather than electoral politics. Advocates of traditional politics have also been supported by the increasing will of Buddhist right-wing nationalist groups to promote Buddhism as the national religion. These religious groups mobilized in 1997 and, although in smaller numbers, again in 2007. Given that the growing malaise towards election politics on the part of the pro-royalist and traditionalist groups has been central to the current political crisis, the monarch's position in the Constitution has become more than just a symbolic issue. This point of concern continues with current prime minister Yingluck Shinawatra (Thaksin's sister), whose party is seeking to amend the 2007 Constitution and to quell rumours pertaining to the overthrow of the constitutional monarchy. Overall, part of the malaise surrounding the Constitution indicates the tension between growing secular forces, conservative religious groups, and traditional institutions in the kingdom. The independence and neutrality of the judicial process has been questioned in the current social conflict between the Thai government and the Red Shirts, largely composed of the rural and urban poor.

Education is another area where the secularization process has been particularly represented in the kingdom. In the twentieth century Western secular education progressively replaced Buddhist temple schools (Lindberg-Falk 2007, 201). Traditionally, the Buddhist clergy had been present in every village, and each monastery had housed a school. Nowadays, of the 31,071 Buddhist monasteries registered in Thailand, fewer than 30 percent have schools in them (McDaniel 2006, 122). In addition, the populace now undertakes more years of education because the National Education Act of 1999 increased compulsory education, mandating nine years of schooling. Under Thaksin's administration, compulsory education rose to twelve years, including all secondary education as well (Pramualratana et al. 2002, 5).[26] The separation of monastic and secular education had a significant impact in the kingdom. At the beginning of the secularization period the Thai state had integrated monastic schools into its education program. To a certain degree, in the Northeast, where some of the hill tribes are located, this is still the case (Chuamsakul 2006). Despite the initial integration of monastic schools into the education system, secular education has changed middle-class views regarding the place of religiosity. The state's secular education system is considered to have created the liberal middle class – the very contingent that now pressures the Buddhist clergy to change their conservative views.

This phenomenon would not have been imagined forty years ago when religious institutions were heavily incorporated into the education system.

The recent secularization of social welfare structures has also dramatically impacted Thai society. The role of the monarchy, however, has somewhat complicated the process of secularization in this area, with the institution's legitimacy resting on a vertical conception of welfare redistribution.[27] In opposition to this notion of social security is a horizontal conception of welfare, better known as the universal-welfare model or the social-democratic model (Esping-Andersen 1990, 41-43). For traditional elites, social inequalities are based partly on the law of karma. Within this traditional structure, elites provide funding to the less fortunate on a voluntary basis; this form of social security and governance has its basis in meritocracy. It is a top-down form of wealth redistribution whose dependence on the patron-client relationship is thought to have been encouraged by the karmic beliefs nourished by a conservative clergy. The core belief is that individuals can gain higher social status and karmic merit by conducting a transaction with people ranking higher in the Buddhist social hierarchy.[28] The 1932 revolution launched an early attempt to provide a legislation-based state where society would be regulated by the government rather than by the law of karma. Equality would be sought through state intervention; however, the military government of this period saw Buddhism, rather than electoral politics, as a cheaper way to gain political legitimacy (Yamklinfung 1990, 101; Keyes 1999, 36-37). Instead of engaging in a secularization process, the authorities decided to modernize traditional values to fit political aspirations – a commonly held practice in Thai politics, even today.

The last element is the secularization of the economy. Whether the economy is truly secular is a point of controversy since there still exists a whole system of economic transactions influenced by the Buddhist concept of *tham bun* (merit) in Thai society. Following the economic crisis of 1997, interest in merit-making activities in Thai society grew more popular as people sought improvement through religion (Taylor 1999, 165).[29] The latest example of merit-based economic theory is the notion of a sufficiency economy, or Buddhist economy, that was advocated for by the king after the Asian financial crisis. In fact, this notion, which stresses moderation and spiritual well-being to counteract the maximization of growth and consumption, predates the Asian crisis.[30] However, international recognition of a Buddhist form of economy as a model for developing countries is new and seems to provide additional legitimacy to the concept (UNDP 2007, v-31). The 2007 constitutional enshrinement of the sufficiency economy and the international community's support are trends that reveal the influential networks consolidated by the royalists, nationally and internationally, to fight the incursion of the new elites in the palace's political and religious domains. What Duncan McCargo (2005, 499) terms the new "network monarchy" is a reaction to the palace's subordination to the country's parliamentary system, dating back to as early as 1932. The recent state incursion into the welfare domain during Thaksin's term of office was also an indirect attack on a Buddhist economy based on merit. In a country where economic access was dominated by patron-client relations, the state's ability to offer this access threatened traditional institutions and required the creation of new networks for the old order to remain politically competitive. In sum, the secularization of the economy in Thailand is a complex issue, as it still contains important religioeconomic institutions, such as the monarchy and the Buddhist clergy. On the other hand, authorities have adopted a modern form of free-market economy. This modernization, in turn, has enabled some new Buddhist movements to emancipate themselves by adapting liberal economic functions to Buddhist practices (Scott 2009, 183-84).

Religious Representation in Modern Thailand

Public space opened in the 1970s and confronted the state and traditional institutions with the concept of pluralism, whether religiously or ethnically based (and, in many cases, these two markers of identity were intimately intertwined). In the past the country successfully imposed an image of homogeneity and tolerance that suited its particular process of constructing a modern state; today secular forces and the growing demands of religious and ethnic minorities are still a challenge to the authorities. Accommodation of religious pluralism requires greater neutrality by the state and its institutions. Despite official initiatives, discontent has been voiced through international forums, world institutions, and conversions. For example, in the case of non-Buddhist groups some ethnic minorities have sought religious conversion as a way to exercise their religious right to differ from the hegemonic monoethnic and monoreligious identity imposed by the central government (Yoko 2004, 285). In such instances, conversion has become a means to resist the universal, centralist Buddhist message, which, by its nature, has excluded these small minority groups.

Religious representation is a delicate matter in the kingdom since it involves coping with the issue of national identity. For example, every ten years the National Statistical Office of Thailand produces a population and housing census. The last one, conducted in 2000, indicated a drop in the number of Buddhists in the kingdom from the previous 1990 census: only 94.2 percent of the population identified themselves as Buddhists, compared to 95.2 percent in the earlier census. The difference of 1 percent continues to be a source of concern for authorities who view the data as evidence that Buddhism may be receding in the kingdom. The 2000 census also indicated that the Muslim population in the country had risen from 4.1 percent to 4.6 percent in the same period. Key statistics from the National Statistical Office (2004) revealed a growing number of churches, temples, and mosques in the country.[31] The figures demonstrate the religion's importance to the majority population's identity, as the Buddhist and Muslim populations together represent 98.2 percent of the kingdom. Interestingly, the numbers published in 2000 by the Islamic Committee Office of Thailand offer a different profile of Muslim communities. They indicate that in 2000 Thailand had a population of 64.110 million inhabitants, of whom approximately 5 million were Muslim.[32] This demonstrates a higher percentage for the Muslim population than the National Statistical Office count, indicating that Muslims comprise up to 7.5 or 8 percent of the population (Gilquin 2005, 40-42). In fact, some national studies show that the country is witnessing an increase in the Muslim population (up to as high as 10 percent of the total population) due to societal factors such as lower rates of contraception use and the tendency towards conversion to Islam within mixed marriages.[33]

The absence of particular categories in the census – such as agnosticism, atheism, and "people indifferent to religion" – shows a continuing alignment with past policies aimed at normalizing religious and minority ethnic groups in the country.[34] In some instances, particular religious and ethnic groups are inseparable, as in the case of the Malay Muslims in the south of the country (Harish 2006, 65-66). However, it is difficult to tell whether the variations between the official and other groups' statistical findings suggest an ideological bias on the part of the authorities in the face of religious pluralism, a lack of recognition of non- or semi-integrated religious and ethnic minorities, or deficient standards in the methodology used to gather these statistics (Toyota 2005, 110).[35]

Conclusion

Old ways of conducting politics based purely on economic development embittered the rural population, who felt neglected by the prosperous, industrialized cities. This situation brought Thaksin Shinawatra, the wealthy Sino-Thai from the North, to power. His election underlined the importance of regional identity in politics. Backed by populist policies and political promises to build a more egalitarian society, his success was directly associated with his status as a righteous Buddhist leader (Winichakul 2008, 28-30; Phongpaichit and Baker 2004, 135-39; Keyes 2006, 21-23). Thaksin Shinawatra could not have appealed to a wide range of the populace without this reputation. His government's involvement in welfare activities, however, confronted the traditional Buddhist notion of welfare that underpins the power base and structure of traditional institutions. This confirmed the prediction of Anthony Gill and Erik Lundsgaarde (2004) that welfare policies would unintentionally affect the way state and religion related to each other.

In theory, the monarchy is above politics and should not be involved in political activities that are considered worldly. However, in practice, history has proven that the monarchy has been anything but neutral in state politics. Although this institution has served as an effective tool of checks and balances in times of political turmoil, critics argue that the monarchy's religious role is reminiscent of the traditional notion that society should be based on a Buddhist cosmology. For most Thais, however, the nation's well-being, as well as that of all Thai citizens, is still perceived to be "in the hand" of the monarch; he *should* be the ultimate and ideal moral leader, for he has accumulated sufficient merit to be reborn as a king. Nonetheless, Thaksin Shinawatra's interest in welfare provision, as well as his success in shaping the state to be the main provider of social safety nets, directly questioned the authority of the influential monarchy.

In the current context religious pluralism provides a means for advocating and retaining the right to observe a different religious tradition. One could question whether religion might move into the private realm, now that the state is moving away from its historical civic religion. The answer is not straightforward, as the legitimacy of political and governing ideologies and institutions is still referenced in terms of Buddhist ethics (Puntarigvivat 1998, 359). For instance, it is common for civil servants to get public funding to attend Buddhist retreats as part of their commitment to acquiring high moral standards. Buddhist seclusions are also offered as group therapy for government divisions or departments where corruption and problematic behavioural issues are recurrent. It is also common for criminally charged politicians to become ordained monks in order to gain public sympathy or portray the image of a reformed individual. In light of these ongoing trends, the secularization process is a delicate, ambiguous, and complex issue in Thailand. These observations are not new to social scientists who study the relationship between church and state (Turner 2006, 215). As well, the normative religious ideology required for state formation now structures, in part, the political conflict in Thai society; here old systems of power configurations – confronted with the democratic and secular views adopted by the modern Thai state – must create their own forms of political legitimacy.

Homogeneous terminology is still widely used by Thai authorities to subsume minorities such as ethnic and religious groups for the sake of a common national identity – one still grounded in Buddhism. This brings us back to the tension between an essentialist and constructivist process of "Thai-ization." But beyond this dichotomy the question of institutional heritage is central. Since the country's religious institutions never suffered Western colonial conquest, as Myanmar, Laos, and Cambodia did, the traditional Buddhist conception of the polity has always sided with a process of modernization, democratization, and secularization. The dialectical modern opposition between the religious and the political spheres is not present in Thailand. The democratization process, assumed to be conducive to a massive impact of secular forces on the polity, has led the authorities to officially espouse a model of respect for and inclusion of religious diversities. The 2004 opening of the National Discovery Museum Institute in Bangkok was an effort to build a new plural identity and was inaugurated during the Thaksin administration. The institute questioned what it is to be Thai, promoted the multiple roots of Thainess, and was a political initiative praised by the new elites and criticized by a segment of the old. Current criticism and the intention of some groups to abolish the museum demonstrate how traditions and conservative views of a homogeneous Thai identity remain strongly institutionalized in the country. It appears that the kingdom's policy on pluralism is still in line with its long-uninterrupted institutional heritage. I agree with the position of Rajeev Bhargava within this volume on the need for a "contextual secularism" to better understand the dynamic interactions between the religious and the political spheres, especially in Thailand.

In sum, the secularization of the bureaucracy and state apparatus in Thailand has not been equated with the secularization of the religiously based foundations of its society. Thailand remains a strong, committed Buddhist society (Keyes 1999, 36). It is also difficult to see a future secular nationalism in Thailand without Buddhist referents (Tambiah 1978, 132). The adoption of a strict model of separation of church and state is unlikely. Rather, the new authorities have opted for opening the religious space and further encouraging the pluralist model of church-state relations. Within this model the Thai state has the opportunity to assume a greater role in promoting respect for the many worldviews held by different kinds of institutions and, in turn, a greater role in promoting a free society. However, this model represents an ideal; reality is another question. A free society has yet to be fully adopted by either traditional Thais or the new elites. The authorities are still unable to provide religious minorities with the sense that they will be treated with neutrality and be afforded equal justice. In other words, although Thailand is more open to differing religious identities, it is still not able to provide a just society where religious and secular worldviews are given equal opportunities for expression by a government neutral to both (Monsma and Soper 1997, 10-12). The Thai case does exemplify one of the main ideas promoted in this volume: the existence of "multiple secularisms."

Notes

I would like to thank the Thailand Research Fund for the opportunity and financial assistance to write this chapter.

1 Thailand Secretariat of the House of Representatives, *Constitution of the Kingdom of Thailand*, 2007.

2 A process of secularization is defined here as a "systematic erosion of religious practices, values, and beliefs"; further, "Secularization is a tendency, not an iron law" (Norris and Inglehart 2004, 5). However, in the context of Thailand the process of secularization must be understood not as the decline of religiosity but as the progressive privatization of established religion – its removal to the private sphere. In Thailand the capacity of the state to reduce its reliance on religion for legitimization of its power by exercising its authority through a more democratic principle such as a system of voting stands as an example of such a "secularization" process. This is why the modern welfare policies and populist strategies of former prime minister Thaksin Shinawatra have been decisive in destabilizing the old royalist elites, whose legitimacy relies primarily on Buddhist referents. The dichotomy between religion and politics is blurred in the kingdom because of the inclusion of Buddhist norms and powerful institutions in the structure of the polity. Given that secular principles coexist alongside constitutional clauses to protect Buddhism in the country, the relationship between religion and politics is now a source of heated debate and growing tension. Nevertheless, religion in Thailand still maintains its stronghold in society, which has not been secularized. It has, on the contrary, "converged with the market economy, consumer practices and the quest for personal and cultural identities" (Kitiarsa 2008, 121).

3 Generally, the elites are understood to be composed of bureaucrats, aristocrats, civil servants, academics, entrepreneurs, state builders, members of the clergy, and military officers. They account for 2 to 3 percent of the Thai population (Muttarak 2004,

508). The old elites consist of aristocrats, military officers, and the clergy. Their vision of the country's economy differs from that of the new elites. The old or traditional elites claim that their rule is rooted in knowledge, expertise, and morality, and they see their interests as consistent with the welfare of the nation. They perceive the new elites as individuals who have bought their way into the highest political institution and who are using their power at the expense of the nation (Suwannathat-Pian 2004, 16-17). Thailand has other categories of elites, such as regional or local elites, that also designate groups with power in society. Notably, intra-elite struggles have occurred in the country between advocates of constitutional rule and supporters of arbitrary rule and between rural elites and urban elites.

4 The new elites are usually referred to as "rural network politicians, elected Members of Parliament who have built influence in a provincial district through distribution of money and business concessions" (Robertson 1996, 924). They usually started as businessmen, as was the case with former prime minister Thaksin Shinawatra. In 2001 Thaksin won the election with his political party Thai Rak Thai (Thai Love Thai), which espoused a nationalist and populist platform. The new elites are part of the country's business elites. In the 1980s the source of power in the kingdom shifted from the military and the bureaucrats to businessmen. This change made a money-based political system and patron-client relationships key to sustaining the new elites' political networks (ibid., 924-25). The business elites' numbers had expanded rapidly in the 1950s as a consequence of rapid economic growth, and they are now part of the Parliament, which as an institution holds more power than it had in the past under military dictatorship (Keyes 1989, 132-33).

5 Thailand has never been colonized and has been able to maintain its political and religious institutions continuously.

6 In this chapter there is a distinction between the Tais and the Thais. The term *Tai* refers to people speaking a language belonging to the Tai-language family. The word *Thai* is used to designate Tai-speaking peoples and non-Tai-speaking peoples who are citizens of modern Thailand (Keyes 1987, 213).

7 After the fall of the absolute monarchy in 1932, the institution's political influence was restrained. The political setting became more favourable at the end of the 1950s (Suwannathat-Pian 2004, 153-64). The monarchy then gained popularity and became a source of power progressively independent from the government. However, recent events suggest that the ongoing process of modernization and liberalization may contribute to an erosion of Thailand's traditional institutions.

8 Thai identity has also been taken to another level by the political authorities. In the early 1930s there was political will to create a pan-Thai identity among the traditional elites in order to justify future incursion in neighbouring countries. It was rooted in the idea of "blood brothers" who were in China, Laos, Cambodia, and Burma. It echoed the German and Italian propaganda of that time regarding the importance of ethnic groups beyond the country's own territory. This expansionist vision continued even in a post-1932 Siam, where there was strong support for the expansion of Thailand's territory in Laos and in Cambodia (Terwiel 2002, 115). These protagonists regarded Siam as the mother country of all Thais.

9 The three-in-one loyalty has been said to come from the British saying "God, King and Country" (Vella 1978, 33).

10 The North and Northeast also have one of the highest concentrations of Christians in the country.

11 The hill tribes, for the most part, practise several different variants of Buddhism or are non-Buddhists. Buddhism in Thailand is dynamic and pluralistic. There have been various religious practices, such as animism, Jainism, and Brahmanism among Buddhist ethnic minority groups. Additionally, a small percentage of Christians (approximately 250,000) are located among the hill tribes. Most Christian converts in the country, however, are Chinese and Vietnamese immigrants (Keyes 1993, 259). The creation of the Tribal Research Institute in 1965 and its dissolution in 2002 should not be interpreted as the end of the country's problems with its minority groups. New environments and government policies are creating new issues (Buadeang 2006, 359). The weakening of the state's established religion brought the issue of social belonging to the fore for the authorities.

12 The authorities officially respect freedom of religion in Thailand, and this right is constitutionally protected. However, religious discrimination does exist. To be labelled "Buddhist," Buddhist religious groups need to conform to the requirements of the Buddhist clergy. Thai Buddhism is strictly supervised politically, socially, and legally. The monitoring of Buddhism is traditionally conducted within the Thai legal setting, as the state is responsible for providing patronage and protection to Buddhism. The duty of the Thai people is to protect and uphold the nation, religions, the king, and democracy (Thai Constitution 2007, Chap. 4, section 70, and Chap. 3, section 37). Buddhist orthodoxy is a serious matter, and the distinctions between mainstream Buddhism – comprising the aristocratic Thammayut sect, created by King Mongkut in the 1830s, and the Mahanikai sect – and other Buddhist schools or new Buddhist movements are well defined by the authorities. Disrespect of the clergy or false claims to Buddhist lineage can result in imprisonment. As for other religious groups, they can proselytize freely in the country. Nevertheless, freedom of religion comes with some form of limitation. The government does limit the number of foreign missionaries in the kingdom, although in practice this is not always strictly enforced. At the international level the Thai government provides some fund to monks from the clergy to travel abroad and disseminate Thai Buddhism.

13 This homogeneous equation, which was originally created to facilitate integration into the Thai nation, is responsible today for the growing sense of exclusion among non-Buddhist religious minorities, such as Christians and Muslims.

14 The Soka Gakkai's presence in Thailand dates back to 1959, when its first member worked at the Japanese Embassy. Today there are about 36,500 members (see http://www.sgi.org/thailand.html).

15 For Thai authorities, the fear of communism is now associated with the growing influence of China in the region.

16 The middle class referred to here is predominantly urban and nonagricultural (Wyatt 2003, 283). It comprises educated individuals with a small family and a profession. They have a house with a long-term mortgage and are inclined to travel, listen to the radio, and watch television. This archetype usually owns a car or plans to have one. They also have credit cards (Paribatra 1993, 884).

17 In the 1970s *phra nak phatthana* (development monks) were members of the Buddhist clergy who did not agree with the development policies of the government

and decided to start independent rural-development projects based on their own interpretation of Buddhism. They feared erosion of traditional local Buddhist values, growing consumerism, and the dependence of the farmer on outside markets. The movement paralleled and joined social-opposition movements led by nongovernmental organizations in the kingdom (Darlington 2003, 99-100).

18 Thailand Office of the Council of State, *Constitution of the Kingdom of Thailand 2540,* 1997.

19 Although the king is the official appointer of the royal patriarch, senior clergymen make the selection.

20 Karma is a universal law that regulates all living beings. It can be defined as the sum of a person's actions cumulated in this life and previous ones as well. It decides the fate of every living being in future existences. This law promotes the view that every individual, in order to advance in the social hierarchy, needs to perform *tham bun* (meritorious actions). Merit creates a channel for worldly and otherworldly orders (Ishii 1986, 29). In the view of Thai academics a large proportion of Thais practise a "kammatic form of Buddhism," which rests on the importance of respecting the law of karma to attain greater happiness and to gain a new social position in the next life.

21 There has been a growing sense of discontent with certain royal development projects in rural areas. Criticizing the king, however, is simply unacceptable in the eyes of the traditional elites, who have reinforced the *lèse-majesté* law, thus further mythologizing the monarch and his absolute position in the political system. In spite of this reinforcement by the old elites, the king has recently invited criticism and encouraged freedom of expression (Streckfuss 2007). Whereas in the 1950s there was an average of one charge per year, in 2008 there were seventy-seven cases sent to trial. The numbers have been fluctuating over the years, but they have risen significantly since the 2006 coup. David Streckfuss (2007) underlines statistics provided by the Office of Judiciary, which confirm that from 2006 to 2008 alone, 231 cases were tried for *lèse-majesté.* According again to Streckfuss (2007, 2010a, 2010b), for political reasons these statistics illustrate only a small portion of those actually convicted, as the authorities have systematically stopped publishing these statistics (Streckfuss 2010a). The conviction rate from current available numbers is around 94 percent (Streckfuss 2007, 2010a). The punishment is three to fifteen years of imprisonment, although some groups have suggested increasing this sentence to twenty-five years. The new elites have also been using the *lèse majesté* law, which has resulted in the current escalation in numbers of cases.

22 Thai scholars, such as Duncan McCargo (2004, 166), have defended exactly the opposite argument by saying that Buddhism is not, in its essence, democratic and is far from being compatible with democracy. In Thailand it has historically been authoritarian and intolerant of dissident voices.

23 Secular law here refers to nonmonastic laws. In Thailand the law has been influenced by many traditional systems of law, such as the Sakdi Na, the Code of Manu, the Rajasat, the Thammasat, and the Law of the Three Great Seals. This contradicts the argument of Donald Eugene Smith (1970, 104), who holds that Theravada Buddhist countries never developed a corpus of civil or criminal law. The new system was influenced mainly by the French, but laws were adopted from the British and European legal systems, with minor borrowing from India, Japan, China, and the United States

(Darling 1970, 197-207). The contemporary legal system comprises a Criminal Code, the Civil and Commercial Code, the Civil and Criminal Procedure Code, and numerous special codes (ibid., 209). The legal system is like Thai society: it is a blend of traditional and modern elements, but its standards are generally comparable to those of modernized industrial nations (ibid., 217).

24 "Muslim 'secular' law" refers to Muslims utilizing their own Islamic tradition of secular law (Reynolds 1994, 449).

25 At the moment, the Yellow Shirt movement comprises mostly, but not exclusively, people belonging to the middle class or higher. Various groups, such as academics, politicians, aristocrats, Buddhist monks, business leaders, Privy Council members, and military leaders, recreated the movement in 2006 (Pathmanand 2008, 130-32). Yellow is also the colour associated with the king and with Thai Buddhism in the kingdom. Wearing the colour is symbolic of loyalty to the monarch. In the literature the Yellow Shirts are often referred to as pro-royalist and anti-Thaksin; the movement is described as primarily connected with a coalition of protesters formed against the former prime minister. The successful 2006 coup is partly attributed to various efforts to mobilize royalist sentiment against the Thaksin government, perceived to be a threat to the monarchy by some groups (e.g., royalists and the military) and by some individuals (Hewison 2008; Pathmanand 2008). In contrast to the Yellow Shirt movement, the Red Shirt movement is associated, although not exclusively, with pro-Thaksin sentiment. The movement is depicted as being composed of lower-class people from rural areas and the urban poor – the majority of the electorate in the kingdom. Both camps have hard-liners and soft-liners. The reality is far more complex than a mere dichotomy, and the two movements are heterogeneous in membership, class, and ideology. It is also useful to specify that the conflict is not a pure class war (Ungpakorn 2009, 84). In fact, the Red Shirts are not Thaksin's puppets and have shown self-leadership.

26 The former Abhisit government had pursued this policy and considered ways to allow some form of free access to university education for underprivileged students.

27 Vertical welfare models rest primarily on traditional networks for social security, such as family, religious institutions, and markets.

28 The benefit is mutual, as both sides gain good karma in the transaction. On the one hand, higher-ranking or rich and benevolent individuals gain more merit and maintain their good karmic accumulation; additionally, they show that they are worthy of their high social position by helping others. Royal institutions, royal projects, and royal charity organizations are Buddhist symbols of such righteous welfare promotion in Thai society. On the other hand, lower-ranking or poor individuals confirm that they are eligible for promotions or donations since they acquire good karma. In such a wealth-redistribution system the social prestige of the institution is directly linked with the level of good karma and social benefit individuals can gain from their donation. In Thailand, however, donations to royal charity organizations and royal projects are believed to be one of the highest forms of merit making. Royal titles are given to substantial donors. These titles, in turn, give individuals higher social status and give organizations higher credibility.

29 Traditionally, in Thai Buddhism the existence of every being is believed to be a condition of the accumulation of merit. The moral purity of the Buddhist clergy enables the lay Buddhist to gain merit by offering support to a virtuous clergy and its monk membership (Taylor 1999, 181). In a more liberal and progressive setting, merit making – even if it still has ritual significance – is now an "opportunistic and compressed social encounter consisting of monetary transactions rather than the day-to-day support of monks" (ibid., 166). An example of such transactions is the billion-dollar industry of Buddhist amulets. In the kingdom the Buddhist system of merit is an economic system generating an important flow of capital. In 1996, a year before the financial crisis, out of 16.428 million households in the kingdom, the average cash donation to religious organizations or royal projects was 12.190 million baht, or 742 baht per household a year (Asia Pacific Philanthropy Consortium 2001, 1-3).

30 The term *sufficiency economy* is understood as referring to "an approach to life and conduct which is applicable at every level, from the individual through the family and community to the management and development of the nation. It promotes a middle path, especially in developing the economy to keep up with the world in the era of globalization" (UNDP 2007, xi). Three key elements are the essence of the notion of sufficiency economy: "moderation; wisdom or insight; and the need for built-in resilience against the risks which arise from internal or external change. In addition, those applying these principles must value knowledge, integrity, and honesty, and conduct their lives with perseverance, toleration, wisdom, and insight" (ibid.).

31 The king, as the spiritual head of national Islam, presides over a national council of Islamic affairs (Gilquin 2005, 43-44). It is not uncommon to see the king giving royal donations to build new mosques (ibid., 19).

32 This number differs from the one given by the population and housing census, which was 60,916,400 inhabitants. Also, minority groups were listed as follows in this 2000 census: population speaking Khmer (2.3 percent), population speaking Malay (2.2 percent), and population speaking a hill tribe language (1.2 percent). Growth in population was noticed in the case of the Malay and hill tribe groups. See National Statistical Office (2000).

33 Contraception use is lower in Muslim communities. In addition, Thai Buddhists usually have to convert to Islam when a mixed marriage occurs (Gilquin 2005, 40-42). The finding of an increase in the Muslim population is supported by key statistics from the National Statistical Office (2007), which has demonstrated that the South recorded the second-fastest growth rate in the kingdom, after the Central region (Bangkok included), during the 2004 to 2006 period. From 1994 to 1996 it held the first position. Additionally, the South maintained a higher than average growth rate than in the whole kingdom for both of these periods. Michel Gilquin (2005) also acknowledges a process of re-Islamization in the kingdom.

34 Thailand's social norms make it difficult to conceive of individuals as being devoid of any religious beliefs. Religion is an integral part of national identity whether a person is a prostitute or an aristocrat. Thailand's civil order is infused with religious values. Here the beliefs of the Buddhist majority weigh on the religious behaviour of minorities. Sometimes the authorities have discriminated against nonconformist

populations. Consequently, people of different faiths may adopt a more discreet attitude (Gilquin 2005, 38). In this context, it is difficult for censuses to provide accurate data on ethnic and religious minorities.

35   In 2002 the Tribal Population Survey of Thailand confirmed that the country had 914,755 hill tribes (Toyota 2005, 110). They accounted for 1.4 percent of the population. Among the people of these hill tribes, between 40 percent and 60 percent remained unrecognized as citizens.

Works Cited

Anderson, Benedict. 1991. *Imagined Communities: Reflections on the Origin and Spread of Nationalism.* New York: Verso.

Asia Pacific Philanthropy Consortium. 2001. "Background Paper: Thailand." In *Strengthening Philanthropy in the Asia Pacific: An Agenda for Action*, 1-11. Manila, Philippines: Asia Pacific Philanthropy Consortium.

Baker, Chris, and Pasuk Phongpaichit. 2005. *A History of Thailand.* New York: Cambridge University Press.

Buadeang, Kwanchewan. 2006. "The Rise and Fall of the Tribal Research Institute (TRI): 'Hill Tribe' Policy and Studies in Thailand." *Southeast Asian Studies* 44 (3): 359-84.

Chuamsakul, Songwit. 2006. "Education and Hmong Culture Change: A Study of Two Hmong Villages in Northern Thailand." PhD diss., Trent University.

Connors, Michael K. 2003. "The Reforming State: Security, Development and Culture in Democratic Times." In *Radicalising Thailand: New Political Perspectives*, edited by Ji Giles Ungpakorn, 317-43. Bangkok: Institute of Asian Studies.

–. 2007. *Democracy and National Identity in Thailand.* Copenhagen: NIAS Press.

Croissant, Aurel. 2007. "Muslim Insurgency, Political Violence, and Democracy in Thailand." *Terrorism and Political Violence* 17 (3): 1-18.

Darling, Frank C. 1970. "The Evolution of Law in Thailand." *Review of Politics* 32 (2): 197-218.

Darlington, Susan M. 2003. "Buddhism and Development: The Ecology Monks of Thailand." In *Action Dharma: New Studies in Engaged Buddhism*, edited by Christopher S. Queen, Charles Prebish, and Damien Keown, 96-109. London: RoutledgeCurzon.

Esping-Andersen, Gosta. 1990. *The Three Worlds of Welfare Capitalism.* Cambridge, UK: Polity.

Evers, Hans-Dieter, and Sharon Siddique. 1993. "Religious Revivalism in Southeast Asia: An Introduction." *Sojourn* 8 (1): 1-10.

Fong, Jack. 2009. "Sacred Nationalism: The Thai Monarchy and Primordial Nation Construction." *Journal of Contemporary Asia* 39 (4): 673-96.

Foran, Tira. 2006. "Rivers of Contention: Pak Mun Dam, Electricity Planning, and State-Society Relations in Thailand, 1932-2004." PhD diss., University of Sydney.

Gill, Anthony, and Erik Lundsgaarde. 2004. "State Welfare Spending and Religiosity: A Cross-National Analysis." *Rationality and Society* 16 (4): 399-436.

Gilquin, Michel. 2005. *The Muslims of Thailand.* Translated by Michel Smithies. Chiang Mai: IRASEC/Silkworm Books.

Glassman, Jim. 2004. *Thailand at the Margins: Internationalization of the State and the Transformation of Labour*. Oxford: Oxford University Press.

–. 2010. "The Provinces Elect Governments, Bangkok Overthrows Them: Urbanity, Class and Post-Democracy in Thailand." *Urban Studies* 47 (6): 1301-23.

Harish, S.P. 2006. "Ethnic or Religious Cleavage? Investigating the Nature of the Conflict in Southern Thailand." *Contemporary Southeast Asia* 28 (1): 48-69.

Hershock, Peter D. 2006. *Buddhism in the Public Sphere: Reorienting Global Interdependence*. London and New York: RoutledgeCurzon.

Hewison, Kevin. 2008. "A Book, the King and the 2006 Coup." *Journal of Contemporary Asia* 38 (1): 190-211.

Ishii, Yoneo. 1968. "Church and State in Thailand." *Asian Survey* 8 (10): 864-71.

–. 1986. *Sangha, State, and Society: Thai Buddhism in History*. Translated by Peter Hawkes. Honolulu: University of Hawaii Press.

–. 1994. "Thai Muslims and the Royal Patronage of Religion." *Law and Society Review* 28 (3): 453-60.

Jackson, Peter A. 1989. *Buddhism, Legitimation, and Conflict: The Political Functions of Urban Thai Buddhism*. Singapore: Institute of Southeast Asian Studies.

–. 1997. "Buddhism's Changing Political Role." In *Political Change in Thailand: Democracy and Participation*, edited by Kevin Hewison, 75-93. London: RoutledgeCurzon.

Jacobs, Rachelle Marie. 2002. "Nirvana for Sale? Buddhism, Wealth, and Modernity in Contemporary Thailand." PhD diss., University of Illinois.

Keyes, Charles F. 1987. *Thailand: Buddhist Kingdom as Modern Nation-State*. London: West View.

–. 1989. "Buddhist Politics and Their Revolutionary Origins in Thailand." *International Political Science Review/Revue Internationale de Science Politique* 10 (2): 121-42.

–. 1993. "Why the Thai Are Not Christians: Buddhist and Christian Conversion in Thailand." In *Conversion to Christianity: Historical and Anthropological Perspectives on a Great Transformation*, edited by Robert W. Hefner, 259-321. Berkeley: University of California Press.

–. 1999. "Buddhism Fragmented: Thai Buddhism and Political Order since the 1970s." Keynote address presented at the 7th International Conference on Thai Studies, Amsterdam, 4-8 July 1999.

–. 2006. "The Destruction of a Shrine to Brahma in Bangkok and the Fall of Thaksin Shinawatra: The Occult and the Thai Coup in Thailand of September 2006." Asia Research Institute Working Paper No. 80, Singapore.

Kitiarsa, Pattana. 2008. "Buddha Phanit: Thailand's Prosperity Religion and Its Commodification Tactics." In *Religious Commodifications in Asia: Marketing Gods*, edited by Pattana Kitiarsa, 120-43. New York: Routledge.

Koninck, Rodolph De. 1994. *L'Asie Du Sud-Est*. Paris: Masson.

Lindberg-Falk, Monica. 2007. *Making Fields of Merit: Buddhist Female Ascetics and Gendered Orders in Thailand*. Copenhagen: NIAS Press.

Litalien, Manuel. 2010. "Développement social et régime providentiel en Thaïlande: La philanthropie religieuse en tant que nouveau capital démocratique." PhD diss., Université du Québec à Montréal.

McCargo, Duncan. 2004. "Buddhism, Democracy and Identity in Thailand." *Democratization* 11 (4): 155-70.

–. 2005. "Network Monarchy and Legitimacy Crises in Thailand." *Pacific Review* 18 (4): 499-519.

–. 2008. *Tearing Apart the Land: Islam and Legitimacy in Southern Thailand*. Ithaca, NY: Cornell University Press.

McDaniel, Justin. 2006. "Buddhism in Thailand: Negotiating the Modern Age." In *Buddhism in World Cultures: Comparative Perspectives*, edited by Stephen C. Berkwitz, 101-28. California: ABC-CLIO.

Monsma, Stephen, and Christopher J. Soper. 1997. *The Challenge of Pluralism: Church and State in Five Democracies*. Lanham, MD: Rowman and Littlefield.

Muttarak, Raya. 2004. "Domestic Service in Thailand: Reflection of Conflicts in Gender, Class and Ethnicity." *Journal of Southeast Asian Studies* 35 (3): 503-29.

National Statistical Office, ed. 2000. *Population and Housing Census 2000*. http://web.nso.go.th/pop2000/pop_e2000.htm.

–, ed. 2004. *Statistical Yearbook Thailand 2004*. Bangkok: Ministry of Information and Communication Technology.

–, ed. 2007. *Key Statistics of Thailand 2007*. http://web.nso.go.th/.

–, ed. 2008. *Key Statistics of Thailand 2008*. http://web.nso.go.th/.

Norris, Pippa, and Ronald Inglehart. 2004. *Sacred and Secular: Religion and Politics Worldwide*. Cambridge, UK: Cambridge University Press.

Paribatra, Sukhumbhand. 1993. "State and Society in Thailand: How Fragile the Democracy?" *Asian Survey* 33 (9): 879-93.

Pathmanand, Ukrist. 2008. "A Different Coup d'État?" *Journal of Contemporary Asia* 38 (1): 124-42.

Phongpaichit, Pasuk, and Chris Baker. 2002. *Thailand: Economy and Politics*. 2nd ed. New York: Oxford University Press.

–, and Chris Baker. 2004. *Thaksin: The Business of Politics*. Chiang Mai: Silkworm Books.

Pramualratana, Phromporn, Suwit Wibulpolprasert, and Sathāban Wichai Rabop Sāthāranasuk (Thailand), eds. 2002. *Health Insurance Systems in Thailand*. Nonthaburi: Health Systems Research Institute.

Puntarigvivat, Tavivat. 1998. "Toward a Buddhist Social Ethics: The Case of Thailand." *Cross Currents* 48 (3): 347-66.

Queen, Christopher. 2003. "Introduction: From Altruism to Activism." In *Action Dharma: New Studies in Engaged Buddhism*, edited by Christopher Queen, Charles Prebish, and Damien Keown, 1-35. London: RoutledgeCurzon.

Reynolds, Craig J. 1994. "Dhamma in Dispute: The Interactions of Religion and Law in Thailand." *Law and Society Review* 38 (3): 433-52.

–. 2002. "Thai Identity in the Age of Globalization." In *National Identity and Its Defenders: Thailand Today*, edited by Craig J. Reynolds, 308-34. Chiang Mai: Silkworm Books.

Reynolds, Frank E. 1978. "Legitimation and Rebellion: Thailand's Civic Religion and the Student Uprising of October, 1973." In *Religion and Legitimation of Power in Thailand, Laos and Burma*, edited by Bardwell L. Smith, 134-46. Chambersburg, PA: ANIMA Books.

Robertson, Philip S., Jr. 1996. "The Rise of the Rural Network Politician: Will Thailand's New Elite Endure?" *Asian Survey* 36 (9): 924-41.

Scott, Rachelle M. 2009. *Nirvana for Sale? Buddhism, Wealth, and the Dhammakaya Temple in Contemporary Thailand*. Albany: State University of New York Press.

Sivaraksa, Sulak, and Ip Hong Yuk. 2004. *Trans Thai Buddhism: Spiritually, Politically and Socially & Envisioning Resistance: The Engaged Buddhism of Sulak Sivaraksa*. Bangkok: Suksit Siam.

Smith, Donald Eugene. 1970. "The Secularization of Polities." In *Religion and Political Development*, edited by Gabriel A. Almond, James S. Coleman, and Lucian W. Pye, 85-123. Boston: Little, Brown.

Streckfuss, David. 2007. "Is It Now Time to Discuss Lèse-Majesté Law?" *Bangkok Post*, 11 April, 20. http://pages.citebite.com/m1a5w1u7u8ysl.

–. 2010a. Lèse-Majesté – The Hidden Crime Revealed in Official Figures." http://facthai.wordpress.com/2010/01/20/lese-majeste/.

–. 2010b. *Truth on Trial in Thailand: Defamation, Treason, and Lèse-Majesté*. London and New York: RoutledgeCurzon.

Suksamran, Somboon. 1993. *Buddhism and Political Legitimacy*. Bangkok: Research Dissemination Project, Research Division, Chulalongkorn University.

Suwannathat-Pian, Kobkua. 2004. *Kings, Country and Constitutions: Thailand's Political Development, 1932-2000*. London and New York: RoutledgeCurzon.

Swearer, Donald K. 1995. *The Buddhist World of Southeast Asia*. Albany: State University of New York Press.

Tambiah, S.J. 1976. *World Conqueror and World Renouncer: A Study of Buddhism and Polity in Thailand against Historical Background*. Cambridge, UK: Cambridge University Press.

–. 1978. "Sangha and Polity in Modern Thailand: An Overview." In *Religion and Legitimation of Power in Thailand, Laos and Burma*, edited by Bardwell L. Smith, 111-33. Chambersburg, PA: ANIMA Books.

Taylor, Jim. 1993. "Buddhist Revitalization, Modernization, and Social Change in Contemporary Thailand." *Sojourn* 8 (1): 62-91.

–. 1999. "(Post-) Modernity, Remaking Tradition and the Hybridisation of Thai Buddhism." *Anthropological Forum* 9 (2): 163-87.

–. 2001. "Embodiment, Nation, and Religio-Politics in Thailand." *South East Asia Research* 9 (2): 129-47.

Terwiel, B.J. 2002. "Thai Nationalism and Identity: Popular Themes of the 1930s." In *National Identity and Its Defenders: Thailand Today*, edited by Craig J. Reynolds, 108-25. Chiang Mai: Silkworm Books.

Thomson, Curtis N. 1993. "Political Identity among Chinese in Thailand." *Geographical Review* 83 (4): 397-409.

Toyota, Mika. 2005. "Subjects of the Nation without Citizenship: The Case of 'Hill Tribes' in Thailand." In *Multiculturalism in Asia*, edited by Will Kymlicka and He Baogang, 110-35. New York: Oxford University Press.

Turner, Bryan S. 2006. "Religion and Politics: Nationalism, Globalisation and Empire." *Asian Journal of Social Science* 34 (2): 209-24.

Ungpakorn, Giles Ji. 2009. "Class Struggle between the Coloured T-Shirts in Thailand." *Journal of Asia Pacific Studies* 1 (1): 76-100.

United Nations Development Programme (UNDP). 2007. *Thailand Human Development 2007: Sufficiency Economy and Human Development.* Bangkok: UNDP.

Vella, Walter F. 1978. *Chaiyo! King Vajiravudh and the Development of Thai Nationalism.* Honolulu: University of Hawaii Press.

Winichakul, Thongchai. 2008. "Toppling Democracy." *Journal of Contemporary Asia* 38 (1): 11-37.

Wyatt, David K. 2003. *Thailand: A Short History.* 2nd ed. Chiang Mai: Silkworm Books.

Yamklinfung, Prasert. 1990. "Buddhist Revival and Modernization in Thailand." *Area Studies Tsukuba* 8: 101-24.

Yoko, Hayami. 2004. "An Ethnography of Local Conversions." In *Between Hills and Plains: Power and Practices in Socio-Religious Dynamics among Karen,* 247-91. Portland, OR: Kyoto University Press/Trans Pacific Press.

State-Society Structures and the Frustration of Movements for Secular Reforms in Lebanon
Civil Marriage and Youth Activism

Elinor Bray-Collins

Chapter 11

How does Lebanon's power-sharing system, which is intended to manage religious diversity, affect the ability of civil society to advocate for political change? More specifically, how does a state designed to protect religious communities and to promote interconfessional cooperation complicate the efforts of a young, postwar generation of multiconfessional activists to lobby for a more secular basis for citizenship and democracy?[1]

Many Lebanese, from all confessional[2] backgrounds, would like Lebanon's system of confessionalism to be abolished. If recent polls are any indication, the majority of Lebanese (58 percent) dislike the fact that political power and representation are determined by confessional identity and would like to see this system changed.[3]

Since the withdrawal of Syria from Lebanon in 2005, many of the questions that have long faced governance in Lebanon have been reopened, and demands for political reforms and, in particular, "deconfessionalization" have once again been voiced. Some of the loudest voices have come from Lebanon's youth, dubbed the "postwar generation,"[4] who constitute the largest youth generation in the country's history. This generation of Lebanese youth has led the largest demonstrations in Lebanese history, mobilized secular political parties free from confessional affiliation, broken political taboos, and brought new life and creativity to Lebanese political demonstrations. The question explored here is why it has proven impossible to achieve even slight gains in secular reforms, especially given the space afforded political activism and advocacy in Lebanon, the substantial popular support for deconfessionalism initiatives, and the significant civil-society mobilization in Lebanese society.

Although it is not known for its secularism, the Lebanese state is technically a secular political system. Lebanon is a consociational state, which, like other consociational systems, is designed to promote intergroup stability by guaranteeing shares of political power and granting each community autonomy over its own affairs. I argue that in providing these protective guarantees to its eighteen religious communities, the Lebanese state ends up sacrificing the rights of its citizens who desire secular lives and offering them the least protection. Moreover, the nature of the Lebanese political arena, produced by the consociational system, makes it extremely difficult for civil-society activists to sustain mobilization and link up with political society in order to change this situation. There are two core reasons for this difficulty that I explore in this paper. First, by granting religious communities both political representation and autonomy over their own affairs on the basis of religious identity (i.e., confessionalism), consociationalism creates more tension between religious communities than it alleviates; the system is too rigid, being unable to respond to the inevitable pressures and demands of social mobilization without the threat of total collapse. Any issue that threatens to interfere with the autonomy of a religious community over its citizens or to erode a religious community's role as negotiator between its citizens and the state – no matter how minor it may seem – becomes politically contentious, if not explosive. Second, the political power and authority that have emerged as a result of the consociational system are both centrifugal and highly informal. The Lebanese state is a weak institution – possibly one of the weakest in the Middle East. The power of Lebanon's confessional elites, in contrast, is strong, resilient, and highly informal. As scholars of developing and divided societies have argued, the combination of a highly fragmented, *non*institutionalized political sphere, on the one hand, and the existence of multiple centres of power and authority, on the other, is a particularly difficult context for activists and other civil-society actors wanting to lobby political society and/or to find a unified voice within the political realm. I illustrate these arguments by exploring two examples of civil-society advocacy in postwar Lebanon; the campaign for civil marriage and the attempts of youth to form a nonconfessional social movement for reform.

A Note on Confessionalism

Before embarking on a more detailed discussion of confessionalism in Lebanon, it is important to clarify the concept. Often referred to in Lebanon as "sectarianism," the term *confessionalism*, as understood here, refers to the practice of assigning political representation according to confessional identity. It is a primarily modern and political phenomenon, as opposed to an ancient, cultural one. Historian Ussama Makdisi (2000) argues that rather than being an "ancient" phenomenon, confessionalism has its roots in the political and economic transformations of the mid-nineteenth century and, as a result, is very much a product of the processes of modernization. Thus, when discussing the nature of the power of confessional elites, it bears remembering that these informal, clan-based networks are *also* products of modernization rather than "traditional" obstructions to it. Similarly, the struggles of youth and civil-society activists against Lebanon's entrenched confessional elites should not be seen as battles between the "modern" and the "traditional." On the contrary, *both* sides are complex products of a combination of modern forces and structures from the local and international spheres.

Lebanon in Regional Perspective

Lebanon's confessionally based consociational political system – at times upheld as a symbol of religious coexistence and as a central component of a country that is still one of the most democratic in the Middle East – certainly has its pitfalls. Debates over the relative merits and shortcomings of consociationalism dominate the scholarship on this tiny country. Whereas some credit consociationalism with Lebanon's long stretches of stability, others blame it for perpetuating cycles of conflict and political deadlock between Lebanon's confessional communities. In a sense, both are correct. The consociational arrangement established in 1943 is associated with nearly three decades of stability following independence (with the exception of a brief period of violence in 1958). It is also precisely because no one group has ever been able to achieve hegemony that Lebanon has not drifted towards dictatorship, unlike most other countries in the Middle East region. Without a doubt, Lebanon is one of the most democratic, tolerant, and open countries in a region still dominated by authoritarian and semi-authoritarian state systems. Until recently, when dramatic revolutions began across the Middle East, leadership in these countries had traditionally ended only with death. Over the past three decades most Middle Eastern regimes have typically had little popular support, have almost exclusively served the interests of the ruling group, and have rarely communicated with their citizenry (Ghalioun and Costopoulos 2004). Religious movements and Islamist movements, in particular, have been seen as threatening the power and legitimacy of these regimes, precisely because they have enjoyed substantial popular support. Thus the "management" of religion has been heavy-handed and has often included violent repression, political oppression, and/ or co-optation – tactics that have been effective in maintaining state power and control. Lebanon, by contrast, is a country of minorities, none able to assert themselves enough to dominate political power. Therefore, to remain one nation, the only option for Lebanon has been to strike an uneasy compromise between communal elites and to divide political power. Thus, in an attempt to ease interreligious fear and hostility, confessional communities are granted political security in the form of guaranteed quotas of representation, freedom from state interference, and autonomy over their own affairs. The Lebanese political system thus mandates that political power and representation in government, Parliament, and every single bureaucratic post is allotted on the basis of religious confession, with quotas assigned to each confession's community according to the size of its population.

The Roots of Lebanese Power Sharing

One of Lebanon's first experiences with government based on power sharing between religious confessions, which helped to entrench the pattern of intercommunal conflict and cooperation in Lebanon, dates back to the nineteenth century before "Greater Lebanon" had been established by the French.[5] In 1840, after conflict broke out between Maronites and Druze on Mount Lebanon, an attempt was made by the Ottomans to set up two separate provinces – one Druze and the other Maronite – in order to reduce tension. This arrangement, however, ended up having the opposite effect, as each community felt increasingly threatened rather than assured of its security (Salem 2004). Following two more decades of social unrest, between 1840 and 1860 (including a massacre of the Christian population in 1860), the Ottoman state decided, in 1861, to establish Mount Lebanon as a legally defined province rather than as a semifeudal emirate. This meant that the province was governed by a nonlocal Ottoman Christian in consultation with a local administrative council. The seats on the administrative council were distributed on a proportional basis among various religious confessions according to the demographic size of their community. This period is important in Lebanese politics because it established a number of patterns that continue to this day, namely political access and representation based on religious identities, confessional competition and conflict, political power sharing, and a practice of intercommunal negotiation through an elected council of confessional elites (ibid.). It was during this period that the groundwork for all future confessional agreements was laid.

The French further institutionalized this system of indirect rule based on religious confession in the Constitution of 1926 when Lebanon was under French Mandate. Confessional rule was then fully articulated in 1943 through an unwritten "gentleman's agreement" known as Al Mithaq al Watani (the National Pact). A verbal compromise was struck between Lebanon's first president, Bishara Khuri, who was a Maronite Christian, and Lebanon's first prime minister, Riad al-Solh, who was a Sunni Muslim. It was the first of Lebanon's grand coalitions and represented the five largest religious communities. It was designed as a temporary measure to overcome divisions and ease tensions between Muslims and Christians in order to achieve the unity needed to secure Lebanon's independence from the French (Melhem 1996). It was hoped the agreement would build a sense of common national identity between Lebanese Muslims and Christians that would strengthen citizens' commonality under a united Lebanese nation. At the core of the compromise were Christian and Muslim fears of domination by the other. More specifically, Christians feared being overwhelmed by Muslim communities in Lebanon and the surrounding Arab states, whereas Muslim communities feared the links between Lebanese Christians and the West, particularly France, and the threat of Western hegemony. Thus, in return for the Christians' promise not to seek protection and suzerainty from the West (i.e., France) and to accept Lebanon as an Arab, not Western, nation, Muslims agreed to recognize and honour the independence of the Lebanese state and to abandon ties with Syria. The National Pact, once again, reinforced the confessional system by formalizing the distribution of high-level political posts in the government according to religious identity and based on the demographic size of each community. Based on figures from the 1932 census – the last official census conducted in Lebanon to this day – the National Pact enshrined the 6:5 ratio of Christians to Muslims in Parliament and the civil service. It also stipulated that the president of the republic must always be a Maronite Christian, the prime minister a Sunni Muslim, and the speaker of Parliament a Shiite Muslim.

The confessional system of 1943 was designed to cope with one problem above all others: Christian-Muslim hostility (Hudson 1976). Essentially, it was effective in this aim for more than three decades, with the exception of a few weeks in 1958 (Hudson 1999). To call the consociational arrangement "stable," however, would be a mistake. Rather, it has been an extremely precarious one. The power-sharing formula has come under serious pressure as the ratio has become increasingly and obviously out of balance with changes in the demographic size of the religious communities. This was one of the multiple major triggers for the breakdown of the system in 1975, which plunged Lebanon into more than fifteen years of civil war. In the end, the solution for ending the conflict (but not really solving the underlying problems) was to prescribe more of the same. The Ta'ef Accord, which ended the civil war in 1989, adjusted the system to a 50:50 balance of power between Muslim and Christian sects and expanded the powers of the Shia and Sunni leaders – a minor reform at best. After nearly sixteen years of civil war, it was a shame that the "mountain of conflict gave birth to such a mouse of reform" (Salem 2004, 17).

In both the Ta'ef Accord of 1989 and the National Pact of 1943 the consociational arrangement between the confessions was supposed to be a temporary political arrangement that was limited in scope but nonetheless deemed necessary. Both the Ta'ef Accord and the National Pact stipulated that the government should work to eliminate the confessional system, which was seen, even by those who had established it, as an obstacle to national progress and as "poisoning the good relations between diverse elements of the Lebanese population" (Riyad al-Solh, quoted in Melhem 1996, 23). In fact, when the National Pact was made, a recommendation was also put forth that a committee should be formed to work for the abolishment of the confessionally based political system. The founding fathers of the second republic did not see the confessional power-sharing arrangement as a viable long-term solution. Since then, however, confessionalism has come to envelop every structure of the country and now essentially "permeates all government branches and institutions, as well as characterises a number of non-governmental, political, educational, and social organisations" (Khalaf 1997, 360). Thus it is not surprising that this committee has never been formed, let alone been active.

Rather than producing a critical juncture in the trajectory of Lebanese political development, the war and the early postwar period engendered a series of socioeconomic and political reversals that reinforced the prevailing and more restricted path-dependent nature of the Lebanese political arena. Many argue that Lebanon has undergone further erosion of its formal, bureaucratic, institutionalized political processes in the postwar era. The incorporation of militia leaders and their informal economies into the state in the early postwar period, the heavy interference by Syria and its manipulation of various Lebanese political figures until 2005, and the strengthening and entrenchment of the clientalistic networks of the political elites are all examples of postwar processes and events that have resulted in "the reversal of what little purposeful power and ability the state and its institutions ever possessed to implement change and policies" (Kingston 2008).

The Pitfalls of Consociationalism

Although, in theory, a consociational system intended to manage religious diversity and protect religious freedoms seems appealing, in the case of Lebanon it has arguably created as many problems, if not more, than it has solved. One of the critiques of consociationalism, when applied to a developing society with a new state, is that the model is intrinsically too static to accommodate the social and political forces unleashed by social mobilization, demographic shifts, and political change (Hudson 1976, 113). Specifically, as Karl Deutsch (1961, 493) and others have argued, social mobilization and modernization generate an expansion of the political arena, an enlargement of the elites, an increase in intra-elite conflict, the stimulation of new ideologies, and the politicization of the masses. Indeed, that the consociational system in Lebanon cannot seem to evolve to accommodate these types of shifts without the threat of collapse has been at the heart of many of the country's problems (Hudson 1988, 229). Interestingly, scholars of consociationalism point to the fact that in the context of industrialized societies with consociational systems, such as the Netherlands, the rigidity of·the consociational system has also prevented it from surviving social and political transitions (Andeweg 2000). In these situations, however, the consociational system has rendered the cleavages less and less virulent, thus leading to peaceful transformation towards more of a majoritarian system, such that consociationalism, as Arend Lijphart (2002, 40) says, has been "a victim of its own success." In Lebanon, however, where citizens often depend on their confessional communities for material well-being, no such evolution has been possible, and confessional divisions have deepened as a result of consociationalism. In Lebanon the rigid allocation of power among religious groups has contributed to a crystallization of divisions based on religious identity and has served only to "set the battle lines" (Choucair 2006, 5).

One of the greatest problems is that the confessional system has prevented a positive systemic response to the inevitable demographic shifts that have occurred over the decades due to different birth rates between the communities and to unequal emigration rates. The distribution of political power is still based on the long-outdated 1932 census and no longer accurately reflects the confessional makeup of the Lebanese population. Thus over time the formula has increasingly lost legitimacy as it has become increasingly unfair. This was one of the main factors that contributed to the breakdown of the Lebanese system in 1975, and it is one that remains unresolved to this day. Indeed, the question of the confessional system's lack of demographic fairness – aside from the fears of certain confessional communities regarding potential consequences of the system's reformation – is one of the main issues that keeps Lebanon in a state of uncomfortable, unresolved, precarious balance. Rather than relieving each community's insecurities about being protected and getting its share, the confessional system has entrenched these insecurities. Indeed, virtually all political issues and debates – no matter how mundane – are coloured by each religious community's fears of domination, if not annihilation, and by a fixation on its share. In such a system compromise – let alone reform – becomes extremely difficult, if not impossible, depending on the issue, as any concession can represent an existential threat to a community. This means issues are evaluated on these grounds rather than on the grounds of ensuring overall fairness and democratic equality (Khalaf 2002). Any attempts to reform the system in order to make it less rigid and brittle inevitably entail establishing forms of political representation that are not based on confessional identity. In the postwar era there have been a few attempts at this type of reform, whether it be reform of electoral law or of municipal representation. Unsurprisingly, these reforms have met stiff opposition from political leaders, who – perhaps rightly – view the reforms as encroaching on their ability to maintain their positions of power both within their communities and vis-à-vis other groups. Thus only very limited progress has been made.

The nature of the Lebanese system has further meant that a central political authority with decision-making and decision-implementation capability has not been able to develop. Institutions of the state are constantly overshadowed by the relationship and negotiations between the country's "three presidents" – the Maronite Christian president, the Sunni prime minister, and the Shiite speaker of Parliament – commonly referred to as the troika, who rule with almost equal power, although in different capacities. Indeed, every reshuffling of top administrators since 1990 has been marred by conflict among the troika members over their respective sectarian shares, and the success or failure of each leader's manoeuvres to legislate or to implement policies is measured in terms of "losses" or "gains" for his respective community (Choucair 2006, 6). The result is an extremely complex political landscape where different sects are continuously vying for power without an arbiter to enforce laws and where disagreements among the members of the troika are not settled in the Council of Ministers or in Parliament but outside of these institutions, often with a foreign power playing the role of arbiter. Thus, although the semblance of a secular, democratic state exists, the reality is that formal political institutions are weak – used mainly by the confessional oligarchs to buttress their informal networks of patronage and power in order to maintain their position in their own communities and compete effectively against each other. The result is at best an ongoing cycle of political and administrative stagnation or at worst conflict, as well as the inability of the state to devise a national strategy for needed political and economic reforms, let alone to introduce the type of "deconfessionalizing" reforms that would grant citizens the option – most would argue the right – to live a life free from their religious affiliation.

Citizenship under Confessionalism

Virtually the entire relationship between a Lebanese citizen and the state is negotiated by the confessional community. The most frequently cited examples of this are the laws regarding family and personal status. In Lebanon all matters relating to family law and personal status are relegated to the authority of religious courts and institutions.[6] The Lebanese Constitution and subsequent parliamentary decisions have dictated that all religious communities must establish their own personal-status court systems autonomous from the state. Currently, there are fifteen religious court systems in Lebanon among the eighteen legally recognized religious communities. None of these court systems, however, are subject to the authority of the more universal dictates of Lebanese law – including its provisions for the protection of the rights of individuals. Neither are these courts subject to the authority of international conventions, such as the Convention to Eliminate Discrimination against Women, of which Lebanon is a signatory.[7] Furthermore, religious officials have access to the highest constitutional court in Lebanon and have the right of appeal if parliamentary laws violate their autonomy. Citizens, in contrast, do not have this right. Thus Lebanese religious officials, in effect, have veto power over reform of the personal-status legal system as it currently stands (Kingston 2012).

There is no civil code relating to these matters in Lebanon, nor has any attempt to create one ever been successful. In fact, Lebanon is one of the few

Arab countries that have enacted absolutely no reforms to religious personal-status laws. Even countries with more repressive regimes, such as North Africa, have made some changes to these laws for the benefit of women's rights. Thus, despite the fact that the Lebanese Constitution enshrines equality between its citizens, there are eighteen legally recognized sets of personal-status laws and thus eighteen different sets of legal rights and conditions for Lebanese citizens, some of which include serious gender discrimination.[8]

Family law and personal status are not the only areas left to the domain of the confessional community. The Lebanese state also provides few, if any, goods and services to its citizens – leaving the lion's share of education, healthcare, and social-welfare services to private agencies, most of which are linked to confessional communities and/or to the networks of confessional elites. In the postwar era, which has been marked by economic decline and unchecked capitalism, Lebanese families have been pushed further and further into the arms of their confessional communities to meet basic needs and to receive necessary social and economic support. Since the end of the civil war Lebanon has seen increasing income disparity. The lower classes have swollen from 20 percent to 60 percent of the population, and the middle classes have deteriorated, dropping from 60 percent of the population in 1974 to 30 percent of the population in 1999. In fact, high rates of poverty now touch almost one-third of the Lebanese population, and almost half of all citizens at some point have depended upon some kind of private social welfare to sustain their well-being (Hamdan 2006). The intensified provision of social welfare along lines of sect and clan generates strong bonds and a deep sense of communal belonging and loyalty, especially between needy citizens and their patrons (Kochuyt 2004). These informal relationships create an experience of citizenship based less on rights and more on privileges – privileges that in turn reinforce clan, communal identity, and affiliation as the factors most crucial and most salient to well-being. This focus on privileges explains the increase in confessional sentiment in Lebanon in the postwar era. In contrast to the prewar period, when expressions of confessional sentiment were described as "nuanced, subtle, and furtive," in the postwar period such expressions have been described as "much more invasive," as intruding into "virtually every national discourse and public issue," and as sparking "confessional hostility and anxiety" (Khalaf 2003, 132). Moreover, 87 percent of Lebanese still describe themselves as "attached" or "very attached" to their sectarian community (Hanf 2003). Thus, although over half of the population express a desire to see the end of the confessional system, it is unsurprising that there is little agreement on the type of system that should replace it.

Repercussions of Confessionalism: The Frustrated Push for Secularism

Since before the civil war and throughout the postwar era, Lebanese activists have made demands for the implementation of secular reforms. The main demand was for the creation of a civil code for personal status – either optional or universal.

None of these campaigns, however, have succeeded. Indeed, they have always been confronted by the powerful counter-movements of religious clerics and confessional elites as well as by strong reactions from parts of Lebanese society.

Eroding Confessionalism: The Case of Civil Marriage

The case of civil marriage illustrates the rigidity of the Lebanese system, its inability to evolve and accommodate social demands, and the degree to which *any* attempt to create a secular alternative for Lebanese citizens – even an optional one – triggers massive fear, opposition, and the potential for conflict. Although religious clerics and confessional political leaders may disagree over much of what is discussed in Lebanese politics, they do agree on their singular dominance and autonomy over the citizens who belong to their sect. Thus the attempts of citizens to seek secular lives unfettered by religious laws and institutions are continually shut down, sacrificed for the purpose of maintaining the authority and control of the confessional communities and interconfessional stability.

As stated, in Lebanon religious courts have complete control over all matters of family and personal status, including marriage. There is no civil code under which Lebanese citizens can obtain a civil marriage; marrying a person from another faith is illegal. One can see why the issue might be controversial. After all, if couples of different faiths were to marry, which confessional community could claim their children as part of its population? In this way the problem once again is connected to the politically contentious issue of demographics and the jurisdiction of religious communities over their members.[9] The irony, however, is that civil marriages obtained in other countries by Lebanese couples are recognized by the Lebanese state. Indeed, the prevalence of weddings obtained by Lebanese couples in Cyprus has created a "wedding tourist industry" there (Forch 2004).

The Cyprus "loophole," however, has not made it any easier for activists to push for the right to obtain a civil marriage. The fact remains that *any* tampering with the Lebanese Constitution – in this case, the creation of a civil code that could open the door to the possibility of other reforms – threatens to question the confessional formula overall (Saadeh 2007). Such questioning is simply not tolerated by confessional elites, particularly those who would stand to lose power (i.e., elites of the Sunni and Christian communities vis-à-vis elites of the Shia community). So, although civil marriages are recognized if they happen elsewhere, resolving the issues surrounding the right of citizens to do the same on Lebanese soil has proven too much for Lebanon's consociational arrangement.

One of the strongest demands for a civil code emerged during the 1990s in the form of a campaign by civil-society activists that concluded with President Elias Hrawi's submission, in March 1998, of a nineteen-page draft bill for an optional personal-status law, which included a provision for civil marriage. Previously, a number of demonstrations in civil society had called for the option of civil marriage in Lebanon. Later that month the Lebanese Council of Ministers adopted the Law on Optional Civil Marriage, voting twenty-one in favour and eight against, with one minister abstaining (Centre for Research and Training on Development 2002). Campaigns for civil marriage had already been in motion for years prior to Hrawi's proposal. These campaigns had been led by civil-society groups, including human rights groups, women's advocacy organizations, and peace-oriented nongovernmental organizations, among others. Touting the issue as a way forward for peace and confessional reconciliation, activists had engaged in months of campaigning and demonstrations. It was Hrawi who brought the bill to Parliament. It is important to note, however, that it is unclear to what extent President Hrawi's actions were a result of civil-society campaigns rather than simply his own political manoeuvring. In interviews with the press, he stated that his bill was "the prelude for a more comprehensive target: to abolish sectarianism as I prepare to leave office."[10] On another occasion he commented, "I have planted the seeds of civil marriage in the country and its people, and one day we'll see how it will blossom" (Chahine 1998, 3). There is strong evidence to suggest that Hrawi's proposal was motivated by the desire to embarrass his rival at the time, Sunni prime minister Rafik Hariri. Many felt Hrawi's motivation was to make Hariri appear as a "traditional and fundamentalist politician" while showing himself to be the "champion of the Christians and the young people" (ibid.). There is little doubt Hrawi knew that the religious pressure on Hariri would be too great and that Hariri would never be able to pass the bill. Indeed, the timing of the proposal was so off that many activists felt Hrawi had, out of his own political self-interest, destroyed any hope for civil marriage in the near future (Bray-Collins 2003, 110).

Regardless of the political manoeuvring between these two political elites, the proposed bill for the creation of a civil code triggered one of the largest political crises since the civil war; the bill was seen as a direct threat to the principle of religious autonomy (Chahine 1998; Zuhur 2002). When the bill finally reached Prime Minister Hariri, who used his veto power and refused to sign it, the crisis in Lebanese society had already grown. Whereas civil-society activists rallied to promote the bill as a vital step towards genuine confessional reconciliation and the dismantling of the confessional political system (i.e., the consociational arrangement), religious clerics and confessional elites came forth with virulently hostile reactions. The first to condemn the bill were the Sunni clerics, some of whom threatened jihad if the bill was passed. The Christian elites, not wanting to be seen as in conflict with the Muslims, soon followed suit and quickly began issuing public condemnations of the bill. A more muted, albeit still oppositional, reaction came from the Shia clerics. Some speculated that this muted reaction from the Shia clerics was linked to sectarian calculus: if the confessional system was to be reformed and a more majoritarian system put in place, the Shias would ostensibly have had the most to gain (Saadeh 2007). The numbers of the Shia community have grown over the decades, surpassing the Christian population, and the Shias currently form the largest single sect and the fastest growing community in the country. The Lebanese Christian population, in contrast, is steadily dwindling, and although under such a bill the Sunnis might gain power in relation to the Christians, they would still lose power in relation to the Shias. Thus the proposed bill provoked "the process of Christian-Muslim bargaining, or more precisely Christian-Sunni bargaining" – the deal being that Christians would not support the "sacrilegious" civil-marriage law if Muslims did not press for abolishing political confessionalism (Chahine 1998, 3).

The push for civil marriage has been reignited by civil-society activists on various occasions since 1998 but each time to no avail. Calls for civil marriage were heard in an April 2010 youth-led demonstration for the de-confessionalism of the Lebanese system. This demonstration, called Laique Pride, was organized primarily through Facebook and attracted approximately two thousand demonstrators – most of whom were educated youth. Whereas some suggest these educated youth should have increasing

influence in the country over the years to come – due to their sheer numbers, if for no other reason (Hilger 2010) – others argue that the ambiguity
of the ideas proposed by pro-secular reformers weakens their campaigns
(Muhanna 2010). The argument here, however, is that the primary obstacle
to secular reforms resides in the system itself. In a country such as Lebanon
that suffers from deep communal divisions as well as unequal socioeconomic
development, the confessionally based consociational system is simply too
rigid to accommodate and respond to reform – even in a case such as civil
marriage where obvious loopholes exist and are tolerated.

Impact of Confessionalism on Civil Society and on Youth Activism for Secularism

> *The conditions of rebellion against the State were not present,*
> *simply because, there was not really a State.*
>
> – *Elias Khoury,* The Little Mountain, *p. 63*

Besides the rigid nature of the confessional system there are other reasons
for the difficulty in achieving secular reforms in Lebanon, namely the consequences of a fragmented and noninstitutionalized political arena for social activism and for actors in civil society. Lebanon is often described as
having one of the most vibrant and diverse civil societies in the Middle
East, comparable with Morocco and Palestine (Hawthorne 2004, 89). Iron-
ically, this vibrancy is perhaps also a by-product of the Lebanese confessional compromise. That no single community is able to dominate and that all
communities implicitly agree not to interfere with each other's affairs
means that there is space and freedom by default. Moreover, one of the
consequences of the fragmentation and permeability that characterize the
Lebanese political realm is that there is also space for social and political
organization, networking, demonstrations, the launching of advocacy campaigns, and so on. Whether a campaign is for gay rights, secularism, en-
vironmentalism, or even "slow food," it is likely the issue has a home in
Lebanon's diverse civil society.

The ability to network, organize, or lobby in Lebanon, however, does not
necessarily mean an increased ability to effect political change. In fact, the
reality is closer to the opposite. Although the fragmented and highly informal nature of the Lebanese political arena can make it appear flexible and
open to change, the argument here is that this openness is somewhat of
a mirage. In fact, the Lebanese system has proven to be extremely resistant

to change. There have been no *fundamental* reforms made to the Lebanese Constitution or to state law in the postwar era.[11] Where reforms have occurred, it has been argued that they were passed only because they were not threatening to confessional political elites and/or because the confessional elites could see some self-benefit in the reform (Kingston 2008). Studies of Lebanon and Lebanese civil society have further argued that the resilience of the Lebanese system and its near imperviousness to fundamental reform are due to the extreme degree of institutional fragmentation of the state and to the dominance of informal and noninstitutionalized dynamics within Lebanese political society, both of which have been reinforced and strengthened as a result of the war and Syrian postwar domination (Kingston 2001, 2008, 2012; Karam 2006). Paul Kingston (2008, 6) describes Lebanon as having a "façade of openness" that masks a political system that has proven to be "highly, if not extremely, path-dependent." The types of political opportunities that exist for sustained broad-based social action in such a political arena are limited. Indeed, the postwar Lebanese political system, at best, allows for social action that is localized and targeted, but this system more often results in advocacy that is fleeting and easily divided. The attempts by youths to create a secular political movement and to push for secular reforms illustrate this situation.

Youth Activism for Secularization in the Postwar Era

Throughout the first part of the postwar era in Lebanon (1990-2005) student and youth movements were "conspicuously absent" as a space and mechanism for expressing some of the aspirations of civil society, especially on the national scene (Kiwan 2003).[12] Survey data from this period demonstrate the pervasive feeling of political alienation and apathy among young people (Khashan 1990; Faour 1998; Chatterji 2008; Economic and Social Commission for Western Asia 2009). It was not until the Independence Intifada of 2005, which ushered in the Syrian withdrawal from Lebanon (discussed in detail below), that youth activism appeared substantially on the Lebanese national political stage. There had been some mobilization, however, by students and youth who resisted the Syrian presence in Lebanon. Much of this activism was driven by two groups of students. The first were youth from Christian sects who supported exiled or imprisoned Christian leaders, and the second were the so-called "independent" youth, mainly drawn from leftist and left-leaning student groups and political parties. These youth identified themselves as independent since they eschewed confessional affiliation and, among other things, promoted an agenda for secular reform, including

the establishment of a civil code for personal status, the deconfessionalization of the Lebanese state, and the like. As one activist of this era stated, "We
wanted our human rights and freedoms to live as equal citizens of Lebanon,
not as members of a confessional community."[13]

The decades of Syrian presence in Lebanon (1990-2005) were characterized by restrictions on civil liberties, including bans on demonstrations,
restrictive interpretations of the laws on associations, press censorship,
and so on. Consequently, youth activism during this era was generally
pocketed in arenas beyond the reach of the Lebanese-Syrian security apparatus – the main two being university campuses and the Internet. It was
within these spheres that most youth activism in the late 1990s and up to
2005 took place. After the Israeli withdrawal from Lebanon in 2000 – and
particularly after 11 September 2001 – there was a turning point in youth
activism that increased the space for questioning the presence of Syrian
forces. This opening sparked the regionalization and internationalization
of the Lebanese question with its accompanying polarizing dynamics,
symbolized by the passage of the Syrian Accountability and Lebanese Sovereignty Restoration Act at the beginning of 2003 and UN Resolution 1559 in
September 2004.

This period of youth activism was significant, as several developments
took place. First, in the years following the Israeli withdrawal, and especially after the extension of the term of President Emile Lahoud in 2004 by
Parliament, Lebanese youth began to take increasingly daring and previously
unheard of actions, crossing "red lines" with regard to their activism against
the Syrian presence. This increased the risk of violent repression by the
Lebanese-Syrian security apparatus, which they endured on several occasions. Second, it was also during this period, particularly after 2002, that
youth mobilization became more broadly based and began to form cross-
confessional alliances – first between Christian and leftist youth and eventually including Druze youth and student organizations. These cross-confes-
sional youth alliances were paralleled by shifts in the positions of confessional
elites at the top levels of political leadership. However, as Rayan Majed (2007)
argues in her study of the 2005 Independence Intifada, it was youth who pre-
empted their leaders and first broke the taboos and defied the fear associated
with speaking out against Syrian occupation. Third, it was also during this
period that youth who had been active in "independent" student groups at
various Lebanese universities sought to form an independent, secular, political movement that could reach beyond university campuses and the realm
of civil society. As one activist of this era states,

Many of us were starting to graduate and we wanted to stay active and continue fighting for our cause. We looked around and saw that there was nowhere for us to go – the Communist Party was too close to Syria, and there was no other left-oriented, democratic, secular party in the country. We knew we would only get so far as student activists; we needed to get organized ourselves and find a way to really enter politics. This is part of why the Democratic Left Movement was formed.[14]

Together with former members of the Communist Party, these students formed the Democratic Left Movement (DLM) in late 2004 – one of its main founding principles being the promotion of secularism and religious reform (Lebanonwire.com 2004).

Lebanon's Independence Intifada and the Disillusionment of Youth Activists for Secularism

On 14 February 2005 former prime minister Rafik Hariri was assassinated by a massive car bomb that also killed twenty-two others. At the time, Hariri was the leader of the Future Movement, the main political group representing the majority of Lebanese Sunnis. Although it has not been proven, the assassination was widely believed to have been ordered by Syria in retaliation for Hariri's gradually emboldened stance against Syria's presence in Lebanon. Hariri had wanted Lebanon to gain increasing independence from Syrian influence and for the two countries to have an equal, brotherly relationship of mutual respect. This emerging position of Hariri's had brought him closer to the group of political parties (mainly Christian but also including the primary Druze leader and his party after 2002) that comprised the opposition to Syrian presence in Lebanon. Hariri had supposedly been warned by Syria against his position in a meeting in Damascus some months before his assassination.

Hariri's death ushered in the largest protests in Lebanese history – known as the Independence Intifada or the Cedar Revolution, depending on who is speaking. The demands of the protestors were, of course, varied, but two of the main ones were for Syrian withdrawal from Lebanon and for reform of the political system, namely secularization and deconfessionalization.[15] The protestors had certain significant successes: most notably, they brought down the Syrian-backed government on 28 February 2005 and ushered in the Syrian withdrawal from Lebanon later that year. The demonstrations, however, did not result in any sort of reform of the Lebanese political system. On the contrary, since 2005 the country has been more starkly divided than at any other point in the postwar era. This is at least in part due to the political vacuum left by Syria and the intensified political competition between Lebanese groups that resulted. As one young activist put it, "We can all agree that we want Lebanon to survive as Lebanon; in this way we have a new sense of nationalism. But we have completely opposed visions of what this actually means. So whose vision of Lebanon is going to win? Will it be the Western-backed coalition led by the Christians and the Sunnis or will it be the vision of Hezbollah and its allies? Whose Lebanon is this anyway?"[16]

Thus the demonstrations betrayed, once again, the deep divisions in Lebanese politics and society and established the dividing line between the two main opposing coalitions that persists today.[17] Although the Independence Intifada has been critiqued as being co-opted or infiltrated by either Western (i.e., American) or Lebanese agendas, there can be no doubt that the demonstrations were historic, and despite what transpired in the months and years following, many of the youth and students involved saw these events at the time, albeit perhaps naively, as the beginning of a new era in Lebanese politics and history – an era when a unified, democratic Lebanon would break free from both Syria and the grips of confessionalism.

Although youth were not the only masters of these demonstrations, there is no question they played a central role. The "independent" youth in particular were key organizers of the demonstrations. Indeed, one of the founders and leaders of the Democratic Left Movement, Samir Kassir, was widely perceived as "the face of the revolution," and the DLM more generally was often seen as one of the "main orchestrators" of the protests (Fattah 2005).

Among other things, these youth initiated a system of weekly Monday demonstrations that employed creative protest techniques and styles that were relatively new to the history of street demonstrations in Lebanon. They also achieved key victories – such as the resignation of the Syrian-backed government on 28 February 2005. These victories injected youth with energy and confidence, and their demonstrations became increasingly audacious. At the protest on 7 March 2005, for example, they held up pictures of security chiefs, calling for their resignations. Arguably, these examples of youth mobilization helped to clear the way for widespread public participation in the historic million-person turnout on 14 March.[18] As one activist said, "We gave our parents' generation the courage to return to the streets and speak out – this had been taboo for such a long time."[19] But to what extent were these students and the other civil-society actors around them capable of forming a movement that could effect change in the national arena?

Underestimating the Power of Structural Challenges

Although in both foreign and local media this movement was depicted as strong and unified, it was far from being so. Moustafa Bayoumi (2005, 34), for example, described the tent city (i.e., headquarters to the demonstrations located in Beirut's Martyr Square) as looking like a "patchwork quilt" of Lebanon's confessional communities. Majed (2007, 37), to give another example, stated that the demonstrations presented a mixture of Lebanese flags and the flags and pictures of the leaders of confessional political parties. Yes, students participated together, she stated, but "chacun à sa façon" – the unity was an illusion. Moreover, certain goals, namely the resignation of the government, gave youth the impression that "the battle for independence and freedom would be quite short" (ibid., 53). The feeling among youth was that they were entering a new era (ibid.) – a sentiment that was unrealistic given the structural context that surrounded the events of the Independence Intifada.

By the end of the month of demonstrations, the confessional leaders had increasingly stepped in, "mesmerized" youth with their speeches, and begun to lay claim to their activism. Of course, the youth who took part in these demonstrations were not a homogeneous group: many were deeply partisan, and others became so in the course of the events of 2005 and afterwards. The purpose here is to highlight the difficulty youth experienced coming together and breaking free from their confessional communities – even in these exceptional circumstances, where they had a large degree of attention and autonomy and where a mobilizing secular democratic party was present in the form of the DLM.

Although all sides attempted to create space for dialogue between the youth from various parties, this youth-led movement became subject to deepening confessional divisions that increasingly paralleled the political manoeuvring of the confessional leaders. Moreover, with the return of political assassinations (including that of Samir Kassir on 2 June 2005) and the subsequent national elections, confessional leaders reasserted their central positions, "old confessional fears" were once again re-energized, and youth were swept back into confessional dynamics – something that was particularly disappointing for those who had considered the Independence Intifada to be the beginning of a project of radical change.[20]

There is no doubt that these massive youth-led protests – which seemed to demand a more democratic, freer, more unified Lebanon and which saw independent youth play a particular role in seeking a politics free from confessionalism – were an important moment in Lebanese history. They were in the end, however, just that – a moment. Despite the efforts of youth to come together across confessional division in order to build a movement that went beyond the single aim of Syrian withdrawal and instead sought a new direction in Lebanese politics marked by greater secularism and the reform of confessionalism, the challenge proved too great given the structures that surrounded it. Moreover, as became increasingly clear at the time and as is glaringly clear now, the so-called Independence Intifada (still called the Cedar Revolution by the many groups within the March 14 Coalition) was not representative of a new juncture in Lebanese political dynamics or of a unified movement for independence. Indeed, in the years since, what has emerged from these heady and hopeful youth-led demonstrations is a Lebanon as starkly divided as ever, as seen at the levels of both youth politics and elite politics (Bray-Collins 2009). On both sides of the divide are Christian and Muslim groups, represented by two almost equally powerful coalitions that hold contradictory positions on the identity, direction, and foreign orientation of Lebanon and that are driven by concerns over "getting their share" and fears of domination by the other. The Lebanese confessional compromise may look different than it did in 1943, but the core problem remains and continues to define Lebanese politics as deeply as it ever has.

The Democratic Left Movement has also been critiqued by both insiders and outsiders as having suffered a similar type of fate. As the political dynamics progressed and confessional divisions deepened, the leadership of the DLM essentially failed to maintain its independence and became part of the March 14 Coalition. It has also been critiqued for the dominance of personalistic, "one-man show" leadership dynamics inside of the party, as well as for lacking clarity and consistency in its positions on secularization.[21] As one DLM insider put it, "The party that promotes secularization in Lebanon has basically become another confessional-style player."[22] The point here is that the struggle of this party to maintain its independence vis-à-vis the current confessional division in Lebanon, as well as to work against the personalistic style of leadership, is evidence of the power of these dynamics and how strongly they have come to characterize the Lebanese political realm.

Conclusion: The Narrowing of Potential for Change in the Postwar Era

The experience of the youth-led intifada, as well as young activists' demonstrations and campaigns for secularism that have emerged since,[23] indicate the limits of civil-society activism in political arenas such as Lebanon's – which has essentially been characterized by frequent, energetic, and colourful campaigns but has most often been temporary and fleeting. In the recent wave of revolutions in neighbouring Arab countries, change has come about as a result of political movements that have been able to create and sustain momentum through broad-based public support and intergroup linkages. Even though Lebanon's political arena has appeared relatively more open to activism than the political arenas of countries such as Egypt and Tunisia, the difficulties facing activist movements in Lebanon are as substantial as in these other countries. Indeed, some may argue that the difficulties are even more substantial since they are less obvious and there is no central authority at which to direct the demands of protestors. Although in interviews many activists blamed themselves (and each other) for the failure of their political activism in Lebanon, the explanation for their failure to build enough political mobilization and to achieve their goal of instigating secularizing reforms lies within the structure and nature of the Lebanese political arena – its division, fragmentation, and noninstitutionalization.

This challenge to activism and advocacy has only deepened in the postwar era. Many have noted that in the prewar era there was a wider variety of mediating actors with a greater diversity of political orientations (e.g., labour unions, student movements, pan-Arab movements, and leftist parties). The postwar era, in contrast, marked by the heavy legacy of the war, has seen the unprecedented strengthening of political ties based on clientelism, clan, and confession. Indeed, virtually all political parties in Lebanon are linked to clans and communities (Messarra 1996). As Antoine Messarra (1996, 64) states: "il est normal et démocratique que dans une société multireligieuse, il y ait des partis confessionnels qui expriment les intérêts légitimes de leurs adhérents, mais il n'est pas normal ... que des partis communautaires accaparent la scène." The strengthening of clan, family, and confessional forms of association have also increasingly come to characterize Lebanon's civil society. Again, during both the war and the postwar periods the significant growth of confessional and family-oriented social institutions has strengthened the socioeconomic foundations for a "communal society." This growth was fostered during the war within sectarian political enclaves and facilitated by significant infusions of capital from external patrons (e.g., Iran and Saudi Arabia) as well as by the continued family-dominated structures of Lebanon's political economy and related diaspora capital flows (Kingston 2012). On the other hand, the war and postwar years have seen the massive out-migration of the middle class and growing socioeconomic disparities – epitomized by increased concentrations of wealth and increased rates of poverty (Hamdan 2006). Moreover, Lebanon in the postwar era is a country with an increasingly "sectarian geography" since confessional communities have remained in the more homogeneous neighbourhoods that were created during the civil war (Makdisi 2000).

A paradox is seen in Lebanon: on the one hand, the increasingly fragmented nature of the Lebanese political system ensures *by default* the continued existence of social and political space for the organization and expression of a wide variety of civil-society interests, including those seeking secularism and secular reforms; on the other hand, the postwar consolidation of powerful channels within Lebanese political society based on confessional community and clan provides unprecedented advantages to the more personalistic and particularistic elements within both political and civil society (Kingston 2008). Those hoping to challenge the strengthening particularism of Lebanon's society and polity are thus at a severe disadvantage – especially when it comes to attempts to mobilize broad-based social movements.[24] In other words, the political structures that could allow opportunities for the emergence of social movements in Lebanon are extremely unfavourable, and this is the case more so now than in the prewar era. Paul Kingston (2012) argues that in comparison to Lebanon's prewar period, when one saw incremental increases in institutionalization, competition, and participation in the Lebanese political system that could be said to have facilitated social action, the postwar period has been marked by a "reversal" in the trajectory of Lebanon's state formation that has reinforced the path-dependent and, hence, highly restrictive dynamics of its political system.

In relation to the other nation-states discussed in this volume, Lebanon is arguably an outlying case that does not neatly fit within the typology laid out in the volume's introduction. This is because the state itself is so weak (i.e., almost nonexistent as a state with its own capacity). Thus, rather than being a nation with a distinct approach to the management of religion, the Lebanese state is more like the board of a corporation where each party pursues its own interests. However, for this reason, it is an interesting case to include. Unlike the other nation-states, each of which has a describable approach to the management of religion, Lebanon is a case in which the various religious minorities have essentially taken over the formal state and divvied it up between them. In theory this is to manage coexistence, but in practice it allows elites to capture and control the state's resources and formal institutions, and thereby secure their own positions of power in the *informal* realms of clan, sect, and family – where the *real* power in society lies.

Lebanese youth pushing for secularism are thus caught in a paradoxical situation: room for advocacy and activism exists, but because power is so divided and deeply informal, it is extremely difficult to challenge, let alone change. In the Lebanese context, as in other divided and developing societies, civil society is not a sphere capable of supporting youth activism, nor are youth easily able to "graduate" to political society without their energies being channelled into confessional and communal politics, as shown by the case study of the Independence Intifada. In Lebanon, without the support of a stronger civil sphere and a less fragmented, more institutionalized political realm, movements such as those of young people pushing for secularism will likely remain precarious and unable to become a viable presence in the national arena, let alone a force for political change.

Notes

1 This chapter is based on fieldwork conducted in Lebanon between December 2006 and February 2007 and between November 2008 and January 2009. The material presented here was gathered through forty interviews with youth in either secular "independent" movements or confessionally based movements. Survey data (Chatterji 2008; Hanf 2003, 2007) and the results of focus-group studies (Economic and Social Commission for Western Asia 2009) were used to contextualize interview data.

2 The term *confession* is synonymous with *religious sect*. The term *confessionalism* (in Lebanon, also often referred to as *sectarianism*) refers to the Lebanese political system – namely Lebanon's consociational state, which is based on power sharing between confessional communities through guaranteed quotas of high political posts and civil administration positions for each confessional community as determined by its demographics.

3 A 2010 poll by Information International showed that 58 percent of Lebanese were "in favour of abolishing confessionalism," whereas 10 percent were "in favour but do not think the time is right." The same poll demonstrated that 22 percent were "against abolishing confessonalism," whereas 10 percent were "neutral" (Information International 2010).

4 This generation includes people under thirty, who were ten or younger in the final years of the civil war or were born after the war ended. The Lebanese civil war occurred between 1975 and 1990.

5 Greater Lebanon was established by the French in 1920. The Lebanese Constitution was written in 1926.

6 The personal-status laws cover all issues related to family, marriage, divorce, child custody, adoption, kinship, lineage, inheritance, and even aspects of nationality.

7   In fact, the religious courts have been safeguarded by the decision of the Lebanese government to express its reservations with respect to those aspects of the Convention to Eliminate Discrimination against Women that infringe upon the personal-status authority of the religious-court system.

8   Both Muslim and Christian religious laws and courts operate based on a system of male authority that reinforces male privilege and control in both domestic and social spheres and discriminates against women in matters related to marriage, nationality, child custody, and so on (Joseph 1997, 171). By granting the sects this authority and by failing to create any civil alternatives to these laws, the Lebanese state has legally mandated gender discrimination.

9   As well, some argue that civil marriage would mean the loss of an important source of income for religious institutions. Being married by a Muslim sheikh costs only a few hundred dollars, but a church marriage can run into the thousands. A Catholic, Maronite, or Greek Orthodox divorce costs between ten and twenty thousand dollars (Forch 2004).

10 The Lebanese Cabinet endorsed Hrawi's civil-marriage plan (Arabicnews.com 1998).

11 There are three main examples of successful reforms in the postwar era: the passage of Disability Law 220 in May 2000; the reinstatement of municipal elections in 1998, after a thirty-six-year hiatus; and the reform of electoral law in 2009 based on the recommendations of the National Commission on Electoral Law, also called the Boutrous Commission (Khoury 2008).

12 Student movements played a larger role in the prewar period of the 1970s. Some argue that the absence of student movements in the postwar era is linked to (among other things) the loss of the Lebanese University as a single campus. In postwar Lebanon there has been the creation of many new universities. These include private universities, and the Lebanese University itself has been divided into several campuses, each located within its own neighbourhood. According to some scholars this scattering has had a weakening effect on the student movements (see Kiwan 2003).

13 MH, interview by author, Beirut, February 2008.

14 SS, interview by author, Beirut, February 2008.

15 MA, interview by author, Beirut, June 2009.

16 AM, interview by author, Beirut, May 2009.

17 The two sides are commonly referred to as the March 14 Coalition and the March 8 Coalition. The dates refer to the days on which each side held its historic protest after Rakif Hariri was killed in February 2005. Although many have predicted that the days of the two coalitions are numbered – and certain party leaders have indeed shifted alliances – the questions upon which these divisions rest remain unresolved, namely external allegiances, the clearly unfair political formula upon which the confessional system rests, and Hezbollah's weapons, among others.

18 It is important to note that the demonstrations by these youth were not the only ones being held at this time, and they were far from representative of the entire country's views on the Syrian presence. Most notably, Lebanon's largest minority, the Shias, were conspicuously absent in the revolutionary demonstrations and the calls for Syria to withdraw. Although some small Shia groups participated, the majority of Lebanese Shias were aligned with Hezbollah. Hezbollah and its allies held a

series of counterdemonstrations, most notably on 8 March 2005, to "thank Syria" for its protection and tutelage during the previous decade and a half in Lebanon and to reject interference by Western countries (i.e., France and the United States) that supported the youth-led uprising and, specifically, the demands for Syrian withdrawal. The demonstration on 8 March had a massive turnout, which no doubt contributed to the historic million-person turnout a week later at the demonstration on 14 March.

19 YT, interview by author, Beirut, January 2007.

20 Another group, called Kafa'! (Enough!), was formed to push for secularism and deconfessionalization. It was organized by many of the same youth activists but could not be sustained and also suffered from personal and political divisions (MA, interview by author, Beirut, June 2009).

21 HZ, ZM, SK, and MH, respectively, interviews by author, Beirut, January and February 2008.

22 MH, interview by author, Beirut, February 2008.

23 Most recently, in April 2010, these demonstrations and campaigns included a youth-led public march, primarily organized through Facebook, demanding secularism (see Muhanna 2010).

24 Another factor complicating the building of political movements has been the growth of nongovernmental organizations (NGOs) in Lebanon in the postwar era. As with adversarial political movements in Latin America and other countries of the Middle East (see Hammami 1995 and Abdelrahman 2004), the growth of NGOs has produced the "NGOization" of political movements, including those initiated by youth. Furthermore, that these NGOs are often supported solely by foreign funds (and primarily by Western donors) can pull these institutions away from their political roots within Lebanese society. As one young activist lamented, "We used to be the dreamers of change, now we are the employees of change" (quoted in Toukan 2008, 22).

Interviews

AM. Tajadod Party member. Interviewed by Elinor Bray-Collins. Beirut, 9 May, 2009.

HZ. DLM member and student activist. Interview by Elinor Bray-Collins. Beirut, 11 January 2008.

MA. Young activist. Interview by Elinor Bray-Collins. Beirut, 2 June 2009.

MH. DLM co-founder and student activist. Interview by Elinor Bray-Collins. Beirut, 4 February 2008.

SK. DLM member and student activist. Interview by Elinor Bray-Collins. Beirut, 7 February 2008.

SS. DLM co-founder and student activist. Interview by Elinor Bray-Collins. Beirut, 8 February 2008.

YT. Young activist. Interview by Elinor Bray-Collins. Beirut, 29 January 2007.

ZM. DLM member and student activist. Interview by Elinor Bray-Collins. Beirut, 14 January 2008.

Works Cited

Abdelrahman, Maha M. 2004. *Civil Society Exposed: The Politics of NGOs in Egypt.* New York: St. Martin's Press.

Andeweg, Rudy B. 2000. "Consociational Democracy." *Annual Review of Political Science* 3: 509-36.

Arabicnews.com. 1998. "Lebanese Cabinet Endorsed Hwari's Civil Marriage Plan." 21 March. http://www.arabicnews.com/ansub/Weekly/Lebanon/19980316.html. Accessed March 2013.

Bayoumi, Moustafa. 2005. "Diary – Beirut's Tent City." *London Review of Books* 27 (9): 34-35.

Bray-Collins, Elinor. 2003. "Muted Voices: Women's Rights, NGOs and the Gendered Politics of the Elite in Post-war Lebanon." MA thesis, University of Toronto.

–. 2009. "Youth Politics and Communal Conflict in Lebanon: Confessionalism from Below." Paper presented at the American University of Beirut conference "Marginalisation and Mobilization of Youth in the Middle East," Beirut, 30-31 May.

Centre for Research and Training on Development. 2002. "NGO Independent Research and Information Service." *NGO/IRIS Monthly Bulletin* 10 (17 May).

Chahine, Jerome. 1998. "The Lebanese Law on Civil Marriage: Balance of Fear." *Middle East Council of Churches News Report* 10 (2-3): 2-6.

Chatterji, Robert. 2008. "Lebanese Student Views on Society and Politics: A Survey." Paper presented at the Germany Development Agency conference "Short Reports from International Development Cooperation," Beirut, 26 July.

Choucair, Joulia. 2006. "Lebanon: Finding the Path from Deadlock to Democracy." Carnegie Endowment for Peace, Middle East Series, Democracy and Rule of Law Project, Paper 64. January.

Deutsch, Karl. 1961. "Social Mobilization and Political Development." *American Political Science Review* 55 (3): 493-514.

Economic and Social Commission for Western Asia. 2009. *Unpacking the Dynamics of Communal Tensions: A Focus Group Analysis of Perceptions among Lebanese Youth.* New York: United Nations.

Faour, Muhammad. 1998. *The Silent Revolution in Lebanon: Changing Values of the Youth.* Beirut: American University of Beirut Press.

Fattah, Hassan. 2005. "A Lebanese Critic of Syria Is Mourned." *New York Times,* 5 July.

Forch, Christina. 2004. "Wedding Tourism on Cyprus: No Civil Marriage for Lebanon." *Qantara,* 28 October.

Ghalioun, Burhan, and Philip J. Costopoulos. 2004. "The Persistence of Arab Authoritarianism." *Journal of Democracy* 15 (4): 126-32.

Hamdan, Kamal. 2006. "The Issue of Development in the Framework of Political Instability: The Lebanese Case." Paper presented at the United Nations Economic and Social Commission for Western Asia expert meeting "Development under Crisis Conditions," Beirut, June.

Hammami, Rema. 1995. "NGOs: The Professionalization of Politics." *Race and Class* 37 (2): 51-63.

Hanf, Theodore. 2003. "The Sceptical Nation: Opinions and Attitudes Twelve Years after the End of the War." In *Lebanon in Limbo: Postwar Society and State in an Uncertain Regional Environment,* edited by Theodor Hanf and Nawaf Salam, 197-228. Auflage, Germany: Nomos Verlagsgesellschaft.

–. 2007. *E pluribus unum? Lebanese Opinions and Attitudes on Coexistence.* Byblos, Lebanon: Centre International des Sciences de l'Homme.

Hawthorne, Amy. 2004. "Middle Eastern Democracy: Is Civil Society the Answer?" Carnegie Endowment for Peace, Middle East Series, Democracy and Rule of Law Project, Paper 44. March.

Hilger, Laura. 2010. "Unprecedented Protests in Lebanon Call for Secularism." *Open Democracy,* 26 April. http://www.opendemocracy.net/opensecurity/.

Hudson, Michael. 1976. "The Lebanese Crisis: The Limits of Consociationalism." *Journal of Palestine Studies* 5 (3-4): 109-22.

–. 1988. "The Problem of Authoritative Power in Lebanese Politics: Why Consociationalism Failed." In *Lebanon: A History of Conflict and Consensus,* edited by Nadim Shehadi and Dana Haffer Mills, 224-39. London: I.B. Tauris.

–. 1999. "From Consociationalism to the Public Sphere, Recent Evidence from Lebanon." In *Ethnic Conflict and International Politics in the Middle East,* edited by Leonard Buider, 92-109. Miami: University Press of Florida.

Information International. 2010. "Abolishing Confessionalism in Lebanon: Lebanese Perspectives." *The Monthly* (Beirut), January.

Joseph, Suad. 1997. "The Reproduction of Political Process among Women Activists in Lebanon: Shopkeepers and Feminists." In *Organizing Women: Formal and Informal Women's Groups in the Middle East,* edited by Dawn Chatty and Annika Rabo, 57-80. Oxford: Berg.

Karam, Karam. 2006. *Le Mouvement Civil au Liban: Revendications, protestations et mobilisations associatives dans l'après-guerre.* Paris: Karthala.

Khalaf, Samir. 1997. "From Geography of Fear to a Culture of Tolerance." In *Conflict Resolution in the Arab World,* edited by Paul Salem, 354-83. Washington, DC: Brookings Institution.

–. 2002. *Civil and Uncivil Violence in Lebanon.* New York: Columbia University Press.

–. 2003. "On Roots and Routes: The Reassertion of Primordial Loyalities." In *Lebanon in Limbo: Postwar Society and State in an Uncertain Regional Environment,* edited by Theodor Hanf and Nawaf Salam, 107-41. Auflage, Germany: Nomos Verlagsgesellschaft.

Khashan, Hilal. 1990. "The Political Values of Lebanese Maronite College Students." *Journal of Conflict Resolution* 34 (4): 723-44.

Khoury, Doreen. 2008. "Lebanon's Election Law: A Cup Half Full." *Daily Star* (Beirut), 10 October.

Khoury, Elias. 1989. *The Little Mountain.* Translated by Maia Tabet. 1977. Reprint, New York: Picador USA.

Kingston, Paul. 2001. "Patrons, Clients and Civil Society: A Case Study of Environmental Politics in Post-war Lebanon." *Arab Studies Quarterly* 23 (1): 55-67

–. 2008. "Can Lebanese Civil Society Incite Social Movements?" Paper presented at the American University of Beirut Sociology Café, Beirut, 19 February.

–. 2012. *Reproducing Sectarianism: NGOs, Associative Networks, and Advocacy Politics in Post Civil War Lebanon.* Albany: State University of New York Press.

Kiwan, Fadia. 2003. "Consolidation ou recomposition de la société civile d'après-guerre?" *Confluences Méditerranée* 47 (Autumn): 68-78.

Kochuyt, Tierry. 2004. "La misère du Liban: Une population appauvrie, peu d'État et plusieurs solidarités souterraines." *Tiers-Monde* 45 (179): 515-37.

Lebanonwire.com. 2004. "Officially Launched DLM Rejects Current State of Syrian-Lebanese Relations." 18 October. http://www.lebanonwire.com/0410/04101806LW.asp.

Lijphart, Arend. 2002. "The Wave of Power Sharing." In *The Architecture of Democracy: Constitutional Design, Conflict Management and Democracy*, edited by Andrew Reynolds, 37-54. Oxford: Oxford University Press.

Majed, Rayan. 2007. "L'engagement politique des étudiants dans l'Intifada de l'Indépendance: État d'âme ou formation d'un mouvement estudiantin autonome?" MA thesis, University of Saint Joseph.

Makdisi, Ussama. 2000. *The Culture of Sectarianism: Community, History and Violence in Nineteenth-Century Ottoman Lebanon.* Berkeley: University of California·Press.

Melhem, Edmond. 1996. "Workings and Shortcomings of the Lebanese Political System." *Middle East Quarterly* 3 (10): 22-31.

Messarra, Antoine. 1996. *Parties and forces politiques au Liban: Engagement and strategie de paix et de democratization pour demain.* Beirut: Fondation libanais pour le paix civile permanente.

Muhanna, Elias. 2010. "Lebanon's Confused Secularism." *Guardian* (London), 23 May. http://www.guardian.co.uk/.

Saadeh, Safia Antoun. 2007. *The Quest for Citizenship in Post Taef Lebanon.* Beirut: Sade.

Salem, Paul. 2004. "Remaking Lebanon: The Persistence of an Imperfect Arab Democracy." Unpublished manuscript.

Toukan, Hanan. 2008. "From Dreamers to Employees: Civic NGOs, Funders and the Process of Change in Lebanon." *Al Adab* 10 (11): 19-26.

Zuhur, Sherifa. 2002. "Empowering Women or Dislodging Sectarianism? Civil Marriage in Lebanon." *Yale Journal of Law and Feminism* 14 (1): 177-208.

Conclusion
Secularism, Religious Diversity, and Democratic Politics

Anna Drake

In September 2010 the French Senate passed a law banning face-coverings in public. Widely criticized outside of the country, the bill fines veiled women €150 and those who force women to wear a veil €30,000. Interior Minister Claude Gueant spoke out in favour of the bill, arguing that it defends "two fundamental principles: the principle of secularism and the principle of equality between man and woman" (MSNBC.com 2011). Similarly, Justice Minister Michele Alliot-Marie noted that the bill "is not about security or religion, but respecting our republican principles" (France24.com 2010). The text of the bill avoids references to women, Muslims, and the veil, yet the government actively promoted the law as a way to protect women from being forced to wear the *niqab* or burka – and it delayed the bill's implementation for six months to facilitate a period of "education" for those already wearing face-coverings in public. Despite the limited backlash within the country, when the law came into effect in April 2011, there were calls for civil disobedience, and two women – both wearing veils – were detained by police after a protest in Paris. Several women have since been fined.

The responses to France's ban on face-coverings capture many of the issues addressed in this volume. The insistence that the bill "is not about religion" sits uncomfortably with its impact upon a specific religious minority. Moreover, the appeal to secularism accompanies this insistence that the bill is not about religion. In setting religion and secularism in opposition, this framing underscores the importance of this volume's subject matter: the relationship between secularism and religion and its effect on larger questions of power, equality, and diversity. France's particular form of secularism upholds a clear separation between church and state, but the state remains empowered to legislate in matters of religion. The legislation, in this instance, ultimately frustrates the pursuit of religious diversity. Significantly, the bill drew a great deal of criticism, mostly from outside of the country, both for its uneven effect on religious freedom and for the Islamophobia underlying the legislation. The veil ban, as a secularist policy, impedes the ability of Muslim women to choose the veil; moreover, it impedes their ability to participate as citizens of the French republic since the bill effectively restricts their movement as citizens who wish to express their religious beliefs in the public sphere. In a context where "the street is the universal home of freedom" (*Guardian* 2011), French women – who "may bare their breasts in Cannes but not cover their faces on the Champs-Elysees" (MSNBC.com 2011) – have grounds to contest the bill in terms of both of the principles (i.e., secularism and gender equality) that the French government uses to uphold it. As the French context shows, when we examine the connection between secularism and religious diversity, our analysis will vary depending upon how we define *secularism*. This variability is particularly evident when we look at East Asian societies, as André Laliberté does in this volume. Secular states may be very supportive of religious diversity, as is the case in the liberal secular states of Japan, South Korea, and Taiwan; or they may seriously limit this diversity through the perpetuation of ancient traditions of state control, as in the People's Republic of China, Vietnam, and North Korea.

There is a lot at stake in this volume's focus on secularism. The stakes become clear when secularism is contrasted with potential alternatives, such as postsecularism and religious pluralism, both of which risk moving away from an in-depth analysis of the power relations that frame state management of religious diversity. Although different interpretations of secularism affect religious groups – sometimes in uneven ways – a focus on religious pluralism risks missing the significant ways that the state is implicated in the power that religion has or lacks in the public and political spheres; moreover, an emphasis on religious pluralism without an analysis of the state's official position vis-à-vis religion may not pay sufficient attention to the institutional structures that lead to the uneven treatment of different religious groups.

Different countries approach secularism in different ways, and the significant variation in their approaches, the inevitable effects on religious diversity, and the multitude of cultural and identity claims that call for accommodation might tempt us to abandon secularism in favour of establishing a "postsecularist" understanding of the relationship between states, religions, and a multitude of other groups. One of the key arguments in this respect is that states can no longer claim neutrality where religion is concerned since in one way or another the different policies states implement under the banner of secularism enable or constrain religious groups. But a postsecular approach has its drawbacks. First, there is the concern that religious claims might lose their particular status if they are treated as one of many identity claims. Second, a move away from secularism might neglect the importance of the state's role in managing religious pluralism. Because the concept of secularism encompasses so many conflicting approaches to relationships between religion and the state – and the significantly different effects of these approaches – it warrants our analytical attention. Those who wish to abandon secularism as a framework would also lose the opportunity to learn from such a diverse array of institutional experiences and miss out on the valuable lessons that contributors to this volume highlight. Given the nature of power relationships between the state and religious groups there is a need to clarify what *secularism* means, why its meaning differs from state to state, and how this affects church-state relations and religious diversity – and we cannot do this if we try to move beyond the concept without really understanding its effects.

Together, the contributors to this volume provide a particular frame for examining the connection between religion and secularism and, importantly, for identifying where conflicting understandings of secularism create problematic state approaches to religion. In their chapter Yasmeen Abu-Laban and Claude Couture note that secularism "is often wrongly conflated with the harder approach to religion – specifically the idea of no religion or the absence of faith in public life." Significantly, this conflation is occurring at a time when religion is, as Peter Beyer notes in his chapter, "making a comeback" and when ignoring its influence is not a viable, or desirable, option. Focusing on secularism allows us to examine this central tension.

The chapters in this volume underscore the many ways that we can conceptualize secularism and how each state's particular understanding of secularism determines its ability or inability to facilitate religious diversity and equal citizenship. The contributors to this volume analyze secularism in a variety of Western and non-Western countries; the contributions in this latter category are particularly important since the approaches of non-Western states tend not to receive as much attention yet yield transculturally important lessons. Contributors challenge dominant conceptions of secularism, exposing the extent to which secularist perspectives mask other agendas. These agendas include particular ideological positions and beliefs regarding the appropriate role of religion in society – as well as *which* religion is preferred – and the forms of knowledge, secular or sacred, that have authority in the political arena. Authors also address the wide variety of practices associated with differing conceptions of secularism, including intrastate disagreement about institutional design and societal norms. Critiques differ by degree and in kind, yet all contributors advocate alternate conceptions *of* secularism – rather than, significantly, alternatives *to* secularism. As they offer suggestions for policy reform, authors draw from this global study of secular societies and point to ways that we might rework the idea, and practice, of secularism to make it more inclusive of religious diversity and better able to facilitate substantive political equality.

Secularism and Secular States

Attempts to understand the secular state and its treatment of dominant religious groups and religious minorities – and of those who reject religion altogether – are complicated by the many ways that states enact secularism. As is clear from the global scope of this volume, policies differ widely between secular states; there are a number of explanations for this variability as well as numerous disagreements about the motivations and aims of these policies. The idea of the secular state and what it should and should not control is something to which we must pay particular attention, especially given the extent to which secular policies and antireligious actions draw global responses (e.g., the criticism outside of France to the veil ban and the international denunciations of the Quran burning in Florida in 2011, discussed below). It has become increasingly clear that attempts to improve the rights of minorities and to uphold religious diversity and equality are made problematic by conflicting understandings of the secular state's role. The lessons that emerge from this volume offer important insights in terms of meeting these goals in established secular states.

Secularism can take many forms and can be understood in many ways, ranging from "antireligiousness and principled superiority to religion" to indifference towards religion (Beyer's chapter). Even the focus of secularist policies differs: some states address the separation of politics and religion, whereas others address state-church separation (Laliberté's chapter). Such differences lead Rajeev Bhargava, in his chapter, to identify "at least four conceptions of secularism" and to argue that "better forms of secular state and much more defensible versions of secularism are available." The range of choice available to states that are interested in some form of secularism is considerable. Institutional design, then, is a key factor, and once we acknowledge that secular state institutions are not value-neutral (Kuru's chapter) and that they can – and do – benefit some religions and disadvantage others while claiming neutrality, we can begin to evaluate whether particular secularist arrangements can accommodate religious diversity and manage inter- and intrareligious domination (Bhargava's chapter). Upon asking these questions, Bhargava finds that "secularism is against some secular states."

States that are only partially secularized can also benefit from an analysis of secularism. In his chapter examining the secular state in East Asia, Laliberté argues that the lack of opposition to secularism is the result of the particular ways that the principle has been interpreted and adopted. The extent of religious influence varies significantly within East Asian societies, with some religions having little institutional strength but exerting a significant amount of influence in areas such as the arts, philosophy, and ethics. This variety is evident in the contrast between China and Taiwan: whereas China is understood by its citizens to be secular even though it operates under a definition of *secular* that does not meet the liberal understanding of the term, Taiwan is a vibrant secular state under democratic consolidation. The difference between these two societies with a similar religious heritage, as Laliberté notes, "reminds us of the need to clearly distinguish between secular states and secularized societies." Even when there is a desire to implement secularism within a state, there may be practical difficulties implementing a boundary between state and religion. This blurring of boundaries, as Laliberté details, occurred alongside Taiwan's significant political transition from a one-party authoritarian state to a pluralist democracy. Ideology influences our perspectives of secularism, but Laliberté shows that states can undergo dramatic political shifts and that "culture is not destiny." Moreover, although a country may be considered secular, the secularization that occurs in formal state institutions may exist alongside strong religious foundations. Manuel Litalien details this phenomenon in his chapter's analysis of Thailand – a secular state that "remains a strong, committed Buddhist society." Litalien notes that it is unlikely Thailand will adopt a strict model of church-state separation. When considering the deep integration of religious beliefs in Thailand's constitutional monarchy and the state's response to demands for social change, as well as the reasons for the lack of opposition to the secular state in East Asia alongside the examination of secularism in Western societies, it is important to keep in mind, as other

Writing about the connection between secularism and religious diversity in the North American context, Abu-Laban and Couture, as noted above, state in their chapter that "secularism is often wrongly conflated with the harder approach to religion – specifically the idea of no religion or the absence of faith in public life." This conflation is problematic. Something is amiss when the justifications for secularism – namely freedom of religion and the ideals of liberty and equality that are so central to the normative foundations of Western society – exclude people on the grounds of their religion (i.e., their presence in the public sphere as people with religious beliefs). There is a dilemma inherent in those conceptions of secularism that, counterintuitively, undermine the acceptance of religious diversity. Similarly, state efforts to offer protective guarantees to many religions, as Elinor Bray-Collins notes in her chapter on Lebanon, can end up failing to protect those who wish to pursue secular lives. Bhargava argues that we need to conceive of political secularism not as being against religion but as being against institutionalized religious domination. Similarly, in his chapter Bruce J. Berman draws attention to the problems that arise when religious knowledge and authority are excluded in a secular culture of modernity. As is clear from the contributions to this volume, religious domination and exclusion can take many forms and must be addressed on several fronts.

Pluralism and Religious Diversity

Even when the secular state claims otherwise, it is not neutral. As illustrated by the example of veil banning in France, the effects of participating in the republic as a religious citizen are felt differently by Christians and Muslims. In other contexts as well, the relationship between religion and secularism is complicated – at times excluding religion from the public arena both institutionally and culturally (Berman's chapter) – as is the relationship between the secular state and religious diversity. Religious diversity can conflict with secularism, as Bray-Collins demonstrates in her chapter's analysis of Lebanon. Religious diversity in secular states can also lead to biases, with states favouring some religions over others (Bhargava's and Abu-Laban and Couture's chapters). Moreover, as Lori G. Beaman notes in her chapter, addressing religious diversity can be particularly problematic once we take into account that we may not be able to reduce questions of religious diversity to religion. As Beyer states in his chapter, secularism "contains the idea that the relation between the secular state and religious diversity is or can be fundamentally problematic." Indeed, Bhargava makes the stronger argument that mainstream Western conceptions of secularism "were not designed to deal with deep religious diversity."

Why, then, focus on secularism? Several contributors ask this question. The discrepancies between a "supposedly neutral" secular state and its inherent biases in favour of Christian religious practices lead Paul Bramadat and David Seljak to argue in their chapter that Canada has outgrown its secularist arrangement. In response to this problem with secularism Bramadat and Seljak call for the adoption of a "postsecular" society. In a similar vein, Abu-Laban and Couture argue that we should replace the conception of secularism as a system that must exclude religion and faith from public life with one that aims to facilitate the peaceful cohabitation of all religious adherents as well as those with no religious affiliation. Although Abu-Laban and Couture do not argue that we should abandon the concept of secularism, their proposal has much in common with the postsecular approach favoured by Bramadat and Seljak. Like many of the contributors, these authors argue that substantive changes are necessary if we are to take religious diversity and substantive equality seriously. Notably, the substantive changes proposed in both chapters identify problems with religious pluralism that are the result of a particular institutional design. Abu-Laban and Couture attribute the uneven impact of secularist policies in the United States to the fact that "the process of disembedding [church from state] was never completed," a circumstance that has entrenched "an extreme and marked tension" between different religions. Bramadat and Seljak note a similar religious bias in Canada, arguing that "the current arrangements with regard to state power and religious pluralism are residually Christian." These observations reinforce the fact that the state is significantly implicated in framing responses to religious diversity.

Although one response might be to call for a postsecular society, as Bramadat and Seljak do, the argument that Abu-Laban and Couture make for something more than the standard neutral (or supposedly neutral) position of the secular state towards religion works, in a way, to bridge Bramadat and Seljak's critique of secularism and Bhargava's arguments for principled distance and contextual secularism. Calls both for contextual secularism and for postsecular societies embody deep-seated criticisms of the way we frame secularism. A shared concern is that state implementation of secularism cannot sufficiently account for religious diversity. And although the terminology adopted by Bramadat and Seljak might suggest a conceptual disagreement with Bhargava, their suggestions about ways to remedy the failures of secularism ultimately complement the call for contextual secularism.

It is clear that, in shaping institutional relationships, secularist practices may actually perpetuate the marginalization of some religious minorities. Indeed, it is this problem that reinforces the need to focus on secularism as an institution and on its relationship to pluralism and religious diversity. One of the lessons to emerge in this volume is the need to ask about the ways we construct the problems that are seemingly inherent in secular states and to what extent we exacerbate them. Beaman draws attention to the ways that our language can perpetuate conceptions of religious minorities as fundamentally unequal segments of society. In her discussion of secularism in the Canadian context she notes that "the words *tolerance* and *accommodation* are used without much reflection on the work that this language does." Because accommodation "relies on the idea that there exists a 'we' who can accommodate a 'them,'" she argues that we cannot separate this language, and this approach, from inequality and cultural imperialism. Identifying this problem is a key first step to addressing it, and Beaman notes that examining this problematic language opens up possibilities for subversion and resistance. Knowing that secularist policies have exclusionary effects – and understanding how these exclusions function – leads her to argue for a shift from the inaccurate language of "giving" marginalized religious groups the rights they already have to a language of reciprocity. This mutuality replaces the idea of a "gatekeeper" – premised on the default hegemony of Christianity – with a discursive framing that takes equality, or "deep equality," seriously and is capable of reconciling calls for equality with religious diversity. In many ways, the problems that Beaman, Abu-Laban and Couture, and Bramadat and Seljak observe in their respective chapters are ones that require an analysis of the way that secularism is constructed and actually operates in society. Without analysis of the power relations at stake – between the state and religion and between different religions and cultural groups – we would be ill-equipped to address these problems of domination and inequality.

Approaching the problem of religion and inequality from a different angle in his chapter, Beyer emphasizes that religion is just one of many things the state needs to adjudicate. He argues that the issues with which increasing globalization and immigration force states to deal – issues that the editors of this volume highlight as being an impetus for the need to examine the role of the secular state – are problems for which religion and religious diversity often bear a significant amount of misplaced blame. Despite "the unease and uncertainty that come with a fundamentally changing global sociostructural situation," Beyer argues that "religious diversity is no more, and is probably significantly less, of a problem than economic singularity." Although Beyer acknowledges that religious conflict and intolerance are clearly significant problems that require immediate attention, he asks "whether religious diversity represents any more of a threat or a challenge that needs to be managed and controlled than anything else." If the problem is, as he argues, largely a question of perception, this seemingly overwhelming problem (Bhargava's "crisis of secularism") becomes much more manageable. Ultimately, this perspective insists that we need to look at religion not through the lens of secularization but in terms of religious diversity. But what is at stake here? Does an emphasis on religious diversity, as opposed to secularization, move away from the analysis of secularism? Beyer's call to re-examine our assumptions about "the place, form, and importance of religion within society, and in relation to the state," certainly mandates a more prominent analysis of religion than many models of secularism support. But ultimately, this is what all of the contributors to this volume emphasize; in one way or another, each maintains that a rich account of secularism needs to take a more complex approach to analyzing religion's place in our understanding of the concept. What is common to the contributors' arguments is the need to place concerns about religion and secularism in the context of the larger question of pluralism – and, in so doing, to open up conceptual room for new policy approaches.

Proposals for new policy approaches, however, still need more robust guidelines. The contextual moral reasoning that Bhargava advocates as part of contextual secularism means that when values conflict – as they inevitably will – we cannot rely on predetermined structures to resolve the conflicts. As Bhargava notes, "each time the matter will present itself differently and will be differently resolved." Bhargava's discussion, however, leaves unclear what guidelines will facilitate this resolution. It is one thing to call for attempts to reconcile these values by finding a mutually agreed-upon middle way, but doing so is another matter given the lack of agreement on the role of the secular state.

The critiques by Beaman and by Abu-Laban and Couture extend beyond religion, most notably in their implications for multicultural policies and cultural pluralism in general. What, then, is different about claims that address religion? What is different about the way that we can and ought to accommodate religious minorities as compared to other minority groups?

Although in his chapter Ahmet T. Kuru does not define the nature of this difference, he demonstrates that at least in some Western states, court decisions appear to indicate that there is a recognizable obligation to accommodate religious belief above other deeply held values. As part of his discussion of the influence of ideology on state approaches to secularism, Kuru examines the reasoning behind the US Supreme Court's ruling in *Wisconsin v. Yoder* (1972). Addressing the conflict between the state's interest in mandatory schooling and parents' possible reasons for seeking exemption of their children from school attendance, Kuru notes the court's emphasis "that such an exemption was permissible only on religious grounds: 'A way of life, however virtuous and admirable, may not be interposed as a barrier to a reasonable state regulation of education if it is based on purely secular considerations; to have the protection of the Religion Clauses, the claims must be rooted in religious belief.'" This framing contrasts with the approach Beyer emphasizes, where religion is one among many things that plural societies need to take into account.

Addressing issues of religious diversity in secular states requires not only that we search for a richer form of equality but also that we clarify where religion fits into a larger conception of a plural society. Berman's analysis of the cultural and political hegemony of secular forms of knowledge highlights a dimension of secularism often overlooked in discussions of the state and religious institutions. Berman notes that the tools of secular culture, practical reason, and belief in human over divine agency, whose development marked such a radical break with the premodern world, now dominate public and private institutions and in doing so prescribe the types of knowledge considered to be legitimate in these spheres. Because religious knowledge and practitioners no longer have the authority or agency they once had, they face institutional and cultural exclusion from the political arena. As Berman notes, although the contextual secularism of the United States allows religious groups considerable scope to participate in politics, the kind of participation is restricted because secular modernity prevents any religious group from claiming that its position on matters of public policy is based on a higher "truth" or on knowledge of the sacred that is superior to the knowledge espoused by any other secular or religious group.

Secularism and the Role of Religion: Democratic Participation and Equal Citizenship

Conceptions of democracy vary significantly between the different states profiled in this volume. There is also disagreement within states over what democracy entails. In his chapter detailing the process of democratization in Thailand, Litalien notes the conflict between the new and the traditional elites as they uphold different democratic ideals. This disagreement exists alongside different religious values and an increasing tension between those who hold religious laws in higher regard than secular ones. Litalien notes that under Prime Minister Thaksin Shinawatra's more secular-oriented government, attempts to promote secular law as a core democratic value met with opposition.

This kind of resistance is unsurprising. The search for ways to institutionalize the secular state in a manner acceptable to religious groups and compatible with religious diversity drives this volume. Contributors offer policy recommendations and avenues for further research, but finding a solution that satisfies everyone seems an unlikely prospect. Given the deep disagreement that sustains conflict between and within religions and that fosters the particular clashes between secular and religious law, it is important to note that acceptance is not the same as agreement and that a more effective and inclusive democratic process may not be compatible with some religious requirements, particularly when these requirements have their expressions in religious law. If the aim is to treat all people as equals, there may need to be limits on state accommodation of religious requirements. The difficulty lies in determining how to strike a balance that avoids responses of either persecution or retaliation.

If we want more inclusive states that fundamentally value both religious diversity and equal citizenship, how should we approach secularism? One response, advocated in Bhargava's and Rinku Lamba's chapters, is to turn to India for inspiration. In marked contrast to America and France, the Indian state has constitutional mechanisms that mandate state intervention *in* religion itself. Lamba's analysis of the work of B.R. Ambedkar examines the circumstances that led the Indian secular state to intervene in religion. The motivation for intervention, and for Ambedkar's stated aim to alter Hinduism, was the pursuit of freedom and equality. Ambedkar's work raises important questions about the process by which we seek equality. Lamba analyzes Ambedkar's arguments for state intervention in religion in conjunction with his broader vision of the way we should constitute a democratic political community. In terms of democratic motivations, it is worth emphasizing two arguments in Lamba's chapter. The first is that constitutional intervention and institutions are indispensable to ensuring that Hinduism will not impede "the development of a democratic political community." The influence of democracy is the motivation for action. The justification for intervention is the need for the state to eliminate religiously sanctioned caste inequalities that pose a serious obstacle to democratic freedom. The second argument is that this reform of Hinduism can be understood as its democratization – external regulation being necessary because changes are difficult to bring about through internal reform. One of Lamba's contributions is to highlight the significance of Ambedkar's democratic motivations. Although this richer understanding of Ambedkar's work is important and the goals of freedom and equality are well intentioned, Ambedkar's justifications for external reform did not sit comfortably with the rich democratic participation he attempted to facilitate. When it comes to both democratic legitimacy and effectiveness, there is an important normative difference between internal and external change. It is one thing to note that religion – or, more specifically, caste differences within Hinduism – impedes the development of an equal democratic community, but questions remain about the extent to which state-imposed reforms that deliberately attempt to change religion (as opposed to state protections for people's rights and freedoms if they wish to challenge discrimination on religious grounds) can be understood as democratization rather than as intervention undertaken on justice grounds.

This issue of state intervention in religious matters is debated in East Asia, as Laliberté notes in his chapter, for obvious geopolitical and historical reasons. Regulation of religious affairs in the People's Republic of China and the other authoritarian states in the region is criticized by liberal states as a major fault of these regimes, and citizens in Japan and in the democratizing regimes of South Korea and Taiwan remain all too aware that state intervention in religious affairs has gone hand in hand with state limitations on civil and political rights. The absence of regulation of religious affairs, Laliberté notes, appears to be a more robust guarantor of democratic justice than state intervention, no matter how well intentioned. This finding suggests that approaches such as Bhargava's may have less appeal in societies with little religiously sanctioned discrimination.

Given the diverse range of secular policies it is unsurprising that conceptions of power influence the ways that societies approach the secular state. As several contributors note, ideology plays a significant role in the ways that we conceptualize secularism. Kuru in particular examines the ways that ideological preferences shape state policies towards religious freedom, belying the claim that secular state institutions are value-neutral. The difference between the two types of secularism – assertive and passive – that Kuru identifies is the extent to which the state allows religion into the public sphere. Even within states that allow public visibility of religion, however, ideological struggles over the nature of secularism lead to different power relations, different conceptions of the role that religion ought to play in public life, and significantly different policies.

The 2006 Danish cartoon controversy and the March 2011 Quran burning undertaken by Pastor Terry Jones in Florida, the latter of which sparked the retaliatory murder of United Nations employees in Afghanistan, highlight what is at stake. In the Danish case editorial decisions to publish (and republish) images of the Prophet Muhammad in various Danish newspapers invoked questions of freedom of speech and respect for religious beliefs; as Berman notes in his chapter, the controversy over the cartoons "raised the issue of what constitutes fair criticism of a religious institution's or community's ostensibly faith-based position on issues in the political arena as opposed to a bigoted attack on its core values and beliefs and a threat to its members." The question is not only how to strike a balance when freedom of speech and respect for religion come into conflict – as they are prone to do – but also how to deal with speculation about intent (malicious or not) and with support (actual or perceived) for antireligious sentiments across the globe. In many respects, offering strong democratic justifications for limiting either freedom of speech or freedom of religion is not enough. This does not mean that we should not offer them, but without taking these other factors into account, democratic justifications may ring hollow and be met, as was the case following the United Nations murders, with the language of democracy used in a significantly different way to counter such justifications. Denouncing both the pastor's action and the United States' inadequate reaction to it, the Afghan minister of education stated, "In a land that claims to be a democracy, how can they allow a religious scholar to burn a Holy Koran?" (*Globe and Mail* 2011).

Top officials from NATO spoke out against Pastor Jones's actions. Immediate responses from General David Petraeus, commander of the American armed forces, and from Mark Sedwill, British ambassador to Afghanistan and NATO's top civilian representative there, condemned "any disrespect to the Holy Koran and the Muslim faith" (*Globe and Mail* 2011). This condemnation, however, did little to quell the anger towards Jones and the larger sentiment behind his actions. Speaking to the *Globe and Mail,* Mustapha Tlili, director of the Center for Dialogues at New York University, pointed out the faults on both sides that perpetuate these kinds of extreme global reactions and noted that "the tendency among demagogues in the Muslim world ... to call for limiting freedom of expression, to say 'arrest them and put them in jail,'" needs to be considered in light of the larger global context (ibid.). Although there are strong democratic grounds on which to rebut the problematic justification offered by the Afghan minister of education for imprisoning people like Jones and those responsible for the cartoons, there is something missing when we talk about democracy and responsibility in this way. The problem is compounded because of the lack of sensitivity (actual or perceived) to Muslim religious beliefs. As Tlili notes, responses to the conflict between religion and freedom of speech are problematic because there is "the rigid, almost ideological, reaction on the part of some Western countries that we have to totally respect freedom of expression" (ibid.).

How, then, ought we to approach the conflict between freedom of expression and religious toleration, both of which are central to democratic institutions? Berman offers a helpful guide, arguing that we cross a line when criticism "turns into a denial of the religious community's and its members' right to enter the political arena in the first place." Speaking to the underlying problem of excluding religious knowledge and blocking expression of the belief systems of religious communities, this statement underscores the importance of democratic participation. Just as importantly, it points towards another issue that underlies many of the chapters in this volume: the need for the meaningful public presence of religious minorities and the institutional support necessary to sustain this presence.

The Secular State and Institutional Reform

The efficacy of minority-group mobilization for democratic change is the focus of Bray-Collins's chapter. In her discussion of civil-society mobilization by those who want a greater degree of secularization in the Lebanese state, Bray-Collins documents the institutional barriers that inhibit change. The extent of youth mobilization shows the desire for reform. Despite the strength of this civil-society activity, the consociational system ultimately stands in the way of secular reform. Lebanon's secular form of power sharing is so carefully designed to accommodate the state's religious communities that it is seemingly unable to respond to the changing social and political climate. As she notes, the tacit acceptance of practices such as civil marriage that the state will not adopt underscores that the problem is not attitudes but an institutional structure with carefully prescribed and limited political dialogue.

The ability of religious minorities to participate in democratic politics is clearly important, but just as important as the institutional structures that carve out space for religious minorities – and that have the institutional capacity to respond to civil-society requests – is the *way* that religious minorities can engage with other citizens and the state. One of the problems with dominant Western secular states is the extent to which religion, at least on the surface, fails to be taken into consideration. This is odd given the influence of religion upon politics in secular states. Berman highlights this influence in his chapter's examination of the role that religious beliefs and institutions play in secular democratic states. Drawing attention to the disjunction between the formal separation of church and state and the actual political practice in the United States, Berman notes that American politics is saturated with references to God and appeals to faith. If it is the case, as Berman states, that "no professed atheist has much hope of being elected" and that the separation of church and state does not prevent religious adherents from forming influential pressure groups and other organizations, then religion clearly has an impact on democratic participation. Moreover, this participation occurs in ways that are permissible within the formal separation of church and state yet compromise this structure – as Berman notes with examples such as public funding for faith-based programs.

If religion enters de facto into the state despite the formal separation of church and politics, how should secular states approach the role of religion when it comes to participation in the public sphere? Several contributors show that religion already influences dialogue in the public sphere. There are also, albeit to a lesser extent, public conversations about religion (notably the Bouchard-Taylor Commission hearings in Quebec). The heated tone of these conversations, however, indicates that much more needs to be done to address the larger institutionalized biases that – much to the detriment of religious diversity and equality – limit the kind of dialogue that occurs. Abu-Laban and Couture note in their chapter the insecurity that plagues the United States when it comes to the place of religion in disputes over visions of the state. They point to a similar uncertainty in Canada, citing the reasonable accommodation hearings in Quebec. One of the things they take from the Bouchard-Taylor Commission is the fact that there was a sustained public debate on religion, something that they note is difficult to imagine in the United States.

Canada's public discussion of religion, as Bramadat and Seljak observe in their chapter, is only a recent development. Despite Canada's more favourable approach to pluralism, multicultural policy has until recently neglected to address religion. Bramadat and Seljak attribute this to "a certain political squeamishness about the complexity of religious issues and an overattachment to an American-style conceptualization of the 'separation of church and state' that is foreign to Canadian law and history." One of the effects of this squeamishness is "that when religious issues do enter the public sphere, the symbols and claims involved tend to be flattened out, depluralized, dehistoricized, de-ethnicized, and decontextualized." Why this is the case, as Bramadat and Seljak note, is not entirely clear; the failure to address religion in its complexity could be the result of unfamiliarity, hegemonic pressures, or general deference – or a combination of all three – but the result is the same. Without "sincere and informed efforts to engage religious interlocutors in honest and meaningful discussions," it is unlikely that we will be able to offer effective political or philosophical responses to religious issues. These obstacles to a rich and productive dialogue have clear policy implications. In the words of Bramadat and Seljak, "the challenge ... is how – or whether – to reconfigure our societies in a way that enables us to engage religious individuals, communities, and claims in a more meaningful, reciprocal, and equitable manner."

The challenge that Bramadat and Seljak outline illustrates the way that the principles underlying Bhargava's concepts of contextual secularism and principled distance shape many of the critiques and arguments in this volume. Some speak directly to the concept of contextual secularism and concur that it is necessary in order to better understand the complex relationship between religious and political spheres (Litalien's chapter) and that its goal "is really a synthesis of the outcomes that the democratic process is supposed to achieve in secular states" (Berman's chapter). For others, the context sensitivity of contextual secularism and the attention that the concept brings to power relations, whether intra- and interreligious or state-religion, make it sufficiently nuanced to counter the significant shortcomings of secularism; indeed, the chapters by Abu-Laban and Couture and by Bramadat and Seljak, all of whom seem on the verge of abandoning secularism, propose remedies that have a lot in common with contextual secularism. It is this common thread – of identifying shortcomings within secular states and approaching them as the impetus to view secularism differently – that may end up saving the secular state.

Works Cited

France24.com. 2010. "Parliament Approves Ban on Full Veil in Public." 15 September.
Globe and Mail. 2011. "Koran Burning Prompts Third Day of Rage." 3 April.
Guardian (London). 2011. "French Police Detain Veil Ban Protestors." 11 April.
MSNBC.com. 2011. "Arrests Made as French Veil Ban Takes Effect." 11 April.

Contributors

Yasmeen Abu-Laban is a professor of political science at the University of Alberta. Her publications include *Surveillance and Control in Israel/Palestine: Population, Territory and Power* (co-edited with Elia Zureik and David Lyon, Routledge, 2011), *Gendering the Nation-State: Canadian and Comparative Perspectives* (UBC Press, 2008), and *Selling Diversity: Immigration, Multiculturalism, Employment Equity, and Globalization* (with Christina Gabriel, Broadview, 2002).

Lori G. Beaman is the Canada Research Chair in the Contextualization of Religion in a Diverse Canada and Professor in the Department of Classics and Religious Studies at the University of Ottawa. Her publications include *Defining Harm: Religious Freedom and the Limits of the Law* (UBC Press, 2008). She is principal investigator of a 37-member international research team whose focus is religion and diversity (religionanddiversity.ca).

Bruce J. Berman is a professor emeritus of political studies at Queen's University, and was director of the Ethnicity and Democratic Governance project, 2006-12. His publications include *Ethnicity and Democracy in Africa* (co-edited with Dickson Eyoh and Will Kymlicka, James Currey/Ohio University Press, 2004) and "Patrons, Clients, and Constitutions: Ethnic Politics and the Failure of Constitutional Reform in Kenya" (with Yash Ghai and Jill Cottrell, *Canadian Journal of African Studies*, 2009).

Peter Beyer is a professor of religious studies at the University of Ottawa, Canada. His work has focused primarily on religion in Canada – most recently on the religious expression of second generation immigrant young adults – and on developing sociological theory concerning religion and globalization. His many publications include *Religion and Globalization* (Sage, 1994), *Religion in the Process of Globalization* (ed., Ergon, 2001), *Religions in Global Society* (Routledge, 2006), *Religion, Globalization, and Culture* (ed. with Lori Beaman, Brill, 2007), *Religious and Diversity in Canada* (ed. with Lori Beaman, Brill, 2008), and *Growing Up Canadian: Muslims, Hindus, Buddhists* (ed. with Rubina Ramji, McGill-Queen's University Press, 2013).

Rajeev Bhargava is a senior fellow at and director of the Centre for the Study of Developing Societies, New Delhi. His publications include *Civil Society, Public Sphere and Citizenship* (co-edited with Helmut Reifeld, Sage, 2005), *Justice: Political, Social, Juridical* (co-edited with Michael Dusche and Helmut Reifeld, Sage, 2008), and *Political Theory: An Introduction* (co-edited with Ashok Acharya, Pearson, 2008).

Paul Bramadat is the director of the Centre for Studies in Religion and Society at the University of Victoria, and a professor in the University of Victoria's Religious Studies Program. His research interests include religion and culture in Canada, with a special interest in the relationship between religion and politics, radicalization, multiculturalism, secularization, and healthcare. He is the author of *The Church on the World's Turf: An Evangelical Christian Group at a Secular University* (Oxford University Press, 2000), and co-editor of various volumes including *Religion and Ethnicity in Canada* (with David Seljak, University of Toronto Press, 2009), *Christianity and Ethnicity in Canada* (with David Seljak, University of Toronto Press, 2008), and *International Migration and the Governance of Religious Diversity* (with Matthias Koenig, Queen's University School of Policy Studies, 2009).

Elinor Bray-Collins is a PhD candidate in the Department of Political Science at the University of Toronto. Her research interests include the political mobilization of youth, communal conflict, and social movements in developing societies, especially in the Arab region. From 2009 to 2012 she was the country director for the Lebanon office of International Alert, a UK-based peace-building agency.

Claude Couture is a professor of Social Sciences and Canadian Studies at Campus Saint-Jean (French Campus) of the University of Alberta. His publications include *Vingt ans après. L'ordre libéral au Canada après Charlottetown* (Presses de l'université Laval, 2013), *La nation et son double* (PUL, 2012), and *Pierre Elliott Trudeau, Etienne Parent and Canadian Liberalism* (University of Alberta Press, 1998).

Anna Drake is an assistant professor in the Department of Political Science at the University of Waterloo. Her research focuses on deliberative theory and practice, and she is currently examining inclusion, exclusion, and protest in deliberative mini-publics. An additional research project, undertaken with Allison McCulloch, takes up the question of how to facilitate substantive inclusion in deeply divided societies. She has published in *Contemporary Political Theory and Studies in Ethnicity and Nationalism.*

Ahmet T. Kuru is a professor of political science at San Diego State University. He is the author of the award-winning book *Secularism and State Policies toward Religion: The United States, France, and Turkey* (Cambridge University Press, 2009), and co-editor, with Alfred Stepan, of *Democracy, Islam, and Secularism in Turkey* (Columbia University Press, 2012).

André Laliberté is a professor of political studies at the University of Ottawa, where he teaches on the politics of Asia and comparative politics. His publications include *The Politics of Buddhist Organizations in Taiwan, 1989-2003* (Routledge, 2004), *Multination States in Asia* (with Jacques Bertrand, Cambridge University Press, 2010), and many journal articles on the relationship between the state and religion in East Asia and on nationalism in China and Taiwan.

Rinku Lamba is an assistant professor at the Centre for Political Studies in Jawaharlal Nehru University, New Delhi. She is interested in contemporary political theory and in modern Indian political thought; her recent and forthcoming publications combine themes from these areas of interest. She has held fellowships at the European University Institute and at the University of Victoria, and has been an invited visiting professor at the Humboldt University in Berlin.

Manuel Litalien is an assistant professor at Nipissing University at the Department of Social Welfare and Social Development. He received his

PhD in political science at Université du Québec à Montréal (UQAM) and was a post-doctoral fellow at McGill University (2010) and at the Canada Research Chair on Democracy (2011). His research focuses on welfare regimes and religion in Southeast Asia and transnational theologico-political movements.

David Seljak is an associate professor of Religious Studies at St. Jerome's University in Waterloo, Ontario. From 2006 to 2013 he served as chair of the Department of Religious Studies at the University of Waterloo, and from 1998 to 2005 he directed the St. Jerome's Centre for Catholic Experience. Along with Paul Bramadat, he co-edited *Religion and Ethnicity in Canada* (2005) and *Christianity and Ethnicity in Canada* (2008). He is also editor of a theological journal, *The Ecumenist: A Journal of Theology, Culture and Society.*

Index

Abella, Rosalie, 129-30

Abhisit Vejjajiva, 234, 244, 258*n*26

Abu-Laban, Yasmeen, 2, 12, 295, 299, 300, 301, 302-3, 308, 309

accommodation: abandonment of, 130; in Canada, 120, 127-30, 128-29, 301; contributions by, 130; and deep equality, 130-32; dismantling of, 130-31; diversity and, 120, 122; and equality, 121, 127, 130, 131-32; in Europe, 80; gatekeeper of, 126, 129, 301; imperialism and, 120-21; as interim value, 130; and labour law, 126; limits to, 12, 126, 304; and minimal impairment, 129-30; and multiculturalism, 124-25; and otherness, 121, 124, 301; power differences in, 12; recovery/reconstitution of, 130; of religious diversity, 36; and religious freedom, 127, 131; of religious minorities, 17, 127; secularism and, 88; and special interest groups, 125-26. *See also* reasonable accommodation

Adams, Michael, 153-54

Against the Gods (Bernstein), 52

Alberta v. Hutterian Brethren of Wilson Colony, 134*n*11

Alliot-Marie, Michele, 293

Ambedkar, B.R., 304-5; about, 188; and affirmative action, 188; beliefs of, 188; on Brahmins, 201-2; on caste observation as contrary to reason, 202-3; on communal electorates, 196; on communicated experience, 192-93; as Dalit, 188, 190; and democracy, 192-93, 199, 203; on "dhamma," 191; education of, 188; on excommunication, 197; on freedom of choice in profession, 198; Gandhi compared to, 200, 205*n*3; and graded sovereignties of caste, 190, 192; and group interactions, 194, 195-96; and groups vs. groupism, 193-94, 197, 204; on hierarchical dismantlement, 202; and Hinduism as religion of rules vs. principles, 188-90; and Hinduism's social order, 189-90; and individual freedom/liberty, 191, 192, 197-99; and individual--group relationship, 191, 193, 195, 197-98, 204; on intellectual class, 201; on internal vs. external reform of caste system, 200-204; on kinship in religion, 204; on like-mindedness/endosmosis, 196, 197; political ideals of, 191; and progress as reform of caste system, 199-200; on public spirit/charity restricted to caste group, 192, 197; on reform of caste system, 197, 198; on reform of Hinduism, 189-90, 192, 200-204; and regulation of religion, 199, 203; on religion and politics, 204; on righteousness, 191; on Shastras, 200, 203; on "slavery," 198, 199, 202; on societies, 195-97; and state intervention in Hinduism, 190, 192, 203-4; and state–religion relationship, 191; on untouchability, 199, 204; on Vedas, 203

Amish, 169
anticlericalism, 9, 11, 50-51, 73, 214
Arab Spring, 8, 59
assertive secular states, 21-22, 305-6
assertive secularism: in Burma, 21; in France, 11, 166, 172, 173, 174, 179-80, 181*n*21; in Laos, 21; and religious diversity, 179; in Turkey, 166, 174-75, 176, 178, 180; in US, 166, 167
assimilation, 113, 121, 239
Atatürk's Principles, 176
atheism, 36, 113, 137

Bader, Veit, 79, 115*n*3
Bakht, Natasha, 134*n*13
Bannerji, Himani, 125
Bauman, Zygmunt, 65-66*n*3
Bayoumi, Mustafa, 283
Bayrou, François, 173
Beaman, Lori G., 2, 5, 6, 10, 12, 299, 301, 302-3
Bell, Daniel, 45
Bellah, Robert, 147-48
Berman, Bruce J., 2, 5, 6, 10, 12, 214, 299, 303, 306, 308, 309
Bernstein, Peter, *Against the Gods*, 52

Beyer, Peter, 2, 5, 6, 7, 295, 296, 299-300, 301-2
Bhargava, Rajeev, 2, 4, 11, 12, 15-17, 57, 187, 191, 233, 253, 296-97, 298, 299, 300, 301, 302, 304
Bhumibol Adulyadej, King, 232, 233-34, 247
Bouchard, Gérard, 99, 105, 114-15*n*1, 156
Bouchard-Taylor Commission, 120, 133*n*1, 156, 159, 308
Brahmins, 192, 201-2
Bramadat, Paul, 2, 10, 12, 14-15, 115*n*8, 136, 300-301, 308-9
Bray-Collins, Elinor, 2, 4, 5, 13, 20, 299, 307
British North America Act (1867), 100
Brodsky, Gwen, 131; "The Duty to Accommodate," 126-27
Brooks, David, 65
Brown, Wendy, 123
Buddhism: in China, 230*n*6-7; and economy, 249-50; and education, 248-49; and governments/states, 216; in Japan, 212, 224, 230*n*6-7; in Korea, 230*n*6; monarchy and, 232, 233, 240-41, 243; and national identity, 237, 238, 253; nationalists in Sri Lanka, 70; in Sinitic states, 21; and social welfare services, 246, 249, 252; in Sri Lanka, 20, 37; as state religion, 216, 232-33, 235; in Taiwan, 224, 225-26; in Thailand, 21, 232-40, 243, 245-48, 250-54
Bush, George W., 60-61

Calvinism, 49
Cambodia: Khmer Rouge in, 21; as passive secular state, 21
Canada: binary oppositions in, 144; Christianity in, 98, 99, 123, 132, 300; civic vs. ethnic nationalism in, 156; Confederation in, 100-101; conservative/community-oriented culture of, 144; cultural power of

churches in, 100; ethnic diversity in, 103-4; ethnoreligious history of, 98; First Nations' spiritualities in, 122; French vs. English, 146, 156; history of Christianity in, 99-100; ideological interregnum in, 98-99, 112-14; immigration into, 99-100; liberalism of, 153-54; modernity of, 157; multiculturalism in, 3, 144, 308-9; Muslims in, 3, 108; *niqab* in, 113; peaceful cohabitation of religions in, 140; postsecularism in, 105-6; racism in, 121, 156; reasonable accommodation of religious minorities in, 3; religion–politics relationship in, 57; religiosity in, 211; religious diversity in, 12, 103-4, 105-6; religious establishment in, 99; religious identity in, 147; as secular state, 3; secularism in, 300; secularization of, 99-102; Sikhs in, 59; Toryism in, 153; transnationalism in, 106, 110-12; US compared to, 140, 144, 157; welfare state in, 153. *See also* French Canada/Canadians

capitalism: and boundaries of secular state, 40; in China, 38; global crisis of, 64; globalization and, 38, 39; Islam and, 59; knowledge and, 53; in Lebanon, 274; reconstruction of, 56. *See also* neoliberalism

Casanova, José, 115*n*7, 222

caste system: annihilation of, 199-204; Brahmins in, 192, 201-2; as contrary to reason, 202-3; and excommunication, 197, 198; external regulation of, 203-4; groups within, 194, 195, 197; hierarchical structure of, 202, 203; and identity, 194; and individual liberty, 197-99; marriage/dining rules, 200; and non-Hindu religions, 193-94; progress as reform of, 199-200; and public spirit/charity, 192; reform of, 197, 198, 199-200; resocialization of, 196; and sectarianism, 192-94; Shastras and, 200; and society, 195-

97. *See also* Untouchables/untouchability

Charron, Louise, 128, 129

Charter of Rights and Freedoms, 98, 102, 103, 124, 128-29, 131

Chen Lu-an, 226

Chicago School, 155

China: Boxer Rebellion, 216, 220; Buddhism in, 230*n*6-7; capitalism in, 38; Christianity in, 213; Communist Party, 8, 216; Confucianism in, 215; cultural revolution, 238; dissidents in, 229-30*n*3; duty of rulers in, 48; emergence as economic power, 5; emperor, 217; established religions in, 8-9, 24*n*11, 219; Falun Gong in, 3; lack of critique of secularism in, 220; local historical personages as deities in, 217; modernity in, 11, 13-14, 219; Muslims in, 230*n*4; nationalism in, 221; prevention of opposition in, 220; Qing dynasty, 217-18, 219; as quasi-secular state, 8, 9, 14, 21-22; religiosity in, 211-12, 212-13; religious diversity in, 210, 298; religious freedom in, 74; religious uprisings in, 216; as secular state, 218; secularism in, 6, 18, 36, 227, 297; secularization in, 210-11; and Sinitic secular state, 19; as state with supreme religious leader, 18; state–religion relationship in, 2, 8-9, 216, 217-18, 227-28; Taiping (Great Peace), 216; Tiananmen Square Massacre, 38

Chirac, Jacques, 173

Christian privilege: elimination for moral reasons, 103; in Europe, 71, 79; in European institutions, 78; and interference with non-Christian faiths, 74; multiculturalism and, 97-98, 106; and shadow/social establishment, 100

Christianity: in Canada, 98, 99, 123, 132, 300; in China, 213; civilization of, 75-76; development of, 48; in East Asia, 215, 230*n*4; East Asian emigrants and,

229; East Asian religions vs., 210, 214; in Japan, 213; in Lebanon, 268, 269-70, 277; other religions contrasted to, 34; principled distance and link with secularism, 88-89; and separation of church and state, 89; in Taiwan, 213; in Thailand, 256*n*11

churches: cultural power of, 100; decline in membership/attendance, 100; modernity and decline of, 101; and social services/healthcare, 99, 101, 102

church-state separation. *See* separation of church and state

City of Boerne v. Flores, 171

Clinton, Bill, 168, 170, 171

Cohn, Norman, *The Pursuit of the Millennium,* 50

Cold War, 7, 38, 39, 45

colonialism: decolonization, and secular states, 7; and India, 11; and Indic states, 21; and indigenous religions, 18; and non-Western secular states, 19; and otherness, 131; and religious intolerance, 137; and secular state, 21; and secularism, 13, 18, 137; and state–religion relationship, 5, 218

communism: democracy and, 55; and millennialism, 62; and religious freedom, 74; Thailand and, 238-40

Confederation, 100-101

confessionalism: about, 267; and citizenship, 273-75; and civil marriage, 275-78; demographic shifts and, 271-72; and expulsion of other faiths, 78; in Lebanon, 265-66, 268-70, 271-72, 277-78, 283-84; and political representation, 272; and reform/political change, 272, 278; sectarianism and, 287*n*2; and secularism, 275-78; and social welfare services, 274; youth movement and, 279-80, 283

Confucianism, 21, 215-16

Connolly, William, 131

consociationalism: critiques of, 271-73; in Lebanon, 266; in Netherlands, 271;

and reform/political change, 278; and religious diversity, 266, 271

Constantine, emperor, 48

Constitutional Act (1791), 155

contextual secularism: about, 84, 87-88, 298; applicability of, 309; in India, 17, 88; internal discord/instability and, 87; and middle way, 57-58; moral reasoning and, 16-17, 57-58, 302; as multivalue/multivalent doctrine, 16-17, 57-58, 87-88; and postsecularism, 300-301; principled distance and, 15, 87; and religious diversity, 23; and religious pluralism, 15; replication of, 2; and rights conflicts, 16-17, 87-88; and situational thinking, 87; and Thailand, 253; in US, 303

Co-operative Commonwealth Federation (CCF), 57, 61

Côté, Pauline, 133*n*1

Couture, Claude, 2, 12, 295, 299, 300, 301, 302-3, 308, 309

Crossman, Richard, *The God That Failed,* 62

cuius regio, eius religio, 31-32, 49

culture: civic, 146; hybridity of US, 140; as less Christian, 102; naive secularism and, 104-5; US as single, 142-43; of US compared to Canada, 144

Curtis, James, 154, 156-57, 158, 160

Dahl, Robert, 54-55

Dalits: affirmative action for, 188; Ambedkar as, 188, 190. *See also* Untouchables/untouchability

Dawkins, Richard, 113

Day, Richard, 124-25

Day, Shelagh, 131; "The Duty to Accommodate," 126-27

Demirel, Süleyman, 176

democracy: Ambedkar on, 192-93, 199, 203; Buddhism and, 244; communism and, 55, 62; and conflict resolution, 55; differing conceptions of, 303-4; and hierarchical structure of caste system, 203; key characteristics as strength vs. weaknesses, 58; monarchy and, 233-34, 241-44; and neutrality of state, 58; pluralist, 55-56; and public significance of religion, 85; reform of Hinduism and, 305; religion–politics relationship in, 57; and religious competition, 221; religious diversity and, 228; and religious freedom, 56, 306-7; religious institutions and, 57; religious minorities and, 307-8; role of religion in, 56; social science and, 55; in Taiwan, 218, 223, 227, 228; in Thailand, 232-35, 244-46, 253, 304; Thailand and, 240-42

Deng Xiaoping, 38

Denmark: cartoon affair in, 56, 71, 79, 306; Muslims in, 79

Deschamps, Marie, 129-30

Deutsch, Karl, 271

diversity: accommodation and, 120, 122; "but clause" problem, 124; in Lebanon, 278; limits to, 124; multiculturalism and, 124-25; as "problem of diversity," 123-24; tolerance and, 120, 122; US and, 143. *See also* ethnic diversity/pluralism; religious diversity/pluralism

Douglas, Tommy, 57

Druze, 268

Durkheim, Émile, 139, 141, 145, 159

"The Duty to Accommodate" (Day; Brodsky), 126-27

Dworkin, Ronald, 85-86

East Asia: absence of resistance to secularism in, 209, 217, 220; Buddhism in, 216; Christianity in, 215, 230*n*4; Confucianism in, 215-16; constitutions in, 219; emigrants from, 229; homogeneity of culture in, 215; influence of religions in, 215; institutional weakness of religion in, 215-17; and Islam, 215; national religions in, 215; neutrality in, 219; noncongregational religious practice in, 221, 225; pervasiveness of religion in public life in, 209; population, 208; religiosity in, 211-12, 213; religious diversity in, 210, 218-19, 228; religious freedom in, 219; religious pluralism in, 221; religious revisionism and, 220; secular state in, 207, 210; secularism in, 214-15, 298; South Asia compared to, 215; state intervention in religious affairs in, 217, 305; state involvement in religious rituals, 216-17; state religions in, 219, 221; state–religion relationship in, 210, 214-15, 217-21, 229; strength of religions in, 210; Taoism in, 216; universal religions in, 215

education: Charter of Rights and Freedoms and Christian dimension of, 102; and religious resurgence, 112; secularization of, 248-49; in Thailand, 248-49. *See also* schools

Egypt: activitism in, 285; Arab Spring in, 8; Muslim Brotherhood in, 221

Eisenhower, Dwight D., 138

Eisenstadt, Schmuel, 19, 65*n*1

elites: democracy and, 55; gods and, 48; in Lebanon, 266, 268, 276, 286-87; secular modernity and, 53; in Thailand, 234, 235, 238, 241, 242, 244, 249, 250, 254-55*nn*3-4, 304

empirical knowledge: and modernity, 52-53; religious right and, 60-61

Engels, Friedrich, 180*n*1

Enlightenment: and modernity, 52; principled distance and, 84; religious resurgence and, 114

equality: accommodation and, 121, 127, 130, 131-32; of Christian vs. non-Christian faiths in Europe, 79; deep, 130-32, 131, 132, 301; difference and, 132; and differential treatment, 85-86; feminism and, 132; formal vs. substantive, 131; human rights tribunals and, 131; intrareligious, 75; and limits on accommodation, 304; principled distance and, 85-86, 87; and religious freedom, 129; and sameness, 132; and special interest groups, 125, 126; state intervention and, 20; in Thailand, 249; tolerance and, 130; of treatment vs. treating everyone as equal, 85-86

Erdoğan, Tayyip, 177

established churches: anticlericalism and, 50-51; in Canada, 100; denominations as oligarchy, 100; in Europe, 78, 115*n*7; in France, 11; and religious pluralism, 51. *See also* state–church relationship

established state religions: biasing toward, 71, 78; Buddhism as, 216, 232-33, 235, 248; in China, 22; and development of liberal democracy, 12; in East Asia, 219, 221; in Europe, 36, 71; in Islamic states, 36; and multicultural equality, 17; in North Korea, 22; and perpetuation of domination, 71-72; religious diversity and, 71; in Vietnam, 22. *See also* state–religion relationship

establishment: Catholicism and, 115*n*7; concept of, 115*n*3; shadow/social, 100, 105

ethnic diversity/pluralism: in Canada, 103-4, 105-6; immigration and, 1, 6; multiculturalism and, 106-7; religious resurgence and, 14; in Thailand, 243-44, 253

ethnicity: defined, 107; and identity, 107; religion and, 106-12; and solidarity, 107; in Thailand, 237-38; transnationalism of, 111

Europe: appropriation of ideas/institutions by non-European world, 33-34; Canada's reproduction of religious establishment, 99, 105; Catholics in, 12; Constitution, 81; established churches/religions in, 36, 71, 78, 115*n*7; evolution away from religious establishment, 5; expansion into non-European world, 33; globalization and, 33-34; Jews in, 12; liberalism in, 153; Muslims in, 78-80, 136; non-Christian migrants to, 78-80; principled distance and, 80; privileging of Christianity in, 71, 79; privileging of churches in, 77-78; protection for religious minorities in, 11-12; Protestants in, 12; religious diversity in, 79; separation of church and state in, 77-78; toleration in, 78; Western secularism in, 77-81

Evans-Pritchard, E.E., *Witchcraft, Oracles and Magic among the Azande*, 66*n*10

Everson v. Board of Education, 167

Evren, Kenan, 175

face coverings. *See* head/face coverings

Falardeau, Jean-Charles, 155

Falun Gong, 3, 227

Falwell, Jerry, 37

Flores, City of Boerne v., 171

France: anticlericalism in, 11, 73; anti-multiculturalism in, 74; assertive secularism in, 11, 166, 172, 173, 174, 179-80, 181*n*21; Catholic school funding in, 82, 173; Constitutional Court, 172; Council of State, 172-73; established church in, 11; face-coverings law in, 293-94, 296, 299; headscarf issue in, 71, 79, 172-74; historical influence on Quebec, 155, 156; Jews in, 51, 83, 181*n*22; *laïcité* in, 132, 223, 229*n*1; and Lebanon, 269; Muslims in, 79, 82, 172-74, 294; National Front, 174; New France compared to, 155; passive secularism in, 166, 172-73; religiosity in, 211; religious clothing in, 113; religious symbols in schools in, 166, 172-74; revolution, 5; secularism in, 90, 293-94; separation of religion and state in, 73-74; Sikhs in, 174; state intervention in, 74; state–religion relationship in, 73-74, 293-94

freedom of conscience: in Japan, 218; and religious diversity, 13; Republic of China and, 218; in Taiwan, 222, 227; in Thailand, 233

freedom of religion: accommodation of, 121, 127, 131; American Creed and, 139; in China, 74; communism and, 74; consociationalism and, 271; democracies and, 56; democracy and, 306-7; in East Asia, 219; in employment, 127; and equality, 129; in Japan, 218; of non-Christian immigrants, 103; and special interest groups, 129; state–religion relationship and, 73-74; Supreme Court of Canada on, 127-28; in Thailand, 243-44, 247, 256n12; in Turkey, 74; in US, 75

French Canada/Canadians: English Canada compared to, 146, 156; marginalization of, 155; nationalism, 155; New France, 99, 155; religiosity in, 158

Friedman, Milton, 62

Fukuyama, Francis, 38, 40, 62

fundamentalism(s): Islamic, 40; militant differentiation in, 6; Protestant, 70; and religious diversity, 40-41, 43; and religious resurgence, 38; rise of, 5-6, 39; world religions and, 43

Gandhi, Mohandas, 200, 205n3

Gates, Henry Louis, 140

Gauchet, Marcel, 214

Germany: citizenship debates in, 113; fall of Berlin Wall, 38; headscarf ban in, 181n21; Muslims in, 79; religious diversity in, 71; religious symbols in schools in, 181n21

Gibson, James William, 66n3

Giddens, Anthony, 10, 52-53

Gill, Anthony, 252

Gilquin, Michel, 259n33

globalization: and capitalism, 38, 39; and changing world, 36; and Europe, 33-34; and fundamentalism, 39; and global society, 39; and homogenization, 23; and modernity, 3; and neo-liberalism, 18-19, 38, 39; origin of

term, 38; and religion, 110-11; and religious diversity, 4-5, 41-42, 71; and religious resurgence, 58; and secularism, 10, 18; and terrorism, 6; and transnationalism, 112

The God That Failed (Crossman), 62

gods, development of, 47-48

Gogh, Theo van, 71

Goldman v. Weinberger, 167-68

Gonzales v. O Centro Espirita, 171

Gorbachev, Mikhail, 38

Grabb, Edward, 154, 156-57, 158, 160

Grant, John Webster, 99-100

Greenfeld, Liah, 145, 146

Greenspan, Alan, 64

Gueant, Claude, 293

Guindon, Hubert, 155

Gül, Abdullah, 177

Gunn, T. Jeremy, 181n22

Gürüz, Kemal, 176

Habermas, Jürgen, 113

Hariri, Rafik, 276-77, 281

Harris, Sam, 113

Hartz, Louis, 144-45, 146, 153, 154

Hayek, Friedrich, 62

head/face coverings: in Canada, 99; in Europe, 79; in France, 79, 172-74, 293-94, 296, 299; in Germany, 181n21; *hijab*, 110; *niqab*, 97, 113, 133n5; in Quebec, 97; turban, 110; in Turkey, 175-77; in US, 168; yarmulke, 167-68

Heilman, Samuel, 66n6

Hezbollah, 288-89n18

hierarchies: caste system and, 202, 203; of gods, vs. of power, 47, 48; millenarianist movements and, 50; and power, 49; religion and legitimation for, 48; between secular and religious, 73

Hinduism: Brahmins in, 192, 202; and caste system, 189-90; exclusionary forms of group life in, 194; excommunication within, 197; family law, 204n1; graded system of sovereignties in, 190; Hindutva movement, 208; immutability of sanctioned practices, 190; lack of central authority within, 190; nationalism, 3, 37; reform of, 189-90, 192, 200-203, 203-4, 305; as "religion of principles," 189-90; as "religion of rules," 188-89; social order within, 189-90, 197; in Sri Lanka, 37; state intervention in, 87, 190, 192, 203-4, 204n1; and Untouchables/untouchability, 188-89, 190-91; as world religion, 20

Hitchens, Christopher, 113
Hofstadter, Richard, 143
Hollinger, David, 142, 144
Holyoake, George J., 137-38, 150
Hoodfar, Homa, 108
Hrawi, Elias, 276-77
Hsing Yun, 226
Hu Shi, 211
Hughes, Everett C., 101, 155
Huntington, Samuel, 19, 39-40, 140, 143-44, 147, 148, 152

identity/-ies: Buddhist, 237, 238, 253; caste system and, 194; ethnic vs. religious, 107-8, 109; intersections of, 111-12; in Lebanon, 271; Muslim, 108; national vs. religious, 33; postmodern/postsecular, 112; religious, 107-8, 109, 122, 146-47; religious, in US vs. rest of North America, 146-47; religious diversity and, 215; religious vs. national, 33; Thai, 236, 237, 238, 250-51, 253, 255n8; transnational, 110-11
ideological interregnum, 14-15
ideological-fragment theory, 144-45, 146
ideologies: in interpretation of religious signs/symbols, 109; and secularism, 297; undermining of hegemonic, 14-15
Ignatieff, Michael, 145
immigration. *See* migration

imperialism: and accommodation, 120-21; and Islamic secularism, 20; and secularism, 18; and tolerance, 120-21. *See also* colonialism
India: Babri Masjid in, 37; Bharatiya Janata Party, 208; caste-based discrimination in, 10; colonization in, 11; Constitution, 82, 83, 88, 187, 190; contextual secularism in, 2, 17, 88; emergence as economic power, 5; individual freedom in, 191; intellectual class in, 192; interreligious vs. intrareligious rights in, 83; lack of separation of religion and state in, 83; nationalism in, 89; neutrality of, 36, 187; opposition to secularism in, 221; principled distance in, 11, 15-16, 83; religious diversity in, 2, 82-83, 298; secular state in, 15, 207, 208; secularism in, 11, 69, 81-91, 187, 298; Sikh Golden Temple in Amritsar, 37; Sikhs in, 37; state intervention in, 83, 304-5; state–religion relationship in, 187. *See also* Hinduism
Indic states: colonialism and, 21; religious diversity in, 20-21; and secularism, 11; tolerant religious cohabitation in, 137
individual freedom/liberty: Ambedkar and, 191, 197, 198, 199; caste system and, 197-99; group and, 197-98; in India, 191; negative, 75, 198, 199; principled distance and, 191; and social/political context, 199
individualism: and communitarian moral responsibility, 145; community vs., 152-53; defined, 145; and denial of culture, 123; local communities vs., 139-40, 150-53; modernity and, 141; in Quebec, 159; and solidarity, 141; in US, 136, 139, 141, 144, 145, 149, 150, 152-53, 159; West and, 141
Inglehart, Ronald, 211, 213
Iran: as Islamic republic, 8; Islamic Revolution in, 3; and radical Islam,

46; Revolution, 37; secularism in, 18; Shia clergy in, 220; theocracy in, 70

Islam: and Arab Spring, 8; and capitalism, 59; East Asia and, 215; East Asian religions compared to, 214; fundamentalism, 40; Imam-Hatip schools, 175, 176, 177, 178; in Indic states, 20; and Indonesia, 24*n*7; international mobilization of, 37; in Iran, 8; and Jews, 51; movements in Middle East, 268; in Pakistan, 8; political movements, 70; and political parties, 3; radical, 46; religions in East Asia compared to, 210; republic of, 8, 9; and secular state, 70; and secularism, 11, 20; in Turkey, 174, 175, 178, 180; "war on," 5. *See also* Muslims; Quran

Islamic states: assertive secular, 19; established religion in, 36; majoritatian secular, 20; passive secular, 19-20; religious minorities in, 20; as secular, 207, 208; tolerant religious cohabitation in, 137

Islamophobia, 79, 160, 173, 174

Israel: as Jewish state, 72; Zionism in, 37

Japan: Buddhism in, 212, 224, 230*n*6-7; Chinese cultural influence on, 6; Christianity in, 213; Confucianism in, 215-16; Constitution, 212, 219; emperor, 217, 218, 219; freedom of conscience in, 218, 219; Kokutai in, 217; Komeito, 212; Meiji Restoration, 218, 219; modern state in, 219; nationalism in, 221; prevention of opposition in, 220; religiosity in, 211; religious diversity in, 218; religious freedom in, 218; secular state in, 220; Shinto in, 219; state control of religion in, 217-18; state–church relationship in, 223

Jews: in Canada, 107-8; citizenship for, 51; in Europe, 51; in France, 83, 181*n*22; Hasidic, 60; Holocaust and, 56; persecution of, 89; religious vs. ethnic identity, 107-8; Western Christianity and, 51; yarmulke, 168

John Paul II, 37

Jones, Terry, 306

Jospin, Lionel, 172, 173

Judaism: defamation of, 56; East Asian religions compared to, 214

Kassir, Samir, 282, 283

Katznelson, Ira, 9-10

Kaufman, Jason, 140

Kennan, George, 152

Kernerman, Gerald, 124

Keynesianism, 56, 63

Khilnani, Sunil, 199

Khuri, Bishara al-, 269

Kılıç, Haşim, 177

Kingston, Paul, 279, 286

kirpan, 127-30

Kiryat Joel, 60

Klein, Naomi, 63

Knilnani, Sunil, 191

Knopff, Rainer, 125

Knowles, Stanley, 57

Koenig, Matthias, 116*n*10, 136

Korea: Buddhism in, 230*n*6; Cheondogyo (the Religion of the Heavenly Way), 216; Confucianism in, 215; kings in, 217; secular state in, 218; Tonghak (Eastern Learning) Rebellion, 216. *See also* North Korea; South Korea

Kurtzman, Lemon v., 167

Kuru, Ahmet T., 2, 11, 12, 13, 233, 297, 303, 305-6

Lahoud, Emile, 280

laïcité, 132, 223, 229*n*1

Laliberté, André, 2, 10, 13, 18, 22, 294, 297, 298, 305

Lamba, Rinku, 2, 10, 13, 20, 304-5

Latter-Day Saints, 122, 180*n*13

Le Pen, Jean-Marie, 152, 173

Lebanon: Al Mithaq al Watani (the National Pact), 269; Christianity in,

268; Christians in, 269-70, 277; civil code and, 273-74, 275, 276; civil marriage in, 275-78; civil war, 270, 287*n*4; compared with rest of Middle East, 267-68; confessionalism in, 265-66, 268-72, 277-78, 283-84; as consociational state, 266; Constitution, 269, 273, 274, 276, 279, 287*n*5; Democratic Left Movement (DLM), 281, 282, 283, 284; diversity in, 278; Druze in, 268; economy, 274, 285-86; elites in, 266, 268, 276, 286-87; France and, 269; Future Movement, 281; goods and services in, 274; independence, 267, 269; Independence Intifada (Cedar Revolution), 279, 281-82, 284, 287; Israeli withdrawal from, 280; Kafa'! in, 289*n*20; Lebanese University, 288*n*12; March 14 Coalition, 284, 288*n*17; Maronites in, 268, 269; Muslims in, 269-70, 277; National Pact of 1943, 270; nongovernmental organizations (NGOs) in, 289*n*24; Ottomans and, 268; passive secular state in, 20; personal-status law in, 273-74; political parties in, 285; power sharing in, 265, 268-71, 270, 271, 307; religious courts in, 273, 275; religious diversity in, 20, 265, 266, 299; secular reforms in, 278-79, 307; secularism in, 266, 284-85, 299; Shias in, 277, 288-89*n*18; socioeconomic disparities in, 274, 286; state as weak in, 266, 286; Sunnis in, 277; Syria and, 265, 269, 271, 279, 280-81, 282; Ta'ef Accord, 270; "three presidents (troika)" in, 269, 272-73; women in, 273-74; youth movements in, 20, 265-66, 277-81, 283-85, 287, 307
Lee Teng-hui, 225, 226
Lefebvre, Solange, 133*n*1
Lemon v. Kurtzman, 167
Lerner, Daniel, 45
Levy, Leonard W., 75

liberalism: absence of feudalism and, 145; and denial of culture, 123; in Europe, 153; feudalism and, 153; Fukuyama and, 38, 40; of US, 145; US vs. Canadian, 153-54; US vs. Quebecois, 154-59. *See also* neoliberalism
Lijphart, Arend, 271
Lind, Michael, 142-43, 144
Lindblom, Charles, 55-56
Lipset, Seymour Martin, 140, 144, 145, 147, 148, 153, 154, 158
Litalien, Manuel, 2, 13, 18, 21, 297, 304, 309
Lorde, Audre, 132
Loyalists, 150-51
Luhmann, Niklas, 35
Lundsgaarde, Erik, 252
Lutheranism, 49

Madison, James, 74
Majed, Rayan, 280, 283
Makdisi, Ussama, 267
Mancke, Elizabeth, 150
March, James, 53
Maronites, 268, 269
marriage: caste system and, 200; confessionalism and, 275-78; same-sex, 133*n*7
Marx, Karl, 47-48, 52, 180*n*1
Masci, David, 138-39
McCargo, Duncan, 250, 257*n*22
McClintock, Anne, 133*n*2
McConnell, Michael, 170
McDonough, Sheila, 108
McNamara, Robert, 66*n*3
Mehta, Pratap Bhanu, 191
The Melting Pot (Zangwill), 161*n*2
melting pot ideology, 121
Mennonites, 107-8
Messarra, Antoine, 285
Middle East: dictatorships in, 267; revolutions in, 267-68, 285
migration: and cohabitation of religions, 137-38; communitarians and, 152;

demonization of immigrants, 151; and disembedding from traditional communities, 141-42; from East Asia, 229; and ethnic diversity, 1, 6; to Europe, 78-80; as guest-host relationship, 122-23; liberalization of, 103; and malaise of modernity, 142; of Muslims, 13, 59-60; and otherness, 122-23; to Quebec, 157-58; and religious diversity, 1, 6, 58-59, 71, 121-22; and religious resurgence, 58-60; and religious revival, 100; restrictions on, 152; and return to countries of origin, 151-52; and secularization, 99-100; and spread of "foreign" religions, 41; and transnational identity, 111; US and, 151-52; to Western liberal-democratic states, 136

millenarianism/millennialism, 49-50, 58, 61, 62

Miner, Horace, 155

modernity: as a-theistic, 52; as based on surveillance and reflexive self-monitoring, 52-53; of Canada, 157; in China, 13-14, 219; China and, 11; and "clash of civilizations," 5-6; and decline of churches, 101; and denominationalism, 148-49; and disembedding from traditional communities, 141; as "disenchantment of world," 52; and elites, 53; empirical knowledge and, 52-53; Enlightenment and, 52; exclusion of religious knowledge/authority from, 299; globalization and, 3; and indigenous knowledge, 18; and individualism, 141; and Islamic secularism, 20; in Japan, 219; Jews and, 51; malaise of, 140-41, 142; as most intense in West, 141; nationalism and, 146; and new forms of solidarity, 141; Protestants and, 141; in Quebec, 155, 157; reason and, 52; religion and, 52-54; and religious diversity, 4-5; and religious resurgence, 112; science and, 52-54; and secularism, 10, 13, 136, 159,

223; and solidarity, 141; and supernatural, 53; in US, 141, 145, 146, 157, 160; West and, 138

modernization: and confessionalism, 267; and religiosity, 213; in Thailand, 236

Modood, Tariq, 12, 17, 59, 78, 134*n*13

monarchy: absolute vs. constitutional, 246; and Buddhism, 232, 233, 240-41, 243; checks and balances of, 232; Constitution and, 248; and democracy, 233-34, 241-44; and ethnic minority groups, 237, 243-44; and *lèse majesté* law, 257*n*21; neutrality of, 247, 252; and politics, 233, 252; and religious pluralism, 233, 243-44; secularization and, 234, 250; in Thailand, 232-34, 252

moral economy, 62, 63, 64-65

Mormons, 122, 180*n*13

Morocco: Arab Spring in, 8; diversity in, 278

Morton, F.L., 125

Multani v. Commission scolaire Marguerite-Bourgeoys, 127-30

multiculturalism: in Canada, 3, 97-98, 144, 308-9; Christian privilege and, 97-98, 106; degree of tolerance and, 125; and diversity, 124-25; and ethnic diversity, 106-7; and ethnic vs. religious identities, 110; and fragmentation, 152; as homogenizing discourse, 125; and ideological fragment, 144; malaise of modernity and, 142; post-ethnicity and, 142; and religion, 106-7, 308-9; and religious diversity, 12; and secularism, 103, 138; of US, 142-43, 149

Multiculturalism Act, 98

Muslims: in Canada, 3, 108; cartoons depicting, 56, 71, 79, 306-7; in China, 230*n*4; in Denmark, 56, 71, 79, 306-7; in Europe, 78-80, 136; in France, 79, 82, 172, 294; in Germany, 79; and identities, 108; and Islam, 108; in

Italy, 79; in Lebanon, 269-70, 277; migration of, 13, 59-60; in Netherlands, 82; Quran burning in Florida, 306-7; religious vs. ethnic identity, 108; schools, 79, 82; separation of church and state and, 59; in Thailand, 238, 239, 246-47, 251, 259*n*33; in Turkey, 24*n*5, 178; in UK, 79; in US, 168. *See also* head/face coverings; Islam; Shia Muslims; Sunni Muslims
Myrdal, Gunnar, 143
The Myth of American Individualism (Shain), 150-51, 152

nationalism: in China, 221; civic vs. ethnic, 156; French Canadian, 155; in India, 89; in Japan, 221; and modernity, 146; in North Korea, 221; in Quebec, 156, 157; religion and, 149; and religious opposition, 221; in UK, 145; in US, 145-46, 149; in Vietnam, 221; in West, 89
neoliberalism: about, 61-65; in developing world, 63-64; globalization and, 18-19, 38, 39, 59; and homogeneity, 6; and justice/equality, 14-15; and moral economy, 64-65; in US, 61-62
Netherlands: consociationalism in, 271; murder of Gogh in, 71; Muslim schools in, 82
neutrality: in East Asia, 219; of India, 187; monarchy and, 247, 252; principled distance vs., 85-86; and religious pluralism, 250; state, 58, 295; in state–religion relationship, 300; in US, 36, 225
Nicaraguan Revolution, 37
niqab, 97, 113, 133*n*5
Norris, Pippa, 211, 213
North Korea: lack of critique of secularism in, 220; nationalism in, 221; as post-colonial state, 218; as quasi-secular state, 21-22; religions recognized in, 24*n*13; religious diversity in, 210; secularization in, 211; socialism

as civil religion in, 213; state control of religion in, 218
North Vietnam: as post-colonial state, 218; religious diversity in, 210; secularization in, 211; state control of religion in, 218

Oakes, R. v., 128
Obama, Barack, 65, 75, 153
Ontario: funding of religiously-based schools in, 97; funding of Roman Catholic schools in, 97; urbanization in, 157-58
Oregon v. Smith, 169-71
Orsi, Robert, 134*n*13
otherness: accommodation/tolerance and, 121, 124, 301; colonialism and, 131; immigration and, 122-23; US and, 144, 151
O'Toole, Roger, 98
Özal, Turgut, 176
Özcan, Yusuf Ziya, 177

Pakistan: Ahmedis in, 72; as Islamic republic, 8; and radical Islam, 46; Sunni Muslims in, 72, 220; Taliban in, 8
Palmer, Howard, "Reluctant Hosts," 121
passive secularism: in Cambodia, 21; in East Asia, 21-22; in France, 166, 172-73; and religious diversity, 179; in Thailand, 21; in Turkey, 166, 176-77, 178, 180; and twin toleration, 11; in US, 11, 166, 167, 168, 179
Patriot movement (1837-38), 155
Peace of Augsburg, 49
Pentecostal church, 61
Petraeus, David, 306
Pew Foundation, 46
Phillips, Anne, 123
Phule, Jotiba, 191
Plaek Phibunsongkhram, 239
pluralism: deep, 131, 298; of political units, 30; of religion, 31; of states, 31. *See also* ethnic diversity/pluralism; religious diversity/pluralism

Poland, Solidarity movement in, 37

Polanyi, Karl, 64

political secularism: and established religion, 17; rehabilitation of, 69; religious domination and, 299; separation of religion and state and, 17

politics-religion relationship. *See* religion–politics relationship

polygamy, 133*n*5, 180*n*13

Posner, Richard, 65

postmodernism, 36, 43

postsecularism, 105-6, 114, 294, 295, 300-301

power: and accommodation, 12; established religions and, 71-72; of European ideas/institutions, 33; hierarchies and, 47, 48, 49; and religious diversity, 294; religious diversity and, 301; secular state and, 305-6; secular vs. religious societal systems and, 34-35; sharing in Lebanon, 265, 268-71, 270, 271, 307; in state–religion relationship, 295, 301; and tolerance, 12

Prem Tinsulanonda, 239

principled distance: about, 11, 84-87, 85, 298; applicability of, 309; and contextual secularism, 15-16, 87-88; defined, 83; and differential treatment, 16, 85-86; Enlightenment and, 84; and equality, 85-86, 87; and Europe, 80; and individual freedom, 191; neutrality vs., 85-86; and public justification, 86; and public significance of religion, 85; and religion–politics relationship, 57, 85; and religious minorities, 86; and secularism, 15-16, 187-88; and separation of religion and state, 84; and social equality, 87; and state intervention, 85, 86-87; as unable to serve as universal template, 23; and unequal preferential treatment, 85-86

Protestants: evangelical, 46, 60-61; fundamentalist, 70; and modernity, 141; and Reformation, 31-32, 49

The Pursuit of the Millennium (Cohn), 50

quasi-secular states: China as, 8, 9, 14; in East Asia, 21-22; religious resurgence in, 14; Soviet Union as, 8; West and, 22

Quebec: Bouchard-Taylor Commission in, 120, 133*n*1, 156, 159, 308; Catholic Church in, 46; Conquest of 1760, 155, 156; Consultation Commission on Accommodation Practices Related to Cultural Differences, 99; diversity within, 133*n*1; English-speaking Canada vs., 157; ethnic nationalism of, 156; exceptionalism of, 156-57; immigrants in, 158; individualism in, 159; liberalism of, 154-59; Ministry of Education, 100; modernity in, 155, 157; nationalism of, 157; *niqab* in, 97; as premodern society, 155, 156, 157; Public Charities Act (1821), 101; Quiet Revolution in, 102, 155, 156, 157; reasonable accommodation in, 308; religious identity in, 147; religious minorities, 156; Roman Catholic Church in, 100, 101, 155, 157, 158-59; societal evolution, 155; sociologists, 155; urbanization of, 157-58; US compared to, 154-55, 158-59

Quran: and Islamic secular state, 19; threat to burn, 75, 296, 306; in Turkey, 178

R. v. Oakes, 128

race: in Canada, 121, 156; religion and, 133*n*3

Ranade, Mahadev Govind, 191

Razack, Sherene, 122-24

Reagan, Ronald, 3, 61, 63

reasonable accommodation: in Canada, 3, 109; and employment law, 131; in labour law, 126-27; in Quebec, 120, 308; of religious diversity, 41; of religious minorities, 3; unreasonable vs., 106. *See also* accommodation

Reformation, 31-32, 49

religion(s): assumption of homogeneity/ consistency/unchangingness in, 108-10; boundaries as non-coterminous with state, 36; caste-type groups within, 193-94; civil, 41, 147-48, 238, 252; cohabitation of, 137, 138, 140; comparisons of differences among, 34; continuation of, 137; definition of, 107, 133*n*4; demise of, 45-46; discovery of other, 32; and ethnicity, 106-12; and fundamentalist movements, 39-40; globalization and, 110-11; and identity, 122; immigration and cohabitation of, 137-38; imposition by backward societies, 146; inspiration and politics, 4; as "isms," 32; and knowledge, 53; Marxist-Leninist views of, 211; and modernity, 52-54; multiculturalism and, 106-7, 110, 138, 308-9; and nationalism, 149; "natural," 32; "of principles," 189-90; as otherworldly reality vs. set of beliefs/ practices immanent in mundane world, 213-14, 225-26; pluralization of, 31, 32; and political parties, 24*n*1; political resurgence of, 2-7; politicized movements, 37-38; and politics, 223; in private sphere, 8, 29; privatization, 75, 113-14, 212; in public vs. private spheres, 37; and race, 133*n*3; role in democracy, 56; secular state and incorporation of, 35; secularism and, 29, 137, 140; secularization, and weakening of, 34; as source of international division and conflict, 31-32; state regulation of, 36; and tolerance, 32; transnationalism of, 110-11; in US, 56, 147-48, 159-60; voluntary participation in, vs. as inherited culture, 148-49; West and systematic/institutional, 42; world, 32, 34, 38, 40, 42. *See also* established state religions

religion–politics relationship: Ambedkar on, 204; in Canada, 57; in democracy,

57; evangelical Protestants and, 46, 60-61; in premodern world, 47-48; principled distance and, 57, 85; religious resurgence and, 46; and right- vs. left-wing politics, 53; and scientific issues, 60-61; in Taiwan, 223, 225-27; in Thailand, 232; and undermining of secular state, 41; in US, 56, 57, 60-62

religion–state relationship. *See* separation of church and state

religiosity: in China, 211-12, 212-13; in East Asia, 211-12, 213; of French vs. English Canadians, 158; index of, 213; modernization and, 213; noncongregational, 221, 225; outside institutional forms, 214-15; and secular state, 212-13; state involvement in rituals, 216-17; in Taiwan, 213, 225-26, 226-27; in US compared to Canada, 158; in US schools, 147

religious, as term, 30

religious clothing: in France, 113; hijab, 110; in US workplaces, 167-68, 171. *See also* head/face coverings; religious signs/symbols

religious diversity/pluralism: accommodation of, 36; assertive secularism and, 179; and biases, 79, 299; in Canada, 12, 103-4, 105-6; challenges to management in secular states, 12-13; in China, 210, 298; and citizenship, 51; consociationalism and, 266, 271; contextual secularism and, 15, 23; deep, 298, 300; and democracy, 228; difference and, 132; and diverse worldviews, 5; as dominant organizing concept of religion, 40-41; in East Asia, 210, 218-19, 221, 228; established religions and, 71; in Europe, 79; freedom of conscience and, 13; and fundamentalism, 40-41, 43; in Germany, 71; global modernity and, 4-5; globalization and, 41-42, 71; and identity, 215; ideological interregnum and, 14-15; immigration and, 1, 6, 58-59,

121-22; in India, 2, 82-83, 298; in
Indic states, 20-21, 22; Islamic pattern of, 22; in Japan, 218; and Judeo-
Christianity, 13; in Lebanon, 20, 265,
266, 299; migration and, 71; missionaries and, 5; monarchy and, 233, 243;
multiculturalism and, 12; naive secularism and, 113; in non-Western world,
18-19; in North Korea, 210; in North
Vietnam, 210; passive secularism and,
179; as potentially chaotic, 41; and
power, 265, 294, 301; as problem, 301-
2; reasonable accommodation of, 41;
religious resurgence and, 42; secular
state and, 30; secularism and, 294;
secularization and, 36; Sinitic form
of, 22-23, 210; and social cohesion,
10; in South/Southeast Asia, 21; state
management of, 298; state–religion
relationship, and state supremacy
vs., 228; in Taiwan, 222, 225, 227; in
Thailand, 233, 235, 240, 243-46, 250,
251, 252-53; in UK, 71; in US, 51;
Western form of, 22; Westphalian
formula and, 41
religious freedom. *See* freedom of
religion
Religious Freedom Restoration Act
(RFRA), 170-71
religious minorities: abandonment of
accommodation/tolerance and, 130;
accommodation and, 17, 127; assimilation of, 239; and contestation, 33;
and democracy, 307-8; demonization
of, 151; dismantling of accommodation/
tolerance and, 131; established church
oppression of, 50; in Islamic states,
20; in Lebanon, 286-87; principled
distance and, 86; privatization of
belief as protection for, 11-12; in
Quebec, 156; religious resurgence
and, 14; and secular state, 12; in
Thailand, 21
religious pluralism. *See* religious
diversity/pluralism

religious resurgence: Enlightenment
project and, 114; globalization and,
58; and intolerance, 14; migration
and, 58-60, 100; millennialism and,
58; politicized religious movements
and, 38; in public spaces, 112; in
quasi-secular state, 14; religio-political movements and, 39; and religious
diversity, 42; and religious minorities,
14; and secularism, 295; secularization
and, 40
religious signs/symbols: and ethnicity,
108-9; and intragroup debate/
disagreement, 109-10; reactions to
news regarding, 108-10. *See also* religious clothing; *and under* schools
religious wars, 31, 32, 33, 49
"Reluctant Hosts" (Palmer), 121
Reynolds v. US, 170
Rioux, Marcel, 155
Roman Catholic Church: and education,
100; and establishment, 115n7; funding of schools, 82, 97, 173; as hierarchy of power, 49; history of, 49; in
Latin America, 209; in Quebec, 100,
101, 155, 157, 158-59; Reformation
and, 31; secular modernity and, 46;
and sexual abuse, 46; and Solidarity
movement in Poland, 37
Roman Christian Church, 30-31
Roosevelt, Theodore, 161n2
Roy, Fernande, 115n4
Russia: Orthodox Church in, 209; reli-
giosity in, 211
Ryan, William F., 115n4

Sadat, Anwar, 37
Sağlam, Mehmet, 176
Saler, Benson, 133n4
Sandel, Michael, 65
Sarkozy, Nicolas, 173
Saudi Arabia: lack of change over time,
72; non-secularity of, 8; and radical
Islam, 46
Scalia, Anonin, 170

schools: de-Christianization of, 102; in France, 82, 166, 172-74, 173; in Germany, 181*n*21; Islamic/Muslim, 79, 82, 175, 176, 177, 178; in Netherlands, 82; in Ontario, 97; religious practices in, 147; religious signs/symbols in, 127-30, 166, 167, 168, 171, 172-74, 181*n*21; state funding of religiously-based independent, 97; in Turkey, 166; in UK, 79; in US, 147, 166, 167, 168, 171. *See also* education

science: communism and, 62; economics and, 62; and modernity, 52-54; Nazism and, 62; religion–politics relationship and, 60-61; theory of evolution in US, 147, 158; in US, 60-61

sectarianism: caste system and, 192-94; and confessionalism, 267, 287*n*2; of neoliberalism, 63; in US, 75

secular state(s): absence of critique of, 209, 217, 220; Canada as, 3; capitalism and, 40; cohabitation and, 150; colonialism and, 3-4, 21; as concept, 29; decolonization and, 7; and degree of secularity, 6-7; in East Asia, 207, 210, 297; emergence of variants in West, 215; incorporation of religious, 35; incremental, 21; India as, 15; Indic, 19; and institutional reform, 307-9; Islamic, 19; in Japan, 220; opposition to, 208-9; and political resurgence of religions, 2-7; power and, 305-6; as protector of religious minority rights, 12; questioning of authority of, 6-7; rationality of, 35; religion–politics relationship and undermining of, 41; religiosity and, 212-13; and religious diversity, 30; Republic of China as, 218; as secular with East Asian characteristics, 218, 219; secularism and, 29, 297; secularization of, 40; secularized society vs., 212-13, 297; Sinitic, 19; in Sinitic cultural area, 219-20; in South Korea, 220; in Taiwan, 220, 222; Thailand

as, 233; three configurations of, 3-4; traditionalist vs. neotraditionalist approach, 217-19; twin toleration and, 210; varieties in non-Western world, 19; as Western hegemony, 7-11. *See also* quasi-secular states

secularism: of American Creed, 140; amoral, 72; anticlericalism and, 50-51, 214; assertive vs. passive, 305-6; in Bouchard-Taylor report, 159; in Canada, 300; in China, 36, 227, 297; Christianity and, 88-89, 98; closed vs. open, 114-15*n*1; and cohabitation of religions, 137, 140; colonialism and, 18, 137; confessionalism and, 275-78; contextual (*see* contextual secularism); and continuation of religion, 137; culture of, 9-10; definitions of, 29, 137, 214, 294; disenchantment of world and, 10; divergent expectations of, 13; in East Asia, 214-15, 298; English Civil War and, 50; as erosion of traditional norms, 141; globalization and, 10, 18; and harder approach to religion, 299; hegemony of, 3, 8; historical/cultural aspects, 13; ideology and, 297; imperialism and, 18; incremental, 12; in India, 69, 81-91, 187, 298; Indic, 11; individual liberty vs. group life and, 191; institutional vs. cultural-ideological, 9-10; Islamic, 11; in Lebanon, 266, 284-85, 299; local communities and, 139-40; moderate, 12, 78, 79, 80; modernity and, 136, 159, 223; and multiculturalism, 103; multiple forms of, 9; naive, 104-5, 113; and non-Western world, 18-23; open, 99; origins in Western historical experience, 5; political vs. existential, 9-10; and postsecularism, 294, 295, 300-301; and principled distance, 88-89, 187-88; Protestant movements decrying, 70; rehabilitation of, 81, 90-91; and religion as voluntary vs. inherited, 148-49; religion vs., 29;

and religious pluralism, 294; religious resurgence and, 295; secular state and, 29, 297; secularization and, 103; Sinitic, 11; and social science, 9-10; state enactment of, 296; in Taiwan, 227, 228, 297; and theology, 137; tolerance of, 137; and understanding of religious life, 73-74; in US, 139; varieties of, 13, 18, 296-97. *See also* Western secularism

secularist, as term, 114-15*n*1

secularization: of Canada, 100-102; of economy, 249-50; of education, 248-49; globalization and, 9; history of, 42-43; immigration and, 99-100; in Lebanon, 307; monarchy and, 234, 250; Muslims and, 246-47; and progress, 103; and religious diversity, 36; and religious resurgence, 40; religious wars and, 32; of secular state, 40; and secularism, 103; in Sinitic culture, 222-23; social change and, 102-4; of social welfare, 249; state independence and, 42-43; of states, and weakening of religion, 34; in Thailand, 234, 246-50, 253-54, 297-98

Sedwill, Mark, 306

Sélim, Monique, 212, 213

Seljak, David, 2, 10, 12, 14-15, 300-301, 308-9

Seljuk Empire, 159

separation of church and state: absolute, 89; anticlericalism and, 50-51; Christianity and, 89; in Europe, 77-78; and exclusion, 73; in France, 294; history of, 48-50; and immigrant Muslims, 59; and role of religious institutions, 57; and societies with supreme religious leaders, 18; and support for religion, 78; in US, 51, 99, 107, 308, 309; and Western secularism, 72-73, 89

separation of religion and state: in France, 73-74; India and, 83; and interreligious vs. intrareligious

domination, 75; as mutual exclusion, 74-77, 89; as one-sided exclusion, 73-74; and political secularism, 17; principled distance and, 84; questioning of, 70; in US, 74-77, 167

September 11, 2001, terrorist attacks, 39, 43, 113, 168

Sezer, Necdet, 176

Shain, Barry, *The Myth of American Individualism*, 150-51, 152

Sharia law, 60, 66*n*6, 214

Shastras, 200, 203

Sherbert v. Verner, 169

Shia Muslims: in Iran, 220; in Lebanon, 269, 270, 272, 276, 277

Shinto, 21, 219

shisuhua, 222-23

Sikhs: in British Columbia, 97; in Canada, 59; in France, 174; in India, 37; and kirpan, 127-30; turbans, 174; in UK, 59

Silvert, Kalman, 54-55

Simon, Herbert, 53

Singh, Gurbaj, 129

Sinitic culture: and religious diversity, 210; sacred space in, 225-26; and secularism, 11, 21-22, 219-20, 222-23; and state–religion relationship, 228; in Taiwan, 222; tolerant religious cohabitation in, 137

Smith, Donald Eugene, 257*n*23

Smith, Miriam, 125

Smith, Oregon v., 169-71

Social Gospel, 57, 61, 101

social welfare and services: churches and, 99, 101, 102; religious institutions and, 224; secularization of, 249; state assumption of, 100, 102

socialism, 212-13, 217-18

Solh, Riad al-, 269

solidarity: ethnicity and, 107; individualism vs., 141; modernity and, 141

Song, Sarah, 123

South Korea: Chinese cultural influence on, 6; Confucianism in, 230*n*5;

Minjung theology of social justice, 220; prevention of opposition in, 220; religiosity in, 211; secular state in, 220; state critiques in, 221

Soviet Union: atheism in, 36; fall of, 6, 38, 39, 43; glasnost and perestroika in, 38; as quasi-secular state, 8

special interest groups, 125-26, 129

Sri Lanka: Buddhism in, 20, 37, 70; civil war, 37; religious diversity in, 20

Stasi Commission, 173

state(s): anti-religious, 166; as belonging in public sphere, 29; boundaries as coterminous with society, 36; concept of, 30; consolidation of sovereignty, 31; definition of, 54-55; with established religions, 166 (*see also* established state religions); as geographical units, 32-33; and healthcare/social services, 102; in late medieval/early-modern times, 30; neutrality, 58, 103; plurality of, 31; regulation of religion, 36; religions moving from singular to plural within, 31; religious, 166; role of, 32-33; as secular vs. religious, 29; secularization of, and weakening of religion, 34; triumph of capitalist liberalism over, 39; welfare, 102, 153. *See also* secular state(s)

state–church relationship: history of, 99; in Japan, 223; and social welfare/services, 100, 102; in Taiwan, 223; in US, 223. *See also* established churches; separation of church and state

state intervention: in East Asia, 217, 305; and equality, 249; in France, 74; in Hinduism, 87, 190, 192, 203-4, 204n1; in India, 83, 304-5; and neoliberalism, 63; principled distance and, 85, 86-87; and reform of caste system, 203-4; in religious communities, 56-57; in Taiwan, 224; in US, 75. *See also* state–religion relationship

state–religion relationship: Ambedkar and, 191; in China, 2, 216, 217-18,

227-28; colonialism and, 5, 218; in East Asia, 210, 214-15, 217-21, 229; in France, 73-74, 293-94; increasing fusion vs. separation between respective authorities, 217; in India, 187; and intervention for social justice/equality, 20; neutrality in, 300; in non-Western secular states, 19; normative vs. non-normative practices, 69-70; in North America, 299; political/historical factors in, 112-13; power and, 295, 301; and religion as otherworldly reality vs. set of beliefs/practices immanent in mundane world, 213-14, 225-26; and religious freedoms, 73-74; state supremacy in, 217; state supremacy vs. religious diversity in, 228; in Taiwan, 223-24, 227; in Thailand, 233, 297-98; traditionalist vs. neotraditionalist approach, 217-19; twin toleration in, 210; variations of, 10-11; variety of arrangments regarding religion as differentiated institution, 35-36. *See also* separation of church and state; state intervention

state religions. *See* established state religions

Stedman Jones, Gareth, 9-10

Stepan, Alfred, 7, 210

Strauss, Leo, 66n7

Streckfuss, David, 257n21

Sunni Muslims: in Lebanon, 269, 270, 272, 276, 277, 281; in Pakistan, 72, 220

Supreme Court (US): in *City of Boerne v. Flores,* 171; conservatives vs. liberals in, 166; in *Everson v. Board of Education,* 167; in *Goldman v. Weinberger,* 167-68; in *Gonzales v. O. Centro Espirita,* 171; in *Lemon v. Kurtzman,* 167; in *Oregon v. Smith,* 169-71; in *Reynolds v. US,* 170; in *Sherbert v. Verner,* 169; and *Wisconsin v. Yoder,* 303; in *Wisconsin v. Yoder,* 169

Supreme Court of Canada: and accommodation, 120, 127-30; and *Multani
v. Commission scolaire Marguerite-
Bourgeoys*, 127-30; on religious freedom, 127-28; on religious tolerance,
129
Suskind, Ron, 61

Ta'ef Accord, 270
Taiwan: Buddhism in, 224, 225-26;
Bureau for Religious Affairs, 227;
Chinese cultural influence on, 6;
Christianity in, 213; Confucianism in,
230*n*5; Constitution, 222; democracy
in, 218, 223, 227, 228; freedom of
conscience in, 222, 227; Guomindang,
224, 225, 226; Presbyterian Church,
220, 225, 226; prevention of opposition in, 220; religion–politics relationship in, 223, 225-27; religiosity in,
211, 213, 225-26, 226-27; religious
diversity in, 222, 225, 227; secular
state in, 220; and secular state vs.
secularized society, 212; secularism
in, 227, 228, 297; state control of religion in, 224, 227; state critiques in,
221; state–church relationship in, 223;
state–religion relationship in, 223-24;
zhengjiao fenli in, 222, 223, 227
Taliban, 8
Tantawy, Muhammad Sayyid, 173
Taoism, 21, 216, 224
Taylor, Charles, 16, 99, 105, 114-15*n*1,
140-41, 147, 148-49, 156, 159
terrorism: global, 6; September 11, 2001
attacks, 39; in UK, 113
Teziç, Erdoğan, 176
Thailand: 1932 revolution, 236, 249;
1973 student rebellion, 241, 244; 1976
repression of student protest and
opposition, 244; 1992 political crisis,
242; 2006 coup, 232, 234, 242, 247;
anticommunism in, 238-40; Asian
economic crisis and, 235, 245-46,
249; Buddhism in, 21, 234-40, 243,

245-48, 250-51, 250-53, 252-54;
Constitution, 232-33, 235, 242-43,
246, 247, 248; democracy in, 232-35,
240-42, 244-46, 253, 304; economic
development in, 239, 245, 246, 251-
52; economic secularization in, 249-
50; education in, 248-49; elites in,
234, 235, 238, 241, 242, 244, 249,
250, 254-55*n*3-4, 304; ethnic diversity in, 235-38, 243-44, 253; freedom
of conscience in, 233; freedom of
religion in, 243-44, 247, 256*n*12; hill
tribes in, 236-37, 239, 246, 248; insurgencies in East Asia and, 238-39;
law in, 257-58*n*23; law of karma in,
243, 247, 249; middle class, 241, 242,
245, 248; modernization in, 236;
monarchy in, 232-37, 240-44, 246,
247, 252; Muslims in, 238, 239, 246-
47, 251, 259*n*33; nation-state in, 235-
36; Parliament, 232, 233; as passive
secular state, 21; political parties, 234;
protests in, 244-45; public space
opening in, 244-45, 250; religious
diversity in, 21, 233, 235, 240, 243-
46, 250-53; religious representation
in, 250-51; Sangha Act (Buddhist
Clergy Act), 238, 239; as secular
state, 233; secularization in, 246-50,
253-54, 297-98; social welfare services in, 246, 249, 252, 254*n*2; as state
with supreme religious leader, 18;
state–religion relationship in, 233,
297-98; Treaty of Friendships and
Commerce, 244
Thaksin Shinawatra, 235, 239, 243, 245,
248, 250, 251-52, 253, 254*n*2, 255*n*4,
258*n*25, 304
Thatcher, Margaret, 63
theocracies, 17, 18, 70
Tlili, Mustapha, 306-7
Tocqueville, Alexis de, 139, 143
tolerance: abandonment of, 130; in
Canada, 301; contributions by,
130; and deep equality, 130-32;

dismantling of, 130-31; diversity and, 120, 122; and equality, 130; in Europe, 78; freedom of expression and, 306-7; imperialism and, 120-21; as interim value, 130; liberal secular state and, 14; limits to, 126; loss of privilege and, 124-25; and multiculturalism, 125; power differences in, 12; recovery/ reconstitution of, 130; religious, 32, 129; religious resurgence and, 14; of secularism, 137; and special interest groups, 125-26; and special treatment, 129; in Thailand, 243-44; "twin," 210

transnationalism: in Canada, 106, 110-12; globalization and, 112; of identities, 110-11; migration and, 41; of networks, 41

Tunisia: activism in, 285; Arab Spring in, 8

turban. *See* head/face coverings

Turkey: assertive secularism in, 166, 174-75, 176, 178, 180; civil law in, 174-75; Constitutional Court, 174, 175-77; Council for Higher Education (YÖK), 175, 176, 177, 178; Council of State, 175, 176, 177; headscarves in, 175-77; Imam-Hatip schools in, 175, 176, 177, 178; Islam in, 174, 175, 178, 180; judiciary in, 174-75; Justice and Development (AK) Party, 176-77, 208; Kemalist state in, 74; *laïcité* approach in, 132; military coups in, 174; Motherland Party (ANAP) in, 175-76; Muslims in, 24*n*5; Nationalist Action Party, 177; passive secularism in, 166, 176-77, 178, 180; religious freedoms in, 74; religious symbols in schools in, 166; as secular state, 207, 208; secularism in, 18; universities in, 175, 177; Virtue Party, 177; Western contact wirh, 24*n*5

Turkish Revolution, 176

twin toleration: and passive secularism, 11; in US, 7-8, 11

United Kingdom: and civic nationalism, 145; established churches in, 115*n*7; ethnoreligious politics in, 59-60; evolution away from religious establishment, 5; Muslims in, 79; religious diversity in, 71; schools in, 79; Sikhs in, 59; terorism in, 113

United States: American Creed in, 140, 143, 144, 146, 147-48, 150, 151, 154; American Revolution, 145, 153; Amish in, 169; assertive secularism in, 166, 167; Canada compared to, 140, 144, 157; community vs. individualism in, 150-53; compared to church, 148; Congress, 166; conservatives vs. liberals in, 166-68; contextual secularism in, 303; cultural hybridity of, 140; denominationalism in, 148-49; disembedding of traditional norms in, 149, 150, 152, 159; and diversity, 143; divisions within, 154; evangelical Protestantism in, 46, 60; exceptionalism of, 144, 145, 149, 151, 152; far-right Christian militias in, 24*n*2; First Amendment, 139, 167; foreign policy, 147; free-market economic "science" in, 65; Hasidic Jews in, 60; historical phases of, 142-43; and immigration, 151-52; "In God We Trust" as motto, 138-40, 160; and individualism, 136, 139, 144; individualism in, 141, 145, 149, 159; individualism vs. local communities in, 150-53; and interreligious vs. intrareligious domination, 75; lack of binary oppositions in, 144; lack of power to legislate regarding religion, 75; liberalism in, 5, 145, 153-59; local communities in, 139-40, 158-59; migration within, 152-53; modernity in, 141, 146, 160; modernity of, 145; Moral Majority in, 37; multiculturalism of, 142-43, 149; Muslims in, 168; nationalism of, 145-46, 149; neoconservatism in, 61-62; neoliberalism in, 63,

65; neutrality in, 36, 225; opposition to secularism in, 221; and otherness, 144; passive secularism in, 11, 166, 167, 168, 179; peaceful cohabitation of religions in, 140; postethnic, 142-43; president, 166; Protestant fundamentalism in, 70; public funding of religion in, 82; Quebec compared to, 154-55, 158-59; religion in, 56, 147-48, 159-60; religion–politics relationship in, 56, 57, 60-62; religiosity in, 158, 211; religious affiliation in, 46; religious diversity in, 51, 225; religious exemptions in, 168-69, 171, 303; religious freedom in, 75; religious identity, compared to rest of North America, 146-47; religious right in, 3, 60-62, 209, 224; religious symbols in schools in, 166, 167, 168, 171; Republican Party in, 61-62; science in, 147, 158; sectarianism in, 75; secular ideology vs. religion in, 24n3; secularism in, 7-8, 90, 139; separation of church and state in, 5, 51, 99, 107, 308, 309; separation of religion and state in, 74-77, 90, 167; as single culture, 142-43; social change and, 145; state intervention in, 75; state–church separation in, 223; twin toleration in, 7-8, 11; voluntarism in, 149; Western secularism in, 72, 74-77
Untouchables/untouchability: Ambedkar and, 188; denial of personhood to, 191; Hinduism and, 188-89, 190-91; Indian Constitution and, 187; and personal growth, 199. *See also* Dalits
Upanishads, 19
urbanization: in Ontario, 157-58; of Quebec, 157-58

Vedas, 19, 200, 203, 205n3
veils. *See* head/face coverings
Verner, Sherbert v., 169
Vietnam: Confucianism in, 215; faith healers in, 212; kings in, 217; lack of critique of secularism in, 220; nation-

alism in, 221; as quasi-secular state, 21-22; religions recognized in, 24n12; religiosity in, 211. *See also* North Vietnam

Wachirawut (Vajiravudh), King, 236
Walzer, Michael, 152
Washington Consensus, 63
Waxman, Henry, 64
Weber, Max, 10, 52, 58, 104
Weinberger, Goldman v., 167-68
West: and individualism, 141; and modernity, 138; modernity as most intense in, 141; "rest" vs., 39, 140; and secular state, 7-11
Western secularism: in Europe, 77-81; in France, 72-74; Indian secularism and, 82; non-Western vs., 89-91, 138, 298; in other societies, 70-71; as restricted and inadequate, 81; self-understanding as universal doctrine, 72-73; separation of church and state and, 89; in US, 74-77
Westphalian formula, 31-32, 33, 36, 39-40, 41, 49
Wisconsin v. Yoder, 169, 303
Witchcraft, Oracles and Magic among the Azande (Evans-Pritchard), 66n10
Woehrling, José, 128
Woodsworth, J.S., 57
Wu Po-hsiung, 226

Xuanyuanjiao (the Religion of the Yellow Emperor), 215, 225, 226

Yang Fenggang, 212-13
Yiguando (the Way of Pervasive Unity), 215
Yingluck Shinawatra, 248
Yoder, Wisconsin v., 169, 303

Zangwill, Israel, *The Melting Pot,* 161n2
Zhao Hui, 225
Zionism, 37
Zolberg, Aristide R., 151-52

Printed and bound in Canada by Friesens

Set in Frutiger and Warnock by Artegraphica Design Co. Ltd.

Copy editor: Robert Lewis

Proofreader: Lana Okerlund

Indexer: Noeline Bridge